#speedwaylife:

Sideways Quotes, Tweets & Comments

Jeff Scott

Congratulations!

Yours in speedway

Jeff Scott

January 2012

Brighton

*"By the second week of battle
We'd become obsessed with trivia."*

MICHAEL DONAGHY

For gawjus

First published in Great Britain by
Methanol Press
2 Tidy Street Brighton East Sussex BN1 4EL

For a complete catalogue of current and forthcoming publications please write to the address above, or visit our website at www.methanolpress.com

Michael Donaghy poem appears in *Dances Learned Last Night Poems 1975-1995* (Picador)

ISBN 978-0-9568618-1-8
A catalogue for this book is available from the British Library

Editor in absentia: Michael Payne
Word Wrangler: Graham Russel
Book Design: Vicky Holtham
Cover Design: Rachael Adams
Cover Photograph: Time Out/Rob Greig

Printed in the UK by Imprint Digital

Introduction

Despite the apparent ongoing lack of national profile or absence of media attention, each season millions of words are written and spoken about British speedway.

Any selection of key moments or comments is – by definition – not a complete record. That's certainly the case here though – in another way – these are also very representative of the day-to-day progression of the 2011 season.

Riders on Twitter definitely provide a unique new dimension above and beyond the usual news sources. It would be good if more riders join up in the future because of the immediate genuine insight their tweeted reactions provide. That said, many riders often still need another job in order to be able to ride so can't afford the posh phones or the monthly cost of web access required to tweet. These less well off riders also usually drive themselves to and from meetings - so don't have the luxury of time on their hands (or, indeed, have their hands free) to share their thoughts, opinions and reactions.

There is minimal methodology to understand about this book. All tweets are marked with an asterisk (*) and, mostly, appear completely unchanged as they were written (except for where I delete repetitive haha's). Wherever possible each comment is attributed directly and appears on the day uttered/written or, alternatively, on the copy date of the print or online publication concerned. If any word appears in [square parentheses] that is usually my editorial addition.

I've deliberately only provided a chronology with no explanation (otherwise this book would have been way bigger). I also assume that each speedway season starts after the strategic decisions of the AGM so that effectively means each 'speedway year' really runs from 1st November to 31st October.

Obviously, I apologise to anyone offended by the language used or the comments chosen! If there have been any inadvertent transcription errors from the media or my contemporaneous handwritten notes, please also forgive them too.

Hopefully you'll enjoy this rather different sideways look at the 2011 British speedway season. Even if not, just by purchasing a copy you've already contributed £5 to the extremely valuable ongoing work of the Speedway Riders' Benevolent Fund. So, thank you!

Brighton

December 2011

1st November

Phil Bartlett "I had a meeting with somebody on Monday about the sale of the club but I can't disclose any information about who that is until things are further down the line. It's still in the early stages and I imagine it is likely to take weeks, more than days. But it is positive news and a step in the right direction. I am waiting for them to get back to me and confirm that they want to go ahead. Until that happens I can't be sure that it is a done deal. The ball is definitely in their court.... There is nothing to stop anybody else from approaching me about buying the club. I am happy to listen to anyone else who is interested. I'm certainly not counting my chickens just yet. It's been a very frustrating period for me and the fans because we all want this to be sorted as soon as possible, which would be in the best interests of all concerned. Whoever does take over from me has to be the right person to take the club forward. Weymouth needs a speedway team but it needs to be run properly."

2nd November

Keith Denham "It's purely and simply a financial decision and not one I wanted to make. Ian [Thomas] took a drop in pay this year to help and we are having to make more cuts across the board in preparation for 2011. Ian has worked with me at Workington speedway for the three years since I took over and I know he is going to be a very, very difficult man to replace. We have had our disagreements, like any other working partnership, but we have never fallen out and I have the greatest respect for him."

7th November

BSPA GRAHAM Drury has agreed a shock return to Birmingham - eight days after leaving the club in a cost-cutting measure. A mystery sponsor has stepped forward to enable Drury to resume his positions as promoter, general manager and team manager after it appeared his four-year spell at Perry Barr was over. Drury said: 'I've agreed a two year deal with Tony Mole (club owner) and myself and my wife Denise are determined to give our supporters a season to be proud of in 2011. There has been a lot of negative stuff surrounding Birmingham of late, but everything is now in place for us to move forward and take the club into an exciting year of racing. I want the fans, management and sponsors to be proud of the team and I'm already in talks with a couple of new signings.'

8th November

Sam Knight "There is only one track spare! I couldn't steal that crown she must have gone round the clock or cock being more apt! at least a few hundred more times lol! Certainly wasn't me posting I can spell! just got in from work and found this can of worms lol! Don't worry Phil (Bartlett) won't be responding on here again lol! But I do have a great idea of a consortium:
• Bankrupt Builder
• Sandwich delivery/Sandwich maker person
• Office Lacky
• Part time cleaner/domestic (rubbish shifter) (hard working 1 day a week person)
• Welder (ultimate plodder! Another goodie who can fiddle the state system)
• Driving instructor (who gives free lessons for sex! Well maybe in the poorer area of
• Stoke on Trent) pmsl
oh and last but not least (drum roll)
• Unemployed Photographer/the one and only track spare! living off the state (well soon to stop once the government sorts the job out)
I think they held their board meeting on Saturday Night? I certainly counted 4/5 of the track spares conquests in their little huddle! lovely how very Jeremy Kyle pmsl So what do you think guys? genius or what? They certainly could do a better job of course. But on a serious note. The facts are even with all these "do gooders", the debts were still there and if not worse, for winning teams attract bigger wages and there still wasn't the gate take to sustain this, even with the school fetes etc.... so all these people who are keen to slate "come on down the price is right" or for the faint hearted who haven't got the balls to do it, live in the so called "golden years" of the past. So long farewell saddos"

9th November

Phil Bartlett "I am talking to someone who is quite seriously looking to take the club forward, I hope to be able to make an announcement very, very soon"

11th November

Barcroftlad "Friday in NZ and I have just seen an interview with Ivan down here to launch his new book. It was interesting to hear him say that he rode in 29 countries and was popular in 28. The one where he wasn't popular was England. Reason was that because of the team emphasis there and he was the stranger who usually won the first race and upset the local chap who was expected to win. I imagine that was only in his early days there because it seems to me that Ivan has always been popular wherever he raced."

13th November

Terry Russell "The Blunsdon facility is now 62 years old and we have to work with what is here. We do our best and spend money on making the place look clean and tidy, by adding additional spectator lighting, regular grass cutting and matters of that kind."

Aaron Summers "[Edinburgh] won the Premier Trophy in my first season as well, which was quite mind blowing"

15th November

Keith Denham "I have done a lot of research across speedway, and no other track pays the amount of money we do for stewards. Last season I was paying over £1,600 at each home meeting for rent and stewards and I'm looking for that to be halved, which I don't think is unreasonable."

Phil Bartlett "We haven't been able to pay the rent in the last couple of months, because not enough people came through the gates this season. Wessex Delivery Partnership have therefore claimed the stadium back and the lease has been forfeited. However, they've jumped the gun really because I had found a buyer. Everything was settled and it was all going through. Had Wessex Delivery waited another two weeks it would have been sorted and the club would have had a new owner. Hopefully the interested buyer will contact Wessex Delivery and go from there..... People have been running me down and voting with their feet by not attending. Well they have got what they wanted. I have never taken a penny out of the speedway – it's the other way around – and I do feel sorry for the hardcore fans who love their speedway and came every week. But I can't keep sustaining £30,000 losses every year. Speedway in this town is not viable as there aren't enough people that support it. Now I can concentrate on my business and my family life, and enjoy it."

16th November

BSPA WEYMOUTH have been closed down with landlords repossessing the Wessex Stadium and the BSPA annulling the National League club. It means the Wildcats' license along with riding assets revert to the BSPA, who will now handle future negotiations with parties interested in operating at the venue. Outgoing chairman Phil Bartlett said: "I think it's a fantastic sport and I wish any prospective person who looks to take the club over all the luck in the world. I can now quite clearly concentrate on my family life and business and actually have a holiday in the summer like most normal working people."

18th November

BSPA FORMER Oxford promoter Bernard Crapper has passed away after a period of ill health. Cheetahs fan Crapper first worked for the club in 1976 and officially took charge with close friend John Payne in 1983 - and with big names such as Hans Nielsen, Simon Wigg and Marvyn Cox in the team, Oxford enjoyed huge success including three British League titles. Crapper was also secretary and treasurer of the Speedway Riders' Benevolent Fund between 1994 and 2008. Payne said: "I'm gutted. I've lost my biggest mate. We went through some great and memorable times at Oxford Speedway. We also had a few lows, but all-in-all we had a fantastic time. I feel privileged that when Bernard took over the running of the speedway, I was the guy that he insisted ran it alongside him."

20th November

Neil Machin   "The stark fact is that some riders are going to have to accept less than they have been earning. If promoters can't live with deals, then they have to say so. You only have to look at what's happening in Poland right now. Riders have been getting good deals and come to us and ask for similar ones - but just about every rider I speak to who races over there is currently owed money. Some are owed thousands and I don't want that to start happening over here."

George English   "As you might expect with having a winning team, our crowd levels did improve and were better than for several years, but not to such a degree that we were able to reach a break-even figure over the season, which was a bit disappointing given our success."

BSPA   STOKE have withdrawn from the Premier League and intend to run at National League level in 2011. Potters promoter Dave Tattum has taken the decision due to the financial climate and having suffered substantial losses over the last three seasons

Phil Bartlett   "My partner Sam [Knight] and I have been slagged off for not bringing people through the gates and not promoting, promoting, promoting. But you have to go back and look over my term. We did school fêtes every year and we've done public displays on the seafront for the past two seasons. We've had riders down there giving out leaflets and we put signs out all over the town pointing people towards the racing on a Friday night. We visited every hotel and guesthouse with leaflets, offering reduced admission to get people to come in. We did a promotion when we invited people in for free, which brought a lot of people through the turnstiles but it didn't earn me anything. We also went out and put leaflets on every single car parked in Weymouth on race days. We did all this, plus advertising in a local resort magazine and our media advertising in the *Dorset Echo* and on Wessex FM. We even won the League in 2008 and finished second in the Standings in 2009. Did all this bring people through the gate? No. Did it make Weymouth viable? No. So tell me what more I could have done to get people through the gates and make Weymouth viable. It's all very well slagging us off and saying you've done no promotional work, but quite clearly we have. I tried everything I need businesswise to try and bring more people through the turnstiles. The failings were clearly in the lack of people coming through the gate. If there were enough people coming through the turnstiles, everyone would have got paid and there wouldn't have been a problem. I'm not going to be the one that keeps propping it up and getting slagged off. Why would I want to do that? There are just not enough people to support it and it was a liability round my neck. Screw that. I've enjoyed the sport and it's been a fantastic time, obviously we had a lot of injuries last year, which completely marred the campaign. Coming bottom is an embarrassment as far as I'm concerned. Last is miles out from winning and it's not right for the town, but the town didn't support it. Even when we were winning the League, did it bring in more people? No, it didn't. I made less than I did last year. I lost money when I'd won the League because I had a better team....I'm going to enjoy not having to run a meeting every week, or having the pressure of finding riders when we get injuries. I won't have to spend my life with the phone glued to my ear while trying to run my six other businesses. I'm perfectly happy that I'm not running speedway and I'll invest the money I save elsewhere. I certainly have no intention of stepping back into another speedway track any time soon."

21st November

Phil Bartlett   "I have only "Banned" to quote your term of fraze, only People that have not and never paid to enter Weymouth Speedway!!! only an Old track spare (slapper) or people that make out they are helping for the good of the sport, only to go running you down behind your back."

BSPA

THREE tier structure remains in place, Elite, Premier and National Leagues.

ELITE LEAGUE

Now includes Birmingham who have exchanged league membership with Ipswich, league numbers are not finalised consequently fixture planning has been deferred.

PREMIER LEAGUE

Still consists of 14 members including new additions Ipswich and Leicester, who have replaced Stoke. The Potters will apply to join the National league at that league's AGM in December. The league continues with the third year of its 3 year plan for teambuilding with a 42.50 team building limit. The Premier Trophy and Young Shield competitions do not continue in 2011. The Premier

League Championship involves each club racing 19 home and 19 away fixtures.

NATIONAL LEAGUE

This league will hold its own AGM in December.

GENERAL

Official Posts ratified so far: The 2010 Management Committee to remain en-bloc with Rob Godfrey to replace Graham Drury as the Premier League reserve member

SRBF Secretary – Paul Ackroyd

SCB Representatives, Chris Van Straaten and Alex Harkess

Super 7even Co-ordinator – David Hoggart

Commenting on this year's AGM, BSPA Chairman Alex Harkess said: "This has been a tough year for British Speedway which has called for harmony and some compromise from our members, we have seen a tremendous amount of goodwill extended between clubs and leagues so that we can look forward to 2011 with optimism. The potential to expand or consolidate the Elite League still remains and will be finalised before the end of the year."

27th November

BSPA   British Speedway's Elite League will have a new look in the 2011 season. The British Speedway Promoters' Association can confirm that both Coventry Bees and Peterborough Panthers will not be taking their place in the top flight after they failed to declare their intent to compete in the 2011 Elite League at last week's AGM. The Association can confirm, however, that the future of the league is secure and the full line-up for the 2011 campaign will be unveiled on Monday at midday. Birmingham Brummies have already confirmed they will be making the step from the Premier to Elite League in an exciting move for the sport. The BSPA can also confirm the structure for all three divisions will be finalised at the General Council and National League meetings on December 7 and 8.

Nigel Pearson   "Yes, okay, there are times where, 2010 in particular, I've done TV meetings where I've driven a long journey home and I've been feeling pretty down, because there have been some meetings that have been pretty poor, and my boss at Sky has been pretty disillusioned with it."

Mike Bowden   "I can't believe the association would not support what has been a successful club"

Dave Tattum   "We have lost money for the past three seasons, but the losses incurred this year were massive and totally unsustainable...to have to stand up at the AGM and outline our financial position to the gathering was quite embarrassing for me, and it's not something I'd like to repeat"

Rob Godfrey   "It's all about getting through a difficult period, eliminating where we think the losses are and making it a better product.....The three seasons we've been in the Young Shield, I just didn't want to be in it by the end because we were haemorrhaging money. Most of my losses came at the end of the season in the Young Shield. There's no secret about that. Basically, the Young Shield bled us dry. So the new system is an upgrade because it takes a few of the problems out and creates more interest all the way through because league matches are what everyone wants. It also stops any possible average manipulation in the Premier Trophy."

BSPA   BRITISH Speedway bosses have moved to set the record straight over the recent decisions made by Elite League duo Coventry and Peterborough not to take their place in the 2011 competition. The top flight has been given a facelift for the new season with Premier League clubs King's Lynn and Birmingham, who boast some of the best tracks and facilities in the country, making the move up. But the absence of reigning champions Coventry and 2006 winners Peterborough has caused much debate. British Speedway Promoters' Association Chairman Alex Harkess said: "Let me first of all say how saddened I am that two clubs of such great stature will not be competing in the 2011 Elite League. But the bottom line is simple. Both clubs left the AGM and therefore failed to declare their intention to take their place in the Elite League. It was their decision and their decision alone. They are, of course, entitled to such a decision however regrettable it may be for the fans of those clubs and for the sport in general. It must be emphasised, however, that the BSPA is a democratic organisation. I sincerely hope it isn't the end of Elite League Speedway at both venues and that, perhaps, they will both return in 2012. On the positive side, we have two excellent Speedway venues moving into the Elite League in King's Lynn and Birmingham and I'm sure the fans of both clubs are in for a treat in 2011 with some exciting racing. And it's also good for the league to have some fresh teams and fresh venues, especially with the coverage provided by our friends and colleagues at Sky Sports." The BSPA can also confirm the Premier League line-up is now complete following Plymouth's elevation from the National League which means no further applications will be considered.

Peter Collins "It was such a boost getting home again to be with the family, to be in my own bed and eating my own food. I am walking unaided and can do the stairs, all the usual things you would expect to do around the house."

Dave Tattum "Stekkers served an apprenticeship in coming over and sleeping on floors whilst he learnt his craft, but it all seems quite different now. Riders want more but not all want to put the club first in return."

Jim Lynch "I've had some good years in speedway but one of my happiest was the last time I was at Belle Vue when we had a very good team with the likes of Jason Crump and Joe Screen riding. I've had a couple of years on the outside looking in but I was delighted when the call came out of the blue to join Belle Vue."

Hans Nielsen "Bernard [Crapper] was always so cheerful and any rider out of form was cheered up instead of getting a telling-off. We had a great team together and up until I joined Oxford, I had not won anything. It was without doubt my best period in speedway, and Bernard made sure we had the best team spirit."

Matt Ford "I can confirm we are a profit making club."

Jon Cook "We need to be mindful that the Elite League was set-up in 1997 by the Elite League clubs of that day to put a league together that would bring weekly televised league racing to the screens and within two years, that goal had been accomplished. We are probably well overdue for pressing the 'refresh' button, that's what we are just starting to do and it's an exciting time. It's certainly a taxing time to be involved but hopefully, we can move the sport on.".....................

Jonathan Chapman "Everyone else voted for [Ipswich] to come in [the PL], but I was the only one to vote against."

3rd December

Keith Chapman "It must have been hard for Niels to find out that he would no longer have a team place at Peterborough through no fault of his own. But he is such a nice guy and after half an hour with him we quickly came to a deal that proved to me what I have long believed about the majority of riders.... racing is about the thrill and ambition and not about the money!"

4th December

Keith Chapman "Over the past eight seasons we have enjoyed our time in the Premier League, but we have won everything we can possibly win and last season things started to feel a bit stagnated.....I also think it was important for the future of British Speedway to be secured by another team joining the Elite League, so after taking our time to look at all the pros and cons, I felt it was the right time for the club to make the step back up."

Alex Harkess "With King's Lynn moving up it created a vacancy for one more Premier League team and Plymouth's application was the next on the table."

Chris Van Straaten "I have worked alongside Colin Pratt for over 25 years through his time with Cradley and Coventry and I feel particularly sad for a man of his stature that this situation has developed."

Mike Bowden "I believe that the riders we have available would make us competitive against most Premier League teams on our own track."

Lewis Bridger "I'm open to all offers and we'll see what happens."

Dave Tattum "This is a new era for the club and one that I hope will put the club on the front foot and set the footings for a more successful and stable future."

5th December

Matt Ford "I am sure people know just what Bjarne Pedersen means to both the club and to me personally, and therefore will recognise just how hard it was to let Bjarne know that the 2011 team cannot accommodate him. At the annual conference we confirmed the points limit of 40 and whilst under the team building rules we could have retained Bjarne, who has an eight-point average, I felt that it could have left us too top heavy. We want to go one further in 2011 and actually be crowned champions so we need to find the right balance and it is the numbers game coming into play that has forced this decision."

11th December

Craig Watson "When I'm the most famous Newport rider and I live in Newport, and I've only got two sponsors, that's a bit of a worry I think"

David Gordon "We have tried to minimise cost on riders. There is no point whatsoever in having a massive asset base and no money to build a new stadium and I cannot stress that point hard enough."

Matt Ford "At this time of economic turmoil in the country, everyone in speedway is going to have to be sensible in their negotiations with me because I won't be putting up my admission prices next year. So there is little more I can pay the riders with points-money. I made it clear last month that we did make a profit as a club this year. But I don't want to go the other way now and pay out more money and become a loss-making club, like a few other clubs who have said they can't afford to ride in the Elite League. If that's because they are paying their riders too much money, I don't want to get caught in the same trap."

Lee Richardson "I've never ridden the Birmingham track and, in fact, I've never been there but I've heard very good reports about the facilities and the track."

12th December

Terry Russell "I thought we would make the play-offs last year, and if we had not lost those meetings at home we'd have walked it, because we had the second-best away record. I have to make sure we win here first, and away second. We want to win away, but we know the pain and the damage of losing at home."

15th December

Nick Barber "I often get a feeling about how the next season is gonna be. Last season, I thought it would be a shit year and it was – everywhere! At the moment, I'm sensing positiveness so, I think, it's gonna be a really good year next!"

18th December

John Anderson "If there are two riders of equal scoring potential available, we are committed to always sign the wilder one, the crazy never-say-die fence-bouncing crowd pleaser – even if he might crash out a few times trying, instead of just opting for safe second places"

Rob Godfrey "Our aim is to attract more spectators to speedway, not try and kill them when they get here"

Paul Cooper "I can't remember the crash. All I can recall is the bike moving out and the next thing it was three or so weeks later. I can't even remember the helicopter ride which is a bit of a disappointment!"

Rob Godfrey "Of course you want to be competitive away but do you want to go and destroy people's businesses?"

Jon Cook "Obviously promotion and relegation is dead in the water now and, in hindsight, it probably was a couple of years ago."

21st December

BSPA WE are pleased to inform fans of Speedway that the BSPA, Coventry Bees and Peterborough Panthers have held discussions with a view to resolving the issues that have arisen between them. We are at this stage unable to relay any information as to the nature or the content of those discussions but we can confirm that all of the parties remain committed to resolving the matter amicably. We thank all of the fans of Speedway, the commercial partners and the members for their patience during this time.

25th December

Mike Bowden   "The minute it's costing me money – I'm off!"

Peter Karlsson   "Whenever you mention Wolverhampton it reminds me of my English home"

27th December

Derek Barclay   "I suggested a couple of years back that Under 16s would be a better concept than Under 15s as this would fit in better with riders making the transition from junior to NL (previously CL) racing, so glad to see it happening now"

31st December

Lewis Bridger *   "Just opened a Box of Cadburys Milk tray.. as I only have under 24hr untill my crazy 3month of training & diet!! ;-(("

. . . .

8th January

Derek Barclay   "No, I have read THREE of his books: the first three...How many is he up to now? Five or is it six all on the same (non-) subject...? And how many people has he upset, offended, broken up their relationships....? Not quite as many as he's bored to death!!"

Julie Martin   "If you dislike them that much why on earth did you buy 3, mind you at least you pay for them unlike some others I could mention??!! ....and as for "breaking up relationships" what a crock of cow poop I almost pmsl when I read this comment from you time and time again Mr P, fortunately I still have full control of my waterworks"

Philip Rising   "British speedway is plagued by a situation where many riders are forced into changing clubs simply because they have got better"

Stuart Douglas   "If I may be so bold, I can honestly say I would not shed a tear, because this [2010 EL] format does not function as a credible sport, nor as a business model."

9th January

Fourentee   "Of course you should be allowed an opinion on the forum. Feel free to point out any post of mine that suggests otherwise. Meanwhile, with respect (and without a smiley if that's your preference), I feel a little getting over yourself might be in order."

17th January

BSPA   THE BSPA is disappointed to announce that the parties have been unable to resolve their differences. The BSPA can confirm an offer has been made to both Coventry and Peterborough which, if accepted, would see them both resuming their membership of the Elite League with immediate effect. That offer remains open. The BSPA very much hopes that, even at this late stage, Coventry and Peterborough will choose to resume their membership of the Elite League; and contribute towards a successful 2011 season. The BSPA would like to make it clear that they would welcome both Coventry's and Peterborough's resumption of their membership of the Elite League in time for the 2011 season: the absence of both Coventry and Peterborough from the Elite League is their own choice. The BSPA regrets that Coventry and Peterborough have not been prepared to accept relatively minor improvements to the BSPA's rules supported by the overwhelming majority of BSPA members but have chosen to maintain their threat of costly legal proceedings that can only damage the interests of the sport, its fans and riders.

22nd January

Nicky Mallett   "Mark fitted in like a glove on a hand"

23rd January

Poole website   Matt brightens the Troops. One member of HM British Forces is proudly wearing the colours of the Poole Castle Cover Pirates when out of uniform in Camp Bastion thanks to the generosity of Poole boss Matt Ford....Matt said "I have the utmost respect for everyone serving in our Forces and I was touched when I read David's message. British Speedway held a Special Forces week last season and it was good to do something to support the troops. It's good to see David already wearing the Poole shirt and cap and let's hope he can persuade his colleagues to follow speedway more."

24th January

Companies House   "Application for voluntary striking off [Wildcats Weymouth Limited]"

25th January

Lewis Bridger *   "I'm in my prime age and never loved life so much I reckon this weeks all bout getting some tatts finished!! :-)"

27th January

Steve Ribbons   "I came on this forum because I thought there were fans out there who genuinely cared about speedway...this is obviously not the case as the low life's have slithered out of their various holes and started personally attacking me (being a cyber warrior is sooo easy!)...So its time to answer an attack with one of my own.....

First a mild one...gibralta, you said ..."all a bit premature prior to getting permission to operate one suspects" what I meant was that I had done some PLANNING for Mildenhall so as not to go at it half- arsed when (if) we were given permission to go ahead.

NOW, to all the others in the snake pit, -

25 year idiot wrote......."I can understand the BSPA having reservations about Steve Ribbons because his previous record in speedway promotions is not good and he rubs everyone up the wrong way, hence the very low opinion most have of him".......

And also........."I learnt a few years back that when Steve Ribbons gets involved in anything to do with speedway, normally things at some point will go t its up which is what I thought would happen with his recent interest in Mildenhall,".......

Ah...25 year fan, jimbo or peachy mead or whatever you're called. i wondered how long it would take you to crawl out of your hole.

I seem to remember that you have an opinion on everything concerning speedway including dreaming up stupid names for non existent teams then posting them as if they were fact!!! Unfortunately they are only facts in the fairy pixy land that you and the fluffy bunnies inhabit!

So,- You say... "his previous record in speedway promotions is not good"... could you be referring to the fact that I didn't like it when Len bought the Rye house stadium out from under the supporters group then told us all to sling our hooks? Or the fact that I chose a [redacted] as a partner at Wimbledon who rinsed the bank account [redacted]? So yes, I might rub those people up the wrong way.

Now then lets examine the statement of... "I learnt a few years back that that when Steve Ribbons gets involved in anything to do with speedway, normally things at some point will go t its up which is what I thought would happen with his recent interest in Mildenhall",

Once again a statement of supposed fact...wanna back that up with a few for instances or even anecdotes? I remember that you had an unhealthy interest in my wallet a few years ago, now I've worked hard and got the money to run Mildenhall you are suspiciously quiet on that subject, but you know everything else...tell me, are you my stalker????

You say ...."I've been going to speedway a long time" well I can tell you mate in all that time,...son, you have learned NOTHING!

Now we come to the next reptile, Blazeaway...you have a serious problem boy and i'd go and see a doctor about that rash mate,...its not good in a twelve year old, sorry eleven and three quarters! As to facts, Wimbledon practice was a shambles because the GRA changed their minds and wouldn't let us lay a permanent shale bends...so you got me there pardner....opening night went ahead because my [redacted],,(sorry partner) insisted on it despite my advice against it! Boston, well the doctor didn't turn up (he was booked with the St Johns and they arrived) its happened before and no doubt it will happen again(it happened at Mildenhall's opening meeting last year I believe) yes, that was a shambles. but so is speedway! I did explain all this a few years ago but with you only just learning to read and write perhaps you missed it. I wonder please if the mods can put a link to my wimbledon story if its still on file?

Also, you said...(and this is a good one)........

"Remember the Conference League riders semi that we had?" You got me on that one. I wasn't even there then having left when Perkins took over so I think that shows how much you have your facts straight. Wimbledon wasn't all it was supposed to be because of the GRA kept changing their minds over track specification. But I did get the place open and you had what,…four years of speedway you wouldn't have had, but i suppose that don't count in your tiny mind. (you being only six years old then)

So why don't you PM me and we can meet and have this out man to boy, - you can bring your conkers and your catapult if you like,,, and I'll bring adult reasoned argument (me being a grown up like)

Now to grandad-speedguy, - John Hyam "Ah yes! Steve Ribbons. Viva Espana" what an incite and depth you bring to this debate. you being a former editor of the *speedway star* an all..... seeing as you believe 'real' speedway stopped after 1954 you never liked the Wimbledon project from day one (yes, I remember you as the only dissenting voice at the press conference announcing we were opening) well I'm sorry Mr Zimmer but your memories going If, by that (so cutting) comment you mean the spanish track, it was Russell paine who was working on that project, not me But I did drive a lorry of all his stuff out there so therefore i'm guilty by association but there you go confusing me with a completely different guy, I think that your carer should check your prescription glasses!!

For those who wonder why I am at loggerheads with the BSPA its down to one man, the so called Conference/National League [redacted] (I don't believe he could co-ordinate his shirt with his underpants. He is a fool and I have told him he is a fool! the very first time I telephone him he berated me for trying to start Rye House and we were on a downer all that season with him once saying to me (in front of witnesses "you lot are just gipsy's, you'll be selling heather next!) I wonder if he has said that to any of his pall's running the dudley club? Lets examine his qualifications shall we. This over blown programme collector is the [redacted]! I wouldn't trust him to run me a bath let along a league!!!

Is it wrong to Post this..yes, but I am sick and tired of thse personal attacks on me because of the fact I deeply care about the sport of speedway racing .I can say all this because I've given up trying to be polite to those people who don't like me behind my back but aren't man enough to say it to my face. Good luck to who ever takes over at Mildenhall cause I'm done with Speedway for good unless their are some serious changes. But for those of you who do try to get off our asses and try to do something for the good of the sport and open yourself up to public ridicule, my advice is.... DON'T, ITS NOT WORTH IT!!!!!!!

I have since found out what went on in the BSPA meeting and It was not a personal attack on me by the NL members –that much I thank them for anyway.

Never scared to hide my identity on line yours sincerely Steve Ribbons"

London Gazette

First notification of strike-off action (for Wildcats Weymouth Limited)

29th January

Nicki Pedersen "They keep saying they're going to bring the top riders back, but they don't seem to do anything about it. It's only going one way and sometimes you need to spend to lift it to a higher level and make money from it. If you just keep reducing, reducing, reducing, it's only going to go one way. I just think the money we used to get as top riders now gets paid to the middle of the road riders. They [promoters] haven't gained anything. The middle riders just have a higher value because they have become more important."

Just down the road "Its great when your relaxing out on your patio enjoying a quiet mid-afternoon nap to suddenly being awakened by 'battle of the tannoys'"

Nicki Pedersen "It's a disaster that they can't figure it out. There is only a month left until the season starts. But I suppose that's British speedway for you."

30th January

Coventry website It is with deep sadness that we have to report that Joyce Blythe, who for many years ran the Track Shop at Brandon, passed away in the early hours of Sunday morning. Joyce had been battling against ill health since the end of last season and sadly her condition deteriorated earlier in the New Year. A great number of supporters of both speedway and stock car events at Brandon will have met Joyce, who was totally dedicated to her work in the Track Shop, both in terms of bringing in and dealing with stock, and also with laying it out and sales on a race-night.

We all send our sincere condolences to Joyce's husband Malcolm and their family and friends at this sad time, and we do ask that their privacy is respected.

2nd February

Philip Rising   "WE have a 'Stop Press' item in *Speedway Star* this week having been briefed that both Coventry and Peterborough appear on the verge of returning to the Elite League with all parties involved having reached some sort of compromise along with speculation that Nicki Pedersen would be returning to racing in the UK ... but, like everyone else, we await some sort of official announcement, one way or the other."

3rd February

Philip Rising   "MUST admit we are as bemused as the rest of you about the lack of any official announcement. *Speedway Star* was contacted on Tuesday afternoon by someone, who we are not at liberty to name at this stage, deeply involved in the whole sorry saga who told us that a compromise had been reached. The editorial and production boys hurriedly re-jigged some pages and dropped an editorial piece by myself about, ironically, the lack of any proper information being provided to speedway fans by either side. We are as frustrated as any on this Forum"

4th February

Julie Martin   "He's a Grade A cock and you can quote me on that"

5th February

Jan Stæchmann   "There is a Danish saying: 'If you won't listen to it, then you will feel it'
- meaning ignore advice at your peril."

6th February

Philip Rising   "THIS thread in essence is not any different to the Coventry Are Back one. The position remains that if Coventry and Peterborough accept the BSPA proposal or the BSPA accept theirs both clubs will return. Otherwise they will not. At the moment both sides appear to be intransigent again and it remains to be seen for how much longer the door will remain ajar before it is finally closed. It is only seven weeks before the first Sky match is scheduled to be televised. The sands of time are running out and with each passing day."

Philip Rising   "EXILED CUDA ... no I honestly cannot say whether all the BSPA promoters are involved or just those from the Elite League at this stage. And therein lays one of the potential problems within the BSPA. If promoters from both EL and PL clubs are allowed to vote then hypothetically you could have a situation where seven EL bosses are out-voted by a majority from outside the Elite League. Steve is right that the BSPA have rejected C&Ps latest offer but one would hope that there is still some wriggle room. Sadly that is looking less and less likely after hopes seem to be genuinely raised last week."

Philip Rising   "I CAN assure you that Flagrag, whoever he is, has no connection with *Speedway Star*. However, from some of my very recent conversations he is currently on the ball. The remaining elements of the dispute that remain unresolved are the distribution of the Sky money for 2011, which is also allied to whether or not legal action continues, and how domestic speedway in this country is governed in the future...ie an independent panel."

Philip Rising   "MAY I also add that, like so many on here, I bemoan the lack of any official announcements from either side. People who do talk are only prepared to do so off the record and anonymously and while I, as a journalist let alone a speedway fan, find that frustrating it is infinitely better than no communication at all."

Philip Rising   "IT is my understanding (and, of course I could be wrong – it wouldn't be the first time!) Coventry and, to a lesser extent, Peterborough allege that a number of rule changes introduced for 2011 were specifically designed to scupper their team building pans and were the result of collusion and therefore illegal even if they were passed by a majority vote within the BSPA. Furthermore, in their view an independent body to oversee the BSPA and actually govern speedway from one AGM to another is the only way to ensure that such collusion, if in fact it does exist, is eradicated."

8th February

Philip Rising   "UNFORTUNATELY *Speedway Star* went to press this afternoon when the mood was still one of optimism. Now it is pessimism. If this ends the way it seems to be going it will be a very black day for speedway, no matter which track you support or whose side in this bitter and ultimately unnecessary dispute, you are on. It did seem as though a sensible and satisfactory compromise was in sight but if the people concerned aren't prepared to grasp the nettle two vital components of British speedway will be lost. Rest assured, *Speedway Star* will do its best to lay out the arguments on both sides and let the jury – that's the wider speedway public – decide."

Philip Rising   "My own view is that agreement has been made much more difficult by the fact – and it is a FACT for a change – that Coventry and Peterborough are effectively speaking as one voice while the BSPA have to embrace a whole range of opinions, with some tracks willing to agree to a but not b and others b but not a and so on. Frustrating is not the word for it."

11th February

Coventry website   BOTH Coventry and Peterborough are fully aware of the need to keep supporters as much up to date as possible but legal constraints have prevented us from doing this so far. We were hoping to give our fans an update today but again the legal requirements of any possible settlement have prevented us from doing so. Please rest assured that as soon as we are able a full update will appear on both Coventry's and Peterborough's websites.

12th February

Philip Rising   "AS far as I can ascertain, and many are being even more tight-lipped than normal, Coventry and Peterborough believed that an agreement had been reached between the respective legal teams on Thursday and that on Friday they would be in a position to announce their intention to run in the Elite League. But, with no formal ratification coming from the BSPA Management Committee, who are mandated to make such decisions, they had to step back yet again. And so the waiting goes on … and on … and on"

Philip Rising   "I WOULD add that the stumbling block at present seems to be a refusal by the BSPA to accept an independent adjudicator/panel to hear appeals over MC judgements on the rulebook and a year's grace before a new regulation (other than for safety reasons or agreed unanimously at the time) to come into force, allowing clubs to do some forward planning for a change."

Philip Rising   "I am sure that if the BSPA would say yes to the independent adjudicator and a 12 month moratorium about rule changes then all the other issues would be rapidly resolved and Coventry and Peterborough would be back like a shot … and we could get on with the 2011 season!"

Philip Rising   "AS I stated earlier, both anticipated being able to confirm their participation but without any confirmation from Rugby had to pull their planned announcements. Probably shouldn't have publicly stated that there would be an announcement but it was a sign of how confident they were that agreement had been reached."

Philip Rising   "TIME, surely, not to put the blame at anyone's door. Just get it settled. C&P shouldn't have walked out of the AGM but most of us have probably had a row and stormed out of something in our lives. It is what happens next that matters. We know for a fact that both Coventry and Peterborough want to run. Presumably the BSPA want them to as well. So, band some heads together, bit of give and take, shake hands and get on with it. And, by the way, it doesn't automatically follow that an independent adjudicator would always rule against the BSPA. In fact, as long as any decisions are properly arrived at he (or she, have to be careful these days) might never come into play."

Philip Rising   "HAVE said before that we would never have got into this mess had the old style SBC been in situ."

Jayne Moss   "A number of riders are ruled out (by 40 point limit) and to be quite honest we haven't had that much interest from riders looking for places, mainly down to the pay scale and what we can offer at Buxton."

13th February

Philip Rising   "I THINK that is what C&P want … a binding commitment for it to happen. Nobody expects it to become operational overnight. And we are not looking at full-time (and expensive) appointments. Maybe a pool of five people willing to act on a panel of three as and when required and for a modest fee and travel expenses if necessary. It shouldn't be rocket science…"

Philip Rising   "ARE you suggesting that people like Tony Steele, and others with an understanding of speedway, are incapable of being independent?"

Philip Rising   "I AM sure most, if not all, promoters would rather be hung, drawn and quartered than see me sitting in judgement on them but you are right. There is a wide selection of people with the utmost integrity out there who would be delighted to play a role if asked."

Philip Rising   "PROMOTERS would not be deprived of their powers. Far from it. No more than High Court judges are deprived of their powers. But, on occasions, there is a need for an appeals procedure. Three people (to ensure a majority vote) taken from a pool of candidates, and yes, referees or ex-referees would be primate candidates, to take an independent view and decision. As previously said, hopefully the panel would rarely be called upon but just having one in existence might sharpen the minds of those making critical decisions."

Philip Rising   "FORMER SCB Chairman Michael Lamb once said to me that it is much easier to impose discipline against people making shed loads of money rather than those who are losing it. So, I understand where you are coming from, which is why I don't think we can realistically expect British speedway promoters to fund league racing without any say. But what is being called for now isn't a full-time speedway czar but simply a procedure which allows for any contentious decisions to be challenged.

Your last point about Sky money is also pertinent and it is imperative that British speedway gets its house in order to ensure that funding continues in the future."

Philip Rising   "I have admitted privately and publicly to those like Ole Olsen and Jos Vaessen that I was wrong about the Grand Prix. The days of the old style World final (and I saw and enjoyed every one from 1962 to 1984) were numbered. And had been since the demise of Wembley. That was always Britain's trump card. It was time for change and while I would contest your claim that I jumped on the gravy train I am proud to talk to friends and journalistic colleagues outside of speedway about the quality of the current SGP series which, in the words of Barry Briggs, stands comparison with anything in motor sport, two wheels or four."

Philip Rising   "DO you not think that a three man panel is more democratic than a single person?"

Philip Rising   "UNLIKE me to put the FIM forward as a beacon of light but the Jury system at GPs works well. Any appeals are put before the Jury President and two others (nominally the referee and the FMNR representative of the staging country). Works well when called upon."

Philip Rising   "I DON'T think it was ever intended to have an independent body making the rules. That is the responsibility of the BSPA, under the auspices of the FIM, ACU and so on."

Philip Rising   "IF I may be permitted an aside, have enjoyed the banter and lively debate on here today, which has enriched a wet, cold and miserable winter's Sunday and which also illustrates how this [British Speedway] Forum can be a force for good when it avoids the personal and banal."

Philip Rising   "IF I understand their position accurately, they would not object to any rule changes agreed by a majority vote as long as there was a 12 month moratorium before they were introduced to ensure, in their eyes, changes weren't simply knee jerk reactions to particular situations at any given moment. While they see themselves as the victims (or targets) last November, next time it could be someone else. And there are plenty of examples of rule changes being hurriedly implemented which are fine in theory but which soon become impractical and counter-productive."

Philip Rising   "IAN Thomas, a genius when it came to working his way round the rulebook to its best advantage, said years ago that the whole thing should be torn up and started again and could be done in half a dozen pages….I would rather get Ian to re-write the rulebook than sit in judgement on the current one. I have known and worked with and for Ian over many, many years and love him dearly but impartiality isn't always his strong suit …"

14th February

Philip Rising "IF you keep reducing expenditure without increasing revenue sooner or later you are left with nothing more to cut and what do you do then?"

Philip Rising "THANKS for your support Bryn but I don't really think the BSPA, who have been or still are contemplating banning *Speedway Star* from being on sale at any of their tracks, would exactly relish the idea."

Philip Rising "THE banning of *Speedway Star* being sold "on the terraces" at all BSPA tracks was discussed at a management Committee meeting late last year."

Philip Rising "THIS is nothing new. It was a regular topic of conversation during the chairmanships of Reg Fearman, Charles Ochiltree and Stuart Bamforth amongst others. Sadly it is the predictable attitude of some when they read things they don't like or agree with. On many occasions we are berated by promoters angered by comments made against them by another promoter. Talk about shooting the messenger!"

Philip Rising "DON'T worry, *Speedway Star* will survive. Tracks sales are important but represent a relatively small percentage of our overall sales and, of course, are non-existent in the close season."

Philip Rising "IT is itemised in the minutes of a MC meeting last September. I have not said it is related to this dispute though we have been informed recently that the BSPA are unhappy with some recent SS content and especially the piece with Nicki Pedersen (costs, etc) which went down like a lead balloon with some."

Philip Rising "We would lose good revenue from Poole sales as we are able to get SS there on a Wednesday night….My wish is to see as many tracks operational in British speedway as possible. Yes, I am in favour of some sort of independent panel (have been for years and have been saying so in SS for as long as I can remember) and yes would favour a 12 month moratorium on rule changes. Proposed such an idea in the magazine earlier this year. And I firmly believe that this dispute can and should be settled asap for the good of the sport as a whole."

Philip Rising "We [*Speedway Star*] don't deal with the Millennium Stadium because they demand 40% commission."

Philip Rising "JUST for the record: I am Managing Editor of *Speedway Star* (Richard Clark is and has been Editor for 15 years) and Managing Director of Pinegen Limited, publishers of the magazine."

Philip Rising "IT was discussed at Management Committee level and I have no knowledge as to whether it has come before the BSPA as a whole."

Philip Rising "I DIDN'T know about it in September, it has only recently come to our notice. How did it get on this thread? As a result of some posters kindly suggesting that editor Richard Clark and I could be candidates for an independent panel but, as stated previously, most members of the BSPA would rather be hung, drawn and quartered than have *Speedway Star* employees involved."

16th February

Philip Rising "AFTER a pleasant round of golf, despite the weather, a long lunch and a few glasses of wine, it would be nice to complete a very pleasant day with news that the central theme of this thread (despite its recent diversions) had been resolved. However, that does not appear to be the case though I would hope (and believe), in the absence of any announcement, it is now down to the phrasing of the final agreement and formal and binding acceptance from all concerned. No news is good news … where have I heard that before?"

Philip Rising "NO one would accept having a panel changing democratically agreed rules – and, remember, the adjudicator system and the rules moratorium go hand in hand. If, at the end of the moratorium, the majority of clubs vote for a particular rule then naturally it has to be accepted by the BSPA as a whole. Peterborough, for example, believe that some Management Committee decisions have been made to favour certain tracks at the expense of others. They argue for the case, as they see it, for a level playing field. Any track that thinks a decision is not fair and transparent would have an opportunity to put their argument to the test. But there might also be an opportunity for a consensus of people to bring their thinking together and strip out a lot of the ambiguities and dubious wording of current regulations that ultimately lay at the heart of this dispute. Incidentally, I don't think Peterborough had a vote at the AGM because neither of their promoters, Rick Frost and Julie Mahoney, had served their three years apprenticeships and acquired full membership of the BSPA."

Philip Rising   "Peter Oakes couldn't attend but he wouldn't have had a vote either. Rick Frost and Julie Mahoney were (as I understand it) in attendance."

Philip Rising   "I DON'T think he's a registered promoter but could be wrong. Either way, he wasn't there so effectively Peterborough had no vote. Not that it would have made any difference but might have added to their sense of injustice having done so much to have cleared Peterborough's debts and coughed up £22,000 for Sundstrom, a young rider who would and hopefully still will enhance the Elite League."

17th February

Philip Rising   "It seems that the news is bad. Coventry and Peterborough out. No matter what side of the fence you sit on this dispute, this is a very sad and bleak day for British speedway."

Philip Rising   "I WAS notified that late last night that emails were sent out to this effect and told by a Coventry source that talks had finally broken down and it was the end of the road. Woke up this morning hoping it was a bad dream. Sadly, that isn't the case."

Coventry website   The managements of both Coventry Bees and Peterborough Panthers regret to announce that neither club will be participating in the 2011 Elite League having learned from the BSPA website that the BSPA has been unable to resolve the ongoing dispute with both clubs on an amicable basis. It is typical of the manner in which the BSPA have conducted negotiations that neither club have been informed of these latest developments directly by the BSPA as normal standards of courtesy requires. The BSPA position during talks has been characterised by delay, duplicity and narrow self interest. Both clubs believe that at no time during the last eleven weeks have the BSPA made a serious attempt to resolve matters, in fact just the opposite. A small number of protagonists have sought to influence negotiations to the advantage of their own clubs and detriment of other association members. The reference by the BSPA to an offer on the 31st January conveniently ignores the terms of that offer which were clearly designed to further disadvantage the two clubs both financially and competitively. In fact a further agreement was reached on Thursday 10th February and both clubs were prepared to announce an end to the dispute on their websites on Friday 18th February. In typical fashion the BSPA negotiators prevaricated on the details the following day and the announcement had to be cancelled. It is clear that in rejecting an independent appeals body and a 12 month rule changing moratorium the BSPA and certain members are only interested in maintaining and furthering their own narrow interests to the exclusion of all else including the desire of the vast majority of the speedway public in having a level playing field for all clubs not just the favoured few. It is a sad fact that the BSPA appears to have little regard for the good of British speedway, its fairness and more importantly the people who keep the sport going, its fans. It is a fact that throughout this dispute neither the BSPA nor its Chairman has acted in the manner reasonably expected of them. From the very first day both the Chairman and the BSPA took the side of those clubs that attempted to "ambush" Coventry and Peterborough at the 2010 AGM and the behaviour of Alex Harkess as Chairman has been lamentable. Coventry owner Avtar Sandhu has made his position clear and has stated that "I will return to speedway any time on any day for the sake of speedway and our fans but not as long as Alex Harkess is Chairman and Matt Ford is Vice Chairman of the BSPA. Their behaviour has been almost criminal in their attempts to keep both clubs out of the sport. Whilst we have been fighting to get into the sport they have been fighting to keep us out. For the good of speedway we have given way on the 60% PL to EL conversion rate, one over 8 point rider, Pawlicki on 5 instead of his greensheet 4 average and even a reduction in the Sky money due to us. However, we will never give way on the principle of fairness and the same standards for all clubs." The desire by the BSPA and certain members to prevent Coventry and Peterborough from participating in 2011 is now apparent even down to the allocation of Sky money to the two clubs which was set at less than one third of what all other clubs would receive, even though they expected both clubs to participate fully in live TV coverage as often as required. In the circumstances and having learnt from the BSPA website that negotiations are now ended both clubs will continue with legal action.

BSPA   IAN Thomas, one of Speedway's most charismatic promoters, has died after a battle with illness. Thomas, 69, left his role in charge of Workington at the end of last season and his last act was to help promote the hugely successful Telford indoor event last weekend alongside Graham Drury. The Yorkshireman launched the sport at Workington in 1970 and was a major player in reviving the Comets in 1999. He enjoyed a glittering career in charge of Hull, Belle Vue and England - and he also had a spell in charge of Newcastle. Colleague Drury, who also rode for Thomas at Hull, paid tribute to a true showman of the sport. "Ian was a true promoter in every sense of the word," said Drury. "I had the pleasure to ride for him and to work alongside him and I am proud to have enjoyed his company as a colleague and a friend. He was very sharp, knew every trick in the book and was always good to listen to. He was also very successful throughout the majority of his career and employed some of the biggest names in the sport like Barry Briggs, Ivan Mauger and Jason Crump. This is a very sad day and my thoughts are with Ian's wife, Dot, and son, Lyndon, who was with me at the weekend at Telford."

BSPA   The BSPA is disappointed to announce that it has been unable to resolve the ongoing dispute with Coventry and Peterborough on an amicable basis. The BSPA made an offer to both Coventry and Peterborough on 31 January 2011 which would have seen them both resume their membership of the Elite League with immediate effect. The offer would also have permitted both Coventry and Peterborough to continue with their proposed legal action, including claims for compensation if they suffer any losses. That offer was rejected. From the point of view of the sport it is disappointing that both Coventry and Peterborough would rather walk away from participation in the 2011 Elite League than accept an open offer to resume their membership, particularly as they could have done so without prejudice to their proposed legal action. Given the proximity of the new season the BSPA has been left with no alternative but to finalise arrangements for the 2011 season without Coventry and Peterborough. In this regard the fixture list will be published shortly."

Philip Rising   "*SPEEDWAY STAR* is a weekly publication and it will be a further six days before our next edition goes to press. In a world of 24/7 news and instant internet access do you seriously believe that stories such as these can be hidden away until someone decides to let them out. All sides in this bitter dispute have handled the PR side badly and by continually refusing to comment publicly – and I don't subscribe to the view that silence was the only legal option – actually increased the flow of leaked and off the record briefings that provided all the conjecture that has appeared here."

Philip Rising   "I WOULD be very surprised if this is the end of the story, just the conclusion of one chapter, which is why (as a fan and someone with a vested interest ie *Speedway Star*) I fear that the worst could be yet to come."

Philip Rising   "I AM not taking sides here but if Sandhu hadn't bought Coventry and Frost baled out Peterborough for how much longer do you think either would have survived anyway?"

Philip Rising   "I REPEAT my earlier post about PR … if a story isn't true DENY IT … if it is CONFIRM IT."

Philip Rising   "WE weren't making any comments of the information we had been given, simply illustrating some of the respective points of view. Peterborough may well be wrong about Andersson but they have contested that. And both Coventry and Peterborough say they have never given the requisite written 30 days notice of intent to withdraw from the Elite League and therefore (in their eyes) remain(ed) members of the Association."

Philip Rising   "WE have published as much as we know and can safely disclose this week. However, if as seems likely there is a continuing legal dispute *Speedway Star* will continue to be constrained by the very limited information either side is willing or able to reveal."

Philip Rising   "THE only way that we, the speedway public, will ever find out exactly who is telling the truth in this dispute and what offers were or were not made, is if this whole sorry affair does end up in court … which is also the worst possible scenario. If the gloves come off and it is open season who knows what might come out. But obviously there are documents and emails that went to and from between the respective lawyers and within them will lay the evidence. If indeed it does go before a judge we might end up with full disclosure but a sport seriously damaged nonetheless.

It's a mess whichever way you look at it."

Arnie Gibbons "I thought Peterboro did indicate that they didn't wish to run in the Elite League"

Speedway Star Q&A

WHEN and why did this dispute kick off?

AT the BSPA AGM last November when Coventry maintain they were "ambushed" by a number of proposed rule changes, some of which were included in a document produced by Wolverhampton team manager Pete Adams.

Coventry, who despite being Elite League champions ended the campaign with a low overall average of just over 42 as a result of their poor start to the season, believe others anticipated the team that they were planning to put together for this year and sabotaged it.

Coventry could have swapped Ben Barker with Kenni Larsen and began 2011 with a team potentially even stronger than the one that finished as league winners.

Coventry were, in fact, the only team at that time with two riders with an average in excess of 8.01 (Bjarne Pedersen at Poole was on exactly 8.00).

HOW did this affect Coventry?

WITH the introduction of the stipulation that each EL team could have only one rider with an average in excess of 8.01, that the conversion rate for riders moving from the Premier to the Elite League (Coventry had lined up Kenni Larsen from Newcastle) be raised from 50% to 70% and an average of 6.18 for Przeslaw Pawlicki, who had ended the previous campaign at reserve, based on the 11 matches he rode in, having controversially missed one and therefore avoided the normal 12 match requirement.

Coventry say that they broke no rules when Pawlicki missed a meeting at Swindon which kept him below the 12 point mark and that his actual green sheet average is 4.00.

Others will argue that if not broken the rule was extremely bent.

SO, how many other tracks agreed?

WE have no voting records but it would appear only Peterborough, who had purchased Lunus Sundstrom from Rye House for £22,000 and were therefore also affected by the raised conversion rate, supported Coventry. But Rick Frost and Julie Mahoney, their promoters, had not completed their three years initiation period and did not have a vote anyway.

Other tracks, and especially those in the Elite League, were in favour of the various proposals that were subsequently voted through and refused to buckle in the face of threats of legal action by Coventry and Peterborough.

The BSPA claim that a democratic process passed the rule changes and the Coventry and Peterborough should have accepted the will of the majority.

WHAT happened next?

COVENTRY and Peterborough walked out of the AGM and as a result did not immediately declare, as requested to do so by the BSPA, their intent to run in 2011.

BUT, didn't Rick Frost say Peterborough wouldn't run because they had lost £140,000 in 2010?

HIS statement was somewhat ambiguous. Some read it to mean that he wanted an improved Peterborough team (hence his purchase of Sundstrom) and an enhanced Elite League product to at least help stem his losses rather than he was ready to quit and walk away.

SO, Coventry and Peterborough were out?

WELL, this is where the waters get muddy. The BSPA constitution demands that any track wishing to withdraw must give 30 days written notice of their intent to do so. Neither Coventry nor Peterborough has done this. And both have continued to affirm their intent to run in 2011 if and when a satisfactory conclusion is reached.

WHAT happened next?

WITH Birmingham swapping league places with Ipswich, the BSPA persuaded King's Lynn to move up into the Elite League to ensure it had the requisite number of tracks demanded by Sky TV. Not surprisingly, King's Lynn moved quickly to sign Peterborough riders including Kenneth Bjerre.

AND then?

THE BSPA and the Coventry/Peterborough camps appointed legal teams to argue their respective case and for the past few weeks efforts to find a deal agreeable to both sides has continued, bouncing back and forth between each side.

WITH no success?

SADLY, no. At various times the stumbling block has either been Pawlick's starting average for 2011, how the Sky money for this year is distributed or the conversion rate. The one 8.01 plus rider per team has resolved itself but could still be an issue in the future. And, more recently, the establishment of an independent appeals panel to adjudicate on perceived contentious BSPA decisions and a 12-month moratorium on proposed rule changes has become the crux of the argument.

From the start of negotiations Peterborough were determined to have an independent adjudicator/panel to give speedway what Frost described as a "level playing field for all clubs."

Peterborough owners Frost and Mahoney believe past Management Committee decisions have been taken for the benefit of certain clubs and to the detriment of others. They also claim that the proposal to increase the conversion rate from PL to EL from 50% to 70% (later lowered to 60% after C&P left the AGM) was not backed up by sufficient research and called for a panel to investigate assessed averages (encompassing both the conversion factor and the assessed average that applies to new foreign riders which wasn't altered.

They also point out that Dennis Andersson has apparently been allowed to sign for Poole on a 4.00 assessed average even though his average in the Swedish ElitSerien is over six points a meeting and he should under the current regulations have come into the EL on 5.00.

WHO makes the decision for the BSPA?

THE Management Committee is mandated to respond to the various proposals and to make ones of their own but whether any final deal would have to be formally ratified by all the full members of the association is unclear.

WHERE are we now?

WE understand that there was at one stage broad agreement on Pawlick's starting average (5.00), the Sky money and the dropping of the legal cases being brought by both sides. Coventry and Peterborough also agreed to abide by all other decisions taken at the AGM last November once afforded an unequivocal commitment to the appeals panel and a 12 months gap between rule changes being proposed and introduced without a unanimous vote to do so.

SO, why hasn't it been resolved?

BECAUSE Coventry and Peterborough are insisting on a legally binding commitment for the introduction of an independent body and the 12-months moratorium. And, to date, the BSPA hasn't agreed.

WHAT sort of panel?

IT is generally recognised that a full-time Chief Executive to administer the BSPA isn't a viable proposition at this juncture, not least because of the financial implications.

One idea being suggested is pool of independent (not BSPA promoters, possibly current or former referees) adjudicators, three of whom could be called upon at any one time to form a panel to arbitrate on BSPA decisions that are contested by one or more members of the association.

Members of the panel could be paid a modest daily fee and travel expenses and their verdict would be binding. The costs would be funded by fees charged against any clubs making appeals that would also, hopefully, deter frivolous ones.

ARE the current BSPA promoters in favour?

WE don't know for sure, some probably are, some not. Many do not feel there is need for such a panel and that the Management Committee, working at the behest of its members who bankroll speedway in the UK, should have the final say.

WHERE do we go from here?

THE lawyers are still making proposals and counter-proposals while the legal costs are spiralling and the 2011 season looms ever closer with no fixtures and no idea whether the Elite League will consist of eight tracks or 10.

Allen Trump "We want the appeals situation taken away from the BSPA themselves. The BSPA themselves are partial, they are biased, they have their own favourites. Coventry has never been one of the favourites- so we wanted appeals to be heard by an independent panel. In addition to that we wanted a 12-month moratorium on new rules, so that a club could not be ambushed – as we were ambushed – by two or three clubs at the last AGM. And when I say we, I mean Coventry and Peterborough. We were ambushed by three or four clubs last AGM in November. Deliberately, premeditated, pre-discussed by them. [They] bounced new rules and regulations on us with one intention to ensure that the side that we had pencilled in for 2011 could not run."

Allen Trump "It's another indication of what we're dealing with at the BSPA. They prevaricate, they're not straightforward, they don't tell you the truth. The management of the BSPA are actually in bed with other promoters from three or four other clubs. The promoter at Poole is the Vice-Chairman of the BSPA – that's like putting a poacher in charge of looking after game. He isn't going to work towards what's good for the sport. He's only going to be interested in what's good for Poole."

Allen Trump "The legal action is intended to obtain an injunction to prevent them continuing with their anti-competitive, discriminatory application of the rules and, if it stops British speedway, it stops British speedway...the purpose of the injunction is basically to say to a judge 'stop this discriminatory application of the rules continuing, because it's illegal because these people are acting against EU Laws, against British Law and any type of Competition Law because it is a premeditated cartel."

Allen Trump "Definitely not – no speedway at Brandon. The only way it will is if they come to us and say 'okay Harkess, the Chairman, has gone' – he's been a disgrace – 'Ford, the Vice-Chairman, has gone' – another disgrace – and 'we'll appoint another Chairman and Vice-Chairman'. And we'll meet them half way. We've given way on the averages and Sky money – just for the good, for the sake of British speedway."

Allen Trump "[Their] weasel wording about the independent panel and the 12 month moratorium, which basically said 'yes – we'll agree to it but it has to go through the constitution of the BSPA, through the General Council and Management Committee meeting formula' which meant effectively we'll kick it into the long grass and you won't see head nor tail of it again."

Allen Trump "Coventry and Peterborough are solid together in this. The BSPA offered Coventry more money to ditch Peterborough to come in by themselves. That's the level we've got. That's how low the BSPA are prepared to sink to ensure one of their client clubs – one of them – win the Elite League. We wouldn't ditch Peterborough. We're in it together – okay – Peterborough are in the injunction with us."

Allen Trump "Anytime, any day we will meet for the good of speedway – Sandhu has said so on our website – but there's no point going back into this prejudicial, discriminatory organisation that masquerades as the BSPA."

18th February

Keith Chapman "We have been supporters of both Coventry and Peterborough returning to the Elite League in 2011, we have actually voted in favour of two resolutions's which is documented and can be called upon in a court of law. We are therefore disgusted by these allegations which are completely fictional and in all honesty totally unprofessional. It seems Mr Trump isn't happy enough with the situation he has left his own club in and wishes to tarnish the credibility of all other clubs at the same time!"

19th February

Rory Schlein "I found that (Jim Lynch) could get through to me in the pits during a meeting, unlike some managers, and I hope that he can do that for me again this year."

Ole Olsen "BSI/IMG in particular are giving a lot of advanced goodies for the spectators so that they feel that they're part of a great event. You go to somewhere like Cardiff, and some of the others, it's amazing – a fantastic event, you've just got to be there. It comes down to small details like the programme, the Methanol Club, the entertainment, the fireworks, every detail is attended to which is important."

Steve Mallett "We are extremely disappointed with the conduct of those clubs which decide to let it be known that they have taken over a rider, but without having agreed terms with us. You would think that clubs would want to make sure the rider they are wanting to bring is actually their man. In the cases of Atkin, Webster and Armstrong, I can reveal now that terms have not been agreed and the paperwork has most certainly not gone through the BSPA office."

Robin Spicer "Last week I returned from my local newsagents where I had purchased my weekly copy of the *Speedway Star*. I sat down and started to browse through the many factual and informative articles on British and overseas speedway. As I reached the National League section, I was interested to see the Weymouth Speedway Track Review, which was never going to be a pleasant read for a life-long die hard Weymouth Speedway supporter like myself. It was at this point that 'factual and informative' turned to fiction. Firstly, I feel I need to give you some back ground information regarding my relationship with Weymouth Speedway. During the 2006 and 2007 season I was one of four 'Directors' of the club, (or so I thought, as myself and my fellow Directors were never officially given directorships), having invested a sizeable four figure sum into the club. During this time we kept accurate records of all monies received by the club and their sources i.e. gate receipts, track shop, food and beverage, sponsorship etc. In 2007 Weymouth Speedway broke even with an average crowd of 487 (paying) plus 30 individuals utilising the "buy one get one free" offer. This gave an average spend of £5.00 per person in addition to their gate money. This was not down to luck. It was the fruits of labour of several people all working together to make Weymouth Speedway a success. Most of these people gave up their time for free, purely for the love of their club. Fellow 'Directors' John Hawkins and Ray Collins, Press Officer Julie Martin and myself along with several other club supporters were the dedicated souls who put the leg work into promoting Weymouth Speedway. We placed tickets on cars in the town, distributed discount vouchers on Weymouth seafront during the holiday season, attended the evening firework displays during the summer holidays handing out yet more promotional tickets, and made sure every hotel in Weymouth had information on Weymouth Speedway. We also employed Paul Oughton and Ross Marks of Influx Marketing for the period of the 2007 season. During this time great efforts were made in promoting the club in the local area, examples of such were a large permanent advertising board placed on Weymouth promenade and the development of our "Speedway in the Community" fund raising initiative. The *Dorset Echo*, local radio station - Wessex FM and Littlesea Holiday Park all became media partners and helped to promote the club to a wide audience. During my time associated with the club, at no point did I see our illustrious leader, Mr Philip Bartlett distribute a single leaflet, attend any promotional event or clean a single kick board (yes we did that too!). In fact, Mr Bartlett often commented that he thought we were wasting our time. Now it is 2011 and we have no club. This however is NOT because the club is unviable as stated in the track review, it is because local businessman Mr Bartlett made the fatal error of thinking he knew best and to hell with everyone else. Mr Bartlett's business acumen really came to the fore when, in 2008 he went to the landlord for a meeting to try and negotiate a reduced rent. During the 2007 season we held 23 meetings on a pay per meeting basis of £1,200 per meeting. After the meeting with the landlord, Mr Bartlett was delighted to have negotiated a new deal and announced that he was now paying £38,000 per annum. Here's some maths - 23 X £1,200 = £27,600 so we were now paying £11,000 a year extra! At the beginning of the 2010 season we were assured that with a new Commercial Manager who could dedicate themselves to finding new sponsorship and promoting the club, this season would be one of the most successful yet. In fact, when Mr Bartlett was trying to sell the club at the end of last season, he informed us that he had had the most profitable season yet as quoted in the *Speedway Star*! Well, I guess I must have been wrong and he must have been right. There was virtually no promotion of the club whatsoever last season, so yes Mr Bartlett, it appears it was in fact a waste of our time, but at least you didn't waste yours. In fact so little work was needed to promote the club last year, the sign outside the stadium, (what was left of it) displayed Weymouth v Isle of Wight 7th May 2010 and did for ever after. No need to change it, speedway fans knew the fixture list and so did the tens of thousands of holidaymakers, didn't they? But hang on, here we are, no club, riders out of pocket, shareholders wondering where their money went, and yet Mr Bartlett did his best, didn't he? Unfortunately Mr Bartlett's outlook on 'promoting' speedway is not uncommon within the speedway fraternity. It is not a matter of 'build it and they will come', look up 'promote' in a dictionary and it will say something like - to encourage the sale of a product through advertising. Speedway has the potential to become a great product but only if it is given the chance. Speedway supporters are a dedicated bunch, they must be to have stuck with a sport that is so poorly run by its governing body, a governing body that cannot ever be impartial by its very nature and a rule book with more holes than a pound of Emmenthal. Unless the way speedway is run in this country is dramatically changed, I fear that many more clubs will be following Weymouth Speedway down the proverbial pan."

20th February

Moira Perrott "I can't see anyway back for Coventry. I've seen but pretended I haven't seen the Coventry writ and far from being something compiled by a top notch expert it reads like it's been cobbled together by one of Sandhu's friends."

21st February

BSPA AFTER discussions between the British Speedway Promoters' Association and Rob Lyon it has been amicably agreed that Mr Lyon will not continue with his role as Team GB Manager. The position will now be considered by members of the BSPA Management Committee. The BSPA would like to place on record their thanks for the hard work and effort put into the role by Mr Lyon over the past two seasons and wish him well for the future.

23rd February

BSPA THE 2011 Elite League fixtures have been released this morning and the full list is available online.

Jon Cook "We are pleased with this year's fixtures as we have delivered as many Friday home meetings as the international list allows and, thanks to the support of our Raceway landlords, we have the advantage of being able to run two Saturday night meetings and on both Friday Bank Holidays. We have lost two home League matches due to the Sport's winter of discontent and as regrettable as that is we have replaced them with at least five Hawks meetings and have applied for another major senior event, details of which we hope to announce soon."

25th February

BSPA Smallmead Stadium closed in 2008, work on a replacement was due to have been completed by the middle of last year, but there have been continued delays. Many feared the closure of Smallmead could spell the end of racing in Reading, but the former promoters of the Reading Racers Speedway team have always maintained local people would like to see the sport return.

26th February

Alun John Rossiter "It's difficult to say, because my biggest problem is that I speak the truth, but unfortunately in this sport the truth doesn't get you anywhere."

Philip Rising "It is bad enough when tracks are forced to close by outside forces or bankruptcy but to lose a brace through internal politics and intransigence is shameful"

Alex Harkess "We don't have funds because we don't get any funds for being in that [Speedway World Cup] event to start with"

Andy Griggs "Troy Batchelor's over here with all the gear and no one to ride for – just like Edward – it's disgusting – and he's British!"

Alex Harkess "We are working hard on under-19s and under-21s to bring them on as best we can"

Andy Griggs "When you think 9 years on I'm still there at Rye House – it's where I started – while Oxford have come and gone and Peterborough have come and gone twice!"

Terry Russell "I am disappointed that Coventry's Allen Trump chose to name me as one of the 'wreckers'. I am not a promoter and no longer go to BSPA meetings. As Swindon co-owner, and through my Go Speed company's tie up with Sky of course, I earnestly hoped both clubs would be in. It is a tragedy for all parties concerned that they're not."

Graham Drury "Ian [Thomas] was a true promoter in every sense of the word. He was very sharp, knew every trick in the book and was always good to listen to."

Rob Godfrey "Speedway always comes first, it has to, because stock-car drivers can drive on anything but speedway riders need a good track to race on"

John Sampford "The public have made it more than well known they are only interested in official fixtures and really only the league and the KO Cup to a lesser extent. This way we are providing ourselves with six more league fixtures, which can only be good."

Paul Clews "Although you never think of the dangers once you are racing, just look at what happened to Adrian Rymel. He basically just slid off and got caught by someone else. It was that easy and sometimes you just have to hold your hands up and say that you have had a good run so let's leave it at that."

Graham Drury "Jason Lyons has a theory, and I go along with it, that whenever a speedway rider gets married, they have a bad season!"

Ryan Fisher "I can kind of see both their sides and the points they have. But I think at the end of the day, Coventry are the league champions. So I would say, 'play by the rules and win again'. It's not the first year they've tried to catch them out a little bit, but when you're a top team, you should be able to play by the rules and suck it up for another year."

27th February

Moira Perrott "It's the one track that really feels like it's run by gypsies. The track is good but everything else is a bare minimum – catering, medical facilities, stadium, the bar.

Moira Perrott "I don't think that a lot of people realise what a success Dudley has been. Not if they don't come from the region. The amazing thing is that it's a complete new group of people not your normal fans!"

Moira Perrott "If there were glimmers, it's not going to happen with all the costs now the season tickets have been sold, the fixtures announced, schedules planned and flights booked. To change now would mean massive upheaval"

Moira Perrott "Who is Allen Trump? To my mind because Coventry needed a second promoter he stayed on in a stay involved sort of position, Sandhu needed a body cos they weren't sure about Rosco. Sorry but I now view him as the man who has taken two clubs out of speedway!"

Moira Perrott "It'll be interesting to see how things go if King's Lynn and Birmingham don't make a good start – they'll soon realise that they've become part of the Big Boys Society and that they've just been dragged along to keep speedway going

Moira Perrott "I reckon Tattum will get a big surprise going down to the NL. The crowd will be okay for the few meetings but they could soon be down to 200-250 fans, particularly if things don't get well"

5th March

Brian Havelock "I do believe that if you have got a feel for a town, you perform better representing that town"

Joe Jacobs "My size [5'5"] has never been a problem because I've always had good balance. Sure, we have handlebars that are cut down and my seat placement and all that is different"

Rob Lyon "We should seriously look at allowing someone of the nature of Barry Hearn to get involved and take the sport by the scruff of the neck and try to bring in a modern way of thinking."

John Campbell "I'm a bit annoyed by journalists who suggest that Newcastle were team of the year. They were the team of the end of the season, but they weren't the team of the year."

Rob Lyon "What have we been doing for twenty years? Every season has got its reasons but a speedway nation that was the nation at one point hasn't won the World Cup for what is now 21 years... It's now 21 years and how do I feel about that? I'm sad, disappointed, frustrated and embarrassed."

10th March

Matt Ford "It was a long, drawn out and complicated process, as I always knew it would be, but I think well worth it as I feel that Renat [Gafurov] will do a good job for us this year. There was a lot of paperwork involved, hours of form completion and many hurdles that had to be cleared but late Wednesday afternoon we received the one piece of news that we wanted, confirmation of the issuance of the work permit."

11th March

Ronnie Russell "I was superbly confident this year and I can't let what's happened [Zengota injury], as tragic as it is, be the end of the season before it's even started. I've put my scouting hat on and I've put out a network of calls all over Europe because I can't afford to leave any stone unturned. We had a very difficult season last year and we've got to hit the road running this time."

12th March

Jonathan Barber "When Allen Trump turned up at our auction, I thought we might be part of his World Tour! I felt like getting a t-shirt done with Allen Trump World Tour on the front and Peterborough, Nuneaton, Ryton on the back. He was saying to Coventry fans at the auction see you at Press and Practice! To be fair, on Thursday evening they were back in but on condition that Allen Trump issue a personal statement saying that the BSPA weren't corrupt. When he said he wouldn't they told them to F off"

Jonathan Barber "Tony Steele asked us at Ryton if we'd been successful bidding to run the trackshop at Leicester. We said, 'they're going to do their own thing'. Tony replied, ' when I buy the stadium for a pound next winter, you can run the trackshop'"

Jonathan Barber "The season hasn't started yet and already I'm sick of people talking about Coventry and Peterborough. Honestly, I don't care. Some people say that it's the end of speedway. What a joke, speedway will carry on without them easy enough"

Jonathan Barber "A bloke came up to me a few minutes ago [at press & practice] and said 'excuse me – have you got any team photos?' I know we're good but we're not that Fing good!"

Jonathan Barber "I said to [redacted] when he first started as a promoter, 'you must think the fans are stupid' and he leant towards me and said, "we rely on it!'"

Olly Allen "When you sign someone, you pay them to do a job like you would a painter and decorator. If you don't do it, you don't keep your job."

Olly Allen "In about 16 years you may be interviewing him [unborn son] for the Star, although not if I can help it. I'm going to point him in a different direction."

Adam Roynon "I was talking to Ryan Fisher and he said 'What's the matter?'. I said, 'Oh, he pulled me out for being mentally unstable.' And Fisher said, 'Well, I've been mentally unstable since I started racing, we have to be, otherwise we wouldn't be here!'"

15th March

Rye House website Rye House Speedway is aware of speculation circulating regarding events at and around Friday's Press and Practice Day last Friday (March 11th). The club has not been in a position to comment before now, but further developments enable it to make the following announcements: An unfortunate incident took place at Rye House stadium very early last Friday morning, and which resulted in Steve Boxall suffering a serious injury to his upper arm. The nature of the incident and its subsequent handling prevents further comment at this point.

17th March

Richard Hollingsworth "The Steeltown Trophy may not be the most prestigious trophy on offer this season but the matches against Sheffield are always very important"

Andy Griggs "It's a mugs sport, it's farsical"

Dorothy Perkins "The early morning incident after the Rye House press and practice last Friday is a bit of departure from the usual team bonding skiing holidays Len usually organizes"

19th March

Robert Bamford "Only in speedway could more equal less. Last season there were nine teams and 32 fixtures while this there's ten teams and 26 fixtures! What is wrong with having home and away twice? They're going to get rid of the 'B' fixtures and instead clubs can make picks for the second phase of five fixtures. What about the fans who've bought season tickets thinking they're getting 32 meetings, but only getting 26?"

Robert Bamford "It's good Nicki is back, but he's got no opposition! He's so fast out of the gate, he'll beat the mediocre opposition hands down. Okay, there is Lindgren, but he's got him beat!"

Robert Bamford   "They say the BSPA were proven 75% correct so, therefore, their costs have been underwritten by their insurers and, thereby, they're got off scott free from the costs or making the changes that would have happened otherwise"

Chris Holder *   "Off to Poland... Not real keen to go tbh.."

20th March

Derek Barclay   "What an unpleasant response. How in god's name do you reckon my response [about Hackney Hawks disabled parking] was "fake concern" I actually despair sometimes about the attitude of people on here"

24th March

Gary Patchett   "There appears to be a stand-off between the F.I.M., PZM and the Polish riders and contrary to what we had originally been led to believe the availability of Polish riders cannot currently be guaranteed"

25th March

Chris Louis   "The last few days has been a whirlwind in the transfer market for us"

Dave Fairbrother   "No one tells us what's going on and we've got the big edition coming out next week. We've got till Tuesday to find out."

Chris Ellis   "We've had more overtaking in two [Ipswich] meetings than in the past 2 years"

Nicki Pedersen [on ekstrabladet. dk as quoted by sportowefakty. Pl]   "I will say only this. Poles are right. I have been testing these new silencers for months now, and cannot say a good word for it. FIM is made up of a few limited old men who are not prepared to listen to riders opinion. I have great respect for the Polish stance on this matter. I have spent 50 thousand Danish Crowns (on new silencers) and, have to say, with poor effect. The 2011 season is however too important for me to give it up."

BSPA

NEW SILENCERS - FIM STATEMENT

THERE have been many rumours circulating during the last few weeks concerning the use of the FIM Homologated silencers in the track racing disciplines. The introduction of the new silencers has now been successfully implemented in all World Championships including SGP and SWC and national Track Racing activities in all countries and leagues in Europe, except in Polish leagues where the situation is still unclear. The Director of the Track Racing Commission Roy Otto stated: "I would like to confirm that the CCP Bureau has no intention in changing the rule of the new homologated silencers complying with the FIM Technical Regulations (Akrapovic, Provide 115, King 2010, Dep Pipes 2010, Dep Pipes T10 – 2010) and these silencers will be the only ones allowed to be used in the FIM Track Racing Championships, including the FIM Speedway Grand Prix and the FIM Speedway World Cup Series". In the interest of the sport the FIM will also take the necessary action to ensure that the riders' participation in other international championships is not prevented.

Companies House   Notice of voluntary strike-off (Wildcats Weymouth Limited) suspended

26th March

Krzysztof Cegielski   "The riders have said they [silencers] are dangerous to ride and they cannot allow the Polish riders to race where the dangerous things are"

Rob Godfrey   "There is an element in them that is going to kill British speedway. I understand we have to cut the noise, but there is an element in the silencers that doesn't work in the dirt and as more clubs are starting to try them, it is becoming apparent there is a problem with them. It's a case of where we see ourselves in a year's time? Do we see ourselves with no crowd or do we see ourselves putting on entertainment?.....we have got to accept that we have to quieten speedway down, which I think we all do, everybody knows that. But we have to quieten it down in a way that maintains what we had and we haven't got what we had at the minute. .....we're watching sub-standard speedway at the moment, so the silencers have had an impact, no question."

Tony Swales   "We always had problems with drainage at Cleveland Park. If the tide was in, the Tees would back up and the water would flood some of the track for about two hours. Some meetings, we were pumping water off at 6.30 for a 7.30pm start and then we'd have to water the remainder of the track for about two hours"

Graham Arnold   "No-one wants to ride – it's terrible out there. The Dragons had to call off a meeting last week cos there weren't enough riders. When you think it costs £150-£200 to ride in a meeting then you ain't gonna do it every week are you?"

Tony Swales   "At Belle Vue, you have to work around the dogs as they have trials from 12 to 3pm on race-day so it's hard getting the water into the surface when you can't do any watering between those times."

Kevin Davies   "Put a Wolves race jacket on PK and he's a different rider"

Tony Swales   "Most of the track curators help each other whenever possible"

Alan Boniface   "I'd be very surprised if the Eagles don't make the play-offs and, if we stay injury free, we could be champions"

Richard Clark   "Those red-tape worshippers at the FIM and their ambition to make speedway bikes sound like 500cc-powered hairdryers"

Mick Hinves   "I just heard the latest bit of bureaucracy – when there's a Sky meeting there's no photographers allowed on the centre green!"

Jonathan Barber   "Mike Western has a Swedish wife so he thinks he knows how to pronounce all the names. So Kevin Long says Lasse Bjerre and he says it like some Greek Eurovision entry"

Kenneth Bjerre   "It was sad in a way to be leaving Peterborough, because that is where I wanted to be, but I am glad to be at King's Lynn now"

Jim Lynch   "There is something different about Rory this year, I can sense a real determination and he wants to do really well"

Renat Gufurov   "Using the new silencers, it's dangerous if there is some grip on the inside because I'm losing power and the bike gets out of control…..I don't like them. I'd like to ride using the old silencers, like we do in the Polish league"

Jon Cook   "I think I speak for all members of the association when I say we are looking forward to going racing now rather than indulging in speedway politics and fall-outs etcetera. We are all in the sport because we love speedway racing…..it's obviously been a difficult winter but I think it's only a handful of fans that are overly stressed about the politics. For most people, as long as their club is going to be racing and the league is looking healthy at the start of the season – which it will be – than they are just looking forward to watching their sport. There are so many other things in life to worry about at the moment and speedway provides a nice escape and that's what we want to be able to present at lakeside from Friday onwards."

Jonathan Barber   "Kevin's having problems with Lasse Bjerre – last week he said 'shit' when he was interviewed and this week he said 'fuck'!"

Jan Stæchmann   "Motorsport is dangerous – it says so on the back of your ticket. No one is forcing them to compete. Do you want to do it, yes or no? Those are the rules. I'll put money on the fact that the Polish riders will compete in the GP as per plan, and as the SWC race off and final is in Poland, then so there will a Polish team."

Dennis Andersson   "I'm not the kind of guy who likes speedway. I like to race, but I don't like the sport as a fan"

Pete Simmons   "Last season I was happy if we got 35 points by the end of the meeting. Tonight we had that by heat 8. I needed a sit down, to be honest."

27th March

Matt Ford [redeclares Poole team before first EL meeting even raced]   "Rafal does have his views on the use of the silencers which conflict with those of our Association and to be honest I could not afford to allow the matter to drift on any further. He cannot commit to being able to ride for us so I have made the decision to move ahead without him."

Jon Cook   "I was particularly pleased with the standard of racing and the amount of overtaking both inside and out, which flies in the face of some of the scare stories we have heard about the new silencers and I didn't feel the noise level was lowered to a level where one's enjoyment of the entertainment on offer was adversely affected"

Stewart Dickson "The problem revolves around an area from the middle of the back straight right round to the crown of the bend between turns three and four. Certain sections in that are exceptionally soft and the real danger is that they collapse during racing. We can't have that, it would be far too dangerous, so having had a meeting with experts in their field, they have told us the correct remedy required to ensure that problem is eradicated."

30th March

Flagrag "In general Elite League speedway gets higher viewing figures than the Netball super league but this is affected by what other programs are on in the same slot e.g. major stories in the soaps or premiership/championship football. Sky no longer rely on BARB figures much now anyway as they don't take into consideration time shifted viewing like recording and repeats. In fact we now have a more accurate system as we have our own consumer viewing panel and online Skyline survey system this is all backed up by our internal viewing monitoring figures collected from set top boxes as this allows us to see how many recorded it along with repeat play outs."

1st April

Bert Harkins "City Rebel, I was always told that the Scots were mean! Why not buy *Speedway Star* next week (it's a good read) and save yourself the entry fee on 17th April? We are very lucky. Motorcyclists coming for the 'Bikers in Paradise' will get a discount. "Normal" visitors to the Park that day will pay full admission price whilst we Speedway folk will have free admission on production of the ad in *Speedway Star*, so that can't be bad, can it? We have a lot to thank Park owner and ex-rider, Peter Sampson for as our free entries won't help to feed the animals and the Museum incurs its own expenses such as electricity, plus building costs for the new extention, etc.."

April 2nd

Gordon Day "We should have walked away from the FIM years ago. I'm sure Bob Dugard would agree if you asked 'what have the FIM ever done for speedway?' we should have formed our own association like Formula 1 or the MotoGP. They haven't got silencers and, if you chat to Boycie, he'll tell you that the sound of 30 bikes at the start of the MotoGP is unbelievable. You have to remember that the noise at speedway is part of the show! It sounds like they're doing 80 when really the average is below 50. Think about it. If you stand on the pavement and hear a car go by without an exhaust you think they're doing 70 when it's only 35 or 40. Okay. We're different to the MotoGP because we're a city centre sport but the noise is still part of our show"

Niall Strudwick "The new silencers will work all day at Lakeside. On a track with a bit of grip, they might be different"

Gordon Day "I got on okay with Pete Toogood and I am sure that he wouldn't have let what happened this Winter have happened. He'd have sat everyone down and not let them leave conference until it was sorted. Now they say the delay is down to the legal people and they always judge things by M-O-N-E-Y so they're never quick"

Jonathan Barber "Funny thing, I missed Phil [Hilton] fall over a step that's been there 35 years and hurt his ankle cos I was here. Course he blamed the step."

Jonathan Barber "It's my first burger here in about five years since I had food poisoning"

John Hazelden "Tell you what [Taylor Poole] looks like Niall Strudwick, only faster"

Jim Lynch "A dreadful situation that shouldn't have happened but I think the people in the sport know who to blame!"

3rd April

Gary Patchett "It's been a nightmare [delay] for the club and we are keeping our fingers crossed for a satisfactory conclusion over the weekend. Should that be the case both Tomasz and Maciej will be flying into the country on Monday for their first meeting in Swindon colours this season."

Mike Butler "Champagne [Leicester opening] moment for me was afterwards when the nearby MCDonald was suddenly and unexpectedly inundated with customers…..the look on the managers face as the queue stubbornly stayed all the way to the door for the 30 mins I was there was amusing as they had to re-open the upstairs seating area and we ruined their previously quiet night."

4th April

Chris Holder *   "Back in uk…. Racing at wolverhampton tonight! We are in wolves way to fukn early!!! Wat is there to do round here!!!!?"

5th April

Sarah Lapworth   "I don't normally like to get involved in the politics of the sport but I would like to set a few records straight on this one. I have spoken to Claes [Nedermark] over the phone this morning to ask him if he had spoken to Mike [Bowden] at all and he said no. When I told him what had happened the kid was practically in tears!! Claes had no idea about this and the last time that he and Mike had spoken on Thursday everything was all OK and there was no indication that this would happen. Mike was well aware that Claes would not be at P&P due to commitments in Poland. Riders get dropped all the time and speedway can be a very nasty world sometimes but there are ways to do things – yes we all hate receiving bad news but am I the only one on here who thinks its only right to tell the lad there and then rather than not telling him at all and letting him find out from others? At the end of the day Mike has messed up on the averages and someone had to go but to say he didn't realise that Claes would be on a 7 point average is a very poor excuse as anyone who does there homework would realise that all Danes and Swedes are given an automatic 7 point average in the PL. Another point raised was the issue of insurance. Yes there was a problem with his van insurance due to his age but this was all agreed last November when Claes signed his contract and I do feel that there has been enough time in between to sort this. Claes has never made any demands and has only expected what was promised to him. Claes even offered to pay Mike back the £2000 out of his wages but this was rejected. I feel that the fact that Mike has gone public over the insurance issue is very unprofessional and should have been kept confidential as it was part of his contract. Another point that needs correcting is that Claes is not a Plymouth asset, you have to ride 12 official meetings before a club can own you so Claes is a free agent and Plymouth are not entitled to a loan fee for him if he does get a PL place somewhere else. I have no grudge against Mike or Plymouth speedway I just wish that Mike could have handled it better and been more professional about things. I'm not gonna ask you all to feel sorry for Claes, he is a big boy and will one day find a club that is genuine but please bear in mind that he has spent over £7000 this winter on his equipment for England…..Claes got a lift to Plymouth from the Midlands only to be told when he arrived that his insurance hadn't been sorted out. He was advised by Mike that his insurance was too high and he was not happy to pay it even though this was in his contract. When Claes returned to my house I advised I would look on the internet and see if I could find any cheaper quotes. I was still searching for quotes up until last Monday when I spoke to Mike who said he was only happy with a quote of less than £500 for the year. We discussed several solutions as after looking for my own car insurance, I did not feel this was realistic. Most of the solutions were rejected then we came to a decision I would still look for insurance quotes but we would also look for a driver for Claes to put on Mike's insurance. The advert for a driver went on Kelvins Facebook after 10pm last Monday and we tried to sort this out all week. Claes spoke to Mike and advised that due to his commitments in Poland he would not be able to get to Press and Practice. As he was without transport he drove home with some friends and was under the impression all was ok and he was returning for the meeting on the 8th. Just as a point to confirm both ourselves and Claes did not know anything about this, all his bikes and clothes are still at our house. Surely if he knew about this he would have taken everything with him last Thursday. Not only has he the disappointment of what has happened he now has to figure out a way to get all his equipment back home. We appreciate so much anyone and everyone who helps these kids and am so sorry that as valued sponsors you have been caught up in this."

7th April

Philip Rising   "GIVEN the mess the British speedway is in and some of the decisions being made by the FIM I would say that the SGP is the shining beacon at present. No doubt you will say that I would say that. And I would … But it's only an opinion, nothing more."

Graham Cooke "I bump into an old friend, Lee Richardson, as he arrives as his old stomping ground. First topic of conversation is about the new silencers are the problems of riding in Poland and then swapping back to the new ones in the UK. Lee is non committal at the moment - there are differences but so far everything seems to be going well. I quiz him about his recent ban in Poland for a bout of "fistycuffs". 'Well it was the third time in the meeting that I'd been knocked off and so I let the guy know how I felt. He didn't like it and swung a punch so I swung back. It carried on back in the pits and now I've copped a ban and a fine for it'."

Rick Frost "The real winners are the fans of Peterborough, Coventry and speedway in general because they will see an enhanced Elite League with ten clubs and that can only be for the good of the sport."

8th April

BSPA The BSPA and Coventry and Peterborough are delighted to announce that both teams will return to the Elite League in 2011. Coventry and Peterborough accept that things said in the heat of the moment could have been avoided. For the sake of British Speedway and more importantly its fans we are all committed to moving on and working together for the future. Allen Trump accepts that he said things in the heat of the moment which could have been avoided in relation to the BSPA and certain named individual members.

9th April

Rob Lyon "When the riders get the helmet on, they are not worried whether it is a black and white, pink, yellow, blue, or whatever colour helmet it is they're against"

David Hemsley "My understanding is that Ken [Naylor] hasn't signed his BSPA contract, and on reflection I think he is unwilling to commit to that level, which is a shame because he's been fundamental to the track being here. But if he feels he doesn't want to commit any further, I'm the first person to say that's not a problem, so if he wants to just be there enjoying the racing, that's what matters to me. Ken's been a personal friend as well as a colleague for four years, and it's sometimes a difficult transition from being a campaigner to the commercial realities of being a businessman, but he has been fundamental to what we've achieved."

Chris Neath "It's really good to be back out there you know, I had a lot of problems which I know haven't been documented but it's been a hard time."

Avtar Sandhu "Ronnie Russell is going to get a big hug from me when I see him, and no doubt a beer or two, and also Jon Cook and CVS who have always been looking for a resolution, and Alex Harkess and Angela Price who orchestrated the final settlement."

Jayne Moss "I am not sure of what we are going to do. I have lost count of the number of riders we have approached, only to be told they cannot afford to race for what we are offering, despite there being a standard pay scale."

Hans Andersen* "Once again an early start :(feel like a human YoYo these days, uk to poland, poland to uk, & again tomorrow uk Poland :D"

10th April

Hans Andersen * "F...:(how the hell am I suppose to get dialed In when practicing on a grippy track AND then they make it as slick as M25 for the meeting aha"

14th April

Derek Barclay "You're right to highlight Uncle Len's on centre green interview: very wise words indeed from the great man (no doubt I'll be accused of bum-licking again!!!)"

15th April

Jon Cook "The [EL 'B' meetings] picks couldn't be totally random because it would be totally unfair for a club to miss out on the play-offs because they have randomly come up against harder teams. Each of the promoters and team managers had a proper input into which clubs they went for, and that was fairer. It means there isn't a huge amount of change to the dates we've given our riders."

16th April

Jon Cook "No-one is trying to say it's better than one home/one away or two home/two away. But at least it is fair in the way it has been allocated."

Stuart Douglas "I have to admit that I seriously considered this winter whether I wanted to continue because of what was happening and I found myself asking what the point of it all was. I felt that all parties were losing sight of common sense, even though sides in the argument appeared to have valid points and really, I watched with dismay as one obstacle after another appeared to be put in the way of progress and a solution to the problems."

Ken Naylor "Contrary to David Hemsley's suggestion that I was unwilling to commit to the level required of a co-promoter, I was in fact fully committed to being Leicester's co-promoter. Unfortunately, it became increasingly obvious that Hemsley wanted it to be in name only – something I was not prepared to do. I was never interested in becoming a businessman as I wanted to concentrate on helping young British lads via the Youth Academy part of Leicester Speedway. It was my intention to run free training schools and I had in fact already acquired three machines and substantial sponsorship to that end. I had hoped that Leicester Speedway would be something special and a catalyst for the sport in general to get back to its Great days. I'm sad and disappointed at the way things have turned out but hope to now draw a line underneath it all and wish the sport of speedway in Leicester every success."

Joe Screen "To be honest we have all probably become a little frustrated as we waited for everything to be ready and although practice did not reveal as much as we had hoped, I think there was enough there to get us excited. I think we have the kind of team which should enjoy the circuit. The young ones were attacking it straight from the off while us more experienced ones were sizing things up but once we get our racing heads on then we will all be giving it plenty of throttle."

Mike Bellerby "We have now got a No.1 [Bjarne Pedersen] we really feel we can trust to do the business for us"

Dick Barrie "It is John Anderson's insistence on excellence in business, be it quality butchery or quality speedway that gives him an edge in what he sets out to achieve."

Jon Cook "There are no excuses to offer for the performances and our problems are most acute within the top five where each rider has yet to find any real consistency, and that is not what we expected when we built the team in this manner."

Renat Gafurov "I had a different engine when I changed bike for the re-run and after the re-run, put that engine in my first bike, which I could use again"

Jim Lynch "[Tomasz Piszcz] thought he was unable to do justice to himself because of his mechanical resources and we felt there was no option but to accept his resignation in the circumstances"

Dick Barrie "[King's Lynn's] new solidly-absorbent safety-fence looked very efficient – 'way better than the air-fences you see on TV – and, should it ever become desirable that Shielfield Park's fence be upgraded at some future point I will most certainly be suggesting we look towards this type of barrier."

Jon Cook "[Piotr Swiderski] gets stuck in and is a delight to watch and it's a bit like watching old school speedway because he never knows when he's beaten"

Paul Burbidge "The politics and in-fighting which dog British speedway had gone from being a source of comedy to something altogether more serious. What would potential new fans and sponsors make of a sport that couldn't decide the make up of its top league by the start of the season? More importantly, what did Sky Sports – the broadcaster and Elite League sponsor that sustains the competition financially – make of it?"

Jon Cook "I've been proved completely wrong over the new silencers, the quality of the racing that I'm seeing now makes up for the slightly reduced noise and the fact that the races are being slowed just by a tad or two of a second"

Alun John Rossiter "You don't have to be best friends with people to race them. I don't want them to be my friend if they don't want to be. That's up to them. We're here to do a job and that job is winning. We'll do it fairly and squarely."

Dick Barrie "Can I remind you of something I've raised a couple of times in recent weeks – the homelessness of Hynek Stichauer? Now our cheery wee #2 isn't quite down to selling The Big Issue yet, or applying to Shelter for a hand-out – but he does want to move up to live in this area, and is actively looking for accommodation! Hynek is currently living in the Midlands, and faces a Clewsie-esque trek to join us each Saturday – he would dearly love to base himself in Berwick or the border area. Any ideas or offers? Ideally, he'd like someplace with local workshop facilities to work on his bike – and with the sport having been staged here for more than forty years, I feel sure there must be a few places in and around town where itinerant Bandits have been accommodated in the past, and could be again. Hynek is clean, tidy and properly house-trained, and would be an ideal companion for your dog or cat – if you think you can help him end his search, please touch base with the wee man"

Allen Trump "I think it's just the legalities of it all. We've been dealing with a body that represents 20-odd clubs without Coventry and Peterborough. Of course, the logistics and bureaucracy of that are what has really dragged this out. That's not a criticism. It's a fact.......we've all won, speedway has won, the clubs have won and so has the BSPA. They've got us back in. the real winner is speedway because you've got 10 clubs in the Elite."

Paul Burbidge "What is vital is such a dispute never happens again. The sport's finances and its reputation with fans, sponsors and television broadcasters simply couldn't take it."

Alun John Rossiter "From the two meetings that I've seen live with my team, and the two I've seen on the television, it hasn't affected the racing"

John Anderson "There are some people who apparently disagree with our choice of our seven riders this year. Well, that is their privilege, although I would hope to have their support for any rider we hand a black-and-gold race-jacket, but let me say this – we have no plans to change this team in the long or short term. In the case of locally-based rookie Tamas Sike, we have every faith in his ability to develop over this first season into a rider who will become a solid scorer for years to come."

Michael Lee "British clubs will never be able to offer all the opportunities that the Poles are given now, with academies in place at every track. I look at them and can see possibly eight youngsters, some I've never even heard of, who could go on to become World Champion. It's difficult but we've got to do something to help our own lads and that's what we want to be about at Mildenhall."

Ben Hopwood "The National League now is what the Premier League was six or seven years ago. I've watched videos of when Carl Stonehewer was a Grand Prix rider and when he was round Workington and I really thought it looked slow."

Kevin Long "I'm very happy to be back. The [Mildenhall] NL fixtures won't affect my job as an events organiser too much, and I enjoy it at West Row. A few people may object to some of the things I ask riders, but really it's only 'Carry On, Are You Being Served', kind of humour and most people get a laugh out of it."

Speedway Star "Some starts were a bit ragged following a starting gate malfunction after the first race which saw the rest of the meeting get underway thanks to elasticated starts"

17th April

Chris Holder* "Can u block people ? Don't want to talk to fuckwits! That's wat facebook is for!"

18th April

Gary Patchett "It's never nice releasing a rider so early in the season but Tomasz [Chrzanowski] has struggled and so reluctantly we have let him go. We wish him well for the future and hopefully now we can all move on and our season starts here"

19th April

Moira Perrott "The only people who'll make any money this season or break even, will be the four that make play-offs. Every rule is done for one person or because they've seen someone else do something and they want to stop it. You have to wonder how teams can be beaten by 60s after all they've done to supposedly equalise things? We can see the have's and the have not's! You can already see that the strong clubs with the biggest voices got and get what they want. Look at Poole. Andersen is clearly on a false average and how do they have rider replacement for

Ward? After they dropped Jason Doyle he can't come back except for the express permission of the management committee. They say crowds are up but then it's the best start to a season I can ever remember. There's only been one postponement – at Poole where, they say if they'd have been patient, they'd have got it on. With the sunshine and Easter things should still be good but there will be a test after that. That said, Peterborough only got a normal crowd for their opener when you would have expected higher than that while they only had 500-600 at the U21 at Lakeside and that's a Super7even event. Last week King's Lynn had a lesson in what Sky do to attendances. Sure they get £3-4k but that doesn't help if you lose 300 or 400 who, sensibly, stay at home and watch it on the telly. Mallett is already saying he's gonna close. Probably as soon as the teams lose one at home, their crowds will start to drop off! I don't know what's going to happen at Weymouth? You have to feel sorry for the landlords who've had two poor tenants who've welshed on the rent deal so you can understand if they're sceptical about people saying that they're going to be different. Somerset is down to Mr Dakota North. With the new rolling averages, it just takes an EF or two and he could be at reserve for a long time. They're calculated by taking the whole of the previous season and adding this season's to it. Matt Ford and CVS wanted two years previously rolling averages but, even with one, it means no one is really going to jump up. Equally it means the reverse is the case. Say Chris Harris drops to a six or so average this season at Belle Vue, he'll still stay on a much higher average because of last season. So you could get some riders dropped on massive averages which means they could get stuck as no one will use them on those figures."

Ronnie Russell "It's a busy spell for us and ideally I would like to see us take seven points from these three meetings. We all know how tough Poole away will be, they are a super side once again this season, but we are very much looking forward to the meeting. And whilst we wish Birmingham every success in the Elite League following their elevation during the winter, I don't want that to be at Swindon 's expense. We have to take points off them, both home and away. All the boys are keen and fired-up for this."

20th April

Neil Machin "Ipswich are still a massive name in speedway and it's great to have them in the Premier League, they are very attractive opposition"

21st April

Gary Patchett "We hope to see a big crowd to welcome the new boys [Klindt & Monberg] when we face Birmingham at the Abbey tonight"

Graham Cooke "On another unfortunately dramatic evening the Robins slip to another defeat. Tonight, the drama was not on the track. As if we didn't have enough to cope with, a major sewer pipe bursts in the main car park and the stadium officials have to manage that. We decide that if someone drives through the effluent and it sprays up at a supporter it wont be the first time at Swindon this season that "Sh*t has hit the fan!" Our start is delayed by 30 minutes.

Keith McGhie "Whatever manager Jitendra Duffill smuggled into the Bears' interval tea is set to be in high demand on Teesside in the future.....[on] a chilly night where fog swirled in off the Tees Estuary at a rate that, at one stage, mildly threatened proceedings."

Paul Rickett

"The Witches were without former Tiger Chris Mills (probably doing the Agadoo at a family wedding by the time the tapes went up)"

22nd April

Elvin King "Chris Mills looked to have a bit of a hangover after being best man the previous day – although he never had an alcoholic drink...[it was] a thoroughly entertaining afternoon meeting that saw one spectator taken to hospital by ambulance with sunstroke"

Mark Hazelden "My prediction is an Eastbourne King's Lynn final. We're gonna be champions. Poole will get to the play-offs"

Jeff Scott   "They're saying over there, it'll be an Eastbourne King's Lynn final"

Nick Barber   "If that happened, I'd toss myself off – not in public! I used to have a team in the play-offs every year but last year I had eight teams and the only play-off was the relegation one at Ipswich."

Jon Cook   "[The new silencers] have closed the gap between the top riders and those below"

Stuart Robson   "We knew it was going to hard – Eastbourne are the second best team in the Elite League"

Jon Cook   "We had such a rubbish winter with the sport but, if anything, the fans have come out more. Obviously, the highest [paying] crowd we've ever had – in our fifth year – means we must be doing something right"

23rd April

Chris Holder*   "survived the trip to torun with craziest fukn driver in Poland"

Rob Godfrey   "[Joe Haines'] had too many clubs in the last couple of years – he's actually had too many this season already – so hopefully we'll be his last club this year. When Joe rang me up, it took me two seconds to agree. He's an Englishman, he's in this country, and it's much easier than signing a rider from overseas."

Jon Cook   "If [Martin Dugard] had enjoyed travelling a bit more, he would probably have made more of an impression on the world scene."

Chris Holder*   "Not a bad night in Polska...can't buy a fucking start tonight! Hopefully make a few starts at Poole tomorrow :-)"

Jon Cook   "Joonas [Davidsson] came to us with a fairly rubbish reputation. I think he was known as 'Joooo3nas'."

Will Pottinger   "Armo first suffered some rib pain after our pre-season go-kart session in Stourbridge"

Jon Cook   "If you work on a working relationship, it lasts past the time when the person is riding for you."

Nicky Mallett   "The riders were left in no doubt whatsoever (during dressing room pep talk) that no-one here at this club was happy at all with the performance in that home reverse against Rye House. They were told straight that a list of would-be replacement riders was going to be drawn up there and then and that every one of them could go."

Jon Cook   "[Dean Barker] is the person who would get the biggest hump if he wasn't on the list. We had so many adventures and there aren't any you can print in the *Speedway Star*."

Keith McGhie on Newcastle   "Top heavy sides are effective most of the time but, when plan A doesn't work, there is no plan B!"

Terry Daley   "[Newport v Stoke was] a meeting which, in all honesty, was a little mundane"

Jon Cook   "[David Norris] left after myself and Deano had an altercation with him at a nightclub."

Stuart Parnaby   "We didn't win anything last season but we came out of it with three trophies. And the three trophies we got are actually better than winning the league because they're called Worrall, Worrall and Birks"

Jon Cook   "I did the deal [to sign Joe Screen] with Martin Hagon sitting at the services near Lakeside."

David Watt   "The biggest thing to happen in speedway for years.....I remember watching videos of old Aussie versus England (Test Series) matches in Aussie"

Fredrik Lindgren   "I can't name anyone but I've seen and I've heard about a lot of riders losing weight, and maybe a bit drastically as well. It's a bit of a worry for me. I don't know how they're doing it. If you do it properly, there are probably no worries. If you eat what you are supposed to, it's fine. It's not good if the rider keeps starving himself and they don't eat as much as they should do. It's hard to ride if you can't hold onto your bike. You've got to have some muscle, strength and stamina. Every rider is talking about losing weight at the moment. With the new silencers, it will be happening even more."

Peter Karlsson   "When you go to the start line for a vital race like that you have to go with a blank piece of paper"

Rory Schlein   "One change I have made, and which is making a big difference, is a mind thing. It may not seem anything special but I was browsing the internet and read about how to control your breathing. It is designed to get your heart rate down and that makes you calmer and less excited. I decided to try it. I don't even know what it is called but now I sit down for five minutes before a meeting and just concentrate on my breathing. If someone tapped me on the head, I'd ignore it."

Rob Godfrey   "I had a bet with the riders at Workington and said 'if you win here tonight, I'll buy you all team kevlars. Naturally, they were all up for that, so it saved me three-and-a-half grand when we lost.......I've got to buy them all a coat now. Every other club probably gives their riders a team coat, but not me, I'd charge them normally!"

BSPA   FANS flocked to Speedway meetings throughout the country in massive numbers on Good Friday. The feel-good factor surrounding one of the nation's favourite family sports shone through on a glorious day with no less than 11 meetings staged.

David Hemsley   "I felt Ilya [Bondarenko] had got around the field coming out of the second bend and he was basically given no room and taken straight into the fence. I suppose that's racing, but you should be given space to get your handlebars through."

Mike Bowden   "We are getting all the team to sign the box and we will be having a raffle for the cake at our next meeting with the profits going to the riders' equipment fund."

Bjarne Pedersen   "That's how speedway is these days in England, the rules are changing every second day, sometimes even in the middle of the season!"

Shane Parker   "Everyone says Aussies like big tracks but I'm a bit different in that I like the little ones; the ones that are technical where you have to think rather than just race with the throttle open."

Bjarne Pedersen   "I'm 32 now and I can't see any reason for thinking about [retirement]. If you look after yourself and get everything done properly in the winter, I think you can stay on top to 37 or 38"

Dale Allitt   "The doctors told [Adam Lowe] he is going to be out for six months, so it looks like his season is over in his first ride"

Bjarne Pedersen   "It hasn't been such a big upheaval for me [going to Eastbourne] as it might have been. I still live in the same place, have the same workshop and everything, the only change is the colour of my kevlars."

24th April

Nigel Pearson*   "Kelvin is pure class always has an opinion which is part of his job"

Chris Holder*   "got to love the immigration que. When six planes turn up at the same time

25th April

Nigel Pearson   "They've been coming back to speedway over the Easter weekend!"

Nigel Pearson   "A big night for the Premier League, which never lets us down"

Nigel Pearson   "Three successive three-alls! You don't see that often at the start of a meeting"

Nigel Pearson   "George English – top man! Well thought of throughout British speedway"

Derek Barclay   "That's only seven quid more than the books Jeff Scott produces and this one actually contains stuff of interest and value... As opposed to pages and pages of utterly pointless non-anecdotes, huge repetition, shocking grammar and harmful personal snipes... If Jeff's pointless and thoroughly objectionable books were given away free with Corn Flakes I'd still say they weren't worth the considerable amount of paper they're printed on!!"

Steve Brandon*   "not sure either Ferjan or Nedermark will provide the answers [for Newcastle], Nedermark the better of the two!!!!"

26th April

Nigel Pearson* "Full English in hotel to start the day, fantastic! Not the best racing [Newcastle v Glasgow] but nice and close last night"

Robert Bamford "Did you know that Swindon have lost successive meeting to Birmingham at the Abbey? Last Thursday and 28 years ago, when we lost 30-47"

Debbie Hancock "If I was Leicester I don't know that I'd have had Sam Masters as a guest two weeks before we go there

Robert Bamford "Why do some promoters think they're up there somewhere where you're not supposed to be?"

Robert Bamford "Nicholls is getting points, but not winning races and he's not beating No.1s"

Debbie Hancock "Dak has bruised his bum cheek and back so he needed a rest"

Robert Bamford "I don't want to knock the guy, but I question his integrity and his pricing"

Robert Bamford "Did you know that Matt Bates has more friends on Facebook than any other speedway rider? He has over 4300, while Adam Shields is on around 2000"

27th April

BSPA BIRMINGHAM are waiting for news of the extent of Daniel King's injuries, after the GB star returned from Poland this week in a neck brace with a possible broken vertebrae. King suffered the blow in a bizarre accident before a race when his throttle cable snapped as he was performing a practice start.

Graham Drury "It's fair to say I've had better weeks in Speedway. I'm stunned by what's happened with KK [2 week ban from Tarnow from riding in the UK] and we can only hope this ban is removed because he loves riding for Birmingham."

Malcolm Blythe "They say it's good to talk. My worst days are Sunday cos that was the day she died but also that was the day when we were together at home"

Kelvin Tatum "There's no doubt Freddie Lindgren has been fast tonight – that's why he's called Fast Freddie Lindgren!"

Nigel Pearson "The telepathy between these two [Holder & Ward] is amazing – they're looking over each others shoulders"

Robolots "George & Linda Barclay Are Back By Popular Demand! Lakeside Training Schools 4 dates so far. Gorgeous Gentleman George & Lucious Lovely Linda Barclay are back with their training schools. Same great days, with excellent training but at a new venue – The home of the Lakeside Hammers @ the Arena Essex Raceway….Track time is 12-4pm. Best riders will also get a ride before the Hawks match and all attendees will be able to watch the following Hawks meeting for half price. Maximum of 20 riders, so we can give riders maximum track time and George will be on hand for tuition. Training can be "Back to Basics", "Improving Skills" or just practice. ALL are welcome. Cost is £40 per rider"

28th April

Chris Holder* "Just flicking through the new NUTS magazine. Rosie Jones faaaaaark bang tidy! :-P"

Rosie Jones* "I have too much going on in my head that comes out in my dreams, last night I: ...... Flew through a rainforest, beat up my bf, bought a private jet, found out Katy perry was a murderer and got a nose job!.. First bikini of 2011 purchased... This excites me!"

Nicolai Klindt* "just had lunch and now doing the last bits on the bike. if there was any grip in swindon i am sure this bike would go for a track record!"

29th April

Nicolai Klindt* "flying off to denmark with jesper from the lovely stansted airport with the more lovely ryanair. got a hole buffet at the hotel"

Nicolai Klindt* "sitting at outrup stadium watching outrup vs slangerup. track looks rubbish, but that's just normal"

Chris Holder* "On way to Polska for SGP…idiots at Luton were not goin to take my engine because they think it smelt like diesel :-S WTF!"

Nigel Pearson "As soon as I heard about the crash I called my friend and colleague Chris Louis at Ipswich. He confirmed Adam [Roynon] was in a lot of pain and later in the evening I was told he'd suffered a broken femur and needs an operation. Our thoughts are with Adam who is already a Heathens hero after only five matches for us."

Gary Patchett* "Eastbourne v Swindon tonight Robins will ride under protest…Bjarne Pedersen shouldn't be riding. Eastbourne took facility for him at Peterboro last night when he was practicing elsewhere"

Scott Nicholls* "U never know. I'm happy at Swindon, but 2012 is another season. Gonna focus on this year for now"

Fredrik Lindgren* "can't believe that Mr Scoop has more followers than me. Where is this world heading towards? What's going on?"

Philip Rising "The style and tone of commentary provided by Tatum and Pearson is at the behest of Sky. Many people, especially on this forum, object to what they perceive to be screaming and shouting but that is what is required, nay demanded, by their bosses in the TV truck. Of course it won't appeal to everyone, no more than the Sun does as a newspaper, but Sky will simply point at their 10 million plus subscribers and say this is how we do it. Also (and I will confess to being friends with both Nigel and Kelvin) I doubt whether many can even start to comprehend how difficult it is to commentate with so many different voices pounding both ears at the same time. And for live league speedway it can be particularly tough. At King's Lynn for example, in addition to be freezing cold and unable to move for three hours, the Sky duo also had to gloss over a number of technical difficulties that at times rendered their own monitors almost useless. Don't worry, they are not looking for sympathy, they enjoy what they do, but occasionally a little understanding wouldn't go amiss."

OAP [to Nick Barber] "Could you get any walking stick stickers?"

30th April

Dick Barrie "We have to sympathise with Newcastle – and reflect how a team looking really sharp can be blunted in a split second by a simple crash, so often not in any way the fault of the rider who ends up on the sidelines. But that's speedway. It is the very risk factor involved in our sport which causes brave young men to test themselves to the limit on bikes without brakes, and it is indeed these risks they are taking which makes this enthralling game so appealing to those of us who only stand and watch."

Steve Mallett "I am seriously unhappy and still actively looking to change"

Troy Batchelor "I don't treat this sport as a joke. I take it very, very seriously and not just on the track. I am definitely working hard at it – fitness training, mental training, working with my mechanics and engine tuner."

Stuart Parnaby "[Greg Blair] seems to be one of those 'hit and miss' riders, he does a bit, gets injured and stops, then he carries on again"

Chris Holder "You've got all the normal things anyone else would have like your tax and all that sort of stuff. You've got to see your accountant and sort all your flights, your food and your life in general. "

Jon Cook "We are working hard on increasing the appeal of speedway racing to the wider population"

Jim Lynch "I think whoever is the team manager at Belle Vue deserves a big pat on the back"

Tim Webster "I want to thank my aunt and uncle at Sutton Coldfield through their Dauben HR and Images Mobile Disco for sponsoring me, because without their input my machinery and form would not be as good as it is."

Jon Cook "I have to say that the [NL] racing was a level higher than my pre-conceived ideas."

Chris Holder "If you have a couple of good Grand Prix rounds, you're straight up there. I think Greg and Bomber were down and out of the top eight for much of the year. They sort of hit their form towards the end and got in the points in the last three or four Grand Prix meetings. They finished fifth and sixth and it's funny how it works."

Jon Cook "[Good Friday crowd of 2750] was the highest paying attendance since Stuart and I moved in here five years ago"

Dick Barrie "For the first time in well over forty years, we get to welcome the Devils from Plymouth to Shielfield Park. They live a long way away. I have been in the city of Plymouth only twice, I think – firstly on a tour in 1966 to race cycle speedway against the local team (they had one very good rider, a nice guy called Pete Neal, I recall) – and just a year or two later to see speedway at their old Pennycross Stadium. I can only remember the track surface being awful – it was some kind of silver sand laid on top of tarmac (there was a stock car track underneath) - and that Adam Roynon's dad Chris was racing for the Devils."

Alun John Rossiter "[Edward Kennett's] always had the talent and the ability, and I've been talking to him a lot this year about how he can utilise that. He's listening"

David Tattum "I am very unhappy about certain comments made about the choice of guest against Hackney. I can assure our supporters that we did our very best to get the best guest available for the fixture, but due to a variety of reasons, those riders mentioned on the forums were unavailable. When we have to book guests, we go for the best rider available and I am appalled with those supporters who feel we would not do so."

Alun Rossiter "I've not seen interaction like that from the fans for a long time, and I think that's fantastic. That's what you get with Nicki"

David Hoggart "Shane Parker must be our new Messiah with what he's done for us this week"

Trevor Geer "Swindon have turned up with a team stronger than they normally are with their guests, but we have taken them apart really. It's a shame that the weather has put paid to it."

Chris Holder* "Pumped for tonight. Little bit nervous...But that's normal for this shit. Heat 1 gate 1"

Nicki Pedersen "I do my best, but the engines and the bikes have to go forward. It doesn't matter how much I want to win if we don't have the right setup."

Joe Haines "I broke all my ribs [12] on the right side, punctured a lung, broke my shoulder in six places, broke the collarbone and broke my back in seven places. I was alright with one lung until I got pneumonia, that's when things started going really badly"

Nicki Pedersen "It has been completely different with me and Tomasz in the last few years. Tomasz has a lot of respect for me and he always has had. He's a true world champion as well. He admitted that he tried to be a bit dirty and it didn't work. I knew the way around it. But next time it is going to go the other way."

Luke Bowen "I knew I wasn't right but last Monday I eventually gave in, went to the hospital, they checked me out and told me I had two broken ribs"

Matthew Wethers "Newport have resurfaced their track this year and it is definitely an improvement. They used to have a fine dust surface which dried out really quick, but the new surface is much better."

Luke Bowen "I came under John Oliver, he locked up and there was nothing I could do but hit his front wheel. From the ref's point of view, it looked as if I had knocked him off, which I did, but I had no choice as he locked up"

Greg Hancock* "The greatest thing about the GP tonight is that it was really safe with the new silencers..:)"

Jarek Hampel "Believe me, it's so hard to give a definition of myself. I'm a bit of everything. Sometimes I'm self-possessed, calm and cautious, but I can also be unwise and inconsiderate. It depends on my mood....I don't drink tea and lemon before a race. And I don't lock myself in the van and do Yoga like 'Mad Dog'. There's no witchcraft either!... Years ago, I didn't know that psychological strength is so important in speedway but Tony Rickardsson once told me in Cardiff that the will to win has to come from your heart."

1st May

Leicester Lion "Our riders aren't gaters. They need to be able to pass opponents, but the track doesn't encourage it. Any rider venturing further out than mid-track only finds loose, ungrippy material, rather than anything which allows them to build up speed on a fast outside line. I'm not saying the track contributed to our defeat. We'd have lost to Somerset on any surface, but a grippier outside would have made the racing more exciting. If we're going to lose at home, the racing has to be better than it is at the moment."

Graham Cooke "Someone recently likened preparing a speedway track to preparing a cricket wicket, and having done both, I can see the similarities. Both are largely dependent upon anticipating the weather conditions and working with them and both are central to the success or otherwise of the event. Both can be doctored to suit individuals or teams but then the similarities begin to wither. Obviously the surface area of a speedway track is far, far greater and unlike wickets, most tracks have some sort of banking. The grass on a wicket can be used to bind the surface together to give it strength to withstand the impact of a small ball, weighing under a kilo, striking it at an angle at up to 90 mph. We don't have the luxury of a strong binding mechanism like grass - we have a clay based substance mixed with stones to make up the shale. When it is wet it moves around and becomes sticky but it can dry in a fraction and then hold together before shattering into dust. It has the ability to be able to draw moisture from the air and from below ground level. I often read criticisms about why we don't water much during meetings. Aside from the fact that the riders don't want waterings because the results can be unpredictable, when the temperature drops as the sun goes down, at about the start of a meeting, the cold air draws moisture up from the base and we suddenly get moist shale on top. If we water too much (and that's probably just a coating of water) the shale clay breaks down so fast into a mush that becomes icy. When the surface shines we know that the moisture content is too high and the racing will suffer. I suppose it's best summed up as walking on the edge of a precipice - just enough and racing is perfect, a little more or a little less and you suffer."

Greg Hancock* "Bummed about the semi but great otherwise"

Chris Holder* "SGP is fukn hard work"

Dakota North* "over washing bikes 3 days in a row is shit! good weekend tho!"

Gareth Rogers "While Keith McGhie (*Speedway Star* w/e April 30th) is right to draw attention to the progress made by Redcar Speedway at the South Tees Motorsport Park - I must correct his repeated assertion that the track was built on a waste tip. The site was previously the Langbarugh Steelworks and became a general Motorpark in the early 1990s. When I first looked at the area where the track now is in March 2005 it was a quad practice track and the current pits was a model car arena. I think the fact that I told Keith how untidy it was plus the fact that Glyn Taylor had to excavate a fair amount of debris may have led to Keith's interpretation. Reading Speedway at Smallmead was definitely built on a waste tip but Brian Havelock and I have now shown Keith the aerial photos of the former steelworks and the current Motorpark which are framed and on display in the well-appointed clubhouse to bring him up to date with the facts. I would be grateful if you could do the same for the readers."

Fredrik Lindgren* [on the red, blue, white & yellow race tabards used in 2011 SGP] "Ask IMG/BSI Speedway, am not a fan of having to change racejacket for each heat"

Steve Brandon* "it's to help with rider identification on the TV & live, it worked last night & looks great!"

Gary Patchett* "Heathens lose at Brum tonight. Don't read anything into this as anyone can cherry pick a team to win one meeting. Ommer um"

Lewis Bridger* "The Check in Cue's at LND Luton is a Joke!!"

Bob Miller "Arena has changed quite a lot since 1984. When we first started Arena was a unique speedway track in the fact that it had no safety fence. I have always laughed at why it's called a "safety" fence. It certainly wasn't called that from a rider's point of view, although of course with the advent of the air fence that has been massively improved, and one of the changes that I have seen over the years that certainly is for the best. The building on the first bend that houses the track shop, sweet shop and cafe etc., wasn't there originally, so the introduction of the Tavern and the viewing from the balcony above the shops is an added bonus for those that frequent it. Also, the pits area is very much improved over how it was at day one too, and best of all, this season we have a much improved box that I work from, cleaner, more spacious and more panoramic."

2nd May

Lewis Bridger* "Polish Club took me out my 2races after winning my 1st race beating there number 1, they achieved 1pt from my 2rides nice 1!! :-)"

Lewis Bridger* "Breakfast at the Holiday Inn LND Luton.. Now chilling on my MacBook Pro.. Going big on Sky Sports HD l8r 4 all my Fans!! :-)"

Lewis Bridger* "[6 hours later] Just got up at Holiday Inn LND Luton.. Hot shower then meet my Boys 2 go do my best at Swindon tonight come on the Eagles!! :-) Swindon it's gunna be 1 of those night's go hard or go home!! ;-) BANG!"

Lewis Bridger* "Traffic due 2 fire on M4!! Arrrgghhh"

Fredrik Lindgren* "Back in sunny UK! Going for lunch at IKEA then we're off to Monmore Green!"

Fredrik Lindgren* "Don't understand the taste of you Brits, at IKEA you choose Meatballs with chips?!? It don't go together should be with boiled potatoes!"

Fredrik Lindgren* "Good win for Wolves tonight! Dropped 2 points from 6 rides so an ok meeting. Swedish League starts tomorrow!"

Steve Brandon* "why can't people just accept change & move on, or should it be black leathers for all?"

Nigel Pearson "And remember it's not where you are in early May but where you are in September in the league"

Charlie Webster "Is the wind affecting you?"

Cory Gathercole "Yeh, I'm really cold"

Nigel Pearson "Lewis Bridger is showing signs of maturity"

Charlie Webster "Simon, great amazing race out there....were you scared knowing how close Scott Nicholls was to you?"

Scott Nicholls "It's all about confidence. That's what Eastbourne are doing. They don't look the strongest side on paper but they're working well as a team"

Scott Nicholls "We were at the bottom – we couldn't get any lower – so we're working our way up"

Joonas Kylmakorpi [after heat 13] "I don't know what the score is"

Nicolai Klindt* "bit disappointed with my own performans tonight, but there is always a new day. was cool to have the helmet cam on tho! good win for Robins"

Nicolai Klindt* "yea we got all 3 points mate, cracking racing. I only got 8 from 5, but struggled abit in the end. Didn't make starts! Cam was sweet"

Lewis Bridger* "Not a Bad Night at Swindon 7pts.. I could of deffo rode better than I did but been busy last 5days!!... A pack of Mckoys chilli.. & a Twix is deffo not the High Protein meal I would of liked but will do the Job 4 tonight!!"

Fredrik Lindgren* "[01.00] Ready for bed now at Stansted Airport. Feels good I'm not Ludwig now he needs to be up 4:30! Me 9:00 so that's sweet!"

Nicolai Klindt* "at holiday inn in stansted now. magic need to be up at 4.00 I need to be up at 5.00.. the feeling of waking up 3hrs late to see you missed you flight and how to spend a fortune to get another one isn't the best thing!"

Chris Neath * "As we're doing overtime on a bank holiday does that mean we get double pay? Course not!"

Speedway Star "The challenge match between two different Valsarna sides was scrapped because of snow"

David Cysarz "It will be punishment for Ferjana? Rafal Okoniewski injury meant that in Sunday's duel with PGE Marmy Rzeszow Betard Sparta Wroclaw was able to drive only six players Pent club. Crane activists failed to download for this match Mateja Ferjana. – *We called him from calling* *for this match, but said the same day is a match in the English league. Do not come to <u>Wroclaw</u>, although it is a priority for the Polish League* – explained Mark Herring in Gazeta Wyborcza. Pent coach the team did not want to admit that the representative of Hungary will be imposed a punishment. Recall that during the tournament Ferjan bound by the agreement with the Newcastle Diamonds. The British club played its home matches on Sunday, and activists in the UK at the signing of the contract require the priority for the league over the other games. Thus, it seems that this season Rzeszow will not be able too many times to use the services of the Hungarian rider. PGE ALSO Marma can not be used as a replacement rider Rafal Okoniewski. We do not know how long it will take a break, "perch" in the starts. On Sunday, cranes will travel to Czestochowa for the match, during which the availability is Newcastle Diamonds. It is therefore possible that the colors of Rzeszow team for the second time in the season will start Ferjan. However, the former participant of the Grand Prix is on the tournament entry list in Pfaffenhofen."

3rd May

Scott Nicholls* "Another early (04.30) start. No bed for the night this time. Swindon,home,home,airport no sleep. Love being a speedway rider! I want my bed. Zzzz...Ah,my little bubba's first day at nusrey/school. Gutted I'm not there to see her x"

Greg Hancock* "Oh yeah, the Swedish League starts today. The weather just reminded me: Snow & Rain"

Fredrik Lindgren* "Saw Nicolai Klindt at the priority queue at my flight to Sweden. Guess Swindon pay him to much money"

Nicolai Klindt* "if you don't know, I'll let you know. it's boring to drive through sweden!"

4th May

Philip Rising "ONE FIM official told me over the weekend that any rider racing in more than one country requires an FIM international licence and once he has it only they have the ultimate power to ban a rider from more than one league. In other words, Tarnow can ban Kaspzrak from racing in Poland but not the UK....

Paul Burbidge "Doyle exploded through the middle of them on turn three"

Philip Rising "IN the UK we refer to 'tracks' and elsewhere, especially Poland and Sweden as 'clubs' and therein lays a huge and fundamental difference. The club culture is far more beneficial and productive and tends to be embraced by the towns/areas in which they operate which has rarely been the case in Britain ... more's the pity.

Philip Rising "We haven't even got a five minute plan"

Philip Rising "I have been disillusioned about our inability to produce young riders for a long time. Years ago it was a thriving junior grasstrack scene that gave us the likes of the Collins, brothers, Chris Morton, Simon Wigg, Kelvin Tatum, Jeremy Doncaster and many, many more. Since that well of talent dried up it has not been replaced. When the Sky money was first put on the table the BSPA declared that some of it would be used to foster young riders. It wasn't and a whole succession of initially willing and enthusiastic people have simply given up trying to do something. Sweden have recently appointed a three man commission, including former World Champion Per Jonsson, to oversee the development of under 21 riders there. We have ex-riders like Mark Loram desperate to help but the excuse is always that there is no money.

Which, yet again, is where the 'tracks' as against 'clubs' culture kicks in. I can remember years ago when Ivan Mauger offered to run some training schools for a number of up-and-coming young British riders. It was turned down because the promoters of the day couldn't agree on a system to determine who got riders that came out of the school. It was even suggested that a draft system like those used in American sports (bottom team gets first pick and so on) be adopted but the in-fighting ensured it came to nothing. We have no infrastructure to develop and nurture young riders. Even those with genuine potential have nowhere to go or no one to turn to who can give them the advice and help they require. Even top class sportsmen like pro golfers and tennis players, athletes, etc, etc continue to receive coaching throughout their careers. Yet we expect a young kid to jump on a speedway bike and get it right immediately. All they do is ride round in circles and perfect their bad habits or techniques. Ally that with the inflexible averages system used to determine team make-up in the UK and it is no wonder that promoters end up importing riders from overseas, more often than not at the expense of British kids."

Fredrik Lindgren* "TV interview went ok I think. Never been brilliant at talk the talk I'd rather walk the walk!"

Greg Hancock* "Dude [Chris Holder], you are already hookin up!! Ride it like ya stole it!! Wooooooo"

Lewis Bridger* "I just Purchased a Charger for my Blackberry at stanstead services but broke top of my phone putting my change in my pocket!! pissed off!!"

5th May

Scott Nicholls* "Micro chip passports...good idea. Is this section ever open at stansted!...I wish I had as much fun at work as the passport control guy. What a miserable old fart. Smile man!"

Keith McGhie "Last September, Richie Worrall....finished rock bottom of the qualifiers and went home from the 2010 Stars of Tomorrow with just a can of engine oil as a consolation prize"

Keith McGhie "Arlo Bugeja....although present and prepared was prevented from riding his first competitive meeting since January by a licensing technicality. That unfortunately left a rather damp crowd further disappointed and standing in light drizzle throughout 15 heats"

6th May

Nicolai Klindt* "on the way to acupuncture to sort out my bastard back."

Chris Holder* "On way [14.30] to lakeside speedway.... Should be only a couple of hours but you never know with M25!!! big decision.. Left on M25.. Or right? Help"

Niels Kristian Iversen* "What happening for 5miles of queue to check a bag inn at stansted ?? Hire some more staff man..."

Jon Cook "It may just be me, but I feel that presentation of meetings on the box is getting rather stale and needs a bit of a revamp or perhaps better, a group of presenters that actually say something worth hearing. It seems everyone wants to sit on the fence nowadays and the good old days of opinions, such as David Norris and Steve Johnston, are sadly missed. Watching the GP last weekend in the company of Peter [Ljung] and Kauko [Nieminen], I think we reached an all time low with some of the 'expert' analysis. To be honest, our two riders were somewhat in stitches at some of the non-comment dross we were listening to. It's not a crime to have a view so why not air it?"

BSPA

Lakeside 48 (Adam Shields 11)

Poole 42 (Chris Holder 42)

Mike Hunter "Michael Breckon, on his first [Armadale] visit, seemed to have left his spectacles at home"

7th May

Peterborough Panthers Thursday's Elite League clash with Poole has been postponed because of the unavailability of the Showground track

Chris Harris "If you get last places and the others score, you're consistently catching up"

Jitendra Duffill "Even after the accident, [Adam Roynon] was in good spirits and trying to make light of it but nobody else felt like laughing"

Bob Dugard "We have just slickened it out a bit because the bikes have a bit less power to get through the dirt with the new silencers"

Speedway Star "The [Leszno v Wroclaw] meeting was witnessed by a poor crowd of around 4,000, and to make matters worse the previous night the stadium had been vandalised."

Bob Dugard "I think you have to say that if we fail to make the play-offs now we will only have ourselves to blame"

Bob Dugard "As a club we were always very anti them [Coventry & Peterborough] not being there, me especially. It would have been a huge mistake to have not had them in the league this season and it might have repercussions long term. It would have been a tragedy, for example, to lose one of the traditional speedway homes like Coventry."

Nicolai Klindt* "thanks for the support dad. really nice to have someone like you that's telling you how shit you are and how good others are. thanks again!"

Lewis Bridger* [after Eagles lose at home to KL] "Smashed it 18pts!!"

Fredrik Lindgren* "Early morning with just a couple of hours sleep. Me no like! Fly fly fly!"

Fredrik Lindgren* "Slept through my flght still freaking tired. Relax more today will be my plan"

Fredrik Lindgren* "In Poland I become such a soup freak, soup really is very underestimated food"

Josie Toms "How gutted I am to see Eastbourne not perform tonight. Firstly our riders didn't seem to be up for it and secondly some of our management are a total disgrace to Eastbourne fans. After the meeting at Eastbourne us fans are allowed into the pits (not sure if every track allowes this) so I asked mike bellarby about cams arm injury he says "didn't know he had one" closely followed by Glen saying "cam had to ride tonight cos if not he would not be allowed to ride in tomorrows long track meeting". Sorry but I miss the point here is cams 1st priority not speedway. He shouldn't be riding just to prove his fitness for longtrack. 5 points from 7 rides from the reserve spot from someone who has riding Arlington for 6 years is a disgrace. Getting back to glens comments he also said" our guests cost us the meetings getting beaten by premier league riders is not good enoug" well if that's his attitude I hope he told them riders that but I doubt he did"

Niels Kristian Iversen* "Won the Danish semi- final today. Dropped 2 points but im happy with the result. Now to the workshop and Pick up the bike for Gorzow"

Niels Kristian Iversen* "Finally at the hotel bed in Gorzow. Bloody satnav cost an extra hour. Bastard. Anyway was billiant to see the Stars won at Eastbourne"

The Sun "TRASHED METAL. Yobs caused £40,000 of damage to loos to nick just £100 of copper at a Speedway club in Ipswich."

Jayne Moss "It wasn't the best of meetings [Stoke v Buxton], firstly with all the problems with the electric and then the weather"

Malcolm Vasey "You would think the [Stoke] riders had been eating raw meat the way we approached this meeting and attacked the track and races. It was a pleasure to watch them and we are so disappointed that the weather has robbed the supporters of what had all the makings of a thoroughly competent team performance."

8th May

Charlie Webster "I am now ready to let people know what I went through as a child. I witnessed and experienced abuse by more than one person. I was very unhappy, confused and lonely. I became a bit like a zombie. Looking back, the mental abuse can take longer to get over. I've always been very quiet about what happened to me because I've been scared and felt people would judge me. When it happened to me, I did not know where to turn. I went through a phase of cutting myself. I've still got scars on my wrist. I thought I was worthless. I hated myself. You believe what is wrong is your fault. But I've learnt survival is the most powerful thing ever. A lot of people will say: 'Why didn't you get out of that situation?' But if you are abused, bullied every day, made to feel you're nothing you believe you are nothing."

Lewis Bridger* "On my way 2 LND Luton 4 Polska again hopefully these No Brainers give me a chance this Week!!"

Scott Nicholls* "Sitting close to Lewis bridger. It's like bike diagnoses n story time at school all rolled in to one! Bless him. He's value for money"

Nicolai Klindt* "arrrg.... thought I could sneak some chain-oil with me in the box, but they said it was too dangerous. even said i would pay for the plane!"

Laurence Rogers "Our telephone has been red hot and we have scoured every continent for a rider we really believe suitable to help us improve our fortunes. Some of our targets are unavailable whilst others are injured. However, the one we want is a huge player and I am confident that we will get our man."

Speedway Star   "A remarkable match [Gdansk v Poznan] produced no fewer than 11 exclusions for Poznan riders, two retirements and a fall. Most of the exclusions were for exceeding the two-minute time allowance as Poznan riders made a strong protest at the state of the Gdansk track."

Graham Drury   "The BSPA are aware of the situation and the FIM have been on the case, this really cannot be allowed to happen. The door is still open for Krzysztof to return to Birmingham, hopefully next week, but I guess we will have to see what happens."

Chris Holder *   "[8am] Flight delayed till 2 hours.... I could be in bed still! :-("

Chris Holder*   "[11am] Still at Luton!!! Don't think in guna make the meeting in tarnow :-(WTF!!!!" [scores 10]

Paul Burbidge*   "Huge meeting poole speedway tomorrow night against Cov Speedway . British speedway's answer to El Classico"

Fredrik Lindgren*   [reaches 993 followers]   "Second Twitter milestone 1000 followers! Let's go for the next on 10 000!"

Chris Neath*   "Super p#*@ed off with today. Started off good then lost the plot for my last 2 rides. No excuses, I rode crap. Sorry guys...it was definitely a lot better and hopefully you will get to see the sort of racing as when they first opened Ashfield"

Mike Bennett   "Mentioned a few concerns I had about the PA and the general presentation and he suggested that I should drop Alan Jones (Press officer) an email with a few ideas that might help future meetings. I took the liberty of offering my services free of charge for one evening, to sit down with their presentation team and run through the "basics" including the expectations of the box announcer, the order of results, the times after the winner is announced etc. I made it clear that I wasn't trying to steal anyone's thunder or try and take somebody's job - living in Norwich would rule that one out (gone are the days of 6 meetings a week and 400 mile round trips!) but, due to my close ties with Leicester since way back in 1986 when I was the resident DJ at the Studio nightclub in Humberstone Gate, and the fact that my partner Tracey is a Leicester lass, I have a real desire to see the club do well.

I was somewhat disappointed to receive a one line response thanking me for my constructive comments and stating "we are on it" when it comes to the presentation.

Clearly, that's not the case and I just think it's sad that the underlying trend in every match report here on the forum is the lack of professionalism from the presentation team"

Bilbo Baggins   "David [Hemsley] has talked about having offered several riders a place to cover for Bondarenko and they have all declined. What worries me is that I am hearing that this is because the pay rates that they are being offered are laughable. I thought that when David took to the mike after the last heat tonight, he sounded desperate, a worried man, aware the tonight, was by far the worst crowd of the season and, that after another bad result tonight, more fans would stay away in the future. He has put a lot of effort in and deserves success but, if he doesn't make some very brave decisions very quickly, things could end up being a disaster. Three team changes are a must as we must change Oliver and Courtney as well as get cover for Bondarenko.

Prepare a proper speedway track upon which the riders can race. The shape is superb but the surface is appalling. Appoint an experienced team manager who knows what he's doing and can concentrate solely on the team, not try to be promoter, team manager etc etc etc . Swap Hall and Sweetman around. Get an announcer who knows about and understands speedway as this fellow is embarrassing and gives the away fans nearly as big a laugh as the efforts of some of our riders. Damn good job that Plymouth and Newport look as bad as we do or, you could give us the wooden spoon now."

Glyn Taylor   "I feel I must defend myself here. Last night I had put 20 tons of new dirt and the riders are telling me there is too much . The problem is in the track shape the surface is good. You who say on here there is no dirt I invite you to come with me on a track walk before and after the meeting. We are going to change the shape over the next few weeks. Both Doc and Graham have been and agree with what I have said."

Jitendra Duffill   "I have to agree with Glynn here, the track preparation last night was superb with plenty of dirt around the outside. Watering was perfect and all the Redcar riders were impressed. The track was smooth and consistent, a great achievement for the amount of time it has been laid, so I'm 100% confident this is not the problem. The reason you are not seeing good racing is definitely the track shape, the straights are far too long IMO and its pretty square going into the turns so its hard to race anyone into the turns. Great to hear that the shape will be altered because I believe that if they took 10 metres of each bend it has the potential to be one of the best racing tracks in the country. The track/stadium is an outstanding achievement given the timescale Leicester have had."

Mike Bennett*   "Note to self- next time you offer the benefit of 26 years worth of speedway presentation experience to a new club, expect abuse from forum!"

Charles Mckay   "What about the events of Saturday at Loony Road (went into bar and met a group of unhappy Buxton fans) no beer as no elec as generator buggered. Lights then came= on and then went off about 3 times – which of course meant the fence went down. Meeting started at 7-50 and two races ran with no track lights. Heat 3 ran with track lights on turns 1 and 2 and half of back straights then for heat four ran with all lights on then rain started. Heat 5 stopped and Priest excluded. Then meeting abandoned. Rain off policy at gate official 2010 policy (month + rerun) policy in programme (3 weeks + rerun –no refunds) I may be writing to SCB and BSPA MC re what policy is and where do fans stand re refunds especially is a meeting is called off between heats 8 and 12 (Dick and Les there from Kent and someone from Ipswich) Also what would have happen if power gone off during race fence when down and rider ran into arco barrier and killed. At inquest Tattum, ref and CofC asked what happen and if there had been any problems with power before hand"

9th May

Fredrik Lindgren*   "Blue sky & sunny in Krakow, don't matter as I'm leaving soon for UK! Had dinner with PK last night what a lovely chap he is"

Fredrik Lindgren*   "Wonder how many hours of my life I'm waiting? There has to be a lot of hours, days, weeks, months, years?"

Fredrik Lindgren*   "My flight is delayed, boring but it don't happens often nowadays. Remember my first years as a pro a lot of delayed flights back then"

Fredrik Lindgren*   "Just had information about my flight delay. The information were that the next information will be in 30 minutes ?!? Expected departure 14:00 GMT+1 if that will be correct I guess I'll be in time for match but can I trust that my flight will depart then?"

Fredrik Lindgren*   "Managed to get a flight to Liverpool instead, has to do check-in & security control again! Speedway life includes solving travel problems! Luckily for me PK is on this new flight of mine so I can catch a ride with him from Liverpool to Wolverhampton!"

Fredrik Lindgren*   "Eating a lovely chicken baguette that I could get with my 13 zloty voucher they gave us when my first flight were delayed. Hopefully I'll score some points today as my new Air ticket was how can I put it? Not very cheap!"

Fredrik Lindgren*   "5 min from the track when I got the news it's a rain off today at Wolves!"

Fredrik Lindgren*   "Off to Stansted, what a day not a very good one! Can't believe how good the weather is more south in the UK! Yea weather god rub it in! Damn rain off!"

Fredrik Lindgren*   "Ryan Fisher just made an awesome save in Heat 7 Poole vs Cov dude that looked sick!"

Greg Hancock* "The race in Gorzow yesterday was one to forget! Hard day for GH with some bike troubles etc. Get that one off the chest quick. The toughest thing was Rafal Dobrucki crashed hard and has a serious back injury. Hoping that he will recover ok from that. Such a bummer!"

Greg Hancock* "2 broken vertebrae for Rafal Dobrucki. That really sucks. Wish him the best!"

Niels Kristian Iversen* "At the airport in Berlin.. The driver was 1h.10m early this morning. Whats up with that.?? Guess it better than being an hour late"

Niels Kristian Iversen*   "Cant wait to get on that plane so i can sleep. And i dont care if im drooling while sleeping"

Niels Kristian Iversen* "Beautifull weather in stansted. I am mega ready to get home and spend the rest of the day with my girlie"

Scott Nicholls* "Like that fine line in competitiveness between racing n getting through passport control quick! :-)"

Dakota North* "looking forward to tonights meeting, need some big points!"

Linus Sundstrum* "have you raced there before"

Nicolai Klindt * "had a hard landing with airbaltic in copenhagen. almost flew into the cockpit! but don't worry, I'm safe"

Nicolai Klindt* "mmh, lovely birds at cph-airport"

Ludwig Lindgren * "ein, zwei, drei polizei! hate german and polish controls they are always such hard asses. i bet they aren't that cool without the badge"

Scott Nicholls* "Little guest booking for cov on sky. Wish I'd had me haircut now!"

Dakota North* "Why is the weather so shit in wolverhampton?"

Dakota North* "Waiting for a nice steak"

Paul Burbidge* "Poole are going through a few air bags tonight"

Nicolai Klindt* "must give Darcy some respekt. he ain't fast, he is very fast!"

Nicolai Klindt* "big crash with auty and andersson. it's like auty is riding over his ability. but so funny to watch fisher, he is really tryin'!"

Mike Bennett* "Oh dear- this is not a good advert for speedway is it? [Poole] Track very patchy. Nigel and Kelvin earning their money tonight! :-)"

Nigel Pearson "Christian Hefenbrock has actually won a GP, you know"

Nigel Pearson "Coventry had a delayed start due to what happened in the winter – lots of arguing off the track"

Kelvin Tatum "[Ward & Holder] ran out of steam, some of the lifestyle...it's very easy just to write in on the calendar 'yes, I can do this. Yes, I can do that'...they just allowed their partying to take over their riding....I just feel Holder, Watt and Darcy Ward have learnt the lessons of last season"

Chris Louis "it's all about Cardiff, isn't it?"

Scott Nicholls "No! It's about winning the British title!"

Kelvin Tatum "I haven't seen much of Kenni Larsen myself – he rode in the Premier League last season"

Chris Louis [to Darcy Ward] "Peter [Johns] might have got the engines going good but you're holding the throttle"

David Watt "I know we've only got one thing to concentrate on but that's pretty hard for speedway riders sometimes!"

Chris Louis "Dennis Andersen really shut the door on him [Auty] there"

Alun Rossiter "Yeh, that's speedway. That's what I keep telling my boys to do!"

Neil Middleditch "Darcy's pulling Tony Rickardsson moves out there – that's a real compliment... He's really serious out there, perhaps, he partied just a little too hard last year – by his own admission.. yeh, he's young he's gotta live!....without a word of a lie, he's one of the best 19 year olds I've ever seen and I've seen a lot of 19 year olds"

Nigel Pearson "Scott Nicholls looks so slow tonight, Kelvin, doesn't he?"

Kelvin Tatum "Where you sit in the changing room does help"

Nigel Pearson "How much tougher is the GP?"

Chris Holder "It's insane! No one really talks to you from when you get there"

Scott Nicholls* "Yer on the road again. Tough night n disappointed but not beating myself up about it. Didn't have me mojo. Sort myself for Sweden morrow"

10th May

Niels Kristian Iversen* "2.30 is just to freakin early for mé to get up. Them 6am flights sucks."

Chris Holder* "Que (at 05.30) is pretty much out the door at Stansted airport this morning! Where is everyone goin on a Tuesday morning?!"

Steve Mallett "We have had to let our heads rule our heart with respect to Mark [Jones]. We had to do something to improve matters and we are preparing the ground for another move. It is now up to the Newport fans who cried out for change to turn out in force and show their support for the adjustment in team personnel. Justin [Sedgmen] has been plying his trade with Swindon in the Elite League so far this season and his acquisition is a real coup."

Dakota North* "week off wish i could be riding somewhere!"

Fredrik Lindgren* "Got some laps in & a few more starts. Apparently starts are very important in speedway I wish I could learn to make good ones!"

Dakota North* "time for cod"

Nicolai Klindt* "västervik is a shit hole when your behind, but a awesome track when your in front"

Fredrik Lindgren* "Feeling good, listening to "Swedish House Mafia - One" powerful! Almost home now in Örebro! Been a good day!"

Nicolai Klindt* "damn! broke my toe nail in half and bloods everywhere. I will see in the morning if I can ride tomorrow!"

11th May

Niels Kristian Iversen* "Almost at home in Esbjerg. Cant wait to get some sleep. Dont sleep very well in vans"

Nicolai Klindt* "a one hour walk from the hotel to the track in flip-flops is not the best thing to do!"

Chris Holder* "Chillin in the sun in Sweden watching the boys wash my bike haha love being the boss :-)"

Lewis Bridger* "Few drinks with my gf for her birthday then a lot of hard work over next few days then of to marbella next week!!"

12th May

Fredrik Lindgren* "Just feels like another perfect day to beat Nicolai or should I say Mr: LeftLegBrakeMan. Surprise if he's in front of real Wolves riders!"

Nicolai Klindt* "thank you freddan! knew I had to be on the gas with you behind me ;) good to beat my "idol" tho, haha. good luck Saturday"

Steve Mallett "I have already had preliminary talks with the sport's governing body about the [NL withdrawal] implications in terms of fines etc but matters cannot continue to be sustained at the present level of attendance. We have one of the best infrastructures for rider development in British Speedway in terms of running training schools, a team in the National League and a senior team in the Premier League but the sums don't add up and a tough decision with respect to the Hornets is pending. If fans want to see the lads continue in action they need to get down to Queensway Meadows and show their support."

Dakota North* "On the route for rugby. The acu what a hassle. All that for nothing farrrkkk"

Chris Holder* "Sick day in Gothenburg! Bit of go karts and lisebergs theme park yewww"

Gary Patchett* [after Wolves use T/R twice on R/R rides] "Meet ref shall have supreme control of the meeting. Except when another one tells him what to do agnst his better judgement!"

13th May

Paul Burbidge* "Just had a ride in the new space pods between Heathrow T5 Business parking and departures. The days of buses here are numbered"

Dakota North* "what's for lunch mate!"

Nicolai Klindt* "just woke up! it was indeed needed with a good nights sleep. woke up next to my mate beaut!" [a dog]

Scott Nicholls* "I heard u've slept with some dogs,but that ones actually quite cute! Ha ha. Good riding last night too"

Fredrik Lindgren* "Don't matter what time a day it is, at Airports you always see people drinking beer!"

Fredrik Lindgren* "Read an SGP preview at aktuellspeedway.se where it says my goal this year is top 8?!? My aim this year is still my secret!"

Lewis Bridger* "Don't you just hate it when your Mechanic's are Smashing a Dirty Burger King & I'm trying to eat my wholemeal Wrap!!"

Lewis Bridger* "This is taking the piss we left Eastbourne at 12:30 & 5hr later still in traffic on route to scunthorpe!! 5mins of racing tonight then it's all fun & games in Marbs bro :-)"

Lewis Bridger* "Rain tonight !!! Why fucking scunthorpe & I swear if Tai gets a Wildcard pick for the British Final they can get fucked !!!... its fucked!! He didn't quallify last year because he fucked up in semi so he crashes his bmx gets injured & gets in!!"

Nicola Sands* "Kelvin Tatum and Nigel Pearson....... speedway's answer to Ant and Dec"

Fredrik Lindgren* "High speed skidding at Ullevi stadium done! Track ok, I'm ok, bikes ok, weather ok, everything ok! Need my trapping gloves on tomorrow"

14th May

Matthew Wethers "I saw the video of Craig's crash, and it did look as though [Taylor] Poole had straightened up a bit and crashed into him, but it's hard to see from that angle. Poole maybe just tries a bit too hard."

Rob Lyon "The referee's decisions were awful – I really don't know what meeting [Barbara Horley] was looking at sometimes, but that's the way it goes sometimes"

Tom Hill "I was told it was a good job that I went back in when I did as the ends of my fingers would have been chopped off as they had gone all dead on the ends!"

Niels Kristian Iversen* "Think its retarded when its says BOARDING on the screen and people are rushing out to the gate only to find out the bastard [Ryanair] plane has not"

Trevor Swales "I reckon he had a personality transplant during the winter...I used to think of [Troy] as a bit of a gating tart, but he's proved me wrong by showing he can come from the back and win races"

John Anderson "situations like this [late rain off] cost the club in the region of £2,500, what with travel costs back for the visitors, referee costs, medical cover, catering and the like."

Nigel Pearson "[Luke Chessell] has been struggling for confidence and has fallen a lot but he seems determined to get out there and practice as much as possible to find a team place elsewhere and we hope he is successful in that."

Nicky Mallet [a few weeks before 'rain' led to the early postponement of Newport v Plymouth on a SGP night that also featured Man U v Barca] "Let's face it, the Grand Prix is watched by massive numbers of British fans and, of course, that includes (both of?) ours. It would have been silly of us to think that we could run a Knockout Cup fixture against the Grand Prix and we are delighted to announce that our fans now have the opportunity to watch both events. Now we have done that, we are seeking our fans to be loyal to us and turn up in their numbers to support the Hornets."

Nicolai Klindt* "hair is still there and looking good. only £20 as well with a wash. not like denmark where you paid £20 just to sit down."

Simon Stead "Scotty Nicholls has been immense, as we knew he would be. He tigers in every race"

Fredrik Lindgren* "So that [Gothenberg SGP] was poor! Feels good to be in one piece at least! Can't wait to get a shower am pretty dirty!"

Scott Nicholls* "Me thinkin must be end of line for gburg gp. Bad times. Thoughts for crumpy"

James Cockle "Weymouth don't run any more so they are not rivals. God forbid that place – I'm not really sorry about what happened there, but that's another story…I'm sad to see it close. I'm not impressed with what Phil [Bartlett] did to it all. I'm not happy in the slightest. Everyone knows everyone is owed money and we are never going to see it again. We're just paying for it now really. Where we would have had money to put into the bikes, we've had to make do with what we've got from the last couple of years."

Steve Mallett "2011 has been the worst start to a season by the Wasps since the sport returned here in 1997 and that simply cannot continue, we need wins home AND away and I will do anything to make that happen."

Steve Williams & Graham Goodwin "We're not in the National League for the short term. It's all part of a long term strategy – tied in with the proposals for the new stadium – for Belle Vue to once again discover its own talent and develop young riders, but we can't do that without the support of the fans…we need them to continue to support us right through the season and to show David Gordon and Chris Morton that the Belle Vue public are on board and sharing in their vision for the future."

Not Len Silver* "Early rain off means me, Pete and John can have our eurovision party after all jedward to win"

John Anderson "These people casting aspersions about our failure to have a guest should know better. I know who most are and I would expect nothing less than a face to face apology from them."

David Mason "We only go to Scunthorpe once a year, we were caught unaware"

David Howe "I don't believe I'm ever going to being a position where I could get in that top two or three at the GP Challenge so I kind of decided instead of throwing thousands of pounds chasing the dream when you probably wouldn't make it, it is better to chase a dream you can achieve and, for me now, that's in grasstrack and longtrack. The last couple of years I've been racing speedway as a living and I have got this other form of hunger now and that's to be in the World Longtrack Championship….I made a lot of mistakes, a lot of bad choices in speedway and I think grass and longtrack is something that I can do and do properly. I'm a better grasstrack rider than speedway rider anyway. I'm breaking into Germany and I'm doing it how I should have done my speedway, I'm taking it very seriously…In old money, I was ten and half stone; I'm nine stone three now. I don't drink at all now, I was never a partier"

Michael Lee "It's very difficult to find good replacements, which highlights the problem in British speedway at the moment"

15th May

Chad Reed* "Really hoping AmericanMX doesn't go to this stupid sound rule what a joke like watching vacuums race around. its the very highest level wtf

Chris Holder* "they done the same to speedway man! FIM... the bikes sound like shit!!!!"

Nigel Pearson* "Sat in Gothenburg Airport teaching Kelvin Tatum how to tweet!!

Greg Hancock* "Congrats to Chris Holder & all who those hydroplaned their speedway bikes [at Gothenberg SGP] last night!:) Hope JC is ok"

John Harvey* "The riders were the only professional part of the evening, lots of uhappy fans @ the bar of the Radisson last night!!"

Fredrik Lindgren* "Was a bad evening for speedway last night, feel sorry for all the fans at Ullevi!"

Paul Burbidge* "Sat in the cafe at Gothenburg airport with the BSI crew. The GP was emotional as ever. When will we get good weather in this city?"

Paul Burbidge* "It's a tough call to postpone any meeting with so many fans in the stadium. Track held up incredibly well in such heavy rain"

Lewis Bridger* "it's my Marbella Possyyyy !!! Haha Gd gp last night fella but that's all history now.. Let's see the real CH in Marbssssss !"

Scott Nicholls* "Saw snoop dogg in hotel,Brighton.Me n blakey are on the town for my b-day,might see if he wants to hook up for a beer!Haha,think he'll wanna"

Gary Patchett* "short term only for Hans. No interest in long term. Great for EL"

Nicolai Klindt* "its always good to watch discovery channel on a sunday. wish i could have me self a full english, just to be fat"

Nicolai Klindt* "anyone who know what you can use as a charger for your macbook pro, if you left yours 1800km away?"

Chris Neath* "Thought it was pretty bad how the [Newcastle] crowd were cheering when Jordan was in the fence. Guess there passionate but there is a line somewhere"

Mike Bennett* "trending on the BSF. . . again!!! Bovvered???... No I was on the mic in the [Leicester] box- for one night only! Trying to give the club some help with presentation basics!"

abc1 "So, how did the Presentation experiment with 'Micman' Mike Bennett go last night?

Mike Bennett enjoyed stroking his own ego, and obviously is a polished performer, BUT, blaming the programme for his own mistakes whilst taking the mickey out of Chris Popple (who did a great job on the centre green) over the tannoy, on the only occasion he got mixed up was BAD FORM! And as for the 'joke' about a Russian rider called (I think he said) 'Knickers Neveron' was corny in the extreme and inappropriate when many children are in the crowd too. We at Leicester may need an improved box man, however I for one hope it's NOT the OTT egomaniac Mike Bennett....I agree that Mike Bennett is obviously an experienced presenter and much of what he did was obviously a massive improvement, I just didn't like the jibes at Chris Popple, which were unnecessary when often Chris (on the centre) is getting info 2nd hand , whereas Mike Bennett had the benefit of sitting next to the Referee to get his info straight from the horses mouth as it were , and still made mistakes himself."

Pixel 8 "Mike Bennett's ego may well have it's own postcode, but so what"

Leicester Lion "I dare say to be a meeting presenter you need to be the sort of person who does "stroke his own ego". But to do the job properly, I think it's essential. A good meeting presenter needs to put on a show for the audience. It's an act. It's about enhancing the customer experience. It's about interacting with the audience, not just speaking to them. The excellent use of Twitter during last night's meeting was a prime example. It's not about simply going through the motions of reading the race line-ups, sponsors' details and the 50-50 draw result (if they can get the colour of the ticket right!). It's about adding some life to the proceedings. The voice needs to be exaggerated. The presenter needs to be prepared to take a few risks and accept that not everyone will love them. The centre green presenter has a wireless microphone, so they have the perfect opportunity to move around - walk around the centre green and take the show to the fans around the stadium, not just those on the home straight. The centre green presenter needs to be visible, which might include wearing something outlandish. I can't stand Porky, the centre green presenter at Wolverhampton. But, like him or loathe him, there's no denying he puts on a good show, and it is a show - he isn't like that in real life. He does many of the things I've mentioned. He interacts with the spectators. He makes a twit of himself with his "dad dance". He exaggerates his voice and has the corniest of catchphrases. People respond to him. He adds something to the atmosphere. He contrasts with the man in the box, whose role is to make the standard announcements about line-ups, race times etc. In my opinion, Leicester needs a centre green presenter in the Porky or Mike Bennett mould. To me, Chris Popple does not seem to be that man. However, he would be an excellent "straight man" in the double act, doing the routine announcements from the box and setting up the centre green presenter to do his stuff."

Mike Bennett "As for "ego stroking??" just answer me this. . . do you honestly think I'm that desperate to have my fragile ego massaged that I would give up an entire Saturday, drive a 6 hour round trip from Norfolk, spend £50 on fuel and return home at 2am when I'm working the following day just to have a few people say they enjoyed the act? I can get that after a home meeting at Kings Lynn thanks or by spending an entire weekend at home with my family so I would appreciate it if my reasons for "performing" were taken in the way they were intended. For many reasons I wish Leicester all the success in the world and just wanted to give a newcomer the benefit of 26 years

worth of experience. If that includes ego stroking then I've missed out somewhere along the way....
You see, even with an ego the size of a small continent, I've never claimed to be perfect! I'll leave
description that to my twitter and facebook followers"

16th May

SGP.com   Polish governing bodies the Glówna Komisja Sportu Zuzlowego and the PZM have
confirmed all meetings in the country will be raced on the new silencer from this Sunday onwards.
The new, quieter pipes have been mandatory in all other countries and FIM events since the start
of this year. However, following a string of protests from the nation's senior riders, the Polish
authorities opted to stick with the 2010 model. This decision was overturned this afternoon,
though, and Sunday's Ekstraliga meetings will take place with riders fitting the same silencers
used in the SGP series and Speedway World Cup.

Steve Mallett   "Kim [Nilsson] had indicated that he would be missing for several fixtures and I felt
that I had to act because we need to be firing on all cylinders in order to pull our season around.
Jason [Doyle] became available after recently covering for Steve Boxall at Rye House and he is
clearly a class act at Premier League level. To fit him in we have handed a reprieve to Mark Jones
and I'm confident he can now do a good job from the reserve berth."

Dakota North*   "Another rain off for me!!! 3 in 17 days haha damit!"

Nicolai Klindt*   "just looked through my schedule and no time what so ever for a holiday! only in
world cup week, but need to be in that."

Fredrik Lindgren*   "Hate when you get these colds, mine started Thursday & it won't go away
runny nose & shite! Well am off to Airport now fly to UK"

Mike Bacon*   "Belle Vue v Peter OFF track waterlogged. Doesn't anyone want to ride the
Panthers?!!!!!!!, or am I looking too deep?"

Mike Bacon*   "Shame about weather in G/burg GP. But that's 2 out of 2 winners so far this year
who ride reg in EL. Well done Chris Holder

Greg Hancock*   "Poland has decided that the new silencers are safe to use so the old ones are
out! What a bummer:(Things r getting quiet. Let's make noise"

Stuart Robson   "Over the years I've not really been the best of starters"

Charlie Webster   "There's been a little bit of criticism of your reserve pairing, what do you say
about that?"

Stuart Robson   "Oh, is there? Don't worry about it.."

Kelvin Tatum   "I fancy that it's the Lakeside Top 5 that's been having abit of criticism"

Piotr Swiderski   "I have a bigger family, less sleep but I enjoy...I'm not asleep on the gate...so
good so far"

Kelvin Tatum   "They probably can't quite believe how hard the Hammers have hit them"

Nicolai Klindt*   "nigel pearson is screaming away on sky sports"

Peter Adams   "He was on the outside there with Lee Richardson which isn't a good place to be...
like everyone else Freddie has the odd blip, he's not a machine...the [Lakeside] track is slicker than
ever, you have to take advantage of the inside gates when you have them"

Kelvin Tatum   "You just said it to me – off air"

Fredrik Lindgren   "I always find this [Lakeside] track boring"

Nigel Pearson   "You'll notice that Lee Richardson isn't wearing the blue and claret Lakeside
kevlars this evening, he had an accident and he's had to send them away for repair"

Peter Karlsson   "You pick your racing line and it's a Sunday ride in the park"

Kelvin Tatum   "He's out with his brother here, so he'll be hoping for some brotherly love"

Nigel Pearson   "I think I might have motivated the Lakeside Hammers this evening by tipping
them to finish bottom of the league in the *Speedway Star*. It's been mentioned in the programme"

Kelvin Tatum   "There's no mistake that Lin, Lynn, Lindgren"

Chris Neath*   "Spaghetti and meatballs for dinner. Pancakes for desert"

Stuart Robson "It's [team spirit] certainly getting better but it's got a long way to go. I also ride at Newcastle and it's a lot better up there. The problem is that the lads are riding against each other in other countries so they tend to keep themselves to themselves."

Kelvin Tatum "The dust flies through our studio once again"

Jon Cook "Clearly if we can't beat PK or Freddie Lindgren, then we're not gonna win the meeting. It's up to the top end....they only come here once or twice a season but we're here every week.... each week the Lakeside faithful – of which I am one – have to wait to see which one of our top end is going to struggle"

Nigel Pearson "Jon Cook's interview was very wise words"

Nigel Pearson "Emil Sayfutdinov - an exciting young Russian – how would you feel about paying to see him every week? There are other stories of GP stars wanting to come to the Elite League which is on the up and up....in February I thought the whole thing was falling apart but now we've got 10 teams and GP riders wanting to join the Elite League"

Fredrik Lindgren "I never liked this [Lakeside] track. I think it's pretty boring but I'm here to do my job and enjoy the crowd"

Kevin Long* "Got to love @freddielindgren honest opinion of the Arena Essex motorway"

Kelvin Tatum "Lunwig Lidgren"

Kevin Long* "Always amazed how Nigel can crow-bar Cradley into his speedway commentary."

Adam Shields "They [PK & Fredrik] actually ride like home riders, probably better than all of us so it's pretty self-explanatory...I'm not quite skilful enough rider to slow down a race. It probably wouldn't help Stuart as he's flat out all the time and the most entertaining rider here"

Nigel Pearson "The Lakeside manager almost feared this [heat 13] race!"

Fredrik Lindgren "I don't hate this track, I do my best riding it"

Lee Richardson I ride against Freddie often enough to not want to make any enemies"

Ludvig Lindgren "It's a bad decision, I'm not best friends with the referee but that's speedway"

Jon Cook "The guy obviously bailed out cos he didn't expect someone of Robert's stature in the sport at this point to come and do that"

Jonathan Barber* "wish Kelvin would stop saying Lee Richardson is making a good fist of things"

Jon Cook "Our so called lesser riders have showed a lot of courage tonight"

Lee Richardson "Lucky I got off – it wrecked me bike and me finger as well"

Nigel Pearson "Sky Sports, the BSPA, everybody has to back Britain – when the [GB] team does well, it raises awareness throughout Britain"

Nigel Pearson "I seem to remember Scott Nicholls being pulled out of the shower at a Grand Prix"

Nigel Pearson "Will he follow them round or will he try to win the race? What's his attitude here?"

Paul Burbidge* "Hammers have too many steady eddies"

Nigel Pearson* "M25 and M1 a constant line of roadworks. Only in this country. Shambles.... These lane closures are threatening my midnight deadline in Walsall for chinese takeaway!!"

17th May

Dakota North* "what to do?"

Peter Adams "And it's obvious we are hurt by the absence of Tai Woffinden but we must also note the scores of riders who should be scoring more than they are."

Niels Kristina Iversen* "Just had a short powernap. Soon its time to getting sideways"

Nicolai Klindt* "västervik lost today but everyone was trying. i had a ok meeting with paid 9, but can still get better. form is on the way up tho"

18th May

Steve Mallett "The attendance for our most recent home match in the [NL] cup was still not good enough but we had a meeting of senior management and decided to persevere for now. However, we do appeal to Newport fans that if they want us to be able to run a second team then they must get down here for the next home fixture against Mildenhall on Bank Holiday Monday May 30th and show their support."

Fredrik Lindgren* "Book a lot of flights in my job, must praise easyjet it's so convenient, from booking to online check-in!"

Dakota North* "fooooood shopping! hungry as the come"

Nigel Pearson* "Cost me £91 to fill my car up today, this is beyond a joke"

Nicolai Klindt* "the new version of quickoffice is pissing me right off! keep closing down on me"

Dakota North* "need to sort out full time mechanic"

Mike Bacon* "if Lasse [Bjerre] bats as fast as he gates, he'll need 20 overs to get into double figures!! Love him really"

19th May

Scott Nicholls* "Saw best team riding in a long time in Sweden Tuesday. Vargarna boys,nicki p n krispysak,heat 15.Nicki p ended up in the fence! Bad times"

Nicolai Klindt* "up up up! new day with loads of activities. two engines for service, a 7km run, office work and much more

Mike Bellerby "It really does make a difference to the riders when they can hear fans cheering."

Dakota North* "cod"

Chris Holder* "Back from Spain today.. Some funny shit went down! Jus bout to get on a bus and off to the horse races yewwww wat a week off this has been!"

Scott Nicholls* "on route to Sheffield for British final "qualifier"...really! Justified over here??? Not so sure. Hay Ho"

Nicolai Klindt* "home after a long day. will start looking for a house to buy in the winter now. but good there is some time so i can find the right one....[Q: Swindon?] nah, dont know where mate. think around wolves or sumah!"

20th May

Fredrik Lindgren* "Star Alliance flight today, remember me of back in the day. Before Ryanair time, oh man I'm getting old!"

Lewis Bridger* "Sunshine in Scunny let's smash it tonight Points mean Prize's Bang Tidy"

Davey Watt* "Hangovers suck !"

Nigel Pearson* "Why would anyone think signing Emil for Bees is a bad thing? Unbelievable! Best Elite League for years!!"

Linus Sundstrom* "cheers mr bigstuff! I see you earning far too much money buying new kevlars ;)"

Dakota North* "Time to do the bike now!"

Nicola Sands* "When did Friday night's change....need to address this work life balance."

Nicolai Klindt* "just picked my dad up from a house party, pissed out of his face. bless him! now gonna play some mxvsatvalive"

billybikespeedway "And Steve Malletts Expetise and Experience at Team Management Is ????
Owning a Speedway team does not make you a good manager, any more than owning a speedway bike makes you a speedway Rider"

Najjer "For a team that was predicted to quite well over the winter months by near enough all Wasps fans (I think I remember that being the case before) and by many other Premier League fans, myself included, it's been a disastrous start to the season. Credit to the Mallett's, they made changes to try and resolve the woeful start and everyone would agree it made the team a hell of a lot stronger and hopes were high again - yet they've just been blown out of site by a team

[Edinburgh] missing their number 1 rider who could only be replaced by two reserves, one of which has barely scored a point all year in Dicken, leaving them with a 3 man side. If I was a Newport fan (perish the thought!) then I would be mightily miffed right now, and rightly so."

Dakota North* "hitting the sack need a big one tomorrow!"

Greg Hancock* "Hangover 2 next Wed! Gotta do it! Never been to Bangkok but wont need to after Wednesday! Stu's gettin married.."

Fredrik Lindgren* "Practice done & dinner done! Now I'm gonna stay in bed and hope that my man flu totally disappear this weekend!"

Jon Cook "By July it's fair to say that riders who currently wouldn't consider UK racing will be more responsive to an approach and that means it's only tonight and the Birmingham Cup matches left for some of the team to show the same commitment and passion for the Hammers that our fans and backroom staff show and expect. Last night was an all time low as it was only our guests and Robert [Mear] that showed any real form. I am not going to make any excuses whatsoever, they know it wasn't good enough and there's only one way to put that right."

Mike Bowden "It was a poor performance [v. Workington] and we were effectively a two-man team, relying heavily on Ben Barker and Jason Bunyan. We will be making changes before next Friday's home match against Scunthorpe. Kyle Hughes will be rejoining us and I am also having talks with an Elite League rider."

Debbie Hancock "Kyle [Hughes] informed the club shortly after last Friday's match against Plymouth that he wanted to take a break from the sport. Although he subsequently had second thoughts on his decision, we felt that the time was right to make a change, and with Alex becoming available following a reshuffle at Newport, we had to move quickly to secure his signature."

Arnie Gibbons "John Stuart Mill's *On Liberty*", Thos. Paine and "*The Rights of Man*" and "*Showered in Shale*" - the three pillars of western liberal democratic thought"

21st May

Nicolai Klindt* [picks his dream team] "1. nicolai klindt 2. nicolai klindt 3. nicolai klindt 4. nicolai klindt 5. nicolai klindt 6. nicolai klindt 7. nicolai Klindt #dreamteam"

Kevin Long* "can catagorgicaly deny, he is NOT having an affair with a Premier League football player!. . .speedway rider perhaps!! ;)"

Olly Allen* [on Joshua Jake Allen] "we have had a boy!!! Yeeeehhhaaaaahhhhh"

Nicolai Klindt* "congratz with the little new one :) thats why u didnt go through last night. your gonna call it nicolai or what then?"

Nicolai Klindt* "the engine i rode on wednesday had done 35 heats before the meeting. amazing it went that well!"

David Watt* "thats not sad mate. I just seen a woman in the airport with a bigger mustache than you ! That's sad !!! Hahaha"

Niels Kristian Iversen* "Tough night for the stars. 12 points, a fucked bike and a soar body for me"

Niels Kristian Iversen* "Fuck you M25.. How can it be traffik jam shit at 23.00 in the night"

Niels Kristian Iversen* "I got sleep to catch. Anyone wanna sponsor me a helicopter ??"

Fredrik Lindgren* "Feels like one big thing in my life is waiting. When have I waited enough?"

22nd May

Lewis Bridger* "In hotel still in Gniezno.. Big meeting today at Poznan, Had a decent Breakfast and 9hr's sleep what else could I want • Big Elbows Bang !!!"

Nicolai Klindt* "just landed in lodz and sun is shining! shorts on shades out, 25 degrees

Fredrik Lindgren* "I'm so hungry now, hope we find a traditional polish restaurant soon! We're in-between Tarnow & Rzeszow at the moment

Fredrik Lindgren* "Starving waiting for food now when Rzeszows two Brits walked in ain't talking to them, it's the Poludnia Derby today! Go Tarnow!"

Nicolai Klindt* rain off in lodz.. lightning and thunder on the parade, haha."

Kevin Long* "Has arrived at Leicester Speedway. . .now going to eat my delicious Tuna Pasta!"

Kevin Long* "Very impressive facility has been created here at Leicester speedway.Long straights with tight, banked bends.Be interesting to see how it rides"

Kevin Long* "Barbara Horley has started the meeting in only a way that she can!"

Kevin Long* "She's now called a break whilst the Sun goes down"

Arnie Gibbons "Easily the best meeting I've seen so far at Leicester"

23rd May

Dakota North* at 08.51 "time to get up"

Chris Holder* "jus got some virus man... Had it a few days but the early morning flight outter polska killed me man!!"

Gordon Kennett "You're looking good"

Peter Oakes "Thank you"

Gordon Kennett "How's speedway?"

Peter Oakes "I've been around too long to say. It's speedway! I'm not sure if you can say it's good or it's bad? Do you come much?"

Gordon Kennett "A bit. I can't stand watching. I like to mechanic coz you're involved and doing something. What do you think of the new silencers? I think they've improved things. The racing is closer and quieter."

Peter Oakes "If you think back to those days at Wembley when you used to step out to that unbelievable noise. You don't get that now"

Gordon Kennett "It's quieter"

Peter Oakes "It is. Even at Cardiff they don't get anything like that noise anymore. It's a shame."

Gordon Kennett "The racing looks better though – closer"

John Hazelden "Timo's terrible – a bucket of worms would beat him round here. I tell you what – send him home! He ain't even on the gas going round that bend"

Kevin Long* "Pearson and Tatum talking nonsensical bo@#% &ks regarding replacement of excluded riders!"

Nick Barber "The best thing about Sky meetings is starting on time and finishing early!"

Mike Bennett* "note to self 'give Trevor Swales some media training tips and enthusiasm pills!'"

Nick Barber "You can see from the team Swindon have that they might be moving on. That's not a Terry Russell team. He spends big and brings in the best cos that gets the big crowds."

Cameron Woodward "It was fun to do [guesting for Plymouth] but not much money"

Dakota North* "Hard night for the team track wasn't as great as it looked before the first heat!"

Lewis Bridger* "One Word for tonight Smashed it !! :-)"

Fredrik Lindgren* "In Manchester with Ricky Kling, flying to Sweden tomorrow! Thanks Joe Haines for the ride from Wolverhampton!"

24th May

Fredrik Lindgren* "Wohoo up & about, free hotel night thanks Mr: Kling!"

Fredrik Lindgren* "BIG Full English Breakfast today that was awesome!"

Fredrik Lindgren* "At David Ruuds place in Gislaved am impressed with his house real nice. I should've become a speedway rider!"

Nicolai Klindt* "yo lew.... wtf is going on about your leg man? haha"

Lewis Bridger* "Fuck knows haha can't keep it on the peg lol just lining her up making points LOL"

Nicolai Klindt* "can understand why woffy got the wildcard but why josh auty. thought steady would get it. bspa obviously don't want the best in the final!"

Mike Bowden "We fully understand the reasons [outside business commitments] for Seemond's [second retirement] decision and would like to thank him for his five years of loyal service to the team."

Terry Russell [cites "rider availability"] "It's regrettable that we have had to make this decision [Second Test cancellation] but we feel it's the correct one in the best interests of the sport."

Lewis Bridger* "On the southern line chilling out wid my MacBook Pro & IBEAT headphones on the way 2 spend sometime with my Gawjus Girl !!!"

Bryn Williams "[Luke Chessell] was ruled out of the rest of the meeting suffering from back pains and facing having to buy a new crash helmet as his was confiscated after being damaged on impact with the safety fence"

25th May

Steve Aston* [to Mike Bennett at King's Lynn v Coventry, his 2nd ever tweet!] "message from the bees fans stop being an arse!"

Fredrik Lindgren* "SINGLE is NOT a status. It's a word that best describes a person who is strong enough to live and enjoy life without depending on others"

Fredrik Lindgren* "Phew, had to print and run out off ink in the printer! Luckily last time I was shopping ink I got one extra black!"

Hans Andersen* "Been to the doctors today and is likely I'M four weeks Away from racing again c",) weeeiii there's a light at the end of the tunnel !"

Lewis Bridger* [prior to getting forearm 'live the life you love' tattoo] "Going 4 tattoo yewwww :)"

Stoke Speedway* "Stoke promoter Dave Tattum is devastated after the clubs Loomer Road base was broken into."

Kevin Long* [to Mike Bennett] "Are you featured in Jeff Scott's new book? Available here tonight ;)"

Double O "Woeful performance from the Bees tonight. Fisher and Sayfutdinov were ok but the rest were awful. One change must happen soon, but unless the Polish Lord Lucan actually rides for us, we have zero chance of the play-offs. Bloody hell our great club nearly closed over primarily a rider who hardly turns out for us. Bees fans may realise that despite all the hype over Sayfutdinov, unless we start performing away from home, the only thing we can look forward too come September is a Midland League against Wolves and Birmingham"

Rob Lyon "The track's not easy to ride"

26th May

BSPA STOKE promoter Dave Tattum has faced with a major repair bill after a break-in at the Loomer Road Stadium. Staffordshire Police are investigating the incident with required the replacement of the dressing rooms' copper pipework and two hot water cylinders. Tattum said: "It's been a devastating blow for the club financially as it is something that you cannot budget for. It has cost around two and a half thousand pounds to replace the pipework and the hot water cylinders which feed hot water into the dressing room area and it is money we can ill afford to keep spending. We have to provide showers etc for the riders so therefore obviously everything has to be replaced and done straight away and ready for the next meeting."

Dakota North* "wills [chiropractor] sister shes i works at the one near the train crossing near the shell servo in shepp, my neck still gets stiff from that man"

Dakota North* "Weather isn't looking good"

Chris Holder* "Movin all my shit into my new house today!!!"

Scott Nicholls* "Gonna try n get to grips with my new i-pad2! Look at me techno geek....err,how do I turn it on?"

Paul Burbidge* "Auty had his chance to be there and didn't qualify. Fair enough, he had bike problems, but these things happen."

Nigel Pearson* "I like Josh Auty, he's a great lad, but I'm with you boys, I disagree with the decision.

Nicolai Klindt* [after Swindon lose 41-49 to Belle Vue]   "is fuming! how can we loose last 3 heats 15-3? was giving it everything in the last one, doing a TR on the fence. better luck next time!"

Lewis Bridger*   "missed the Gym Bad :-/ had good workout tonight, deffo going 2 join a boxing club next week to help out with some new circuits !!!"

Paul Rickett   "It probably took until Friday afternoon before Richie Worrell's bike stopped glowing red"

Scott Nicholls*   "Bad day at the office n a crash for good measure. Might be a tad stiff in the morning,n not in the right places!Will enjoy couple days off"

Dakota North*   "What a shit night! Wish these doctors would hurry up an strighten my finger bra starting to hurt haha Fucking hell, xray doesn't look good. Ahhhh needles in the fingers. In hospital for the night fingers straighten in a cast waiting for surgeon to pin my fingers"

Dakota North*   "On a positive I got the clutch working good in my second ride happy with the new gear"

27th May

Dakota North*   "Fingers are sore this morning! Still waiting to find out when they will do the op"

Niels Kristian Iversen*   "Bloody Q for security starts outside terminal this morning.."

28th May

Chris Holder* [to Lewis]   "yewww on way to GP praga u got some tickets bro or wottt !!?? :-)"

Hans Andersen*   "well done [Greg], Keep it up was rootin for ya All night without doubt the best rider on display tonight. Age is just a number..."

Jan Staechmann*   "hats off. 14 years ago you won in Prague, and now again!"

Niels Kristian Iversen* [to Nicolai Klindt]   "because you look like a dodgy fucker. They think your trolley is full of weed. ;)"

Chris Harris   "Turning up [at Prague SGP] was probably the biggest problem. I should have stayed at home. I burnt my clutch out in my first ride and everything was downhill from there really. I'm really not that confident that my bikes are performing at the moment. We keep trying new things, but they basically aren't fast enough in a straight line"

Dick Barrie   "I was recently asked what I thought of the new-look Ashfield strip. Sadly I had to admit, despite living in Glasgow all my life – that because my contract for the past thirty-odd years has demanded my presence at Radio Forth's Edinburgh studios every Sunday – I haven't had an opportunity to see a Tigers' meeting on the revised lay-out. Or indeed the original shape, so well-spoken-of when they first took the team there from Shawfield. In fact, the only actual meeting I have ever attended at Ashfield was a wee while ago – I remember being taken there on the top deck of a Glasgow tram, and that Ken LeBreton was racing! In truth I can honestly recall more about the tram ride – right across the city – than the speedway. We stood on the third bend among a huge crowd, and (being about six) I could see very little of what was going on down on the track! That would have been over sixty years ago – things have moved on a bit since then."

29th May

Sheffield Speedway   SHEFFIELD Speedway have issued the following statement in the aftermath of the postponement of the Premier League meeting at Glasgow today, Sunday May 30, 2011: 'Sheffield Speedway received a telephone call from Glasgow Speedway at approximately 12.30pm informing us that the meeting had been postponed. We were told this was because it was raining and the weather forecast suggested it wouldn't improve so the decision was taken. This is in direct contradiction to what two members of our own team told us. They had travelled up last night and arrived at the track to inform us there was in fact no rain. For this reason we have asked the Speedway Control Bureau to conduct an inquiry into the postponement.'

Scott Nicholls*   "Like it at check-in when someone clearly speaks no English n the assistant thinks they will understand by repeating themselves but louder!"

Scott Nicholls*   "I love the snug seating arrangement budget airlines have! Just like being back in the womb!"

Mike Bennett* "fighting a losing battle with these varifocals! Just want to see my speedway stalkers from a distance and read my programme - simples???"

Dakota North* "bikes basicly done! wish i could play xbox kinda hard with cast on"

Eric Thornton "Claes Nedermark – what a find he is turning out to be"

30th May

Niels Kristian Iversen* "If i didnt know better, i would have thought my driver was the guy inside "the stig" fuckin hell he is on it this morning"

Niels Kristian Iversen* "Just been to the Cinema watching hangover 2. Fuckin brilliant movie."

Chris Holder* "U won't believe it... But coventy is rained off.... Wat a waste..."

31st May

Graham Drury "Due to the lung injury, Ales [Dryml] is unable to fly for two weeks, so he's got his mechanic to drive him to Prague to see his usual doctor, and on Wednesday the surgeons will be opening his shoulder up to see what the damage is. Until that operation takes place, we won't know what the long-term prognosis is, so whilst at the minute we're using rider-replacement for him, if we feel going forward that he's going to be out for any length of time then I will scour the world to see if I can get a replacement in for him."

Chris Holder* "4hours to the track from the airport! Who's idea was it to fly to this joint!"

Nicolai Klindt* "yeeeeew, finally i had a good meeting outside denmark! mechanic worked good and bike was sweet. on the way home!"

Lewis Bridger* "Killing the Gym in Wimbourne !!!"

Fredrik Lindgren* "Decided to go to UK next Mon & prob watch British Final at Monmore! Sky Sports if need track info from track specialist give me call!"

Niels Kristian Iversen* "Back at stansted airport. On the late flight again today. Me like"

Niels Kristian Iversen* "Been gokarting with the rest of the indianerna. Now to the track."

Dakota North* "very annoyed im not racing tonight [Sky meeting] at the oak tree"

1st June

Graham Drury "Our phone has not stopped ringing with calls from speedway supporters from all over the country to confirm that Emil is riding. His inclusion will add to a great night of speedway as these two big clubs fight it out to be the top team in the Midlands, and we're looking forward to his first appearance in such a hotbed area of the sport."

Nicolai Klindt* "just been at my acupuncture specialist who said i was low on energy. so is eating a big salat with a banana/strawberry smoothie"

Lewis Bridger* "Poole Aus vs GB test match have a very different motor to test tonight give it X2 heats if no good back to what I no !!!"

Gary Patchett "We didn't have a man of the match sponsor this time, but if we had then it would certainly have gone to Darryl Ritchings. His performance was vital, and I'm personally delighted for him."

Fredrik Lindgren* "This is awesome relaxing in the sun almost nude with shades on!"

Dakota North* "Just finshed first session in the oxygen chamber"

John Anderson "As someone who was unfortunately placed in a similar situation [heart attack] less than a year ago, I know how stressful running a speedway club can be. Ian Rae's workload, ironically recognised by the club with a special presentation on Saturday night, was incalculable, and it is just awful he's fallen ill just as we have a bright light shining in from the end of the tunnel."

Wayne Russell "[Swindon Test] was supposed to be ring fenced but Birmingham are racing and Ipswich have the Star of Anglia that night. If the series is drawn, we'll stage the meeting later in the season but we won't if it's decided"

Flagrag "The two main reason that we now only normally have one pit reporter is cost of fuel to get two reporters there and Charlie has now taken on a full time role for Sky sports news which often means she is working early morning or late at night on day of meeting or early the next day. When you take into consideration a Sunrise shift often means a 3:30-4AM wake up and a late shift means getting home at 2am its difficult for her to do as many meetings now"

Philip Rising "As for Charlie Websters interviewing 'technique'.... like so many of her predecessors in that 'role' she often forgets that she is speaking to people whose native tongue isn't English, probably doesn't understand most of the questions herself, let alone the answers, and rarely has a proper follow-up. Does that sound like a bigoted old journalist? Probably..."

Mike Bacon* "Just seen highlights Somer v Sheffield PL. Superb racing. Come on Sky, more from the PL please"

Scott Nicholls* "Poole/Australia v England,no team GB,no great Britain,3 lions,united kingdom.... anyone know what the hell we're called now! Pc gone mad!"

Peter Butcher "Two days before a Test Match and the only name announced for either side is Rob Mear - unless something's emerged today - another PR triumph!"

Nicolai Klindt* "i need and i want more speed. what is up with the bikes? no matter what we so it never seem to be perfect! maybe new engine?"

Lewis Bridger* "Hello Pvl.. Goodbye Pvl... The Worst decision I have ever made !!! Sorry guys.."

Jason Doyle "Tai took me out, although it's all water under the bridge as long as he doesn't do the same again"

2nd June
Dakota North* "wake up"

Fredrik Lindgren* "11:45 I just had breakfast, insane!"

Nicolai Klindt* [at almost the same time] "what... massive lie-in last to days. think i've needed it. now shower, breakfast and workshop time. we make winning bikes"

Andy Povey "Our [BSPA website] hit count went mad during February and March – much more than in the season – we had to buy extra bandwidth which now we're not using. Everyone was logging on to see if this mystery statement ever materialised!"

Lewis Bridger* "Just had a S-bed now Going out for a run now everything is soughted with new ignitions and everything else ready 4 tommorow"

Mike Bacon* "I'll be tweeting from Foxhall Stadium tonight . . . Star of Anglia. First one since 1996 WOW!. Sun out, speedos ready"

Trevor Gordon "Correct me if I am wrong but didn't Swindon cancel the second Test because of the apparent non-availability of riders. From what I can see the only rider from the First Test who would have been unavailable last night was Ben Barker who rode for Birmingham. So why cancel the Test?"

Martin Neal* "sheffield 34 bears 16 after 8. On the plus side, we got a free salad with our pizzas at pizza hut"

Chris Schramm "The track was a bit drier than usual and caught the Ipswich riders out."

Scott Nicholls* "Lovely Bbq with friends at ours. Chilly now so gonna head inside. Can gear them bloody speedway bikes at foxhall.Need quieter silencers!Haha"

Niels Kristian Iversen* "At chiquito with my hot girlie. Ordered my food red hot aswell.. I like hot.. And a XL sparkling water with ice."

David Watt* "Has gone off the rails over the last year but am turning everything around and will be on top from now on!"

Graham Drury "Emil asked if every track in England was like Birmingham because it's the best track he has ever been on!"

3rd June
Chris Van Straaten "I'm sure there will be a lot of children with British colours splashed on their face. It should be a great night for the whole family."

Niels Kristian Iversen* "At stansted airport. I think my car can find this place on its own. Danish final 1 tonight but now i can feel a chicken sandwich is waiting"

Niels Kristian Iversen* "sitting at the gate watching people get their bags checked by ryanair crew. I hate when they do that. Plonkers... BUT i guess that is what you have to expect when your flying with the tight ass express"

Chris Holder* "Gettin the car washed on the Poole speedway account cheers ;-) not jus a good speedway club"

Lewis Bridger* "In the Botany Bay pub.. waiting for my lunch in the garden.. got shorts n flip flops on the gooo getting a tan"

Lee Richardson* "you on holiday?? Lol.."

Lewis Bridger* "till 2pm yuuupp midlo taking me 2 lakeside :-)"

Lee Richardson* "nice 1 brown nose..."

Lewis Bridger* "looks better than turning up wid 1 of the aussies tho ay !!"

Mike (e)Bennett* "on a bit of a (e)mission today!"

Gary Patchett* "Josh G has broken his femur at Plymouth. Gutted for him. He was going so well"

Lewis Bridger* "The M25 can Lick my Bollox haha !! The M25 is a joke!!!"

Steve Mallett ""We have recently strengthened our team and did not want to lose momentum so have made this decisive move. Charlie [Gjedde] has an excellent pedigree racing at the highest level both in this country and abroad and will no doubt make an impact."

Fredrik Lindgren* "First swim in a Swedish lake, check! Amazing day! Love Swedish summer proper good!"

Niels Kristian Iversen* "Had a pretty shit meeting tonight. So up and down couldnt make it work. Bike lost power in the end so 8 points to mé. New day tomorrow."

Peter Johns* [explains to Lewis] "bi means 2. We have secretly fitted 2 pistons, don't tell anyone!"

Craig Boyce "[Adam Shields] picked up a bit of unexpected grip and it just got away from him. The sun was playing a funny part at the start of the meeting but that's the same at most tracks."

Rory Schlein "We were up manure creek without a paddle before we even got here with Troy pulling out at the last minute."

Chris Harris "Lakeside has never been one of my favourite hunting grounds. I tried a few things and I felt I had some good speed in some races. But if you don't make good starts, it's hard to pass here"

Chris Holder* "Mega traffic on m25!! And it's nearly midnight!!"

Rob Godfrey "I think we've got to put another call out to Sky to come here again. Okay, the Somerset v Sheffield meeting was good, but Scunthorpe was voted the best track in the country and arguably we get one bad meeting out of 10."

John Campbell "I don't want to give Kalle too big a build up because he can be challenging on occasions, not least when he doesn't answer his telephone when I call and doesn't answer the next time I call and then again and again, but when Kalle is at his best, he is such a character that he brings the team together. He acts like a clown and well get involved because, I think, we can't believe what he's up to."

4th June

Trevor Geer "It's amazing how many people think we have had a dip in form when, in fact, all we have done is lose that one [home] meeting with a depleted team."

Mike Bowden "We were missing Ben Barker and really, he's got to make up his mind whether he wants to ride for his country occasionally, or the club which pays his wages."

Sebastian Alden "I took one look at it [Berwick track] and thought, 'that's different' because it is big, but has narrow entry into the bends."

Paul Burbidge "Seeing Sky Sports' Nigel Pearson or *Speedway Star* editor Richard Clark test the latest JRM is about as likely as seeing Poole co-promoter Matt Ford visit Brandon wearing a Coventry scarf"

David Hoggart "We think staging a meeting [Scunthorpe-Sheffield v Buxton] in just 59 minutes must be a record. Hats off to our track staff and officials. It was a bit of a logistical nightmare but we did it in double-quick time and a big thanks to them all, especially ref Chris Durno."

Dick Barrie "As a final note on the Charlie Gjedde saga, I will say this: I was hugely excited when your promotion showed such great ambition to sign him this past winter. It was the biggest-name signing by the Bandits since 1991. Watching him here and at most of the away fixtures, I observed an emerging pattern. Charlie was at his best on greyhound-style tracks where he could go into the turns really quickly, almost backwards, turn sharply and accelerate out again. Places such as Newcastle, Edinburgh – and yes, Belle Vue. On the faster tracks where it is important not to scrub speed off, where you need to ride close up to a board fence instead of around the line, like at Workington, Glasgow – and yes, Berwick -- his style wasn't so suitable. Did Mr Gjedde become overly-apprehensive after he saw spectacular accidents here involving Matty Wethers, Jason Bunyan, Jesper Kristiansen and Tam Sike, all happening around the second turn? For whatever reason, Charlie apparently decided he could not and/or would not ride at Berwick with any confidence. Away, on the white-line tracks he had no such problems, but it was crystal clear his self-belief in being able to race at Berwick was shot to pieces. It was due to this factor – and I totally disregard talk of the rider deliberately riding to lose – that it was merciful to end the relationship. Ominously, internet sources were for several weeks apparently (I don't read 'em myself) suggesting Charlie Gjedde was 'working his ticket' with a view to relocating to a circuit nearer to his Swindon base – as to that I could not possibly comment – but one thing I do know...... Your promotion were absolutely correct to accept Charlie Gjedde when he was offered to them by Belle Vue prior to the season beginning, and your promotion cannot be faulted in any way for the way the rider was treated, encouraged and protected here, even as the tide of public opinion turned – perhaps deservedly – against him. But that was then and this is now."

Stewart Dickson "This sport can be really cruel at times and this is something that Josh [Grajczonek] simply did not deserve. He was having the season of his life and to see him in the obvious pain he was is so cruel for the lad. He is young and strong and very determined and he will come back in the fullness of time, but that will be small consolation for him."

Rob Peasley "OXFORD Cheetahs fans awoke to a rude shock last Wednesday – to find news plastered across the front page of the local paper that the City Council might be interested in redeveloping Oxford Stadium for housing. The initial story, carried in last Wednesday's *Oxford Mail*, made for very grim reading and seemed to end all hope of a return of the Cheetahs to the stadium that last hosted speedway in 2007. However, it has since become apparent that the closure of the stadium would not appear to be the council's first preference. It is understood that stadium owners, Risk Capital Partners (RCP), who own the Greyhound Racing Association (GRA), wrote to the council stating the venue was unlikely to continue trading for much longer and were thus seeking advice on the best way forward thereafter. Thus the stadium was included in a list of potential sites for redevelopment. There is a need for extra housing in the Blackbird Leys area. On Thursday, City Council deputy leader Ed Thomas was interviewed by Radio Oxford to clarify the situation. He confirmed that the council's opinion had been sought by RCP in the event that the stadium closed, but that the council would prefer for the stadium to remain trading as a sporting venue. He added that the council would also like to see the return of the speedway. The council are looking at 75 different sites for possible redevelopment."

BSPA WORKINGTON skipper Tomas Topinka was ruled out of Friday night's clash at Edinburgh after a bizarre collision with a mechanic on the parade lap.

Nicolai Klindt* "no racing this weekend, so having a day of and spend time with the boys. but need to wash my dirty kitbag first"

Fredrik Lindgren* "Back in business queuing at an airport. Nice not."

Fredrik Lindgren* "Hot hot in Poland too, not the nicest to sit in a traffic queue but hey what to do? Tarnow here I come!"

Fredrik Lindgren* "At hotel in Tarnow now! Try and get a little more sleep in before todays action. 2pm a sponsor thing & 4pm practice starts. There are good times & there are bad times. We don't go to new places all the time, but I enjoy my life & what I do."

Fredrik Lindgren* "A quick shower & I'm awake again, soon Zurek soup quick & easy to get some energy. Then I'm off to some school promotion work with sponsor!"

Dakota North* "waiting for sudden sam [Masters] at the oak tree"

Dakota North* "Fuck I'm over driving [to Workington]"

Shane Hazelden "People say riders can be a bit thick but you have to have a good brain to work things out in split seconds at times."

Anthony May "How many more letters to this magazine, disgruntled conversations on the terraces and people who switch off is it going to take to get it through the SGP's thick heads that we DO NOT want to see racing on super slick tracks!"

Philip Rising "Those who believe that you simply have to throw a load of dirt on to a track to produce a perfect racing surface are at best being naïve."

Chris Holder* "Practice in Poland today…. Cos I don't ride enough through the week :-/ apparently 3 times is jus not enough these days"

Chris Holder* "Love priority boarding :-D"

Speedway Star "Heathens are now without a home fixture until Tuesday, June 21, when they welcome the Isle of Wight to Monmore Green – or Monmore Wood as fans now call it."

Fredrik Lindgren* "I'm so old now that I'm out on internet looking at furniture!"

Brian Owen* "wouldn't bother washing the car before going to speedway tonight. Could be a dusty one!"

Nick Barber "No one has said anything about there being a fanzone at Cardiff again this year? Usually it would have been in the *Star* by now"

Keith Denham "We did so well to win the match, virtually with just four men, yet Somerset made it so unpleasant. They were clearly revelling in our misfortune…..I thought Sam Masters was totally unprofessional and out of order when he went for Gary Irving after Heat 14 and fully deserved the fine he was given by the referee. There was a second incident involving Christian Hefenbrock and Richard Lawson and, like the other one, was completely unprovoked by our rider. Some of the things that went on the pits were completely out of order."

Steve Mallett "Charlie's [Gjedde] debut is one of the best individual performances I have seen from a Wasps rider and bearing in mind I used to travel the country with Craig Watson as his sponsor when he was in his prime, that comment does not come easily for me to say…..I just hope crowd sizes continue to increase. Things now appear heading in the right direction and we just hope the famous saying that a good team will bring in a good crowd is true and not just a myth!"

Charlie Gjedde "Well there were some issues at Berwick which I would prefer not to go into and the truth is both the club and I decided it was better for everyone that I moved on."

Christine Donovan "Some cocky bloke strolls up so I say 'who are you?' and he tells me 'I'm Jonathan Chapman owner of King's Lynn'"

Ashley Wooller "Cam was moaning he needed a second [long track] bike and Marcel Gerhard – who used to be champion and who used to help Joonas who now helps Cam – said 'when you fall off you don't want to ride again that day'"

Kevin Coombes "It's a very exciting but very simple sport"

Peter Boast "I know we're not speedway and we don't expect to be part of speedway. But we have speedway riders racing for us [UK Flat-track] and we use speedway tracks."

Chris Neath "All the people that like to say about home advantage here, it's not true really as anyone who can ride a speedway bike should be able to get themselves around Rye House. It's one of the easiest tracks to ride in the country. All those years we were invincible was because we had a team of track specialists, not a specialist track."

Brian Andersen "[New silencers are] not such a big deal for the GP riders but it is very hard on those trying to earn a living in the various leagues."

Neil Machin "Coops is struggling with a crisis of confidence. He is on a long road to rehabilitation after that dreadful crash last year and it is a long, long process for someone who sustained those kind of injuries. There was a time when Paul had to re-learn simple things such as tying his shoelaces and not many months down the line from that he's riding speedway again. Paul, being Paul, expects to carry on where he left off but it's not as simple as that."

5th June

Niels Kristian Iversen* "I bloody hate M25.. Its midnight and there is a 3 lane que and its solid.. Sort it out ffs. Havent mooved for 5min."

Hans Andersen* "My healing is gettin there I THINK... Having new X-rays taking tuesday so fingers crossed."

Trevor Geer "I thought we were going to get slaughtered, the way we started the meeting. Our riders did not look up for it at all. But we had a good team talk at the interval and it seemed to do a bit of good. They were up for it after that. It was a constructive talk. All the riders were trying to help one another. The track was a little bit different to how it has been in other weeks and we just had to get out and ride it like the King's Lynn boys were."

Kevin Long* "this forces the issue of team changes now, with Risager and Schramm sidelined. Cant afford to let the season slip away!"

Niels Kristian Iversen* "Weather is very good in poland. Good job i got a pair of shorts in the suitcase. Might get some sticky onions in these jeans."

Chris Holder* "Too nice a day to be racing (Polish) speedway! Should be at the beach droppin in on some locals yewwww"

Fredrik Lindgren* "During the winter I hardly drink any coffee but in the season it's like I'm addicted to coffee sometimes, very strange."

Paul Burbidge* "Hart replaces Auty in British Final. Was Stead overlooked or did he decline?"

Nigel Pearson* [in Bolton with darts work] "come on lads, first time I've ever watched a [Dudley] match on twitter!!"

Tim Hamblin "The flashpoint saw a Dudley rider manhandled by a [Buxton] starting official and disqualified, visiting fans cheer a heavy fall by home guest Jason Garrity and a minority of them chant obscenities at referee Dave Dowling. Dudley had controlled the meeting and were all but over the line after late wins for Richard Franklin and Jon Armstrong, the latter spiking the double-point tactical guns of Adam Allott, left them eight up with two to go. But in the penultimate race Tom Perry fell while holding a second place that would have guaranteed the win. It meant Dudley had to avoid a home 5-1 in the last to clinch the win, and tempers rose when the starting marshall leaned into Dudley rider Ashley Morris and tried to pull him forward to the line. Morris reacted angrily, words were exchanged and the rider was disqualified. Armstrong then twice shot into the lead only for referee Dowling to call an unsatisfactory start on both occasions. Armstrong had clearly got a flier on the first running; the second looked marginal. With the Dudley support now seething and a handful chanting obscenities at the referee's box nearby, Armstrong hit the front yet again. Garrity tried to go round him but was clearly going too fast and crashed on the third bend – bringing, regrettably, a big cheer from many of the visitors who realised the meeting was now won. Ironically, the rerun with just Allott and Armstrong remaining saw the former get arguably the biggest flier of all, but with the result now decided nobody cared.

Referee Dowling...confirmed afterwards that Morris had been disqualified "for failing to comply with the start marshall's instructions after repeatedly being asked to come to the tapes". He said the marshall's behaviour would be discussed with Buxton chairman Jayne Moss, adding: "The reaction from the rider also puts him under question as well." Dudley chairman Nigel Pearson, who was working elsewhere and not at the meeting, said: "I am not going to criticise our supporters because they have made this club what it is. But as a club we cannot condone foul language."

Chris Holder* "Jus swapping all the "do not disturb" signs on peoples rooms to "please clean" hahaha cracks me up everytime!"

Jim Brykajlo "Why would millionaire businessmen like Trump, Sandhu or Frost listen to Harkess who's a small fish in comparison."

Scott Nicholls* "not under estimating anyone,but I'm only there [British Final] for the win"

Lewis Bridger* "Yewww chilling in tin tins hastings"

Nicolai Klindt* "wish a had a sponsor who could buy me a new engine. have to sell more newspapers i guess!"

Scott Nicholls* "How crap is X-factor Poland! No offence,but I reckon I could win it!"

Gary Patchett* "No chance Scotty. U don't speak Polish and I've heard u sing on the showers!!"

Keith McGhie "The attitude of Scottish referee Jim McGregor towards Juul's predicament angered the Bears management and Duffill, who is a qualified ophthalmic optician, pointed out: 'It was a freak accident while he was watching Heat 1 – it wasn't just a bit of shale, his whole eye was full of shale. I 'phoned the referee and said we had a rider with an eye injury and was told he'd allow an extra minute, which we got, then Peter was excluded from Heat 2, while the medical staff were still attending to him!'"

Rupert Rigby* "I'll take your advice and not follow you, clearly a pleasant, expletive free public proflie is too difficult for you!"

Chris Holder* "I think u should jus fuk off to be honest haha"

George English
"A win's a win but we deserved all three points – and might have got them but for a blatant bit of cheating by a visiting [Somerset] rider."

6th June

Lewis Bridger* "Just fucked a Moth up with my Guerne Mx boots & nearly put a hole in my wall"

Rupert Rigby* "Fed up with reading your tripe as well so you're correct that not following you is a good idea!"

Fredrik Lindgren* "where is my call? I can do track inspection! Tell what lines is best at Monmore!"

Fredrik Lindgren* "Just told Nigel Pearson they shouldn't use me today Sky Sports I know how much he appreciate his job and I don't want to take that from him!

Keith Denham "A few people may have disappointed that we dropped Charles [Wright] but I am afraid we are not dealing in personalities, we are dealing in points scoring. Charles hasn't been doing enough of that recently"

Hannah Marie Coates* "Australia aint got talent cos all you ever do is fuck yourself up! X"

Dakota North* "easy coatsy there fighting words!"

Colin Barber "Polish EL and British EL are almost two different sports ! They both have their positives and both have their negatives, it is easy to enjoy both. Many years ago there were quite a lot of large tracks in the UK and most people thought that racing on the smaller tracks was not so good. Well, here in the 21st century things are different in the UK, most of the tracks are smaller and more technical, however in my opinion the racing is no worse than it was and certainly deserves better attendances."

Kelvin Tattum "That's exactly what I was going to say. You just took the words out of my mouth Nige, thanks for that"

Nigel Pearson "so win win win for Wuffy Wuffy Wuffy"

Jonathan Barber* "Frampton 250/1 for me"

Charlie Webster "How crucial is the first corner?"

Nigel Pearson "Again it was entertaining speedway, Kelvin"

Kelvin Tattum "It was the class to the front"

Nigel Pearson "Again the stats will change"

Kelvin Tattum "There is a pattern emerging here – the big guns are up there"

Nigel Pearson "Tom Perry a young lad from the Dudley Heathens who do ride on this [Wolverhampton] track, by the way, while they search for a new track in the Dudley area"

Nigel Pearson "I'm finding this British Final the most exciting in a number of years"

Edward Kennett "I've just got to keep it up"

Charlie Webster "I talked to Neil Middleditch earlier, he stood there and talked to you"

Edward Kennett "I really want to ride abroad in Poland that's what I really want to do"

Kelvin Tattum "He just clipped the corner of the bouncy castle"

Nigel Pearson "Bouncy castle, huh, I like that!"

Kelvin Tattum "I just gotta say the introduction of the wild card slot has reinvigorated the British Final"

Kelvin Tattum "Beware the man with one arm!'

Nigel Pearson "Jeh-Ran"

Ben Barker "Yeh get out of my way I'm coming through I wanna be British Champion and get to Cardiff....I've got people in Tenerife and people at home watching me so I've gotta make that final"

Nigel Pearson "We've had passing in almost every race"

Kelvin Tattum "Tell you what this [Monmore Green] is a fabulous venue for a Grand Prix, Nige!"

Fredrik Lindgren* "I agree with Kelvin Tatum, I want a GP at Monmore Green!"

Tony Millard [on old clip] "Nicki Pedersen missed his meeting with a groin strain but no sign of that here tonight"

Fredrik Lindgren* "Pete Adams looking very good on the television!"

Nigel Pearson "Tonight's meeting at the British Final has been more exciting than any Grand Prix we've seen, I would argue!"

Kelvin Tattum "A lot of talk of Edward Kennett not having enough ambition Nige"

Kelvin Tattum "I don't like the way [Lewis] keeps kicking his foot off the footrest – very vulnerable!"

Kelvin Tattum "He wants his briddle, British title back"

Neil Middleditch "I'm just looking for heart. I think a thinking man can pick my team for the World Cup"

Chris Harris "He's pretty good around here but most of the riders are here tonight"

Nicola Sands* "You know you work too late, too often, when the cleaners and security guards know your name!"

Chris Harris "I'll just watch the start and then that'll be it"

Nigel Pearson "Going off the outside, the outsider literally"

Kelvin Tattum "You can almost hear a pin drop in the crowd can't you?"

Nigel Pearson "Those speedway bikes are heavy as well Kelvin"

Fredrik Lindgren* "I think a Championship in a one off meeting shouldn't be decided with a Finalheat! It's the same shite in Sweden! What you think?"

Nigel Pearson "You look at that and try telling anyone the magic has gone from the British Final!"

Edward Kennett [after being excluded from the final of the British Final] "I just gotta say happy Birthday Mum – sorry Mum – Huh huh"

Chris Harris "As the night went on the track went slicker and I went slower"

Olly Allen* "starts were good but caught up in every dog fight going!!! One o those nights"

Nicolai Klindt* [to Scott Nicholls] "well done boss! you was a bit out of breath in that interview after the final haha"

Lewis Bridger "It wasn't my night, I'm 21-years-old, I'm going to be in Cardiff sooner or later. When I get there, I'll show everyone what I can do."

Nigel Pearson* "I thought the ref had a nightmare, what do you think tweeps?"

Lee Richardson "[Wolverhampton] isn't my favourite place. This is by far my worst track. I used to hate Lakeside, but this is a place I just can't get on with for some reason."

Mads Korneliussen* [on getting a UK passport]   "i don't feel danish anyway :-)"

7th June

Stein Waalen   "[Monmore Green] Track - typically British; too much heavy, loose dirt, would actually be more fun if it was slicker but with an even grip....or grippy but with an even grip if you understand what I am saying. When riders have problems staying on the bike there is something wrong. But as long as Kelvin Tatum continues to tell us that the track is perfect it must be!

Lewis Bridger - an accident waiting to happen. Someone needs to learn him how to ride a speedway bike, you just can't crawl all over it. Loses a lot of speed going out of every turn because he takes his foot off the footpeg while hanging on the inside of the bike which means he doesn't get his wheels straight early enough. He also does not have a single "tactical" fiber in his body, it is full gas from stop until finish.

Ben Barker - what can I say? I mean he is a bit overrated. He looks a bit overweight, looks to have very slow bikes (or can't get the setup right) and has a strange gating technique... and he has too hot a head! Now he won a heat and just gets too fired up about it in the interview afterwards. Stuart Robson - age is taking to him, but he is still a exciting rider....and he has got the biggest b**ls in the world after all those injuries he has had.

Olly Allen - so much potential, good gater, but just can't hold onto a lead. Seems to chose the wrong lines all the time, and can't defend his line when he is leading.

Lee Richardson - not sure what to say. So far he seems out of depth and are just getting points on his experience.

Jordan Frampton - I like this guy, neat style and very gutsy, too bad he lost it when he was leading.

Richard Hall - what has happened to this guy, didn't use to be one bright talent? Now he just makes a mess of every turn.

Leigh Lanham - to me it seems like Leigh has been like this forever, classy style, hard fighter but never gets many points.

Ricky Ashworth - hot and cold, his style needs a longer track. Could actually be good in Poland!

Jerran Hart - just filling up the numbers"

Colin Barber   "I thought that the track for the event was fairly good bearing in mind some of the tracks we have seen in the GPs in the past-(no dirt at all until about heat 12) .There certainly didn't appear to be any holes or bad ruts even after 22 heats of speedway so the track curator certainly knew what he was on. I think one must remember that as I said in an earlier posting that Speedway in the UK is a slightly different sport to what it is on the Continent, much closer and more intimate"

Mads Korneliussen*   "just got to skavsta airport with coolman doing all the driveing, now 5 hours sleep in hotel VAN then fly fly over the rainbow to the uk. Hallo sunny UK. Two engines to service for tomorrow, better get my hands dirty, a lot of work"

David Hoggart   "The Oak Tree Arena is a fabulous venue with good food and cider by cask"

Speedway 365   Belle Vue Aces new state-of-the-art venue has been given the title of National Speedway Stadium by the BSPA

8th June

David Watt*   "Hopes Leigh Adams is ok"

Graham Drury   "Obviously Ulrich left the club under a cloud last time but we are all grown men and we have moved on. A lot of water has gone under the bridge since then and we are delighted to welcome Ulrich back."

Phil Morris   "The SRBF helped me several times when I was on the injury list, so I would like to help them out. I will also be doing something for the Under-15 lads who I have been helping to develop since I joined the Team GB set up last season."

Colin Barber   "It is all about Money. So far as domestic racing is concerned Poland get the biggest gates and is on a 'roll' at present. GB although in the main the racing is good the sport has been in the doldrums for a number of years, if the past is anything to go by the curve will be reversed and better days will come to pass. it happened in the 60's and seventies with the advent of the Provincial League and the the British League. The downturn started in the late eighties but hopefully something will be done in the future to reverse the trend. I believe Poland has in the past had similar trends."

Nicolai Klindt* "how can they cancel a meeting at 10am because the forecast says there its going to rain at 4pm? #danishspeedwayisadisaster"

Mads Korneliussen* "Needs parts, balhams it is. What could I have as race food today, need to be fast."

Fredrik Lindgren* "Not sleeping very well, "too many mind"."

Niels Kristian Iversen* "It was Nice with a home cooked meal. Salmon with mashed potatos and steamed veggies. Proper stuff.."

Nigel Pearson* "Voice recognised in Merry Hill shop"

Paul Burbidge* "Gutted to hear Leigh Adams has suffered a serious back injury Down Under. First rider I ever interviewed…. broken back, suspected spine damage, broken ribs, punctured lungs"

Dakota North* "Can't stop thinking of you mate"

Nicolai Klindt* "having a very nice meal at my moms place with Luke Corbett - no restaurants beat my moms diches!"#bed."

Linus Sundstrom* "Going for a run in a minute, will try very hard to drop a few kilos now!"

Fredrik Lindgren* "Felt like my head & body wasn't responding today, bad match! Hope my bro Ludvig is ok, bad crash!

9th June

Kylie Adams "He has no feeling in his legs at present except a little bit in one thigh. But, that situation could certainly change and improve in the weeks and months ahead. He faces a long hard road to recovery. He's currently in intensive care but could be moved out today into the special spinal unit. He's actually very stable and probably a bit too well to be in intensive care. He's very alert and talking. Leigh has no head injuries at all which is wonderful news. He's just very sleepy due to the pain medication being administered,"

Nicolai Klindt* "can't wait to ride tonight in swindon and tomorrow at coventry. isn't it how is should be if you love your sport? i think so"

Nicolai Klindt* "there is some right strange characters in this world. doesn't hope i ain't one of them"

Nicolai Klindt* "arg! forgot my shades at home and the sun is out so have to buy a new pair. poor wallet"

Nicolai Klindt* "flying billund now and there is ppl here for once! on route to abbey stadium. will it be a win? i think so! first time with a full team of winners."

Ludvig Lindgren* "first time ive been knockt out! nice with a nw experience hahha iam all fine shoulders are abit bashed but just some rest now will do me god.. ts always nice to be knock out, then you know your alive haha. did you get the crash on video?"

Fredrik Lindgren* "Checked in at Heathrow Airport with an engine, don't fly with engine much always worries me. But was ok fly SAS to Copenhagen"

Robert Bamford "£16 to get in to see Todd Kurtz at No. 1, who's going to pay that?"

Niels Kristian Iversen* "Pisses mé off when ryanairs website makes errors.. Its All the fukin time. I hate that i need to use that airline"

Dakota North* "had a tirm today, look like a dick!"

Dakota North* "its cold tonight!"

Fredrik Lindgren* "Feeling both refreshed and tired after a run on the treadmill in my hotel gym"

Ludvig Lindgren* "gaaaaaaa sick of reading and sleeping and watchin tele! strange tho cuz thats the only things i do when iam not injured! And oh yeah iam feeling sorry for myself!"

Terry Russell "Good evening and welcome to the Abbey Stadium for the first of our Elite League meetings against Coventry this season. My notes for this week are written with mixed emotions as this Club has been a big part of my life since 2004. We have come a long way as a club since that time, racing in four sets of Elite League Playoffs and two Playoff Finals. We are yet to lift that trophy, but what a ride it has been. I can officially announce that this season will be my last at Swindon Speedway. Having spoken of my intentions to Gary previously, I wanted to make the announcement as early as possible to give the Club as a whole as many options as possible with a view to moving into 2012 and beyond. My last official function will be this year's end of Season Dinner & Dance taking place at Blunsdon House Hotel on Saturday 5th November, 2011. I have become increasingly busy in other areas over the last couple of years both within the Sport and in other business. With my involvement in other areas of the Sport there are often occasions where there could be seen to be a big conflict of interests through having a heavy involvement with one particular Club. With these things combined something had to give. I have enjoyed being a part of Swindon Speedway. It is a special Club with lots of fantastic people involved. It still amazes me the amount of people willing to give up their spare time to help Swindon speedway. The Track Staff team are superb and their dedication to the cause is second to none. Everybody working for the Stadium has been friendly and helpful whilst I have been here. You guys, the fans, have been terrific. I have had involvement in other Clubs over the years as it has made business sense. With Swindon, that was not the only reason. I enjoy coming here, I like the people here and I have wanted success as much as all of you. I'm sure that in some quarters more will be made of my decision than is actually written, but that is par for the course nowadays!! I'd like to think my stay here has been a positive one for all, and I'd like to thank you all for your continued support. We still have plenty of points to race for in 2011 yet along with a Knock-Out Cup starting next week against Poole. Let's get behind the lads and show them the support that they deserve.Enjoy the racing."

Kevin Long* "Chris Louis practising after the meeting at Ipswich speedway. Racing return to aid injury crisis?"

Kevin Long* "Lasse Bjerre asked me for a second time tonight why I dont "do the talking" at King's Lynn, because I said, you have Mike Bennett"

Linus Sundstrom* "In bed now [22.10], alarm set on 03.58! Off to arlanda in the morning and fly to warszawa with big L. Home meeting with daugavpils tomorrow ZZzZzz"

10th June

Hans Andersen* "A couple of bikes sat waiiting for monday c",) I'M All excited by the thought of riding again just hope things Will be ALL OK"

Hans Andersen* "Cant wait to show the people WHO doubt my comeback *angry* just finished over tree hours Physio And feel great c",)"

Chris Holder* "Early morning mistake by the costa guy left me walking outter here with a free ham and cheese toastie :-) cheers bro"

Niall Strudwick* "Tired after racing last night. 4 hours sleep before work isnt good"

Nicolai Klindt* "gotta love a early morning when u gotta do the bikes yourself. reminds me of when i was a young star on 16 riding like a star"

Nicolai Klindt* "this years first full English"

Nicolai Klindt* "bike stripped, bike washed, bike build. been on the gas and must admit i'm loving this mechanic bit. maybe I should sack Luke Corbett"

Kylie Adams "Leigh is very sleepy today following yesterday's marathon operation. He has access to morphine as a pain killer and that almost instantaneously puts him back to sleep. The doctors are unsure if he will need further surgery but that will become evident in the next few weeks. His breathing is a little shallow as he still has bruised and swollen lungs and he constantly has to clear his throat, but he's not too bad considering."

Mads Korneliussen* "why can't people just say things as they are, insteod of all the bullshit"

Dakota North* "Rain fuck off! For oneday please!"

Ludvig Lindgren* "worst day so far!"

Lewis Bridger* "On my way to Somerset to get my head down and ride properly.. Been riding like a p***k lately time to turn it around!!"

Lewis Bridger* "All the way down to Somerset for a poxy rain off !! :-/"

Robert Bamford "I'd be embarrassed to receive the trophy they gave to Scott Nicholls! It looks like it's been damaged. Couldn't they have done something with it or shined it up a bit?"

Niels Kristian Iversen* "If this traffic continues i will make practice at midnight... Bastard friday traffic. And damn you roadworks."

Scott Nicholls* "Rain,sun,rain,sun. Trying to predict this weather is almost as hard as trying to tell what a women is thinking! Ouch,I could be in trouble"

Paul Burbidge* "Track looked superb in Copenhagen - the riders are saying it's the best ever and they know their stuff. My money is on Hampel this time"

Linus Sundstrom* "Just saw a kid about 12 yrs old with 4 cheeseburgers, 4 packs with chips and 2 big macs. My mechanic asked him and he says he will eat it all"

Chris Neath* "Awesome night at Plymouth. Wicked little track and a good performance all round. Only dropped points to Barker who was on it. paid 13. Tiny little place, right up my street!"

Olly Allen* [wonders if Red Bull sponsorship influences choice of Copenhagen SGP wildcard] "that could explain the wildcard choice maybe?? Just a thought!"

Nicolai Klindt* "you think so? hmm.... i want to say one word, bu won't let it out in cyber space"

Olly Allen* "do it!! Say it!!! Say what a lot of people are thinking! I dare you...."

11th June

Nicolai Klint* "absolutely freaking rammed in stansted. don't know if I'd rather be queing up on m25 - atleast you can sit down while listening to the radio"

Nicolai Klindt* "sitting next to a guy with a freddie lindgren cap on in stansted. it must be amazing to be such a big superstar!"

Nicolai Klindt* "in copenhagen airport waiting for the check-in to open. wish i could have been in parken, but need to look after my job. i'll be there!"

Nicolai Klindt* "crumpie is looking fast. looks like he is on one of my engines tonight!"

Terry Russell "I thought about packing in at the end of last year, but with Leigh [Adams] retiring, I just thought the two of us going in one go would be a bit of a blow, because we both started here in the Elite League together. I thought I would start this season and see how things went, but obviously we had a torrid winter for one reason or another which impacted on my business that I do in the sport. With the best will in the world, although I try not to get involved on a lot of things, I get clawed into problems that might happen between this club and another club, and it actually creates a very big conflict of interest with my main core business, which is working in the sport on behalf of everybody. To do my job properly, it's necessary for me to be not involved in the day-to-day running of any one club. I need to be neutral. GoSpeed is my main core business and I need to expand that because that is how everyone in the sport earns money. What you won't see me doing is coming back into any other clubs. That won't happen. The other thing I'm adamant about and more so now, is that I believe this is a great club and a good business, but you need to live here in this area. I believe if I lived in Swindon and I was working in the office here on a daily basis, and going out and working in the local community, I could make a big financial success of this place. But I live two hours away, so I get here at three o'clock on Thursday and leave at 11 o'clock on a Thursday."

Peter Adams "it's easy to say we don't look much like a team who were second favourites for the title"

David Watt* "My cabin bag must way 20Kgs today and had no issues at Luton ! Screw you Stansted / RyanAir !!!"

Trevor Swales "We have seen that Nicki and Troy haven't always looked like the most natural pairing in Heat 13 and Heat 15 so far. They are both hard first-turn riders and haven't always looked for each other....you are always going to get little clashes and differences of opinion when people are racing"

Fredrik Lindgren* "Before everyone asks me should they bet on me tonight! I'll say: Yea go for it sell your house put everything you own on me! 'no guarantee'"

Mads Korneliussen* "100% standing still on the motorway in fu&king germany, for 30 min now, hate this country"

Nigel Pearson* "in hotel room just finished my Sunday mercury speedway column, brummies boss Graham Drury not a happy man!"

Nigel Pearson* "Copenhagen revives memories of my stag do here in 03. Thankfully I've grown up since then."

Niels Kristian Iversen* "Bored at the Hotel in Gorzow. Gonna hit the gym now. Get a sweat on…. Its something like 10.000 degrees in my room. Aircondition dont seem to work properly"

Linus Sundstrom* "Just landed, poor old guy on the plane smoked a cigarette. They fined him €1000 and two polices took him straight when he walked out"

Joonas Kylmakorpi "I think most of the people who complained about the silencer didn't have a clue! There's only a few people in the world who know what they're talking about and they didn't complain."

Marc Lyons "For any one person who feels the sport is well run there are probably a dozen who would disagree."

Stuart Douglas "The [KO] cup obviously has a special place in my heart, we haven't won anything else and we worked hard to get it"

John Swain "I would like to say how polite and well spoken Connor Dugard and Brandon Freemantle are on the car park at Eastbourne on a Saturday night."

Speedway Star "The moose caused considerable damage to the vehicle and Pedersen was thrown out of his bunk by the force of the impact"

Peter Adams "Credit must go to the promoters for the rule changes which were implemented during the winter which has created a more unpredictable league. The policy adopted at the AGM with the rules has resulted in a fascinating push for the play-offs and it's good to see clubs like Eastbourne very much in the shake-up after their tough season last year"

Dick Butler "Here we are, years down the line, still continually using an outdated, ambiguous and sometimes grossly unfair rulebook to the detriment of the sport. I am fully aware that several of our senior referees have volunteered to rewrite and simplify the regulations so that they are fair to all, make sense, can be understood by everyone and, most importantly, can be implemented in an accepted and fair manner for all and not on the whim of someone on the management committee. The only chapters that cause real problems are 17 and 18 which are managed and controlled by the BSPA (information from the SCB) and these clearly need a fresh look by someone not involved with any club who would or could be biased."

Graham Drury "People need to realise that KK isn't on any financial guarantee with Birmingham Speedway, he is simply on points money and he flies over here from Poland and employs a mechanic so it's hitting him in the pocket. I've had a lot of conversations with KK and in many ways I feel sorry for the lad, we will continue to work with him to try and get it right but if he cannot sort it then we will need to look elsewhere."

David Watt* "did Freddie Lindgren just look at the inside when he was off gate 3???"

Lewis Bridger* "Feel sorry for Nicki P.. :-/ don't have the best of luck does he"

Lewis Bridger* "yewww final for Dicky Holder happy he made the final after a bad finish to praga Gp !!"

Fredrik Lindgren* "Hip hurt am in a bit of agony, head bashed up a bit! No final again damn it, it's world championship tough game! My mind is now at Cardiff!"

Fredrik Lindgren* "Stopped at a service station got a tuna sandwich & water! Another 10-11 hours in the van to Tarnow. Glamorous life!"

12th June

Nigel Pearson* "Wish Mikkel B Jensen had UK passport - me and Chris Louis would be battling for his signature!!!"

Linus Sundstrom* "Back to uk tomorrow! Last meeting we did was birmingham home, who are we racing tomorrow? Oh yes, birmingham at home"

Jan Staechmann* "On the Harris incident. I called it as I saw it and, more importantly, as a rider. It's my opinion and that's what I'm paid to do"

Dakota North* "so bored guys!"

Nicolai Klindt* "saw a funny thing today. i was emptying my bladder behind the pits and saw a 8 year old having a fag. then he saw me and hid himself!"

Chris Holder* "need some more quick engines..can't keep floggin the one that is good!! Gotta save it for Cardiff yewwww"

Mike Bennett* looking forward to a "guest appearance" on the mic at Peterborough speedway tomorrow. That will please my fan club!!! :-)"

Dakota North* "goodnight twitter"

13th June

Fredrik Lindgren* "Another Monday and not racing at Wolverhampton. That's not good, not really racing in England at all at the moment it's bad!"

Mads Korneliussen* "breakfast in wroclaw airport not the Best I've ever got, but it is food"

Chris Holder* "I hate sketchy landings!! Especially wen the runways wet!! Farrrrrkkk"

Chris Holder* "So happy to be goin back to Poole tonight not to airport! Not gunna miss Sweden tomorrow !"

Chris Holder* "These average speed cameras work or wat? I wanna get home!"

Linus Sundstrom* "Just boarded the luxury ryanair boeing 737-800 aircraft. No Ludvig Lindgren here today so i might get some sleep! u forgot 800 series aircraft! with 4 overwing exits 2 on the left and 2 on the right. and i hope u haven't forgot to insert the metal end in to the buckle and to secure pull on the loose end of the strap"

Hans Andersen* "Bikes are being unloaded and My stomach is full of butterflies like never before fingers crossed I'll be okay"

Ludvig Lindgren* "F*%%ing printer won't print! Sick of it! Throw it out the window"

Ludvig Lindgren* "just got flowers from valsarna! how rad is that!"

Nicolai Klindt* "at the hotel in dauga, laying on bed chilled out. been a very hard day for me. been sorting toolbox and workshop out....gonna miss dauga when we are leaving tomorrow! and ofcause i gotta drive all the way because some knob forgot his driving license at home."

Mike Bennett* "Bugger! Change of plan so no guest at speedway Peterborough for me tonight! Real work gets in the way sometimes!!"

Mads Korneliussen* "11 points and a burned forhead again, nice to help poole get the win but have to stay away from tapes"

Graham Drury "I was instructed prior to the start of the meeting that they had a very strict curfew of 10pm, so that it did seem very strange that when 10pm came and there were only six points in it, they were very determined that the last two races would still take place, and Heat 15 took place at 10.15pm! So it seems to me there's a curfew if you're winning and there isn't if you're losing, which seems a bit naughty, but there you go!"

Trevor Swales "They lost the meeting and we did nothing wrong. The comments from Birmingham insinuate that we cheated and we are very disappointed by that as it is clearly not the case. Yes, we do have a 10pm curfew, but it is not set in stone and we can run beyond it if it is absolutely necessary."

14th June

Linus Sundstrom* "Lifting with Nicki Pedersen to the airport making the old man happy. Just looooove these early flights"

Nicolai Klindt* "where is all these people going on a tuesday? massive que in riga airport. went on a de-tour on the way, through lethiania or what's called"

JUNE

Nicolai Klindt* "funniest thing just happened. geezer had the same bag as me and obviously took mine. had to sprint and force through to get him! and he was gonna complain cuz he bag didn't look that shit when he put it on the plane."

Fredrik Lindgren* "Extra promotional girls at last SGP! Are organisers going in the right direction?"

Fredrik Lindgren* "Off to Västervik soon! Dackarna team meet up 14:00 we're being forced onto a boat trip. It's total bollocks, that's my own opinion!"

David Watt* "take a life vest mate. They might throw you over !!!"

George English "This is yet another blow for Mark, and for the team...I've never heard of a break re-breaking with no crashing before and I can only wish Lemo the best of luck and hope for as early a come back as possible."

Neil Middleditch "Ben Barker in particular was very emotional when I told him he had made the starting line-up, he was made up. It was a big moment for the lad and we know we will get nothing less than 100 per cent from the boy. Despite all the doom and gloom portrayed by some members of the media I feel really positive and excited about the King's Lynn meeting and we are going to give it everything we've got. We need the fans to do the same."

Lewis Bridger* [isn't selected for Team GB] "That decision was way to early & the wrong 1 mark my words.. Ill prove what I'm capable of !!! angry pissed proving a point is what's fucked me :/ X2 Dream's destroyed this month nothing to lose now is that a good or bad thing :-/ !!??"

David Watt* "Feeling much better after having a sleep. The bed in the van is ok but not ideal !!!"

Chris Holder* "whinge whinge fuckin whinge!"

Mads Korneliussen* "Burned forehead painfull today got to stay away from them tapes. Well bikes to do, then polska later tonight"

Nicolai Klindt* "get a new helmet"

Ludvig Lindgren* "shoulders are killing me atm! why do i have to sleep in weird positions?!?!?"

Lewis Bridger* "Always in poole but ride the track like a wanker about time I ride it like a local haha bring on tomoz eagles vs poole"

Fredrik Lindgren* "Arrived in Västervik in time! Time for boat thingy"

Fredrik Lindgren* "Boat thing cancelled we're going to the rowing club. Everyone here except Rune the pole!"

Dakota North* "It's times like these you learn to love again"

15th June

Mads Korneliussen* "Driveing back from polska, is getting a cold, in summer time wdf. Super start to my b-day"

Fredrik Lindgren* "I drove by myself, of course I came on some strange way back home. Terrible sense of direction! Lucky for me speedway just go round & round."

Fredrik Lindgren* "Don't like reporter Conny Blomander from Nyheterna today! He has quoted me wrong written something I never said. Whatever it is I hate that!"

Conny Blomander* "Att du hatar och inte gillar mej bryr jag mej inte om. Men du är INTE felciterad" (The fact that you hate and do not like me I care not about me. But you are NOT misquoted)

Niels Kristian Iversen* "How lovely it is to get to the carpark after 5 days and nothing less than 11 bird shits has covered my ride."

Mads Korneliussen* "*Speedway Star*s meeting at Coventry on Friday has been canceled!! what a fu&king joke who i paying for me plane tickets, thats booked. WTF"

Nicolai Klindt* "hvad kan man forvente af et udskud som iver som prøver at være med på toppen af poppen" [what can you expect from a scum who eagerly trying to be on top of the pops]

Ludvig Lindgren* "puh why wont this f*#%ing printer work!"

Alun John Rossiter* "That Bsf have a load of dick heads on there"

Jan Staechmann "I think it's great that the FIM are looking to move major events outside of Europe [at Balakovo]. But what they seem to forget is that someone has to foot the bill for getting the riders to and from those venues, and that's where the film breaks, because it's just expected that the riders will go wherever for the same money, and I don't think that is fair. IF there had been a bit of communication along with the proposed venues, then the riders and federations might be more open to it. With the greatest of respect, I have been involved on the 'inside' of this for the past 5-6 years, so I know how flawed it is."

Phil Morris "This was the exact reason we did not enter a team in the U21 Team event. The BSPA and U21 management had this very conversation and decided the costs were way and above the budget that is available. We did the best thing and pulled out prior to the season to avoid any of the upcoming issues."

Mike Bowden "It's all very well for the paying public to ask for team changes, but although there are riders out there, it's finding them that is the problem. We have been used to success here at St Boniface in the past five years and so have the crowds. It all depends on the people of Plymouth – do they want speedway in this city or not? If it comes to it, I'd go back to the National League, but I would say that if the club started costing me money, I would walk away from it. Hopefully, though, if we stick with the Premier League, things will get better."

Linus Sundstrom* "Back on the road again after a chicken salad"

David Hoggart "We fully understand and support Ben's wishes to prepare for the biggest event in World Speedway and recognise the difficult decision Plymouth have made to support him. Mike Bowden feels that Plymouth's opportunity in the PL Pairs cannot be fulfilled without his number 1 rider and has graciously withdrawn which opens the door for the next club in line, Ipswich, to compete."

Lewis Bridger* "Tonight at poole only 5pts but a tough 5pts away at num5 :-/ but plenty of pace & this is what matters"

Linus Sundstrom* "Time to go back and spend some time on the sleepshelf! About 500km left to our destination"

16th June

Jason Crump [35] "It's not that I don't need to ride, but I don't feel that I need to ride three, four or five times a week. We've got a great life without that."

Nicolai Klindt* "for all swindon fans: the reason why i'm not riding tonight is because of flights"

Lakeside website Mindful of the fact that many of the riders involved in the meeting [Hackney v IoW] have to take time off work, college or school, as do their parents, by making an early call we hope to have caused the least inconvenience to them and our fans.

Chris Holder* "Good to see the BSPA knockin down the Money for the pairs!! Wat happened to winning 5k...? useless %%€s"

Scott Nicholls* "ha ha,I got the wild card & no hotel! Come on the brits. What a shambles"

David Watt* "Love drivin to a speedway meeting with the windscreen wipers on !!! Hahaha. Isn't it summer ??"

Chris Holder* "Goin to be difficult to team ride tonight because I can't turn my head!! Haha neck is a bit of a problem!"

Mads Korneliussen* "Called off in sweden due to unfit track, what a joke, just got to love my job. It did not look like the hat done the track for two years. Have not hat the best off luck this last two days, called off today and tomorrow. WTF"

Niels Kristian Iversen* "Just had a inconsistant 18 holes today. Got beaten by Bjerre. Not happy bout that. But good with a day off to recharge. Busy week ahead"

Linus Sundstrom* "Looong way home from denmark now (malmö) . Satnav says 635km and we gonna be home by 03.48"

Nicolai Klindt* "well, i'm not off to bed. got loads of packing and washing to do before bed. got to go to austria saturday now, so wont be home for a week."

David Watt* [to (absent) N. Klindt after 25-65 Swindon home loss] "confidence isn't an issue in the Pirates pits mate. You might want to have a look closer to home !!!"

Darcy Ward* "beach party tomorrow down sandbanks... Now that's keepinitreal

17th June

Paul Burbidge* "I'm in Hong Kong and missed what appears to have been a mad meeting at Swindon last night. What the hell happened?"

Paul Burbidge* "Tough year for Swindon fans. T.Russell pulling out, hammered in the KO Cup, fireworks stolen and Leigh Adams badly hurt. It never rains ..."

Sam Masters* "Whaaaat [Plymouth] rained off already!! Need to race this is killing me!"

Olly Allen* "Just seen a dude at the gym drying his chest hair with a hair dryer!! Never seen that before"

Mads Korneliussen* "I was not put on this planet to do paper work"

Niels Kristian Iversen* "Been in the office All morning takin care of business. Now to the airport, a busy week starts now. Next one is tomorrow in Divisov"

Nigel Pearson* "Come on, get me over 3,000 followers tweeps. I was never sure about Twitter but I'm loving it!!"

Fredrik Lindgren* "Am ready for my speedway marathon! Ride a bike every day for the next 11 days. Start at Eastbourne tomorrow ends at Vetlanda Tuesday June 28. E'bourne, Torun, Wolves, Målilla, K'Lynn, Swindon, 2x Cardiff, Gorzow Wolves, Vetlanda. Places to race my next eleven days!"

Hans Andersen* "nothing beats the life of a superstar the human YoYo forwards & backwards on day after another"

Ludvig Lindgren* "just had mi dinner now iam ready for bed!"

Scott Nicholls* "Comb overs....why?! What is the point. We can see u're bald!"

18th June

Fredrik Lindgren* "Here we go again! just having my breakkie at Sthlm Skavsta Airport or Nyköping that is! Back in the groove"

> **Nigel Pearson*** "hope the boy Clark didn't lead you astray yesterday mate!! He said he was meeting up with you, I thought "poor scotty"!!"
> **Scott Nicholls*** "he was my in car entertainment system. Surprisingly a pub was mentioned!"

Rob Godfrey "The forecast was horrendous so if the fans want to blame anyone, they should blame the BBC weathermen because they were 100% wrong. It rained, but not like they said."

> **Lewis Bridger*** "spoke wid the wife, the J.D school comes with the relationship.. Like a Bonus an amazing girl with special Advice !!"
> **Scott Nicholls*** "oh god,starting to feel sick! U brown noser! :-)"

> **Lewis Bridger*** "Just in Subway Bexhill Hmm today I'm feeling a Subway Club.."
> **Chris Holder*** "Frankies and bennys mmmmm"

Nicolai Klindt* "arrived to mureck after a long drive. it looks like a big lakeside with red shale to me!"

Niels Kristian Iversen* "That was a very wet one today everything is covered in shit. 10 points and trough to the next round."

Kevin Long* [after 62-28 at Berwick] "many question the fans commitment in following Ipswich speedway away from home;hardly surprising given tonights result.Truly shocking!"

Jon Cook "You can mention any name in the world and believe me, we've spoken to at least a dozen of them, but British speedway is still not particularly attractive to most of them who are pretty well committed to their foreign engagements, quite apart from those in Sweden and Poland."

Nicolai Klindt* "was 2nd in today's euro. semifinal at mureck. had good speed and track was sikk [bit rough] so leg was back and cable tight"

Mads Korneliussen* "sådan mand. så kan du købe dig en flot lighter med nøgne damer på for alle de penge du har tjent idag [such a man. so you can buy yourself a nice lighter with naked ladies on all the money you earned today]"

Nicolai Klindt* "jeg har da aldrig tjent så mange penge som i dag! woohoo.... (I've never earned so much money that day! Woohoo ....)"

Chris Neath* "What am I gonna do this week? Bikes are all ready and I've got 5 more days to kill before Redcar."

Fredrik Lindgren* "Things not working great in the UK at the moment! We've been racing to little over here with Wolves lately. For me 5p/5h"

Dakota North* "Need to sort this out, hand still giving me trouble, going to get another operation"

Lewis Blackbird "We took scalps of some of the best riders in the league, such as Kyle Newman who is riding Elite with Poole, which makes you realise they are just names and anyone is beatbale."

Nicola Sands* "I'm already looking forward to you and Kelv's moans about the road trip!"

Lukas Dryml "The track was probably better than other weeks when it has been too dry. This track needs some grip and some rain."

Gary Patchett "I see that the conspiracy theorists have gone into overdrive in light of Terry's recent announcement and would move to assure our fans that this is not, as some would believe, the first step towards an end to speedway at Swindon. I shall be making my own enquiries with a view to securing a partner, or partners, who I feel I can work with and with whom I can, jointly, move the club forward. This is an Elite League club and as long as I am involved at Blunsdon it will remain so."

Stewart Dickson "I sensed before the [Leicester] meeting that their heads were right down before the meeting and if we were to race to our capabilities then we could get the win, however the margin that we gained [28-62] was far greater than we could ever have hoped for. I said to the lads to fill their boots on nights like this because they do not come along too often, and to their credit they did just that."

Lukas Dryml "Lewis was wild. He didn't look...I had a word afterwards. I said to him 'you didn't need to do this because you are fast enough and you are a good rider here'."

Simon Lambert "I am chuffed to bit because I have been told I have created history by being the first rider to win this event three times."

Jellyman "I've been wondering. Is your username [Parsloes 1928 nearly] a typo?"

19th June

Lewis Bridger* "not happy bout not racing in Polska at the moment but they treated me like a F5kn Ku▼t & enough's enough Ill be back !!!"

Hans Andersen* "Just been told by the Danish media that I'M not In the World cup sqaud (not even by the national coach) know I'M not fit but there's a month"

Jan Staechmann* "always nice to find these things out that way, isn't it?"

Hans Andersen* "Think it's a bad move by the national coach not to inform. He'll struggle to cross a burned bridge one day....."

Niels Kristian Iversen* 'Having lunch at the hotel. What to dó after?? Meeting is 8.30pm. Got some time to kill. Boring. Im not a fuzzy eater, and my english might not be perfect. BUT how can you not understand "NO fries, i want boiled potatos and vegetables" ? Still a good meal, gotta give him crédit for that."

Nicolai Klindt* "hoped to get the call for the world cup, but got told of my maliniak dealer that i'm reserve. nothing seems to go my ways these days"

Nicolai Klindt* "so think i'm applying for a austrian license an passport for next year, after i saw how much they loved me down their."

David Watt* "Had a crappy day. Spent the morning in hospital and then only got paid 8 and we lost. My eyes are killing me !"

Chris Neath* "Think I offended mums friend today when I rode my pit bike through the house. Oh well getoverit! That's why we got wood and not carpet!"

Chris Holder* "Playin wheres wally on the plane with wuff"

Nicolai Klindt* "just arrived to holidayinn berlin and already in the world comfiest beds. but not happy that I have to pay for wifi!"

George English "People expected us to take Plymouth apart, but they proved a tougher prospect than anticipated and they certainly adapted to the tricky surface left after torrential overnight rain better than we did. But congratulations to them as they deserve a lot of credit for the spirited show they put on."

20th June

Tai Woffinden "I must be honest and say I don't like the Eastbourne track, I don't enjoy riding it and that's why I was so poor on Saturday. I'm not going to make any excuses, it's just the fact that I hate the track."

Andy Povey* "Media Accreditation sorted, money in the bank, so nearly all sorted for British Speedway Grand Prix @ Millenium Stadium on Saturday"

Graham Drury "I've been in regular contact with KK on his travels and he seems to have found the right set-up and obviously did well in Italy at the weekend. Anyone who thinks the lad doesn't care is mistaken. He has been hurting badly during this poor run of form because he knows he has cost us the chance of league points and cup progress, although we were poor as a team in the cup."

Fredrik Lindgren* "If I could choose my dad chris holder would be my daddy!"

Fredrik Lindgren* "Just realised darcy ward is the funniest geezer in the world of speedway!"

Nicolai Klindt* "can't wait to go downstairs to the massive breakfast buffet.... my bed was nice n comfy too. Would love to be in it for a bit longer! Got a stupid 'o clock flight to catch though"

Mike Bennett* "looks like I WILL be at the Norfolk Arena on Wednesday night after all thanks to another change of plan in Aberdeen this week!"

Nigel Pearson* "just spoken to the legend Johno... could be a messy weekend in prospect!"

Ludvig Lindgren* "chillin at petes with tai. watchin sum tele"

Greg Hancock* "Back in Sweden and just got a message from Johno!! The Eagle has landed he said!! Beware in the UK! Johno's Baacckk!"

Nicolai Klindt* "bless me.... lost my filling in my tooth yesterday morning. last night a piece of the tooth came off and now the hole thing just broke!"

Dakota North* "Fuck I hate airports. See you later Uk for awhile"

  Nicolai Klindt* "finally arrived to england. going to watch the mighty wolves tonight for the first time this year, hope it will be good"

  Gary Patchett* "anyone tell u it was rained off before u got there"

Fredrik Lindgren* "Unlucky with the weather today at wolves back to Stansted now!"

Nicolai Klindt* [to Nigel Pearson] "you are looking like a star on skysports with your new haircut!"

Lewis Bridger* "Tonight went no good 4 me but head up.. Turn negatives into Possitives & I have something interesting to test on Thursday at Johnos meeting!"

Steve Williams "Although the riders were willing to carry on, they were pointing out how dangerous the track had become, so it seemed the sensible decision to call a halt after 12 heats before anyone got hurt."

Cameron Woodward* "I'm struggling at the moment man. hopefully sort myself out soon"

21st June

Chris Hunt "We need to have a successful team on the Island, you can't just go through the motions of being also-rans. It's a hard sport and we have to try and keep the public happy."

Scott Nicholls* "Wanna support a speedway legend? Steve "johno" Johnson's farewell,Thursday,swindon. All action guy on & off track! Turn out for a top bloke!"

Mike Bennett* "Norwich Airport security on go slow this morning!"

Niels Kristian Iversen* "Thanks to everyone who remembered my birthday yesterday."

Fredrik Lindgren* "Back in Sweden a fair few riders on the Skavsta flight today. If it would've been cancelled Elitserien would struggle."

Nicki Glanz* "I couldnt get a decent mecanic for my comeback saturday so i wil have to settle for Nicolai Klindt"

Niall Strudwick* "waiting for our coach to devon :)"

Lewis Bridger*
"I went for Hypnotherapy today & it is pritty Heavy stuff trying to connect with your sub concience or watever let's see if it works"
Scott Nicholls*
"what cam,flywheels combo did ya sub-conscious come IP with! :-)"
Chris Holder*
"hahahahahahahahahahaha"

David Watt* "Bloody rain offs just mean I'll be even more busy later ! Gotta get some before we smash the little robins tomoz"

Hans Andersen* "Not offen you Can take something positive from scoring just two points! But being less painfull racing and not feeling shit afterwards is a+"

Hans Andersen* "Weiiii.... Can almost sense home and my bed ;) Not much i'll sleep In that this coming week. Poland, sweden then of to Latvia oh dear...."

22nd June

Fredrik Lindgren* "Had some difficulties falling a sleep last night, everything is not perfect. Let's go for breakfast"

Ludvig Lindgren* "running abit late to the airport! coach driver step on it!!!

Ludvig Lindgren* "2 rain offZ in 2 days! oh ma life that sucks third time lucky at Kingslynn 2nite hopefully!"

Nigel Pearson* "Two coaches of Heathens fans heading to Cardiff plus loads more in cars... great support for legend Greg Hancock"

Lewis Bridger* "Off for a Haircut then back to Wirebrush the Weapon for Thursday night !!"

Nicolai Klindt* "waiting for my haircut at wow with a cup of coffee!"

Nicolai Klindt* "an hour left to poole... heading down for the knock-out cup against poole speedway. think it's gonna be tough to pull a 34 point defeat back! any news bout the weather?"
Chris Holder* "pissin down... :-P"
Scott Nicholls* "your team managers told me porkies then! I thought that was a promoters job..."
Chris Holder* "nah its fine scotty I jus wanna upset Nicolai ;-) u know wat these Danes are like"
Scott Nicholls* "ha ha,he's just worried about his new haircut getting destroyed!"

Fredrik Lindgren*
"K'Lynn awesome track!"

Phil Chard "Then Gafurov, in a thoughtful voice, said: 'It's all been worthwile. I'm happy I made a good job over the winter sitting the English exam in Moscow and passing it.'"

Linus Sundstrom* "Been a relaxing day with some good fun playing buzz, minigolf & tennis! Back to work tomorrow again. Hope weather is good in b'ham tomorrow!"

Mike Bennett* "olly allen should be in the starting 5 for the World Cup round at Kings Lynn. He could be a match winner! Retweet please tweeps!"

Mads Korneliussen* "Bad meeting today for me. But we won. Lost my grandmother today RIP 103 years old, not bad. Not the day I wanted this way, but that's life!!"

Rob Lyon "We got out-trapped a little like we have been doing, and it has become a bit of a trend."

Shane Parker "Age means you take a lot longer to get over a knock – you don't heal as quickly as you used to – but you never lose the experience and track craft and don't forget it overnight."

23rd June

Fredrik Lindgren* "No joke got hit by a big stone where it's very very awkward for a male person to get hit in the last heat. Still suffering, no joke not fun"

Nigel Pearson* "Let's get this party started. Johno's Farewell at Swindon tonight, see you there!"

Linus Sundstrom* "Love boarding when its pissing down, lucky me i have priority! Watching people queing outside in the rain trough the window"

Lewis Bridger* "Styling it up at Swindon tonight with Corn Dog.. Going to be 1 fukkn Epic weekend can I hear a Wooohhhaaaa 4 all the cardiff Fans.. Bang !!!"

Lewis Bridger* 'I hate people that take sides.. If it aint your buissness don't get involved !!"

Niels Kristian Iversen* "Sort out that shit ryanair website.. Dosent work half the time"

Ludvig Lindgren* "at the ferry on my way to polska for sum action! fricking shit boat tho!"

Nicolai Klindt* "I love tesco!... all those cheap things you can buy in tesco is unbelievable"

Fredrik Lindgren* "Arrived at Swindon and what's on TV, Wallander in Swedish on BBCfour! Come on Kurt solve the crime!"

Nicolai Klindt* "cant wait to get my house in england!"

George English "We might have had more but the referee [Dale Entwistle] had a very poor night, telling me he did not see a first bend incident that resulted in Kyle Newman being put over the fence by an opponent. If you can't spot something on the first bend of a race, there's not much hope for anyone."

Marc Lyons "Steve Johnston bade farewell to British speedway, and the popularity of this journeyman rider was underlined by a class field in front of a slightly above average crowd at Blunsdon."

Graham Cooke "The track [at Johno farewell] did cop its fair share of criticism. Once again we found ourselves with too much loose shale on turn 2. One lesson we are all learning is that the new silencers are not only making life difficult for the riders, they are also making our life difficult preparing a track. It seems that the fall off point (where the engine suddenly loses power) is much lower than on the old bikes and it only takes a little bit extra shale on the track for the engine to suddenly drop revs, straighten up the bike, stop the spinning back wheel and allow the tyre to really grip the surface and cause mayhem as riders lose control. I suppose the easy answer is to take all the dirt off tracks and run them absolutely bald and slick, but that's not how we want our speedway at Blunsdon - that would just add up to processional racing with no passing. We are the first to admit that we haven't got it right at Blunsdon but then our problems are magnified by the exceptional speeds and the banking at the old Abbey Stadium."

Poole Daily News "A TRANSSEXUAL speedway fan said she broke down in floods of tears after being told she was not allowed to use the ladies' toilets at Poole stadium. Victoria Saxe-Coburg said she was told by security in front of other spectators there had been a complaint about her from another spectator. The 55-year-old from Bournemouth, who had a gender reassignment operation more than 20 years ago, said she was told to use the disabled toilet. Stadium manager Shaun Spencer-Perkins declined to comment on the incident. Ms Saxe-Coburg was watching Poole Pirates' speedway victory over Wolverhampton Wolves on the evening of June 8. She is a speedway fan of more than 40 years standing and has been watching Poole since moving to Dorset four years ago. "It was said within earshot of everybody," said Victoria, of Springbourne. "They asked me to use the disabled toilets and I turned round and quite catgeorically said 'no'. I've never had any complaints before whatsoever. I have been a model fan. There's been no problems. I felt humiliated. There were quite a few people nearby. I always stand in exactly the same place. I felt so humiliated and angry that I felt as if I had to go to the opposite side of the stadium. I was in floods of tears. I saw the stadium manager afterwards, who said things were not handled well." Ms Saxe-Coburg got a letter from her GP confirming the operation and met stadium staff again on Wednesday night during the Pirates 54-40 victory over Eastbourne. She said she "did not get very far" with her complaint and staff were "not happy" with her using the ladies' toilet. She did not use the toilets during the match. "I very much doubt I will go again," she said. A Poole Pirates spokesman said the club only leases the stadium. They said the incident involved a member of the stadium staff, not an employee of the club. "

24th June

Nicolai Klindt* "decent night in poole, but still fuming after chris holder made it on me from 4. think I got a concussion after bike in my face, but yea!"

Graham Cooke "The first visitor of note to the [pits] gate is Sweden's Magnus Zetterstrom. He is rejoicing in getting a completely unexpected call up as a GP reserve to the main event after the bizarre situation that has befallen GP rookie, the Russian Artem Laguta. Artem has been prevented from coming to Cardiff because he has not got his Visa sorted. Magnus finds it almost incomprehensible that such an oversight should be made on Laguta's part. 'We've all had lots of time to get paper work sorted out so it's no excuse, but I'm glad it's given me a chance to compete here. I'm just going to go out and have fun and let's see what I can do.' He's a nice chap is Magnus. I hope he goes well."

Nicolai Klindt* "you guys up for the trackrecord or is it going to be a wheelie competition at practice?"

Stoke Speedway STOKE Easy Rider Potters promoter Dave Tattum has confirmed that the Potters have a new centre green presenter in former rider Chris Simpson. Simpson (36) used to ride in the mid nineties before retiring in 1997 after breaking his collarbone three times within a six month period and has since turned his hand to centre green presenting. Chris has been doing the centre green at Elite League Birmingham for the past couple of seasons and has also done the music at Coventry for a number of years and has also done a number of Grand Prix's including the British Grand Prix at the Millennium Stadium back in 2008 and 2009. Simpson makes his debut on the centre green for Sunday's National League KO Cup semi final against Midlands rivals Dudley alongside announcer George Andrews. Easy Rider Potters promoter Dave Tattum said 'Chris and I had a chat a few weeks back and we agreed to give things ago over a couple of meetings and see how things go. I'm delighted he has come on board as I feel the presentation of a meeting is important. We're now moving forward on the track with our first piece of silverware and we're now looking forward to improving things off the track and I feel Chris is a good addition to the club as we aim to move things forward. I've heard good reports on Chris and have also seen him when we have travelled down there and he comes from our area'."

Chris Holder* "Gotta pay to go into Wales... They should be payin u! Haha"

Gary Patchett* "look on the bright side fella. They don't charge u to get out!!"

Ludvig Lindgren* "in Gniezno chillaxing all cool. Why would any one be in cardiff when you can be in Gniezno watchin the u21 semi final???."

Nicolai Klindt* "fuming and i mean fuming over the ryanair website is going 'error' all the time when i wanna book tickets"

Lewis Bridger* "Pritty pumped in Cardiff.. Wid doyley & Corn yewwww !!!"

Fredrik Lindgren* "Practice over and done with! Now try and find my hotel later dinner with some sponsors!"

Nigel Pearson* "Fantastic draw for the Dudley heathens at Newport in dreadful conditions. Top of the league with best fans in the business!"

Fredrik Lindgren* "Back at hotel after awesome dinner at an Italian restaurant! Get some rest now."

Chris Neath* "Fuck you bouncers of worcester your all a bunch of wankers!!!" Same old shit!"

Joe Screen "It wasn't mega, mega heavy, but it was consistently raining and it did make conditions greasy towards the end. It was just down to technical, old-school riding and me and James are one of the oldest pairs in the group."

Jason Lyons "Conditions were terrible at the end and there was so much water there. I suppose with the shape and size of the track, we got away with it. If it had been held on something smaller and tighter, we wouldn't have kept going. All credit to Somerset – their track holds up for the wet ones. I've done this for three years and now I've had a first, second and a third, so maybe I shouldn't come next year!"

Shane Parker "The track to start with was a joke. Obviously we had the prediction of rain, but we went out there and it was dusty. They watered the track after the first heat and then it started raining. Then the track was that slick and they didn't have the equipment to get it decent enough for us to ride on."

Tony Jackson "I'm sure that a league match would have been called off"

Magnus Zetterstrom "There was no room booked for me and there were no ferry or flight tickets. I had to deal with this myself...Financially, I should have said no, but from a sporting point of view, I love to do this."

Kenneth Bjerre "Everybody is World Champion when they're practising"

25th June

Fredrik Lindgren* [07.00 on day of Cardiff SGP] "Upset with my brother now, my phone rang and woke me up! I answered Hello, with a scrubby voice. No one there he must've rang in his pocket!"

Graham Cooke "Back in the [Millennium] stadium, the inflatable helmets are being pumped up. It does seem as if a disproportionate amount of time is being taken on a feature that will only be in place for about 30 minutes before the GP starts, but it keeps quite a large team of people happily employed.... Once the flame throwing has been passed as suitable the next entertainment is to watch the start line girls go through their routines on the start line. These four have been flown in from Poland apparently (although one wonders if we couldn't have furnished four locally born beauties for the job). They strut and jig and open their umbrellas in a sequence of moves and then make their way off track. It doesn't take much asking for them to stop on their way back to the pits for a special Blog photo. Perhaps they thought that appearing in the Blog would be a giant step towards fame and stardom!"

Scott Nicholls "This year, with respect, you wouldn't really regard them as top, top riders, but on the night, Tai, Eddie, Ben Barker, there was some stiff opposition, and you could see how much it meant to them, which was nice."

Mike Hunter "The club will be scrutinising the next set of Green Sheets when they arrive this week to find suitable guests. It's much harder to predict these days with the new method of calculating averages."

Paul Bellamy [celebrates 2011 as the 'Year of Innovations'] "Grand Prix coverage was at the forefront of technology and innovation and I am very proud of that"

Scott Nicholls "Everyone seems to think that there's a big, big problem between me and Bomber and there really isn't. There's a rivalry there, and yes, there was a time when we didn't particularly get on. But, sadly that more people surrounding him causing more problems than he was himself. I think now that he's grown up a little bit, he's standing on his own two feet a bit more and doing what he wants to do, we get on better."

Krzysztof Cegielski "I am always here for Leigh if he wants me. Whatever I can tell him to help lift him, I will do because I know it is a new situation for him now. ...I was in the same situation as Leigh. One day your life is completely different. But after that day, I wouldn't say everything was bad. It was different, but still good."

Scott Nicholls   "I put everything into [Ipswich] and there wasn't really a lot coming back. On the flip side of that, living five minutes down the road and a Thursday night was handy, that was money in the bank to me really."

Stuart Douglas   "The points gained versus points lost and its effect on league position I can live with, because you are either good enough, or you're not. But the emotional aspect troubles me. I feel it is fundamentally wrong to have the satisfaction of victory snatched away in this manner. So, what's the solution? The old aggregate home/away system skewed the table equally badly, favouring home tracks like Poole and Swindon massively. Ironically, the new, fairer track at Swindon prepared by Ronnie Russell would no longer yield the same distortion it once did… my view is that we should have a review of the scoring system. It's ridiculous that you have the opportunity of picking up more points away from home than you do at home."

Scott Nicholls   "I don't really understand why they brought them [new silencers] in, I really don't. I think there's only one club in the country that has got a noise issue and that's Birmingham, but then the junior riders go round at the end of the meeting, late at night, and use the old silencers. If someone's going to complain, it's more likely to be ten o'clock at night than it is seven. It's an FIM rule, we're not an FIM-governed body, nor are Sweden, nor are Poland……For Roy Otto to go into the press and say that so many riders tested them and they've done this many races, well, I don't know a single top rider who's been asked to test them. They're definitely having an effect, they are affecting the engines. There have been more engine failures this year than there has been for a long time, the maintenance bills have rocketed because you have to have the engines serviced more regularly. When do you see Tomasz Gollob or Jason Crump scoring 15 points one day and then going to a track and scoring four?…..I find it strange that they bring them out last year and, in that time, they haven't made any changes. Those shoes don't fit, okay we'll give it a year and they will fit – no they won't…. We know money is limited in the sport, but I'd be prepared to bet everything I own that next year riders will be saying 'my maintenance bills have gone up, I need more money'. And you know for certain the clubs will say 'we haven't got more money', which I'm not disputing, but what do you do then?"

Dakota North*   "Someone let us know how chris holder does in the gp!!!!!"

Scott Nicholls   "They moan that teams are doctoring points, but they stick a rule in place that makes it open to that."

Mads Korneliussen*   "trying to do 100 things at ones this morning, not good booked worng flight bye bye 186 pounds, pissed off "

Scott Nicholls   "I think every rider that has had a kid, at some point, normally when they're about two, has a dip in their career. Interaction starts happening, you do start looking at things differently, you do start weighing up what's more important."

Chris Holder*   "I swear greg hancock was following me round yesterday! Everytime I turned around he was there!! Wats he playin at…"

Scott Nicholls   "To be honest I was certain what my World Cup future was, and that was there wasn't one…During the Coventry thing a while back, I was nearly out of a job in England. There was no support coming for me to get my job back… what did British speedway do to secure places for top British riders?….. we all know that when we ride in the World Cup, financially it's the worst pay-day we get with the exception of testimonials and farewells…I want a little bit of proof that the BSPA are actually behind the riders and want to support them. It's almost as if they're not bothered whether we succeed or not. So, if they can't be bothered, why the hell should we?"

Niels Kristian Iversen*   "Motorway Que + Niels = Moody bastard.."

Scott Nicholls   "As a rider you're expected to turn up with your equipment and everything in tip-top order because you're paid to do a job. I agree totally with that. But, at the same time, they're effectively our bosses, so they should be laying a good foundation for us to perform. If you turn up for work and it's a shambles, how can they expect you to do the job?"

Nicolai Klindt*   "fuming over not being at cardiff! why did I even bother to help nicki glanz when he touch the tapes….."

Scott Nicholls   "Anyone who's been in the GPs, if they're being honest, will tell you that when things are going good, it's fantastic, a buzz, really enjoyable. When they're not, it's the worst thing that can be happening to you. It has such a knock-on effect on the other leagues and, the fact is, the other leagues are our bread and butter. It also affects your family life and your friendships, because it does wear you down."

Fredrik Lindgren* "Just wanna get out of here, vanish! Right now hate that you have to wait around for everything!"

Scott Nicholls* [after 5 points at Cardiff as wildcard] "Sorry people. Rode my balls off but just didn't happen for me. Did the best I could & will do my best to be back & better next year… Frustrated because I wanted to do better & had a tough couple of weeks but I won't give up & got my 2 special girls to make me smile"

Speedway Star "[Alan] Carter collared the newly-crowned champion [at press conference] and appeared to be telling him his whole life story and perhaps recounting, word for word, what he has written in his new autobiography"

Fredrik Lindgren* "I know now why I've been enjoying the GP's this season. It's been going ok. Now I remember how it is when you don't enjoy them! It went bad but saw a couple of Freddie Lindgren flags around! It's nice to see, thanks for your support!"

Niall Strudwick* "had a awsome night at cardiff with Sarah :). Well done greg hancock for winning, knew you could win bud :)"

Greg Hancock "The only thing I could do was pray. I couldn't close my eyes, but I wanted to. I hit a big lump of dirt coming off the corner, it shot me forward and then I had time to clean my underwear!"

Andy Povey* "Knackered and my feet feel as if they have walked a 100 miles today. Will sleep well tonight. Well done greg hancock. Fantastic performance. Once a Bulldog, always a Reading Bulldog. Great times, great guy!"

Roman Chyla "I was watching, here in Poland, online coverage broadcasted by Sky Sports 2 HD, and there was no Jan, only Kelvin and Nigel, plus Chris and Charlie in the Pit area. Both pictures and sound were excellent. Anyway, what about the final, the first attempt. My view was/is that Mr Grodzki (don't we have better referees than him?) should have called all 4 riders back. Emil did such a flyer that everyone who had eyes could see, if not, they should go to the Specsavers :-) If he excluded Emil as a cause of stopping the race then he was wrong again. It all started with Nicki who pushed Chris and he in turn pushed out Emil who had no one to push (only the fast approaching safety fence). Of course he tried - as much as it was physically possible - to avoid Barry Briggs' invention by correcting the line of direction he was going. The end of it was for everyone to see. What happened to Gollob? In his first race he looked as good as any, if not better. In the remaining outings he looked under power, no speed at all. All he could do was watching as other pass him by. It was a sorrowful site. And yet before Cardiff he was telling everyone in Poland that he spent 70K PLN, or about £16K in preparation for the British GP. During the close season he claimed to spent nearly 400 thousand PLN, or about £90K on tuning his engines,. Most of them was paid into account of the Swedish tuner Jan Andersson, who prepared ten power units (the minimum cost of tuning one engine is apparently 25 thousand PLN, or nearly £6K). Five others went into the hands of Polish top tuners. One engine was also sent in the hands of Joachim Kugelmann. Tomasz apparently tested the engine prepared by Kugelmann in the recent Swedish league match between Hammarby and Dackarna Malilla (45:39). Gollob scored in that meeting eight points, won two races, and was only moderately pleased with the engine. Those tuned by Andersson turned out not to be suitable for the new silencers so in the end Gollob tried various settings himself to no avail. Eventually he gave up and put them aside, because he finally realized that he needs to replace the whole lot to give himself a chance for another title. For the Danish GP Gollob came with three brand new engines. In Cardiff he (presumably) did the same."

Magnus Zetterstrom "Bring some of the youngsters and I run away from them really easily. I'm fit, I did as lot of training through the winter and, as long as the head works, I think you can ride a bike as well."

Chris Holder "That 1st corner was EPIC! nicki nearly killed us all!"

Greg Hancock "I almost had a tear in my eye because I felt so darn good and the people here are amazing."

John Sampford "No disrespect to Ben [Morley] who has raced his heart out. It's a hard business, but it's a man's league and Ben is only 17......young minds soak up experience and knowledge without even realising it and he'll be a better rider for the whole experience."

Lewis Bridger* "In RSB Cardiff chilling out with a Couple of Jd's haha with a Friend surpose to be rough in here but drinks drink !!!"

26th June

Paul Bellamy "A lot of major sports have an iconic trophy that is recognisable throughout the world and runs through everything the sport does. The brief we set was a [new SGP] trophy that represented the world champion and the SGP series, and also provided something the champion could hold aloft and say 'I'm on top of the world.' We also wanted something fans could relate to, so the idea is we will have the trophy on display at Grand Prix rounds in our fanzones and then fans can have their photograph taken with it. It allows them to live their dream, hold it aloft and say 'I'm champion of the world' too."

Fredrik Lindgren* "Off to Luton Airport early flight to Poland. Not feeling the best think I'm about to get sick."

Chris Holder* "And where off again! Polska bound!"

Fredrik Lindgren* "Having the worst morning! First I find out some crap! Then my engine I was gonna take on the plane were overweight, so had to leave it... plus one mechanic at the Airport! Sick of shit!"

Chris Holder* "dude u must of went to the wrong chick! One was a sgp fan! Mine engine 34kg! No worries!"

Nicolai Klindt* "two people told me i had the biggest talent in danish speedway, but is wasting it. and if i want to be the best i must be 100% serious all the time. i would say i am very serious, but then they said i need to be more than very serious! people looking in from the outside always knows it better. But what dó they really know ?? f all"

Mads Korneliussen* "sig de skal lukke røven lige nu, og gå så ud og ryg en smøg, folk skal bare passe deres egen kage [themselves they have to shut your ass right now, and then go out back and a cigarette, people just need to look after their own nest]"

Hans Andersen* "told you All along to stop focuss on pink goggles and new shades"

Philip Rising "THE fact that the Millennium Stadium is hosting some Olympic soccer next year is muddying the waters a little but why would anyone want to go anywhere else? It is a fantastic show at the Millennium with the 23 races the top billing and a crowd of 43,640 says it all. BSI want it there, the Millennium Stadium want it as do the city of Cardiff. Don't panic, I'm sure they will all get it together."

Gary Patchett* "At Stoke Speedway waiting for medical cover. Tatt selling loads of chips"

Nicolai Klindt* "når jeg vinder gp i cardiff næste år vil jeg stå med en hotdog i hver hand [when I win gp in cardiff next year I will stand with a hot dog in each hand]"

Chris Holder* "Gotta love a bit of room service!"

David Watt* "Is at the track way too early for my liking !!! Got 4 bloody hours until I get to ride"

Charlie Webster* "Last night's Speedway GP packed out! 50,000 amazing crowd...have to confess I watched some if 3D later, wow!"

Philip Rising "OFFICIAL attendance was 43,640 which, given the economy, the current state of domestic speedway in the UK and the lack of British riders. is quite remarkable and a great tribute to the loyal fans of the sport in this country. BSI are quick to point out that no matter what they do, and the huge amounts of money they spend ensuring that the whole package can stand alongside any other sporting event held in Britain, ultimately it is the fans who make it happen."

Hans Andersen* "Made Myself available for UK racing again so only time Will tell what happens"

Philip Rising "The Olympic people demand that the stadium be exclusively theirs for several weeks beforehand. Might make sense as far as brand new stadiums are concerned but not with the Millennium. Seems that the rest of the world must come to a halt when the Olympics demand"

Philip Rising "THE British Grand Prix requires a stadium with so much more than just a speedway track. For example, over 500 people availed themselves of hospitality on Saturday, many of the corporate boxes were taken. I am sure that given how much BSI want to remain at the Millennium, and how much the Millennium want the event (now rated second only to Wales rugby internationals) a date will be agreed especially if the Olympic committee can be persuaded that the stadium doesn't have to lay dormant throughout June"

Fredrik Lindgren* "Nicki cried when I passed him in last heat & didn't finish, that cost me a bonus point! Polska change the rules! 10p/5h should've been 10+1"

Nicolai Klindt* "ive changed my background and lock theme on my phone now, so hoping for better days!"

James Sarjeant "In that last one, I gave Ashley [Morris] too much room and he went for the gap. I should have been a bit hard on him but he's a mate and we raced fair and hard."

Kevin Jolly "We are looking at stopping the [Mildenhall] riders doing the track walk because the idea is to psyche out the away team but it's not working."

Pete Hill "Promoter Len Silver did his best to keep the dust down but it was a losing battle on a heat wave afternoon, when the water cart did more laps than the riders."

Terry Daley "The meeting suffered from the late withdrawals of David Howe, who had previously won no less than six individual titles at Newport, because of injury and Ben Barker, who had been on reserve duty at the British Grand Prix, due to food poisoning."

Pete Hill "That though paled into insignificance compared to a surreal penultimate race. Tyson Nelson, failing to meet the two-minute allowance, was forced to go off 15 metres but, for some reason, Josef Franc refused to move to the inside gate, causing referee Chris Gay to lose his patience with the argumentative Bandit, excluding him for delaying the start. Franc still refused to accept the decision, returning to the start line again to demonstrate before being thrown out of the race. That performance cost the visitors any faint hope of a race point"

John Anderson "It was very tricky for our lads to get to grips, or in fact get any grip, on that [Rye House] dust bowl this afternoon"

Fredrik Lindgren* "On the road again, towards Berlin this time! Tomorrow Bee crush time!"

27th June

Lewis Bridger* "Woke up at 4am with loads of drive.. I want to be one of the Greatest riders in the World & i need to work hard 4 it from now on !!!"

Chris Holder* "ur dreamin lbr! U still asleep! Hahaha"

Lewis Bridger* "mate ur living the Dream & I want to be Living the same one.. I can be there if I work hard enough !!"

Scott Nicholls* "less talk mate n just race ya bloody bike! U've got talent so let that do the talking!"

Dakota North* "Had a good sleep for once! :)"

Dakota North* Just had a game of mini golf, tired as now took it out of me!"

Chris Holder* "Back in Uk... Sun is shining yewww summers back!"

Niels Kristian Iversen* "Met Kenni Larsen in the Airport. He asked me if i had been on the lash all night ?? Told him its just how i looks"

Niels Kristian Iversen* "Awesome weather in UK. Shades out cruisin up M11."

Mike Bennett* "connect with me on Visible.me! It's a great tool for managing our public identities"

Fredrik Lindgren* "On a serious note greg hancock what's up with all these retweets? You're such a twitslut"

Linus Sundstrom* "Alive again! Had a nice 2hrs sleep when i came home. Time to do some job in the workshop making it all ready for tonight"

Nicolai Klindt* "chilling in the garden listening to bbc radio 1 xtra and doing office work, while watching luke corbett washing bike. only clutchplates to do! i'm gonna make them that hot, i will smoke them from the starts tomorrow"

Lewis Bridger* "Me & corn are about to smash the gym"

Fredrik Lindgren* "Arrived in UK now and must say weather feels a bit funny today I really hope the rain stays away we can't have another cancelled home match"

Mike Bennett* "Once again Rob Lyon proving he is one of the best team managers in speedway. Shame the "powers that be" didn't see that?"

Fredrik Lindgren* "Damn it no max & not all 3 league points! And one engine destroyed in heat 13, that rain before last heat didn't help either damn it! 14p/5h"

Nicolai Klindt* "just thought about the funny times i had last year at wolves Ludvig, freddie lindgren and luke corbett. defo missing them at times"

Alun Rossiter "I'm bitterly disappointed with the refereeing though. For the referee [Paul Carrington] to tell me that a rider under power, leaving the pits, can't get to the start line in 30 seconds – it's his watch that tells him that, not what he thinks can happen. He said 'I believed that he couldn't make it' – well, let the watch make that decision."

Marc Plummer "The home camp were even more aggrieved when Lasse Bjerre charged home in Heat 8 as they weren't even aware he was in the race!...Panthers planned an official protest until discovering no specific rule had been broken...[Kenneth] Bjerre was lucky not to be scraping himself and his machine off the fence after being on the receiving end of a ruthless [Nicki] Pedersen overtaking manoeuvre in Heat 13 which certainly tested the boundaries of being acceptable."

Nicolai Klindt* "goodnight to all my twitter followers! i know there's not many compared to others but i will get there :-)"

Fredrik Lindgren* "Down at Stansted again, terrific driving down by the PK! Sleep few hours before that early flight"

Ludvig Lindgren* "oh my life when is this shit gonna end??? off to bed sweden 2morrow LETS GO!"

28th June

David Tattum "There has been a misunderstanding between the promotion and the medical staff and that's all it was...It hasn't been a nice time but we will put it right and ensure that it never happens again. It is not the first time in the sport that somebody has had to wait two hours for an ambulance. If we look back, these are things that do happen"

Nicolai Klindt* "let's gooo..... up and showered, now making coffee and a piece of bred with french brie cheese before heading for hagfors. roads at 04.37 danish time. damn I feel like toast being burnt for 10mins"

Nicolai Klindt* "just found out i ain't going poland anymore this year, so think i will have a major fall out with my bank account. guestbookings in uk, yes!"

Linus Sundstrom* "Another early morning today, loves it! Had a strange night last night with some positives and loads of negatives 2',3,R,R,2...bike problems.. Sorted now so it wont happen again ;)"

> **Lewis Bridger*** "I can't keep waking up after 3hr's of sleep me thinks maybe the Fermo Fusion Fat Stripper that's full of Caffine is not helping"
> **Lee Richardson*** "in the real world your young but not in speedway terms...;) he he...I'm a veteran!! Lol"
> **Lewis Bridger*** "LOL a Veteran earning a fuck load of cash"

Philip Rising "BYDGOSZCZ and Leszno don't even start to compare with either Torun or Gorzow or even Gorican ... but even those venues, magnificent though they undoubtedly are in speedway terms, lack the facilities required for a British Grand Prix. Hopefully the current negotiations with the Welsh Assembly will reach a satisfactory conclusion. It is hard to think that they would want to be responsible for Cardiff losing such a prestigious event and one that brings considerable financial benefit to the city."

> **Hans Andersen*** "Got a 2010 GP Rolling chassis for sale, only used it for sweden and GP last season. Any one In need ????"

Lewis Bridger* "i need x2 chassis for next season if you are getting rid of any mate !"

Sam Masters* "yeah keen how much?"

Hans Andersen* "hi mate, looking at around £1200 she's sat at My house In UK…"

Sam Masters* "okay man get back to you this afternoon ;) in need for one and another one at end of year for next season"

David Watt* "Man this hotel room is bright ! I'll give up trying to sleep now and have a go later !"

Nicolai Klindt* "try and close your eyes… might help, haha"

Niels Kristian Iversen* "Steaming inside cause of shit ryanairs useless website. Its almost everytime i am booking flights the bastard thing does error.."

Chris Holder* "Tgi Fridays jack Daniels chicken strips!! Now that's wat I'm talking bout mmmmm"

Linus Sundstrom* "New record when we filled up the van today! 222 liters, 3200kr"

Nicolai Klindt* "pissed off…. team mate fucks up my pass and can't find my freaking race jacket now"

Fredrik Lindgren* "On my way back home after racing on the most boring track in Sweden, Vetlanda! Another loss for Dackarna & I'm just pissed off!"

Fredrik Lindgren* "One positive thing about Vetlanda, IT'S a Quick drive to home afterwards ;)"

Fredrik Lindgren* "nearly at home so not so long before Zzzz…."

Hans Andersen* "Getting slowly back to the rhythm of racing, just not a 100% happy with my engines lacking speed so on the Hunt for new ones… Danish league tomorrow, poland thursday, latvia saturday, poland sunday and sweden tuesday before holiday as not In Danish squad ;-)"

Fredrik Lindgren* "Done some office work in the back of my van. Eleven straight days of racing & travelling & riding & 1 rainoff & racing is finished"

Fredrik Lindgren* "What matter the most? Entertaining racing? Your team winning? Would you not have em both? or does it not matter about racing when you win?"

Ray Blackwell "The sport needs to get back to having personalities and characters that generate the passion that's missing from the terraces, and before anyone starts the, 'we don't need trouble' argument, speedway always had the villains and the characters from the pioneer days, and we've never had to worry about crowd issues, and never will… BSPA pay heed… allow the riders to be characters and entertain.. you may get a shock and see the crowds come back"

Alun John Rossiter* "Last few beers with my mate Jono then home for some red wine and cheese :-)"

29th June

David Watt* "Just seen a huge moose !!! First 1 I've ever seen so excited now and I can't go to sleep"

Nicolai Klindt* "at ferry… it said 4:10 when i look at the time table on the way, but says 4:20 on their board down here. bless me for rushing!"

Jeff Dooley "Neil Machin's putting Shawn [Moran] up in a nice 5 star hotel in the centre of town, he definitely wouldn't have done that in the past"

Scott Nicholls* "What a cockhead I am!Land at stansted,go to get bus to carpark only to remember I don't actually have a car here!Hitchhike it is! Away 2long

Scott Nicholls* "….I like making people laugh.be nice if it wasn't at my expense though :-)"

Nicolai Klindt* "woke up after the nicest sleep in a long time. was dreaming loads of stuff if i remember right. now food and then office work"

Paul Burbidge* "Chris Harris is set to ring the changes to his pit crew and bikes after a tough night in Cardiff"

Lee Richardson* "lewis bridger spectating from the burger van!!! DAD (JD) told me your flipping burgers tonight!!!"

David Watt* "brilliant ! Love ya work Rico"

Lewis Bridger* "think u will find Jd earns more selling & Flipping Burgers than you 2 earn"

Lee Richardson* [to David Watt]   "give him a wave on the first corner!! ;)"

Niels Kristian Iversen*   "Feels Like im in a relationship with my suitcase at the moment"

David Watt* [to Greg]   "Re-lived the final in Cardiff. WTF is up with that [Nicki] Dude ? Hahahaaha. I was his team mate and had it every night !!"

Fredrik Lindgren*   "what's with all the nicki hating????"

David Watt*   "who said anything about hating him ? I like him. I just don't like somethings he does on a bike"

Darcy Ward   "Middlo had said we needed a heat win in the final race…fortunately Rory Schlein lifted a bit and I was in the right place at the right time. I've had a lucky year like that."

David Watt   "Eleven again and I'm not even getting into Heat 15. It's frustrating. How good have you got to be to get into that race!"

Nicolai Klindt*   "can't freaking sleep… too hot in here! and i'm twit-dicted. anyone els who's twit-dicted?"

30th June

Nigel Pearson*   "Heading into voiceover"

Nicolai Klindt*   "fuming here…. forgot my snus at mortens house! need something to calm me down. flying with crapair now, baaah"

Mads Korneliussen*   "Just love this 20min ferry to sweden just enough time for a piss and an icecream nice combo"

Lee Richardson*   "no good having breaks this long from racing!! Especially when I'm paying mech to sit around doing nothing!"

Linus Sundstrom*   "hahahaha greg presing a instead of s on his phone and telling klindt to reload his anus instead of the snus!"

Lewis Bridger*   "got x2 new Jrm's at Richard Kowalski Tuning Workshop Polska Kurwa! :-) 5peedwsy Yellow tops new boxes !!"

Paul Burbidge*   "The Aussies are selling advertising space on their SWC race suits to raise cash for the seriously injured Leigh Adams"

Nigel Pearson*   "Busy day sgp highlights show with Kelv went well, spent afternoon on phone on Heathens business, press statement later"

Hans Andersen*   "Ahhhhhhhh i've had it with using others stuff, i know people just want to help BUT your always more comfortable using own bikes & engines"

Nicolai Klindt*   "on the track side it was very rough to start with, but after heat 8 it went more smoth and better. but very slick. so kerb for me, no fence!"

Scott Nicholls*   "bad night for robins,tough 1 for me.Some time off soon,which I really need.lot going on recently n mentally drained.make good use oftime off"

Jeff Povey*   "HOW the F can you guys at Swindon cope with that piss poor excuse of a track ?!? Ronnie needs to piss off NOW !"

Ronnie Russell   "Scott Nicholls is set to change engine tuners, following a difficult first half to the season in which he has burned out three new engines at great personal expense. He's had his troubles with his engines this year and let's hope it will get sorted soon."

Scott Nicholls   "Don't know where this engine story has come from. I didn't quote that n bit p*ssed off to be honest"

Nicolai Klindt*   "how cool am i…. just had a piss on m25! thats what i call #wolfpackbehaviour"

Ludvig Lindgren*   "been helpin freddie all day building fking sofa and chairs!"

Matej Kus   "My impressions were is that [King's Lynn] is a very smooth track with a lot of grip but consistent so nice"

Nigel Pearson*   "just listened to a fantastic hour of bob harris country on Radio2. I was brought up on Country Music, not a lot know that!"

1st July

Mads Korneliussen* "28 krona for a diet coke thank fu€k i am geting out of sweden, who do you think you are???"

Mads Korneliussen* "Just seen two men getting busted with 30 cartons off Marlboro each at stansted ha ha ha sad idiots"

Niels Kristian Iversen* "And now the trip goes to croatia.. Only 1139km to go"

Jon Cook "Our Team Manager Neil Vatcher has started to really find his feet with the team and his calls from the use of Rider Replacement at No.2 to changes in the meeting were spot on. He and the boys have a great rapport and his arrival at the Club has been a big positive."

Nicolai Klindt* "anyone flyin stansted-poznan? i need someone to hold my hand. im affraid of hights and ryanair!"

Nicolai Klindt* "on the bus going from the hotel to the airport. got bad vibes there bout mega que at secrurity..."

Lewis Bridger* "Cant Believe I have got rid of 4,870 peeps of fBook.. setting up a fans page l8r for everybody that wants to Follow my Progress !!"

Lewis Bridger* "Yewwww just bought new Pro T-1000 Loco skate wheels and pro alex barrow bearings skate sesh tonight !"

> **Nicolai Klindt*** "do you have any cheap tricks to give me for tomorrow? no ones there, so i gotta take the position as national coach i think."
>
> **Jan Staechmann*** "someone should be there. Poor show. Yes, tell them to go hard, or go home :o)"

Ludvig Lindgren* "off to Norrtälje soon. gunna be sweet to check out the nightlife there! heard that greg hancock is the true nightlife king up there!"

> **Lee Richardson*** "u in the hot tub or running lbr???"
>
> **Lewis Bridger*** "1st Hottub Rico then run now shower do u wanna no wat im doing now !?"
>
> **Lee Richardson*** "not really lbr! But u keep telling everyone on here!!! Lol..."
>
> **Lewis Bridger*** "Follow me.. Follow me.. The life of LBR this is how i Roll people wanna no my shizzle ya kno !! :)"

Nigel Pearson* "Massive hype followed by disappointment... That's British sport for ya!"

David Watt* "Don't you just love border control ?? NOT !!!!"

Stoke Speedway Stoke Speedway very much regret that because of essential planned stadium work which is still incomplete, that the match against Buxton tomorrow has had to be cancelled. Supporters will be aware that serious damage was done to the premises earlier this month when thieves stole materials and damaged the area in which the riders and medical staff are accommodated. Temporary renovations enabled the facilities to be used in the interim but further work this week has revealed the necessity for the electrical supply system to be enhanced in order to conform with standards now required for the issue of a new electrical safety certificate and it has not been possible to complete this work in accordance with the estimate that was provided to us.

Hayley Armstrong* "Seathing!!! Just found out that the Stoke Potters V Buxton meeting is off. All thanks to the incompetent promotion team. For fuck sake Mr T"

Ross Jackson "with the scores tied at 18-18 by the end of the sixth, it was clear divine intervention would not grace North Lincolnshire"

2nd July

Rob Godfrey "Rolling averages have not done him any favours whatsoever, because a true average for Joe [Haines] at the moment is three, and rolling ones suggest he's a six."

Nicolai Klindt* "still got freaking 475km left to daugavpils. already done a bit over 6hrs"

Hayley Armstrong* [to Nicolai] "you're the king of twitter. You make me laugh! believe me, supporting a national league team, I need a laugh. stoke #shitpromotion"

Richard Frost "He was happy to sign for the Autogate Aces on a double-up basis at the start of the season only to suffer the disappointment of having it rescinded when Tomasz Piszcz had his average recalculated to a lower figure. That allowed the Aces to accommodate Mark Lemon instead but, when Piszcz left, the arrival of Dawid Strachyra pushed Lemon out and Frampton was reinstated."

Nicolai Klindt* "just arrived to lovely daugavpils 5min ago with a frigging sore ear. they had reserved VIP parking for us and everything!"

Jordan Frampton "I want to be in the Elite League one day but it's not just down to your ability. It depends on whether your average fits and whether your face fits."

David Hemsley "The priority now is to start winning at home again and get the whole project back on track."

Mike Bowden "It is good news for Ben [Barker] that he is having a successful run personally, but disappointing for our supporters that he is having to miss out on so many of our team fixtures."

Paul Cooper "I really don't know why more clubs don't get together like [Sheffield/Scunthorpe] because there are so many benefits and opportunities for young British riders. I agree that Neil Machin and Rob Godfrey have always had a lot to do with each other's clubs but other clubs could do the same."

Nigel Pearson "We have the best fans in the league [at Dudley], it's only the actions of two or three which ruin our reputation"

Nick Mallett "We were chasing a rider who is based in Europe and it looked likely that a deal could be done soon. However, and it appears very much in keeping with the bad luck which seems to dog this club at every turn, the guy picked up an injury which could sideline him for a while. Nonetheless our search goes on and I continually look to see who is out there and doing what."

Hans Andersen* "if you are ever to be nation coach then you have to turn up for practice as well......"

Nicolai Klindt* "yeye, im coming in a bit! the national coach had just had a 2hrs sleep and will now go to the track in daugavpils to see how his fellow countrymen are doing."

David Watt* "Gorican is one of the best places. Such a cool set up here ! Even got WiFi !! Better get ready for practice !!"

Nicolai Klindt* "i just love when poeple blank me, best feeling in the world!"

Lewis Bridger* "What a Lush day.. Been for s-bed with Jade Davis haha.. Now waiting for Claire at Toby Carvery in the Bourne :-)"

Lee Richardson* "what a life lbr!!! I've been ripping out and gutting another place I just bought on my only day off..come an give me a hand..lol"

Lewis Bridger* "ur a harcore trooper Rico.. Day off & ur still bringing in the dollar :-)wat ya last bit a HAND or summing haha !!"

Ludvig Lindgren* "dont you just hate it when i need to print something and the f*cking printer has runned out of ink!"

Nicolai Klindt* "going for some food. got dust everywhere and sweating like a fat bird walking"

Hans Andersen* "Just like to thank the national coach aka Nicolai Klindt for helping out In the pits c",)"

Nicolai Klindt* "think i will apply for the danish national team manager job for the sgp next year. i did a pretty good job today i would say!"

Ludvig Lindgren* "how the hell can u [Nicolai] have 1k followers people are crazy these days"

Niels Kristian Iversen* "Cowshit meeting"

David Watt* "Aaaaarrrrrrrrrrgggggggghhhhhh ! Bloody hate speedway sometimes !!!"

Terry Daley "There wasn't a great deal of exciting racing and most of the entertainment surrounded visiting team manager Richard Hollingsworth. At one stage he infuriated home fans by doing his own piece of track grading before soon jumping in front of the tapes as the riders were at the start for heat 6. All extremely strange behaviour."

Rob Godfrey "It was a 50-50 decision in Heat 15 and unfortunately for us, the referee [Christina Turnbull] went with the home team, as most of them do."

Robert Branford "I've been using money I'd had saved but that's obviously been going down but I've been lucky that my mum and dad came over and they'll be here a month or two. It's great to have them both here, dad helps me out a lot, although we argue all the time! He knows what I'm capable of and gets annoyed when I'm not doing it."

Rob Godfrey "So [Michael Palm] Toft is going to be either hero or zero, but even if it's zero, it'll be no worse than what we had anyway."

Ben Hopwood "That's the case with the National League unfortunately, the fixtures are too far apart. It cost me £100 to get here today....to be honest, I haven't even noticed the team scores, I've been so busy trying to improve my team performances."

Kozza Smith "Shielfield is a big track and I think that what you have to realise is that a race is over four laps"

Pete Hill "The last time Rye House won at Berwick, Jim Callaghan was Prime Minister"

Nick Mallett "To be frank, it is simply not good enough by the stretch of anyone's imagination for four riders to only score ten points between them. It is my opinion that now is the time for me to unwrap everyone from their cotton-wool existence and spell out some home truths. Obviously I would never go public in what I plan to say to any rider, be it good or bad comments....as someone who has ridden myself, I am fully aware that no one ever goes out to deliberately underperform"

3rd July

Scunthorpe Speedway Away wins are a rare commodity in speedway but the Henderson Insurance Scunthorpe Scorpions claimed their second of the season last night at Newport.

Red5 "So here we are no one going through for the GP Qualifyer Final. What has got to be done for this to change, Training Teaching and Track time. Support with Finance proper support and an infrastructure that gives GB a chance. Poland do it, Sweden, Denmark, Ausies come over here and take over the team places that our riders should have! It really is a sad state of affairs and the BSPA are to blame, Self centered individuals who want the money from the sport but wont give back.

All it wants is World Cup failure and it will complete the season of hell for the fans.

Wolverhampton British Final £20 and just to put money in CVS till. Promoters walking around like they were doing a good job, fat ar---es living of the fans, nice blazer with a badge and a freeby entry. By the end of August the promoters should be making the rules for next year, get round the table and know the rules before play of finals. Rules should be in Public domain by then, so contracts can be sorted and agreed, if a rider knows by October where he will be next season he has a chance to obtain local sponsorship to help him along. Elite Teams MUST have 3 Brits minimum, not Double uppers. BSPA Super Seven, All monies after basic expenses should go to training fund,Appoint a Team Manager and give him the budget to do the job. Enter the World Under 21 WC, bring youth on.This has to be a long term position, Test Matches Seven man team, Two against Aussies in GB, Two against Poland Home and Away,Two against Denmark Home and Away. Sky coverage, give riders the chance to mention their sponsors, Tatum and co should give sponsors the opportunity. Cameras should Pan on Signage. If Sponsors do not get anything from the sport they will be gone. Yes there is lots to do before the end of the season if we as a nation are to climb the ladder internationally."

Niels Kristian Iversen* "Nothing is better than a allnighter in the van, been pissin down the past 400km and its still wet when arrived to Leszno. Happy days, NOT"

Mads Korneliussen* "5min from the track and they call it off, only 24hour round trip. Polska is stupit, they could have called it off yesterday"

Mads Korneliussen* "989km to go for a sleep then testing tomorrow"

Mads Korneliussen* "So my tweet earlyer was misunderstood, 24 hour drive for nothing is stupid, not polska. Sorry polska. I did not mean to affend you"

Dakota North* "hello"

Linus Sundstrom* "Wonder how much you save in a year if all meetings goes ahead like they should do? Spending far too much on flights and shit for nothing!"

Nicolai Klindt* "this year [Denmark] swc suit looks absolutely crap! easy to see it ain't maliniak who designed it"

Mads Korneliussen* "Driving on the way to Denmark. Still about 6 hours to go. 2nd night in the van in a row. Gotta love it."

Lewis Bridger* "Hopefully my Ktm150 will be rebuilt for next weekend so i can put in some Hot laps !!"

Nicolai Klindt* "out of me skin here! just got on board on the ferry from latvia and it's absolutely shit. no wifi or anything here.."

Malcolm Vasey "Stoke may move back to the PL but that is not my decision and as far as I am aware nothing has been decided"

Hans Andersen* "Having a blast on the ferry Think the average age is 45-55 on this ferry!"

Michael Lee "I know it's the same for everybody, but that was a bad track. I'm just glad we came away with all our riders intact. It was my first visit to Buxton in eight years and there doesn't seem to have been much development, which is sad because it has all the makings of a great little speedway"

4th July

Rob Godfrey "I thought Michael's arrival ignited the whole team. He breathed life into the rest of them"

Philip Rising "WEMBLEY was the spiritual home for international speedway and, in its day, one of the world's top stadiums. But, having seen every World Final there from 1962 and covered numerous soccer events, including the 1966 World Cup final, it was also vastly over-rated in my opinion. It has never been any easy place to get to, by road or public transport, the facilities used to be very poor, disgusting toilets, inaccessible bars and food outlets (not that you would want to eat anything) terraces rather than seating for the majority and a race track that wasn't anywhere near as good as many remember through (as you say) rose-coloured spectacles. It did, of course, have a great atmosphere generated by a crowd double that we now get at Cardiff but the fact that you arrived not knowing who would be World Champion and left knowing who was was a major factor too. You are right, there were no World Finals rained off at Wembley but the huge cost of staging a British GP to the standard now required (and I am talking about the overall show here not just the racing itself) almost demands the extra insurance of a roof. But the roof also cuts out daylight and helps generate the atmosphere inside the Millennium which would otherwise be impossible in mid to late June. I have been lucky enough to witness many top sporting events around the world and honestly think the current British GPs stand comparison with most if not all. It is also worth remembering that the Millennium authorities enjoy having speedway there and bend over backwards to be helpful and co-operative. I am not sure that would be the case elsewhere and certainly not at the new Wembley where efforts by Barry Briggs to have a permanent speedway museum established are falling on deaf ears."

Philip Rising "TRUST me, speedway will get no more noticed at Wembley than the Millennium. I have been to the new Wembley several times and while I recognise and applaud its virtues to say that it wipes the floor with the Millennium is rubbish. And look at its location... would you like to spend a weekend there?"

Philip Rising "YOU obviously don't go to London much ... which is much more expensive then Cardiff. And, of course, Wembley isn't in London for starters. Nigel Pearson is no more likely to get Talksport interested just because an event is at Wembley rather than the Millennium....British national newspapers have absolutely no interest in speedway for many reasons, including a general dislike of motorbikes, and until such time as there is a British 'Tomasz Gollob' will remain apathetic and even that might not be enough."

Ludvig Lindgren* "On the coach to the airport! Lady next to me is smelling shit but hopefully I stink worse"

Ludvig Lindgren* "i need sleep but i cant sleep why is the world so cruel against me?gotta w8 for linus sundstrom and his neck pillow on the flight!"

Nicolai Klindt* "you two [Hans & Casper] can piss off with your ferry. you should have been on ours. think it was too cheap!! finally arrived in sweden after the worst boattrip in my life and i have been on a few i would say. but anyway... västervik here we come!"

David Watt* "Back in the UK and back in traffic on my way to peter johns racing with some engines that need his love !!!"

Andy Povey* "Is on a train heading to the BSPA HQ in Rugby"

Ludvig Lindgren* "oh and how nice is it to wait in the que?? cant w8 'till passport control!!!"

Dakota North* "just had a nice dinner with danae"

Hans Andersen* "practice practice practice AND after that even more practice practice practice ;-)"

Fredrik Lindgren* "Some huge queues at Stansted when we arrived today. Hopefully I'll be able to work today, don't want more cancellations"

Fredrik Lindgren* "New date for our rainoff yesterday in Poland is Wednesday! Just got info so has booked my flights and sorted all, late bookings cost £$€ !!"

Lewis Bridger* "Okay mate i will work a date out or something uk is so bullshit for testing ay ?"

Darcy Ward* "on the gas brother!! for one ride then meet this guy called Nicki"

Lee Richardson* "Feel sorry for anyone that paid to watch the wacky races at belle vue tonight.."

Rory Schlein* "Another max but lucky know one got hurt tonight track was dangerous as"

Jim Lynch "I guess there will be complaints from the Lakeside management and riders about the condition of the track in the first half of the meeting. But people must understand that if we put on a slick track it would be like giving the keys of the castle to Lakeside. Craig [Cook] didn't like the track early on but he still went out there and had his best meeting for us."

Fredrik Lindgren* "Have I done this before? Yes I have! On my way from Wolves to Stansted on a Monday night!

Fredrik Lindgren* Love is floating, me & PK alone in the car listening to Heart FM! Think we might be clicking!"

Reverend Michael Whawell "Darcy attempted the most hair-raising last bend - spectacular to watch; could have killed somebody......and he didn't score many, either."

Chris Holder* "The long drive back to Poole! Jet ski time tomorrow onlygettingbetter!!!!! LTD!"

Hans Andersen* "Just chillin In Hultsfred sweden, not a lot to dó but what are the chances In a Pro riders lifes these days to completely dó nothing !"

Dannii Simmonds "Think I better set the record straight here! My name is Dannii Simmonds, wife of Mark! The comments I make on the Plymouth forum and the updates site is that of a speedway supporter NOT that of a riders wife. I have followed speedway long before I met Mark, my father rode at Exeter until he died racing at Exeter 30 years ths year. I follow the updates in support of my team (usually I know whats going on before anyone else as I have my own personal updaters- our daughter!!!) I was completely shocked at the updates from Najjer, and agreed with Adam74 that the updates were a disgrace on Friday evening, this was against both teams, not just Plymouth. I then joined the updates on Saturday as I didnt go to Plymouth (a seven year old and Transformers 3 beckoned!!!) The comments about Mark didn't bother me at all, hes a big boy and can look after himself but when I read the comment made about a member of the track staff I was horrified. The comment was relating to heat 4 after the fence was damaged and went something like...another bloke with long hair comes over to have a look...oh no, its a SHE MALE. Well, THATS

MY SISTER YOU ARE TALKING ABOUT YOU ARSE!"

Chris Holder* "I'm officially darcy wards spell check.... Has asked me over 100 times on the way home so far! #Neveradullmoment"

Ludvig Lindgren* "feel absolute shit after the crash my stomach is hurting like hell and knee is swelling up! oh and a bent bike.....again. oh and f*ck being positive from now on Im gonna do what i do best and that is staying miserables and negative!"

5th July

Fredrik Lindgren* "Phew nearly missed my flight because of some valves in my bag. Stansted security, it's ok they search my bag but not that it took 25 min"

Rory Schlein* "Easy jet gets my vote over ryainair every day"

Mr S Bear "Proud Potter [Malcolm Vasey] claims that recent problems at Stoke "have not been of our making" Therefore who was responsible for the following? At the Under 21 QR meeting there being no flag marshal on the second bend Allowing the first running of the Buxton Knockout cup meeting to start with a generator in a worse state than the Greek economy especially a generator which runs both the track lights and the air fence which is surely a health and safety risk Amending the readmission policy following the Buxton meeting and therefore asking fans for £4 who attempted to use their programmes to gain free admission as per the terms of entrance in their programmes especially as the revised readmission policy is not a BSPA/SCB regulation. Running an amateur meeting with no ambulance cover.

Having fans wait 2 hours for a paramedic to turn up especially when the paramedic claims he did not receive a booking. Telling these fans that "at least it was a nice day" Malcolm your team may be good but off the track the promotion at Stoke seems to go from one cock up to another and the public relation side of the promotion is a diaster and therefore it is little wonder that you met many former regulars who no longer go and many neutrals limit their visits to the bare minimum."

Hans Andersen* "Oh In case any one knows any In need of second hand race sults, boots etc I'M selling out"

Nicolai Klindt* "Tai's comment on after match parade was Ben forgets i have to race him for next 10 years-unlucky Ben!!" classic"

Lewis Bridger* "I want to be a Hero in the SWC i need a shot.. Hope somebody will stand up & realise i should be there SWC round 2 !!!"
Chris Holder* "hahaha well get on the gas then!"
Darcy Ward* "talk the talk then walk the walk son"
Lewis Bridger* "so barker is going to do a better job in Gorzow than me.. ?? Bullshit"
Nicolai Klindt* "u uk boys not even gonna go gorzow"

David Watt* "Can't resist ! I'm going on the jet ski with darcy ward and chris holder. Let the games begin !!!"
Chris Holder* "Jus finished jet ski'n with darcy ward and david watt. way to many near misses!!! haha could of ended in tears"

Lee Richardson* "Had a sleep and shower, and just had sum lunch with nickki p! Were off to vastervik in an hour! Straight in the van to Poland afterwards!"
Nicolai Klindt* "don't bother coming mate. you will leave with nothing"

Ludvig Lindgren* "still feel like shit feels like ive been demolished by a truck in diffrent words I feel how Nicolai Klindt looks"

Nicolai Klindt* "is it true what i heard - that you am #flippinforaliving???"
Lewis Bridger* "haha like fuck am I.. It makes me sick even smelling the greasyyy burger vans just lee richardson and david watt winding me up KUNTSSS!!"
David Watt* "I seen him flipping burgers. Turn 1 at Poole. JD says you're a good worker !!"
Lee Richardson* "dad (Jd) said your talents will be wasted at gorzow! He said you're 1 of the best burger flippers he's had!! don't worry lbr dad (Jd) got bigger plans for you than the world cup! Glastonbury festival is coming up!"

Mike Hunter "The [WTC] meeting will lose virtually ALL of its appeal if the Russian team isn't there in full"

Colin Barber "Oh I don't think that is so, Gollob is still a bigger pull than the Russian. After all you see Gollob once a season normally at the Millennium stadium - currently you see Emil at Elite league tracks (when available). Tomasz is still probably the biggest pull in the world and I don't think many people will beat him around KL, he can still produce magical moves that Emil has even dreamt of yet!"

Mads Korneliussen* "Busy flight, hate it Ryanair why is everyone flying on a tuesday night, i don't get it"

Jayne Moss "Feel free to show us how its done then"

Kenni Larsen* "I dont care what people says. Mads korneliussen has fully deserved to be in the danish national team. Who else should it be"

Fredrik Lindgren* "All alone in my hotel bed!... And now I can't sleep damn it!"

6th July

Niels Kristian Iversen* "I Like Copenhagen airport but shit mé the foods are pricey. 104.dkr for a sandwich and a juice"

Hans Andersen* "hi mate, Might not get to ride no more In uk this season SO Might have Them 2 rollers for ya early..."

Lewis Bridger* "hey mate, really speedway can be shit when you havn't got the meetings & $$$$ rolling in ay.. Well put them down to me 4sure"

Scott Nicholls* "Not been on for a bit. Lewis Bridger still going on about the bloody swc!If his results were good as his Twitter effort he'd be world champion!"

Chris Holder* "hahahahahaha yep"

Lewis Bridger* "Head is down mate im ready to walk the walk after all the talk the talk but no Fueking meetings till the 18th"

Scott Nicholls* "then lift ya head up mate, stop the talking & prove the doubters wrong with ya ability from the 18th!"

Jan O. Pedersen [48] "I've bought a bike from Nicki Pedersen and I've done some laps in Poland. I would love to start racing competitively again but I wanted my first rides in England to be in front of the Cradley fans."

Lee Richardson* "In the van on the way to Zielona gora! Gave crumpy a lift think we might head into town for some lunch"

Hans Andersen* "Just a bit of info: reason i might not race anymore In UK this year is due to ONLY ONE 8 point rider per team RULE. ballocks"

Ludvig Lindgren* "Gotta love the weather in England! sun, rain, sun, heavy rain...worst rain ive seen in my life here in the uk is absoluteley smashing down!"

Roman Chyla "Chairman of Zielona Gora team in Poland has come up with an idea of running Polish League matches in 2012 on Saturdays, instead of Sundays. He argues that fans increasingly moan about Sunday evening matches because not everyone lives locally and when they come home it is very late. Next day, Monday they have in prospect an early morning rush and going to work. He conveniently does not mention that Saturday is SGP night. I wonder what BSI will have to say to that, because right now it looks as though Polish club chairmen see themselves as pipers who can call any tune they like (money talks)."

Crazy Sue "After discussions over the last few days and in agreement with the people involved in the troubles of the last few days, we will still be covering Plymouth's updates as and when we have a texter...this will start from the meeting this week as a texter and updater has already been arranged. The 'removal' of the Plymouth section on Updates was a measure intended to take some heat out of the situation, to stop the gawpers making things worse, not just for us but for those outside of updates and mentioned on the update also. We were not requested to remove the section, we were not requested to stop covering Plymouth home meetings, the moving of the

Plymouth section was my decision and mine alone with no pressure being brought to bear from the promotion or anyone else. The Plymouth section will be moved back to its rightful place in the next day or so (it was never deleted, merely moved safely to another area out of the public eye), to allow further cooling of the situation. As the owner of the site, I am ultimately and legally responsible for whatever is written on there and because of that, I take full responsibilty for the upset and distress the comments cause, I can only apologise from the bottom of my heart for this and I will endeavour that it doesn't happen again. Hope that clears up a few confuzzled things over the last few days."

Lewis Bridger* "Fu€k i knew i should have gone for the Bigger Gb Xbox i have just used up all my memory just installing Forza 3 tracks cars etc.."

Niels Kristian Iversen* "Does fastfood make you go fast ???"

Linus Sundstrom* "Have a 2007 gm engine for sale that i used 90% of the meetings in PL last year. Done 4 heats since service. Contact me if you're intrested :)"

Philip Rising "The old one-off World Finals had run their course... Bradford, Norden, Vojens ... please! And how often would GB be allocated a final now anyway ... once every four years, five, ten? As previously said, I have been lucky enough to attend many top class sporting events (Champions League, Ashes cricket, etc, etc) and the British GP at the Millennium is right up there with any of them in my opinion. Speedway isn't missing a trick ... Cardiff is ideal and from what I gather will continue to be so for a long while yet"

Mads Korneliussen* "Lost at poole today, I hat 10/5. Poole boys was Very fast"

Nicolai Klindt* "i felt good today... 3 blinders from gate 4 and what? thanks alot to luke corbett for some good work! 14+2p/6heat"

Nigel Pearson* "Productive day on dudley heathens duty in the media, back to the proper job tomorrow!"

Lewis Bridger* "Got my new Xbox setup down at my Gf's with all the Extras was a right nightmere with the HD leads at 1st but we got it hooked !!"

Linus Sundstrom* "Gahhh, i was so ready for my first EL max tonight but threw it all away in ht 15 with a silly crash! Good team performance tonight"

7th July

Lee Richardson* "I'm at the plaza in Wroclaw lbr, where are you??? Casino it might have been! Lol"

Emma Richardson* "you stay out of there!"

Lee Richardson* "u cheeky minx thought u wanted me to come home as only been home 1 night in nearly 2 weeks! Thought u were asleep??? X"

Lewis Bridger* "fukk no way man i love that joint haha Concusion or no concusion im a winner in there!!"

Lee Richardson* "exactly. u always been a winner at the park plaza!!!!"

Lee Richardson* "Going home!!! Looking forward to seeing my wife and boys! Been home only twice in 2 weeks! And now 10 days off!!"

Chris Holder* "On way to the world cup... Let's get it on! at vojens... Rekn it will rain? Always does!"

Linus Sundstrom* "Just landed in västerås, now off to grandma to get some propper food before tonights meeting! Yoyoyo go with the flow"

Lewis Bridger* "What is going on with my Season had 3weeks off i need to make $$$$ Bad !!"

Lee Richardson* "no Poland then lbr???"

Lewis Bridger* "u no im not in poland at the moment.. Taking backwards steps to move forward"

Lee Richardson* "get back there lbr!!! Need to be riding in Europe mate!! Get some meetings in germany and Denmark!!"

Lewis Bridger* "yea i no m8 i have some meetings in Germany coming up plus Summin else maybe in the pipeline haha"

Fredrik Lindgren* "Been for some food at Ikea, #meatballs #yummy on our way to B'ham pissing it down with rain where I am!"

Dakota North* "Time for bed goodnight"

Lewis Bridger* "Im going to Kill the Gym tonight Circuit training to the Max then a 20kg Cycle"

Jan Staechmann* "Sat in BA lounge in Manchester waiting for flight home to see ma & pa, & then SWC starts Saturday at Vojens, w Darren Fletcher & Steve Saint"

Niels Kristian Iversen* "5k run now. Then i better get some ink for the printer. Got 2 extra yellow, black and red but no blue. Guess what colour the printer need ??"

David Watt* "Talking crap with the boys in Denmark out side the hotel !!!"

Nigel Pearson* "Phone red hot today, just want to confirm I AM NOT buying Swindon Speedway. Where do rumours start?!"

Speedway Star* "STOLEN SPEEDWAY BIKES! Taken in the Gorton area, 2 black bikes, 1 is a laydown Jawa, the other is a Weslake"

> **Fredrik Lindgren*** "Oh boy, all hotels full down by Stansted Airport! So stupid not to have booked this one before. Will be a night at the Airport floor!"
>
> **Kenni Larsen*** "like me yesterday mate. Buy a sleeping bag at bishop stortford services."
>
> **Mads Korneliussen*** "did it last night, not to bad. Good for your back"

Graham Drury "It was the biggest one-point thrashing you are ever likely to see at Perry Barr!"

8th July

Kenni Larsen* "On my way to Dk. My god the roads in Sweden are boring!"

Lewis Bridger* "Fat Burners = Bad news for sleep"

Niels Kristian Iversen* "Hates when the shuttlebus takes off right in front of your nose. Is it really that hard to wait 3 more sec. ?? #buswanker"

Fredrik Lindgren* "Slept better then expected on the concrete floor! Am through security control and it's still 2h to my flight to Billund, DK"

Fredrik Lindgren* "Almost the whole Danish team on this flight. I eat bacon for breakfast!"

Gary Patchett* "It's raining in Vojens. What a surprise. Why do they keep going there ;-)?"

Hans Andersen* "at least some of you boyz Got some Jetski practice In the other day so advantage Aussies :)"

Linus Sundstrom* "boarded the wizz flight to gdansk, last meeting tomorrow before the break!Been on a plane every day so far this week"

BSPA Newly-appointed Lions Team Manager, Jason Attwood, said: "I am pleased with the support David Hemsley has given me during the negotiations to sign Kauko. In my eyes he is a proven Premier League number one.

Not Len Silver* "Just had a call from the Borders agency, looking for a Kurt Shields whose visa has expired, Kurt who I said?"

Jan Staechmann* "A bit strange seeing someone else in charge of the National Team, but very nice reception from the boys. I wish them nothing but the best."

Linus Sundstrom* "Finaly at the hotel in gniezno,not gonna do alot more today!Might go down the supermarket & buy myself some sweets as its friday"

Paul Burbidge* "For the first and only time this year, I'll be covering an SGP/SWC meeting from home tomorrow night. Roll on King's Lynn!"

> **Linus Sundstrom*** "Bored so looking around here on twitter,loads of speedway riders have on there profile "pro speedway rider"? When can you call yourself pro?"
>
> **Jeff Scott*** "when you have a van to write it on?"
>
> **Linus Sundstrom*** "By the look of it, its when you have 2 bikes and a van with your name on!"
>
> **Nicolai Klindt*** "when you are only doing speedway. no school, no work, no nothing!"

Linus Sundstrom* "Nicolai Klindt is a pro all the way trough! Just look at his kit with painted arai's and fly high edition kevlars"

Nicolai Klindt* "haha, yea but i don't have any "sundström business partners". that's a bummer!"

Nicolai Klindt* "i'm gonna grow my hair again!"

Claudia Staechmann* "i forbid it you are much hotter with short hair"

Nicolai Klindt* "i may do, but it's long is cool!"

Lewis Bridger* "Im on some next Bike ride in the Rain i love this training makes me feel invinsible"

Linus Sundstrom* "I know that seb alden is sniffing around here on twitter nearly every day, get your fingers out and join the crew maaate!"

Derek Barclay "My, of my were there traffic problems! Still, was grateful that my good friend Christina [Turnbull] was slightly behind us in the appalling traffic queues so getting there late [for Hackney v IoW] but before the ref meant missed no action!....Outstanding performance (and what a HUGE improvement on previous AE showings..) was from Brandon Freemantle - holding off Nick Simmons on a T/R in heat 13 could be a real watershed in this young man's career"

9th July

Neil Middleditch "Bridger is a bit like Ben, if he can get a bit more focussed, I know he's got the talent but he's lost his way a little bit."

Lewis Bridger* "Can't believe what Dickhead's were out tonight 1word for it Dickheads !! unreal 2mandown #matefuckedoff #pussy"

Kenni Larsen* "ahhh så er man i gaten. Russiske tøser. På med kyskes bæltet for her kommer FAR!! (ahhh, then you are at the gate. Russian girls. On with the chastity belt because here comes the DADDY!)"

Speedway Star "Ex-referee Daryl Clark has been jailed for six years for a string of sex offences"

Lewis Bridger* "Finds it so funny how I only get x1 night out from a pair of shoes !!"

Graham Reeve "We are such a close sport that our Child Protection policy will only work if people think about it. The charges had nothing whatsoever to do with speedway and we do have a very rigorous vetting system. If any rider or their parents has any notion of what they might consider a strange approach, they should make it known to the Child Protection officer at the track, to myself or Gary Thompson at the Auto-cyle Union."

Speedway Star "Engine tuner Tommy Nicholls has called on the authorities to do spot engine checks to put paid to rumours doing the rounds at the moment. Illegal carburettors and illegal silencers, so the whispering goes, are allegedly being used both here and abroad.... 'if they were involved in an accident that resulted in a death, that bike would be confiscated and checked over. Should anything be found illegal, the insurance would lapse for everybody involved' he claims."

Graham Drury "I have to say that it is unlikely that Birmingham Speedway will be signing Hans Andersen, there have been enquiries behind the scenes but it's a complicated issue."

Anders Mellgren "I love this life. I live for riding speedway. I love this sport so much and this is what I want to do."

Speedway Star [advert] "Attention all riders. To any rider who has bought a Danish illegal copy of the Briggo Dirt Deflector. The Briggo Dirt Deflector arm is made of superior material and has a proven safety record. You can swap your copy arm for a Briggo homologated arm for a one time price of only £25.00. This offer is for 1 month only and finishes on 1st August 2011. Keep our speedway tracks safe...think of your fellow riders"

Colin Pratt "[Przemyslaw Pawlicki] is such a clever rider for one so young, and I am convinced he would make an impression in the Grand Prix given the opportunity."

Dick Barrie "It is only fair to also mention the Rye House riders – representing a club guilty in the past of making complaints and offering excuses at the drop of a grain of dust – were helpful and supportive during last Saturday's long-drawn-out proceedings"

David Helmsley "Sergey started the season like I thought he would, but he has lost all his form, lost his confidence on the track and is riding like a novice. He needs to go away and sort himself out."

Dick Barrie "When I was in Oz earlier this year, there were reports on TV of a suspicious package having been reported to the Darwin police. Following a major security scare, it turned out to be a bottle of shower-gel."

Neil Middleditch "Edward Kennett has got his professional head, a few years ago he didn't seem to be very motivated but he is now"

Danny Warwick "Being without a team place at the start of the year, I was a bit upset, you don't let life get you down and just keep working hard. I've been working this year for Renat Gafurov"

John Hall "We knew we couldn't make Norway if we did the Pairs as it would have meant driving all the way from Somerset to Newcastle, and that would have killed us. And there's going to be trouble again because we can't ride at Scunthorpe, so the s**t is going to hit the fan. But what can you do? We were committed to the FIM and the longtrack and Leicester knew that when we signed."

David Helmsley "I am learning all the time, and what I have learnt here is that the rules are there to be broken. It's dog eat dog out there and I am happy to mix with the worst of them."

Chris Holder* "Looks like the rain is coming! NOOOOO!"

Scott Nicholls* "u're in vojens,what do u expect! I'm sure vojens probably means "gonna piss down" or something in Latin"

Nicolai Klindt* "just need a shower, then i'm ready to go to vojens as a 'supportive reserve'"

Lee Richardson* "could get use to the limo bit!! Maybe us boys should travel like this!! F$ck chav air!!!"

Paul Burbidge* "Hope the rain clears up in Vojens - I hear they've had a downpour. Not a cloud in the sky over sunny Dorset!"

Nicolai Klindt* "boring in vojens, just waiting for the cover to come off so we can have a track walk!"

Nicolai Klindt* "good crowd in vojens. track looks slick as f*ck tho..."

Nicki Pedersen* "you know these tracks in the World Cup & GPs, they're never going to be grippy like the league meetings"

Lee Richardson* "Robbie Williams....one word....awesome. Take that were bloody awesome!!! 86,000 can't be wrong"

Dave Rattenberry "There's a lot of good people in speedway and I enjoy it and there are also a lot of arseholes"

Chris Holder* "Ahh race off it is! Hopefully some more dirt in gorzow :-)))"

Nigel Pearson* "Lesson learnt – every speedway track should have covers as well as an air fence!"

Fredrik Lindgren* "On my way back home from Vojens, we'll drive all night! Serious thinking going on, need some drastic change with my gating! Gate practice!"

Chris Neath* "I hope len wasn't dropping hints when he told me 'nothing lasts forever'. Don't he know I'm a Rye House lifer!"

Niels Kristian Iversen* "Tonight was a struggle. Im happy my teammates did the goods. Its awesome we are strait in the final. Got a week now to sort out my shit"

Niels Kristian Iversen* "Just watched tonights meeting. A fucking donkey ón crutches could have done ny job. Only way is forward. Final it is"

Nigel Pearson* "Best job in the world, Speedway World Cup, Matchplay Darts next week, Italian SGP then the new football season"

Ian Rae "[Alex Edberg is] one amazing young lad and received great support from the collection [£1012.22] from a crowd limited in numbers thanks to the dodgy weather."

Pete Simmons "I'm convinced the [Leicester] airfence saved Lasse's life. Both he and Nieminen were flat out as they headed towards it. It was one of those crashes where you are reluctant to run over and see what the result is. Lasse being so small helped, his body absorbed the impact, he's not all arms and legs."

10th July

Scott Nicholls* "Some dickhead just moaned that there's not a wardrobe on the plane. It's Wizz air!! Funny times"

BSPA IPSWICH'S Danish youngster Lasse Bjerre has suffered a suspected broken femur in a crash at Leicester

Chris Hunt "We are sweating on the fitness of Gary Cottham following a workshop accident whilst working on his bike, he needed 30 stitches in one finger"

Scott Nicholls* "It's pretty funny to watch other peoples arguments...not funny when it's ya own though!reckon I look like a right tool.Cruel world sometimes"

> **Scott Nicholls*** "Well done to the Tossers, [danes] at round one of the swc. :-)"
>
> **Nicolai Klindt*** "cheers fella! only cuz i was such a good national coach/manager. but ain't getting a ride so going in for emil on monday"
>
> **Scott Nicholls*** "maybe u should be rider/coach at swindon then!"

Dakota North* "Goodnight, off to work the old mans quarry's tomorrow, il show you what real men drive. CAT"

Troy Batchelor* "Wants to be in my house now ! Not stuck in traffic fuck"

Nicolai Klindt* "have no energy atm. just done my room and changed it with help of Luke Corbett and now waiting a minute before going chinese with pappa"

> **Darcy Ward*** "Can't wait to get home and do abit of fuk all"
>
> **Rupert Rigsby*** "Jeez, another one to unfollow, must be an Australian speedway rider trait!"

Alex Harkess "Matthew Wethers was the only [Edinburgh] rider using a Prodrive Silencer [at Newcastle], the rest were all using King. For his last ride Matthew borrowed the silencer from Kalle Katajisto's spare bike and had his best ride of the night. I don't think he will switch back now."

Mike Bennett* "The bigger the crowd, the better the meeting for me so bring it on!"

11th July

Scott Nicholls* "What a silly time [03.45] of the day to have to get up this is. I love my bed!"

Neil Middleditch "The Poles don't frighten me as much as I thought they would. Being champions it's a big ask for them, the pressure is on them"

Gary Patchett "Ronnie [Russell] has stood down by mutual consent. This will allow him to fully focus on the preparation of the track and relaying the top bend which has been badly affected by the ingress of sand from the dog track. Jan [Staechmann] was the only candidate considered for the [team manager] position and is very enthusiastic about the role. As a former rider he will be able to relate to the riders from that perspective."

Roman Chyla "I think you're right about that "thing" between Ryan and Jason, but tell me why would you put Dave (Watt) instead of Troy (Batchelor). In my opinion, right now Troy is having the best time of his riding career. He is doing very well at Leszno and not too bad in BEL either. Dave on the other hand has only 19th CMA (7.79) in the Polish second tier League One."

Laurence Rogers "Whilst at the grass track at Bridgnorth yesterday I heard that Charlie Gjedde's workshop had been destroyed in a blaze on Saturday night with bikes and equipment all lost in the fire. Tried to contact Charlie last night and he sent me a text this morning that it was true. This is a massive blow to the popular Dane who now needs to rebuild his stable of bikes and riding equipment etc"

Hans Andersen* "Making My way towards UK to check up on things AND Cut the grass at My house..... Not been able to dó it since i broke My leg"

Mike Bennett* "Hmmm same as last year - heard but not seen for most of the night!"

Hans Andersen* "Sorry for All the tweets forks, just trying to beat Greg Hancock to Twitter slut champ haha"

Lewis Bridger* [on Ben Barker after 2 rides, nil points] "GOONRIDER that's all im saying haha"

Fredrik Lindgren* "Looks like we'll have to beat Team GB in the Race Off Thursday! Sweet as!"

Mike Bennett* "Nobody told me it was Bomber in heat 14"

Nigel Pearson [after KK race win] "This is what frustrates Graham Drury"

Neil Middleditch "Ben isn't usually a nervous person but it is a big meeting"

Nigel Pearson "Ben rides for Plymouth in the Premier League and Birmingham in the Elite League and now here he is in the Word Cup"

Kelvin Tattum "He wouldn't be human if he wasn't nervous tonight"

Neil Middleditch]after Scott falls on a t/r] "I'm speechless!"

Sam Ermolenko "I think when Scott Nicholls goes out and makes a mistake on the first corner, it puts everyone under pressure"

Keith Huewen "There's a couple of Dryml brothers who're going to be going home with some dirt this evening"

Chris Louis "It looked like he went down a bit easy but you did touch him"

Tai Woffinden "Guess it's the Dryml sisters"

Keith Huewin "Minus Tai again, he's going to have to calm himself down"

Mark Loram "What they (Buster at King's Lynn) do in five minutes is the equivalent of 15 minutes at any other track"

Nigel Pearson "Scott is still a class act – on his day"

K Kasprzak "Silencer and I put wrong set up and wrong engine – must completely change set up...I try best to try to make the points for Birmingham for rest of the season"

Nigel Pearson "Chris Louis seems to think that Ben Barker has rode himself into the team in Gorzow, I'm not so sure about that"

Neil Middleditch "I said to Ben to go out and prove me wrong...his chin was on the floor – to see that smile was really worth it!"

Kelvin Tattum "Harris was literally the meat in the sandwich"

Nigel Pearson "Heroic display from Chris Harris"

Kelvin Tattum "Moley recognises that"

Nigel Pearson "DNS off the outside is Does Not Start"

Nicolai Klindt* "heard your in gorzow?"

Lee Richardson* "no mate afraid not"

Nicolai Klindt* "i'll take ur spot then"

Rob Peasley "I couldn't believe what I was seeing there. With all those people down in the Team GB pit, surely someone should have spotted that Woffinden needed to finish behind Topinka in that final race. Such tactical naivety... If we could have got the Russians out of the race-off, it would have made things just a bit easier on Thursday.... Just noticed that tonight: Ben Barker - scored 6 out of a possible 9 Scott Nicholls - scored 6 out of a possible 18"

Bagpuss "Saw Olly there tonight (not in team shirt though) but not King, Stead or Bridger, and as squad members you'd think they would be. The team spirit didn't seem as good this year"

Gaz W "'Here comes the British joker, Scott Nicholls'. Has there ever been a truer statement?"

Bagpuss "Regarding the organisation side of things the overflow carpark wasn't signposted (the usual entrance wasn't in use) which seemed a bit daft and Buster definitely needs to get some extra loos when 5k people are expected!"

Lewis Bridger* "LMFAO !!"

Lewis Bridger * [2 hours later] "I am so the happiest man alive right now"
Peter Johns* "why is this then, you had the call?"
Hans Andersen* "don't brung your strongest engine as track Will be slick assss"

Charlie Webster* "Speedway banter in the petrol station in the middle of nowhere...and a milkshake and some sweeties keep me going on drove home!"

Charlie Webster* "Home but listened to Ibiza set live on drive back from DJ Laidback Luke and ate too many sweeties now 'wired!' with my dancing head on!"

12th July

Paul Burbidge* "Lewis Bridger joins the GB ranks to replace Scott Nicholls, who sits out Race-Off to look after partner Sophie, who recently had surgery."

Lewis Bridger* "Great job from Team GB tonight i just hope we can kick ass Thursday"
Lee Richardson* "now you're in you after all the noise you've made you better produce the goods...;)"

Nigel Pearson* "Morning all, in Farnham hotel ready to head to voiceover for swc highlights show with Kelv. Good effort by GB last night, Poland 2 strong"

Dakota North* "Steak night!"

Mads Korneliussen* "Ryanair sort your fu&king website out!! Plonkers"

Mike Bennett* "back to the day job for the rest of the week after speedway World Cup last night. Good to catch up with Nigel Pearson again!"

Chris Holder* "Flat out like a one legged man in an ass kickin comp this morning!! Not use to all this work burnout"

Nicolai Klindt* "jobs done! now town and then accountance to answer on loads og question"

David Watt* "Love riding bikes but all the other stuff that surrounds it can go and get f..."
Chris Holder "Yeeeeeeeep"

Nicola Sands* "there are days I wish Ryanair didn't fly! Certainly would not call them awesome!!"

Hans Andersen* "Driving up an down England to try find a job ;-) finished down South so now aiming north"

Hans Andersen* "Sooo made up to midlands now :-) wonder if anyone around here has a job for me"

Hans Andersen* "Might be able to Cast some light over My UK future end of the week."

Linus Sundstrom* "Today i swear im not doin anything! Trallalallalalla . Did not even watch the SWC yesterday"

Scott Nicholls* "Thanks for all the nice tweets. What a sh*tty night that was! Feeling rather 2nd today! Wanna wish the boys all the best for race off"

Mads Korneliussen* at 23.45 "Can't sleep, workshop it is then"

Chris Neath* "Ritchie Hawkins quote 'Chicks dig scars'. Seems like they like pink pants 2!"

13th July

Richard Hollingsworth "(Richard Hall) is having his best season in the Premier League so it is a surprise he is available and full credit to Rob for signing him".

Lewis Bridger "I don't like the kid full stop. [Ben Barker] tries to like me but I don't like him. It's got to work, though, because we are doing it for Team GB. It's nothing to do with me and him and it's the same with Edward because we have problems at the moment....There are a few things Barker says and he comes out with snide remarks...I have no problem with Edward but the thing with my girlfriend is a bit messed up. He'll get over it, though, and I'm sure we'll sort it out in the future. We've spoken on the phone and we were fine and we need to get over it because Neil has made it clear that he'll be really angry if we let it affect the team atmosphere at all. It can't happen and I'm certainly not going to mess it up"

Fredrik Lindgren* "Checked some statistics in British EL! My average is actually better away from home! That much for a Monmore specialist! H/10:00 A/10:23"

Lewis Bridger* [c28 hours after WTC call up] "Workshop time finished around 15hr's in 48hr's prepping for SWC can't wait !!"

Chris Neath* "Drunken chat with Ritchie and he just told me he's died 3 times racing. WoWww! warrior"

Jan Staechmann* "BA bacon sandwiches in the lounge at T5! Love it! Wifi is abit slow mind. Is that to give you extra time to enjoy the bacon rolls I wonder?"

Nicki Glanz* "Its 8:23 and iam soaking wet! Good if i was a woman, but not when your working flat out"

Nicolai Klindt* "another nights sleep done! fuck me i'm getting good at this!"

Nigel Pearson* "Heading to Heathrow to meet up with Sky Sports colleagues for SWC trip to Berlin! Keith Huewen is driver to Gorzow, hat and gloves ready!"

Chris Holder* "Cancelled flight! And cracked screen on my phone! It can only get better!"

Bryn Williams "I understand the FIM told Buster to change the light bulb in his red light. I think they got a short answer"

Philip Rising "RED faces at the FIM ... it would seem that the sport's governing body are powerless to prevent Emil Sayfutdinov riding for Russia in the SWC race-off at Gorzow tomorrow despite their protestations to the contrary. Apparently there is no actual evidence that Sayfutdinov declined to ride at King's Lynn on Monday and that his complaints about payments, etc, etc do not constitute a formal refusal to participate especially as the Russian federation say ultimately they simply did not pick him! Without any paper trail supporting the FIM's case and the Russian federation's position it would appear to leave the way clear for Emil to return. As a fan and a spectator, that's great news and will greatly add to the competitiveness of the race-off, especially with Grigory Laguta riding as well. But as for the authority of the FIM? Well, that's another matter"

Hans Andersen* "Seems like All i dó these days is driving along the roads.... Would rather ride My bike :("

Lewis Bridger* "at the Hotel now in Frankfurt in total 15hr's of driving but going to be worth it polish mechanic on route from torun with my new baby !!"

> **Lee Richardson*** "oh yeah keep the foot on the footrest!!!"
> **Lewis Bridger*** "Okay mate try my hardest !"
> **Peter Johns*** "only points for finishing not style!"

BSF "Race-off Lineups: Farce – 24 hours to go and still no lineups on speedwaygp.com. Can't imagine similar situation in any other pro sport"

Graham Cooke "A massive upturn in work, a feeling of disillusionment with the sport, being tired after Cardiff and the helpful comments from a correspondent on the British Speedway Forum received just after I'd got home from a full on day at the track last Thursday, made me seriously question whether I actually wanted to carry on"

John Turner "On top of the earlier crashes, it led to the referee inspecting the [Belle Vue] track, which was a mix of slick and grippy with some ruts on the inside of the bends, a combination which gave some of the inexperienced riders a tough time."

14th July

Dakota North* "had a rough night sleep. Off the the dentist this morning arggghhh!!! My week sucks. Off to see the new potter movie today, 3d no one spoil it for me I'm kinda looking forward"

Dakota North* "Dentist time. Last time I was here was in 02"

Dakota North* "teeth are all good:) Nice! Lamb salad for lunchtime"

Scott Nicholls* "Sorry I've not tweeted any replies.won't be at race off.Sophie had big op few weeks ago & family comes 1st.feeling pretty stiff anyway too!"

Nigel Pearson* "In Poland trying to get my head round tonight's events at Belle Vue?"

Chris Morton "The track was patchy early on. There were some ruts on the inside which created problems but we were working on it from Heat 2. Some riders were revelling in it and others were struggling to cope in the early heats. I apologise for the meeting being a shambles but there were so many incidents and not all could be blamed on the track. Belle Vue is not an easy track to ride and young riders can find it difficult, no matter what the conditions are."

Fredrik Lindgren* "Isn't it fantastic that everyone drinks beer at airports no matter what time it is. 90% in this cafe have a beer 5:30 in the morning"

Nigel Pearson* "Overcast in Gorzow after thunderstorm last night (woke me up cheers). Team GB massive underdogs tonight"

David Hemsley "Richard [Hall] has upped his game since coming to Leicester but we are in the same situation as we found ourselves with Mathieu Trésarrieu and need to have a captain who is not elsewhere when he should be leading the side. It is not a good advert for the sport or the people of Leicester to pay to see a six man team operating the rider replacement facility."

Steve Mallett "We have attracted increased coverage from a variety of media outlets, have set-up two highly-successful websites, completed several extremely large leaflet drops throughout Gwent and the valley and recently did so outside the Millennium Stadium before and after the Grand Prix. Anybody willing to give their time to work for the good of the club can easily contact ourselves and any fresh ideas will be listened to."

Paul Burbidge* "Davey Watt has been issued with the wrong licence and may not be able to ride in the SWC Race-Off tonight. Rory Schlein is on standby"

Paul Burbidge* "I've just heard that Davey Watt's licence issue should be sorted in time for him to ride"

Paul Burbidge* "I've just been told Davey Watt has been cleared to ride in the SWC Race-Off at Gorzow tonight. Great news for the Aussies."

Lewis Bridger* "Starting to get my mindset ready for tonight's SWC Gorzow this is my last tweet then im in the zone ill do my best Great Britain"

Fredrik Lindgren* "At the stadium in Gorzow. Inspected the track it's 'hard & fast' or maybe it should read 'slick & slow'"

Mike Bennett* "what a shocker- SAAB in for MOT and they reckon a spring needs replacing but they can't get the genuine part? Could only happen in Norfolk!"

Chris Louis "Lewis is showing his inexperience at this level"

Neil Middleditch "He's just not gating into the corner with them"

Nigel Pearson "Lee Richardson not available for Great Britain tonight by his own choice"

Nigel Pearson "Nice guy Jim Lawrence – he's British that's all I'm saying"

Nigel Pearson "And we do deal in big ifs when it comes to British speedway"

Nigel Pearson "We do have some good British youngsters coming through the system"

Nigel Pearson "I dunno about you but I thought Britain would be out of contention at this stage [heat 20]"

Nigel Pearson "In what is turning out to be the best Elite League speedway season in five or six years, I would suggest"

Lee Richardson* "you listening to sam PJR!!! think he might want to have a look on the side of some of the Aussie engines"

Peter Johns* "I don't listen between races, would rather watch without shouty man too! So what was he saying?"

Lee Richardson* "at the end he said english riders should use tuners abroad as uk tuners aren't good enough for polish tracks"

Peter Johns* "I work for 2 of the British guys, the other guys do use forein tuners! 3 of the ozzies use me!"

Paul Burbidge* "The FIM should throw the book at Russia's Roman Povazhny for launching a bike at the doctor during his altercation with Jonsson"

Keith McGhie "Whenever Masters was around life was never dull, although frequently his opponents' lives looked precarious"

Nicola Sands* "Is Tatum Kelvin involved in another buy a round of drinks shocker?As often as halley's comet #onceinalifetime"

Lewis Bridger* "To all you cunts slating me blow me.. Fuk u all got no idea the passion & hardwork i put into speedway.. Most GB fans r 2faced kunts !!"

Lewis Bridger* "& once again i don't care what people r going to say fuk u all"

Lewis Bridger* "Proved tonight none of u r true fans !!"

15th July

Nicola Sands* "Berlin Tegel quite possibly the dullest airport to arrive 2 hours too early at..."

Leigh Adams "I am remaining positive. Thanks to the public for giving me the personal space and time I need. Hopefully one day I'll be able to travel around to thank everyone. I am hugely relieved to have recently been given the OK to stop wearing a neck brace that was driving me crazy. Not having the neck brace makes everyday tasks that bit easier. I'm happily propelling myself around in a wheelchair and I'm already looking ahead to a lighter, more agile design to aid my increasing mobility. My plans for the future will require some initial lifestyle changes, but remain relatively unchanged. My goal is to enjoy time in Australia with my family and to continue with my plans to conduct Speedway training schools across the nation and to develop junior speedway bikes"

Nigel Pearson* "Nursing a thumping head thanks to Polish Lager. Tatum's fault, led me astray. Should have gone to bed when Jan Staechmann did"

Kevin Long* "just goes to prove Lewis, that both on and off the track you are not ready yet to represent your country; Lose with dignity Sir!"

Lewis Bridger* "I appoligise to Everyone who has seen my nasty tweets last night, i no it's no consulation but i am very sorry, very bad move on my behalf"

Scott Nicholls* "good move mate. As long as u know hand on heart u gave 100%,then u can do know more"

Darcy Ward* "dude you need to stop writing on here or delete it"

Scott Nicholls* "as much as what u tweeted was way wrong to do. There is some truth in it. Move on fella"

Lewis Bridger* "i messed up but will move on and learn to keep my mouth shut"

Scott Nicholls* "wouldn't be u then though!"

Lewis Bridger* "but at the end of the day the fans have there own opinion and they pay my bills so they are aloud to say what they want it's just upsetting to see when u put 100% in"

Fredrik Lindgren* "Just seen the crash from last night Heat 16 and I must say well done and thank you Tai. That could have ended up nasty, stupid move by me"

Ludvig Lindgren* "I hate it when iam not checked in and my flights leav in 2 hours"

Hans Andersen* "Hmmm turn up In Gniezno and where is everybody ??? Know we're not suppose to race for a couple of hours BUT no fucker of any kind"

Chris Neath* "It seems like speedway is having its first twitter scandal"

Olly Allen* "What is all this scandal regarding bridger on twitter? Someone fill me in!"

Paul Burbidge* "Poland are big faves but speedway is a funny old game"

Leigh Adams* "Neck brace gone, thank god, was driving me mad!"

Peter Johns* "Come on swc track prep guys, let's have a track so some real HP can be used!"

Jonathan Barber "I think its a case of [Lewis Bridger] can give it but not take it, he had been slagging ben barker of on twitter for the last couple of weeks and he had not reacted to any of it, bridger also got his friends to write malicious threats on ben barkers wall on facebook and ben did not respond, so the picture I get is he can dish it out but when the boot is on the other foot its a total different kettle of fish, he needs to grow up but can't see that happening any time soon."

Mike Hunter "Fairly heavy drizzle pre-meeting made this match rather an endurance test, one-sided and far too long without much good racing. The major incident of the night was a frightening crash in Heat 7 from which Mark Simmonds seems to have been fortunate enough to emerge with only a broken wrist. He was caught between Jesper Kristiansen and Tim Webster approaching the first corner and burst forward at speed straight into and through the fence boards. He flew high into a lighting pylon before landing….Lyons, though, was frankly a poor substitute for the missing Ben Barker. His recent form has been good but he seemed to settle far too easily for a series of modest seconds and thirds, perhaps not fancying the conditions. There was little positive to be said for the other visiting [Plymouth] riders, other than a reasonably competitive Hughes and one or two moments of promise from Jaimie Pickard."

16th July

Peter Adams "Although we are out of the play-off picture, we are still over the points limit"

Ulrich Ostergaard* "Just been out running 11 km in 49 minutes..love it:-)"

Chris Van Straaten "We will see what we can do over the next ten days. We owe it to the Wolverhampton supporters, who have been tremendously loyal. At the start of the season, you have riders who don't want to come here because they are booked up. But towards the end of the season, their commitments fall away and they can be interested."

Dennis Andersson "That's speedway. Sometimes you have to eat dirt."

Dick Barrie "The return tonight of the Comical Crew gives me a chance to pay tribute to Ian Thomas, the man most-connected over the years with speedway at Derwent Park, who passed away earlier this year. I knew Ian for at least half a century, and we squabbled bitterly for most of those fifty years. From our cycle-speedway days in the early sixties right through to a wee tiff over something I said (I think it was that "99% of Workington fans give the rest a bad name") just last season, we had our differences. But never, ever to the extent that we wouldn't shake hands before and after public hostilities were over – often with Ian having scored a point or two in the clash. He held a huge personal psychological advantage – an unyielding conviction that all Workington, Newcastle or Hull's opponents were rubbish. Mind you, it didn't stop there. He felt exactly the same about Scots, people from the south of England, those who voted Labour, vegetarians, homosexuals, the entire BSPA management committee and every writer or commentator who dared to disagree with him. Xenophobia for Ian started where the 30mph signs stopped, coming out of Ilkley in West Yorkshire….He could be thrawn, perverse and a twisted wee git – and I'm sure he spoke as kindly of me. But we always shook hands, and for fifty years we agreed to disagree many, many times. I'll miss him. A lot."

Billy Hamill "I remember England being a force in world speedway and hope the new [National Speedway] stadium will help the drive towards re-establishing that."

Dennis Andersson "Matt is a good promoter. He thinks speedway and knows speedway. It's great to have a promoter who gets into you whatever it is."

Alun John Rossiter* "Got Charlie Gjedde sponsor coming over to take some stuff for there new work shop After the fire last few things left from my racing days!"

Lewis Bridger* "Practice at Arlington is Cancelled due to poor weather once again, hope we can get another go at practice tomorrow morning !"

Nicolai Klindt* "got what you need in life? i do…."

Chris Neath* "Thinkin about renting a house up north for rest of season. Will be cheaper than all the fuel if league split goes like its looking!"

Nigel Pearson* "Lunch by the river in Gorzow sunshine. Perfect prep for tonight. Spagboll ordered! Kelv, Chris, Sam and Keith buzzing about tonight"

Nigel Pearson* "Still working on getting Kelvin Tatum on twitter. Might as well talk to a brick wall"

Scott Nicholls* "ah maaaaaate! As kt would say. Think he knows he'd become an addict"

Scott Nicholls* "Damn I'm good.just packed my bags faster than the guy at check out could zapp them through…guess goes to show women are better on checkout"

Mike Bennett* "can anyone get close to Poland in the speedway world cup tonight? Good luck totroy batchelor chris holder mads korneliussen niels kristian iversen"

Rory Schlein* "Watching at home track looks good grow some balls Jim [Lawrence] just cause he polish and ya in Poland. Sorry Jim your having a shocker"

Greg Hancock* "I say that was the bad call by the referee! Ward was in front with no sight of Hampel at that stage. Glad Hampel was OK though!!"

Cameron Woodward* "Come on Aussie come on, come on. Gollob is a star"

Nicolai Klindt* "wtf! gollob just change the cam-timing between his two heats #shouldntbeallowed"

Fredrik Lindgren* "He did not! Just put oil in, in a weird way. But he is weird, weird & fast!"

Nicolai Klindt* "just looked like he did. and yep weird and very fast!!"

Fredrik Lindgren* "That's the SWC for this year. Congrats Polska! We still have some way up to the top. Better to beat the Danes then go home with nothing"

David Watt* "Well were beaten by a great Polska team tonight but it still sucks to get silver !!!"

Troy Batchelor* "Gollob had race after race and he changed the cam timing in between WTF ?"

Chris Holder* "so did i ;-) haha"

17th July

Dick Barrie "Speedway riders are self-employed. If they can't race, they can't earn money to feed their families"

Chris Neath* "Seems like I'm now sending strange random DM's as well. So before anyone asks no it isn't you in the album you can't open!"

Fredrik Lindgren* "Yea I got a DM from you as well. So there is no photo album which I might be in, phew got a bit worried there hahaha"

Chris Neath* "I'm saving those photos for when your World Champ!"

Lee Richardson* "Landed in Rzeszow nice weather here…going for some practice…engine didn't turn up from ups!!! Arrrggghhh!!"

Troy Batchelor* "#givebatchelorawildcard nuf said"

Chris Holder* "fukn turn it up!"

Darcy Ward* "#shouldntbeallowed"

Troy Batchelor* "did u get your money ??? How many points"

Darcy Ward* "not all I'm happy Aww 17 you know"

Troy Batchelor* "easy pickings down in premier league ad a reserve hey"

David Watt* "For all those asking, the Aussie suits will go on eBay in a few weeks. Please be patient and offer as much as you can please. Thanks all"

Chris Holder* "How hot is it in polska today!!!!! Like Aussie!!!"

Lewis Bridger* [to Lee Richardson] "I am fully aware that im in the paper thanks for making it even more public like you didn't no what you was doing"

Nicolai Klindt* "it's funny to see how some people have gone fat and downhill"

Niels Kristian Iversen* "What a c&nt of a meeting. Blow my new rocket to bits in heat 1. Chain snapt in 2nd. Then you get the feeling its not your night. Lost by 2"

Hans Andersen* F…angrylikehell things not going the way it should but Will find the solution soon ! Pissed of with some people that for sure…."

Chris Holder* "Can't beat a bit of nirvana on the long trip to hotel"

Fredrik Lindgren* "Bedtime in Berlin, unfortunately not sharing room with Greg Hancock no bromance tonight. I'm all alone that's how I roll!"

Greg Hancock* "#nobromancingberlinoranywhere"

18th July

Chris Holder* "Love an early start…. NAAT!!! this is f*%ked!"

Charles McKay "The Supplementary Regulations no 2, which of course is not available on the internet, states that the Premier League will be split into two sections no later than 17 July. Yet BSPA web site says it will be spilt once teams have completed 10 home and 10 away which of course is not the same because at the cut off date 8 teams haven't completed 20 fixtures, Plymouth have only done 15 but Sheffield 24. What happens if the four extra that the Tigers have completed are not against teams who will be in their section do these no longer count. What happens if say Sheffield have raced team A twice at home but team A are not in the same section in the second phase as Sheffield? Is the second match omitted from records? Otherwise Sheffield will have raced one more, possibly even more, meetings than other teams and does omitting this/these extra meetings cock up all the rider averages etc. Remember speedway is a professional sport run by professional people."

Graham Drury "I think it's fair to say that if we had permission to take Hans we would have signed him, that's how close it was, but I'm not sure why were denied permission when we were, you will have to ask other people that. But we are also more satisfied that KK has now got back to somewhere near his best and he had a fine World Cup. It's nice for Birmingham Speedway to have a World Cup winner in their side and we will welcome him back with open arms against Lakeside on Thursday."

Dakota North* "Flight booked, 20 days and il be back in sunny England, Ready to tear it up"

Dakota North* "just checked it's about 17 days till I'm back in Uk, so the way things are going il be straight into my team spots"

Scott Nicholls* "Landed back in the UK from Poland & it's still only 7am!Not up at 7 when in bed in UK! Normally awake though thinking about it,thanks 2 Maya"

Chris Holder* "Passport control can go and get…"

Nicolai Klindt* "feel sorry for all those who been at the airport this morning, waited in security, waited for bags and to get a lift home. i just woke up!"

Hans Andersen* "pissed off with some polish fans, they don't get the whole picture AND havent Got a F*%£ing whats going behind the scenes"

David Watt* "don't stress man ! They'll love you again in 5 minutes !! It sucks right now but You WILL get through it"

Chris Neath* "next door seem to have found a dog and the bloody thing hasn't stopped barking for the last 2 hours"

Fredrik Lindgren* "Just woke up and got the message that the meeting at Wolves tonight is cancelled #whattodo"

Hans Andersen* "Best Drylm qoute ever: maybe you see mé In hell BUT i always ride the fast line hehe"

Chris Holder* [to Darcy] "Nothin worse the. Havin to wait around for other peoples stuff!! Wen all you wanna do is get out of this place!! You owe me"

Fredrik Lindgren* "Forgot my phone charger at hotel I stayed yesterday, been out on a find a charger mission but didn't get lucky"

Chris Neath* "Putting the bikes in the van for pboro tonight and it hammered down. Not gonna be a happy bunny if I'm rained off again"

Chris Neath* "And to make things worse I just realised I left my gear bag open on the drive and everything is soaked!"

Taylor Poole* "Raining all the way here"

Taylor Poole* "And for once its sunny in Glasgow. #surprisedhappyverykeen"

Chris Holder* "Late call to race at Peterborough tonight! Bit of runin round but I'm here now"

Fredrik Lindgren* "Have had an AWESOME day in Berlin today! Feel so relaxed. Now it's time to pack up and head to the airport, late flight to Sthlm"

Fredrik Lindgren* "Landed ok at Arlanda but now they have some technical problems with the doors. We can't get out! Come on I need to catch my bus to Örebro!"

Fredrik Lindgren* I'm out but we had to make a detour to get out amazing it's 2011 and we can't open doors. But we can tweet.

Fredrik Lindgren* And I'm on the bus and soon we are off, it will only take 2h 45min to get to Örebro with this bus"

Ludvig Lindgren* "Arlanda is a f*cking good airport that way with the busses but i reckon the driver will do it in less ;)"

Fredrik Lindgren* "Even though I will be home pretty late. One thing is certain, I will not miss the 6:05 flight out of Stansted tomorrow!"

Edward Kennett "It was pretty dangerous out there, you certainly couldn't do any overtaking because it was going to be one-line, so I think it was the best thing to call it a day."

Ludvig Lindgren* "3 days, 3 meetings, 3 rain-offs! yipphey! at stansted airport with woffy any one wanna come?"

Ludvig Lindgren* "actully we are at the hollyday inn!"

Nicolai Klindt* "no one wanna come if your there"

Ludvig Lindgren* "well if u were here people would screem and think it was fricking Frankenstein with ur bloody hair cut! baldylocks"

Chris Holder* "Goodnight at Peterborough now same in sweden tomorrow please"

Linus Sundstrom* "Bedtime! Not looking forward to that alarm ringing 4.15 .. ZzZzZzzzz"

19th July

Chris Holder* "Watchin people try and sit in the 1st 4rows on the plane wen the tray tables are all down and a sign on them sayin 'do not sit here' dumbass"

Lewis Bridger* "Deffo time for a Tattoo in desperate need to get some pain & express my feelings ! #lifeshardattimes"

Nicolai Klindt* "just woke up from the a deep sleep and had a meal nothing beats - maxi hamburgers. now in the front leading the way to kumla and picked up a salad for later. i'm not that bad with fastfood, but it always makes you fast"

Fredrik Lindgren* "World record in changed & cancelled meetings this year. My match in Polska Sunday are changed, I'll be home a little this weekend"

Fredrik Lindgren* "We can never find this damn track in Norrköping haha every year we make some wrong turn. But we'll get there in the end"

Troy Batchelor* "Rained off in gislaved fuck it meeting is on tomorrow and I have to ride in uk yay :l Makes me feel even better the forecast is shit for kingslynn tomorrow and Sweden is sun sun sun #stupidrules"

Linus Sundstrom* "Rain rain rain... What a shit season this have been, far too many of them!"

Chris Holder* "Today started good! With some clay shooting! And go karts!!!! But then pissed dwn and meeting cancelled! So stay here and race tomorrow!"

Ludvig Lindgren* "was at kumla today what a shit meeting and shit track! 2 meters from the fence from the first to last heat!"

Nicolai Klindt* "västervik got smoked proper today at kumla. track was sooo boring! win the start, cruise on the outside and 3 points in the bag."

David Watt* "Shocking night. Feel so sick had to pull out after 2 pointless rides. I'm so tired and I slept until 3:30 this afternoon too ! wasteoftime"

Hans Andersen* "Oh well as promised i'll Cast some light on Elite League future, sad to say but wont be riding any more this season as 8+ rule :(maybe next"

Lewis Bridger* "Harry potter was mint now some chillaxing time"

20th July

Rob Godfrey "It's not often you get teams that challenge for league titles and I really think we have one this year. We have a bunch of talented riders and it would be great that after three years of building a National League side we can reap the rewards"

Fredrik Lindgren* "Once again in Skavsta Airport heading towards UK, long drive up to Manchester from London Stansted Airport later"

Niels Kristian Iversen* "Ready to board the plane from sweden with a load of speedway riders. Kings lynn-panthers tonight. Should be good"

Fredrik Lindgren* "Don't feel great boarding your flight knowing the meeting tonight most likely will be cancelled. I hope we race tonight!"

BSPA IT has been declared that in the Second Phase of the 2011 Premier League, teams will be split into the following groups.

GROUP 1: Glasgow, Somerset, Edinburgh, Redcar, Scunthorpe, Newport, Leicester

GROUP 2: Sheffield, Workington, Ipswich, Rye House, Berwick, Newcastle, Plymouth

Clubs will issue their Second Phase fixtures in due course.

PREMIER LEAGUE CHAMPIONSHIP - HOW IT WORKS

The 14 teams initially race each other in Round 1 with a total of 26 meetings (13 home and 13 away). Round 2 (Second Phase) sees the league then split into two groups of seven teams (at an agreed cut-off point), with everyone then racing each other in their group for an additional 12 meetings (6 home and 6 away). Those additional 12 matches are then added onto the points gained from the 26 meetings in Round 1. The league table at the end of the season will then show a total of 38 meetings (19 home and 19 away). The team that finishes top after these 38 meetings is declared 2011 Premier League Champions

Fredrik Lindgren* "Looks like we might get lucky with the weather today. Now in B'ham lunch at the San Carlo Italian restaurant"

Fredrik Lindgren* "Had a great pasta dish here with an awesome sauce! Love pasta WITH sauce! Apparently Bon Jovi has been here at this restaurant as well!"

Ricky Wells* "yeah twitter is pretty shit..but i think it will take over facebook in a few years"

Chris Holder* "Practice all over... Now jus gotta kill few hours. #wastingtime"

Chris Neath* "I've deleted twitter off my blackberry, ipod and ipad and re-installed them all so I'm hoping I will stop overloading your inbox with spam"

Niels Kristian Iversen* "Just cocked my speciality. Rice with turkey and chilisauce. Should get mé out of the gate tonight"

Alun John Rossiter* "Apparently I've said something on here about the BSF about the Lewis Briger saga gone through my posts not me there must be another ajrosco"

Nigel Pearson* "stopped reading that rubbish three years ago mate. People getting personal who have never even met you or don't even know you"

Alun John Rossiter* "agree Nigel just clearing my name no angel wouldn't be dam right rude on here !!"

Alun John Rossiter* [to Lewis] "as I would know passion can some times over take you and people can be dam right horrible some just don't understand !"

21st July

Fredrik Lindgren* "Had time to sleep like almost how long that I could this morning and what happens can't even make it past 9 o clock. Getting old!"

BSPA [NEWPORT Hornets] have signed Brendan Johnson after his release from a short-term deal at Dudley, and former Carmarthen rider Steven Jones to replace David Gough and Tom Young. Johnson became available after Richard Franklin, the rider he replaced for Dudley, was declared fit to return to the Heathens. Newport general manager Laurence Rogers said: "With David Gough having sustained facial injuries in the recent meeting against Dudley, and with new averages in force the opportunity to strengthen up the side became available.

Gary Havelock "Historically, the teams that do well have track conditions that are consistent and the recent improvement coincides with our upturn in fortunes."

Arnie Gibbons "Please don't pretend that the racing at Beaumont Park is good. Most meetings have had no more than two or three passes, making it one of the least exciting tracks to watch racing at"

Rory Schlein* "Last night well what can i say if we keep that up we can kiss good bye the play offs"

Niels Kristian Iversen* "Just booked a load of flights and done other paperworks. Boooriing..."

Mads Korneliussen* "yes i burned my forhead for the 3. time this year. Stupid i know. Hurts like hell"

Ludvig Lindgren* "draw today iwas poor but funny thing happend Lindbäck was busy throwing his fist in the air so AJ passed him on the line in heat 15!"

Lewis Bridger* "Not the best of nights at the Abbey stadium 5pts but gave it 100% and this is what counts"

Simon Stead "I spoke to him and said after the meeting different bike Magic [Janowski] – no same bike, was the reply. Different engine – no same engine, different Magic then – he just laughed and said yes!"

Nicolai Klindt* "10min from home and then massive que on m6. thats why we love england! cant wait to get to wolves..."

22nd July

Nicolai Klindt* "scotty will have his bum checked out by maya tomorrow so everything will be perfect ;-)"

Scott Nicholls* "ha ha, yer she'll check it for me bless her. Not sure what treatment she will do though,probably slap on a plaster"

Nigel Pearson* "Walkabout Blackpool. Feel old."

Mads Korneliussen* "Why is there a life jacket under the seat, when u fly. You don't get a parachute when u are on a boat???"

Lewis Bridger* "Life is just one massive lesson. u never stop learning new things !!"

Mads Korneliussen* "Only 3 hour drive before i hit my bed, giveing it like a F1 driver"

Justin Sedgmen* "Any one no how to ride a speedway bike I need lessons !!"

Linus Sundstrom* "Off to airport, lucky me that its my mechanic that takes me so i can sleep!"

Ludvig Lindgren* "Off to Skavsta! oh i reckon it wont be a pleasant flight today!"

Rory Schlein* "Peterborough tonight. A proppa race track"

Brendan Johnson "Winning it [British U18s] last year was a magical feeling, not just for me but for my parents and all those who have stuck by me. I feel ready physically and mentally to go into the championship and put myself in the frame."

Jon Cook "We have moved rider-replacement away from No.2 as it's a waste of Lee's [Richardson] talent to have him come out in the easier Heat 8 against a team of this top end strength. We can also then pick our riders for the r/r rides as the heats and scores dictate."

Paul Burbidge* "If Matt Ford's bid to sign Martin Vaculik comes off, can't wait to see what he does for Poole speedway on a 4 pt average. Class act. Bargain"

Gary Patchett* "Think you'll find he's a 6. Averaged over 7 last year in Poland"

Paul Burbidge* "Is that another rule the BSPA have changed on the quiet? When did this happen? Even on a 6, he's good value"

Gary Patchett* "riders on ass ave have always been judged on what they have achieved elsewhere. Under 6 is 4. Over 6 is 5 always has been. just been extended to cover riders over 7 and 8 too. Makes league more competitive as riders judged on ability."

Paul Burbidge* "Fair enough, Gary. Looks like I need an up-to-date rulebook, although it will probably be out of date this time next week"

Chris Neath* "Wow, what a squeeze. 4 bikes and 2 lots of gear in a kitted out vito van"

Niels Kristian Iversen* "No golf today either, bastard.. But some Tour de france while takin care of things it not a bad thing. Them guys are tough, doping or not"

Nicolai Klindt* "haircut in a min by Lacie and hopefully they will ask me for a coffee. gagging for one here! then telford it is to visit vcostums.

Olly Allen* "Don't go ginger again buddy...it's just not your colour!"

Nicolai Klindt* "i wont mate. maybe ill try blond or black or maybe even go silver!"

Olly Allen* "maybe it's a bit too early in life for silver?? I say dark hair"

Nicolai Klindt* "some people is constantly doing my freaking heading. even when you tell them they don't stop!"

Chris Holder* [en route to Lakeside] "Love the traffic in the Uk!!"

Chris Neath* "Looks like its retro for me tonight. Forgot my bike covers so going Andrew Silver style. retro old skool"

Fredrik Lindgren* "Checked in at this hotel by the airport and did I get astonished when I realised they have same bed & bedside table as me at home! Haha even the bedside table lamps are the same just a different colour here, but the bed is in the same colour! Home sweet home! Haha"

Linus Sundstrom* [to Chris Neath] "nice to see you riding as good as you loaded the van tonight mate!"

Matthew Wethers "I also watched Tim Webster's rides and was really impressed. Although he fell off a couple of times, I felt he was competitive. A fast rider can learn to stay on, if you're not fast you are not going to score points"

23rd July

Malcolm Simmons "May I remind Nigel Pearson that when England was still great in the 70s, we had an abundance of English riders who were great (and a lot of them were southerners, which proves we can ride speedway bikes after all!). We won the World Cup in 1973, '74, '75 and '77. We should have won in '76 had we not got too complacent. And don't forget the Danes who won in 1983-88. I know Nigel is going to say it's the World Cup, not the World Team Cup, but look at it...it's still the same competition. Looking at the riders we have at the moment, it's going to be a very long time before we see these glory days again, especially when some of the riders don't even want to wear the England body colour."

Philip Rising "World Champion Tomasz Gollob faces an uncertain future following the breakdown of his marriage. *Speedway Star* has declined to publish all the gory details but it has been headline news not just in Poland but also Denmark and Sweden"

Rob Peasley "I think the Hackney revival was very worthy, and an attempt to recreate the Cradley success. However, not all clubs maintain the same interest over years of inactivity. When I recently interviewed Dave Perks (available in Backtrack Issue 43), I think he hit the nail back on the head, saying how special speedway was to Cradley, since they didn't have a good football team or anything like that, so speedway is therefore the main sporting attraction."

Derek Barclay "Low crowds..? Well, there were actually only three 'stand-alone' Hawks fixtures at AE.. The first was Dudley, so - fair play as ever to the superb Heathens hordes! - that was well attended. The IoW match was blighted by one of the worst nights for traffic in East London/west Essex for years and then there was Buxton...As an experiment it does appear to have been abandoned but I'd personally NOT call it a failure...

The voices of doom and gloom on here will doubtless say they were right; but frankly if you're pessimistic and down-beat about things you will often end up being right... It's those who take a leap of faith as Cookie did for a bit here, who make things actually happen so fair play to all who tried"

Bryce "Speaking as one of those Hawks fans, I could just about cope with Lakeside as being a "home" meeting. Rye House just isn't. I've no animosity towards the place, it's just nowhere near East London. It's a trip to the countryside for us. It will never feel like a home track for Hackney."

RocketBen 1 "There was no Hackney merchandise either and programmes were not even Hackney programmes, little things like that just add to the mickey mouse approach this was unfortunately given. If it was approached the right way, things could have been a great success and the partnership between Rye and Lakeside would have blossomed with riders being able to progress from the NL to the EL without having to club hop. I doubt this will signal the end of NL at Rye from next season, however I'd love to see the Raiders name brought back, Raiders meetings always used to draw decent crowds and having sides with riders such as Boxall, Allen, Bowen, Mear, Burchatt, Betson, Halsey and Powell, all who have gone on to PL at least helped get the fans excited."

Derek Barclay "I think the Hackney idea had far more attraction and viability if just at Arena Essex.. And remember the Lakeside promotion did brand the Hawks as a separate club with an excellent programme in (retro) Hackney stylings for example. It was - strangely, considering his impeccable Hackney background - Uncle Len who let the experiment down by making literally no effort to style as a stand-alone third tier club"

RocketBen 1 "How you can call the short comings of both promotions Len Silvers fault is beyond me. How people can suggest the Hawks racing solely at Lakeside would have made them successful is also a lot of rubbish (stronger word should be used but it's a family forum)"

Nicolai Klindt* "having a nice cup of tea before a nice plate of english breakie and then of to freaking derby"

Alan Dick "The league is the holy grail and we are spending a lot of time looking at ways of making our chances of winning that greater"

Chris Harris "If [Ben Barker] keeps doing what he's doing, doesn't talk too much and let his racing do the talking, he could get there. Ben is very outspoken and says what he feels, which is usually good."

Neil Middleditch "Eddie lacked at little bit of speed, as did Lewis, but we knew it was going to be a tough, tough meeting.'

Lewis Bridger "After what everyone had put on my wall, I just felt that I didn't have anything to lose and didn't want to do speedway, to be honest. It was just anger really. I checked my Twitter, which I probably shouldn't have done. I just saw everyone turning their backs on me there, saying I wasn't good enough now and I was never going to be. I put so much effort into it and to then have everyone slate you is pretty hard. But I need to start thinking a little bit more before I open my mouth."

Bob Dugard "Lewis has had a lot to say for himself and given himself an impossible thing to live up to. He has almost backed himself into a situation where people are looking for him to fail, which is not a good place to be. I'm still totally confident the boy has enough talent to do it but he has got to be sensible in what he says. He wants to play it all low key at the moment, doesn't he?"

Niels Kristian Iversen* "At MOT with the Merc. First time there. Shouldnt take long"

Jon Cook "Who makes way is likely to be determined by availability as the Premier League fixture list has proved problematic so far and is likely to continue when it's redrawn for August and September."

Paul Bellamy "As always, we want to ensure fans are getting value for money so, as well as joining forces with the stadium and the Welsh Government, we'll again be working with Cardiff & Co to offer fans booking advance tickets the chance to reserve hotel rooms at reasonable rates."

Ben Morley "I think I live in the workshop and Mum and Dad run up and down the country just to help me out. It's madness going out there if I have a crash and bend something it could turn into half a season's wages! The sport is so expensive, you have to find sponsors but everyone says they are in recession. This year I sent out 75 sponsor letters and I only got two replies saying sorry but there's a recession on."

Chris Holder* "Go kart sesh tonight with the boys... See how many laps we get before we get kicked off"

Nicolai Klindt* "all this house buying thing is actually much more stressing than i thought it would be. but we're getting there!"

Trevor Swales "Troy lives, eats and sleeps speedway"

Graham Drury "It was with great reluctance that I felt I had to release Kevin [Wolbert] and James [Wright] because they both have their positives. I'd like to think they can both ride in Birmingham colours again at some stage in the future"

Linus Sundstrom* "Promotion day done, hope it pays off! Now time for some workshop and then maybe down rye tonight"

Craig Cook "There is no comparison between moto-cross and speedway. Yes, a speedway track can be grippy and rough but the big difference is that you have a suspension on a moto-cross bike. The two sports are like chalk and cheese...the only similarities are that the bikes have two wheels and engine!"

Chris Neath* "Freaky shit! The moment I sent the tweet about Amy Winehouse she came on the cd player"

Fredrik Lindgren* "Unbelievable what happened in Norway yesterday! It's less then 300km away from my home"

Fredrik Lindgren* "Bought a new living room carpet today, freaking expensive these things!"

David Watt* "Sick go-kart sesh with the boys. Somehow we are all still ok and nobody got kicked out !"

Ove Fundin "When I qualified for my first World Final in 1954 nobody told me that there was a practice at Wembley on the Thursday before. I knew nothing about it. I had never even seen the stadium before I arrived, by tube, on the Saturday...I didn't even know I needed a mechanic for the World Final"

Fredrik Lindgren* "Have decided to have a quiet evening at home. Relax time! Or have I?"

Neil Machin "Shane Parker was brilliant for us at Workington but I believe certain members of the team owe an apology to our supporters. I really do hope they learn from it and show a better attitude in terms of preparation. I'm not going to question their effort, that's for other people, but you can win or lose meetings in the workshop."

Andrew Dalby "I believe only two sides, Sheffield and Leicester, have managed to fulfill their home and away requirements, while a few others, including ourselves (Newcastle) and Berwick, have managed one or the other."

Brendan Johnson "The BSPA don't always look at the bigger picture at times and I think this move to Under-19 status, which brings us in line with other countries, is a real plus."

Ludvig Lindgren "This is the first time I have seen Berwick and I think it is an unusual and hard track to ride, but hopefully there should be some home advantage in it"

Shane Hazelden "If you ask the doctors, I shouldn't have ridden but I'm stubborn. The break hasn't healed and the dislocation is temperamental to say the least. I can just about pull the clutch in but when the adrenalin starts pumping you forget about the pain."

24th July

Matt Ford "In the middle of a domestic tsunami in British Speedway during the close season, Alex [Harkess] proved a giant as the man who held the sport together in this country. The fact Elite League speedway has a ten-strong division in 2011 is testament to him and the quote brilliant job he did and I salute him for the results he achieved."

Nigel Pearson "[Greg Hancock] always eats sensibly, he has never been a heavy drinker and I reckon the guy can carry on for another three or four years at that level....It's easy to take a pop at our young riders because we don't have any permanent riders in the four rounds of the World Under-21 Final, so British riders are a target for criticism. But I'm not prepared to do that. I am currently working with teenage hopefuls like Ashley Morris, Tom Perry, Darryl Ritchings and Richard Franklin with my own team Dudley Heathens so we are doing our bit to give the kids a chance...there are some British riders who could take a look at Greg and learn from the man. I'm not going to name names but I know too much about what goes on behind the scenes in this sport and we need more discipline amongst many of the boys. We do have naturally talented riders who can do well in the sport but they need to want it – and want it through hard work rather than expect it to be handed on a plate."

Barry Briggs   "He's been around Chris Holder and [Darcy] watched what happened to Woffinden. If you get your backside knocked out, it can take you a year to get over it."

Craig Boyce   "My heart fell out of my backside"

Steve Shovlar   "Hilarious moment of the meeting was when Shamek Pawlicki slid off under pressure from Andersson. Instead of jumping back on and gaining a point as there were only three riders, he pushed to the centre green, rolled around on the floor in a tantrum bashing his fist on his bike. If there had been a tree close by he would have ripped off a branch and hit his bike with it ala Cleese and Faulty Towers. Funny stuff."

Linus Sundstrom*   "Been out for a quick run, never been in this bad shape before i think! Must try to run/walk more often when im not racing"

Troy Batchelor*   "Heading to Wroclaw in the taxi with edek kennet .. Hungry as..."

Lewis Bridger*   "Well I must say I live a crazy lifestyle & being single at the moment is pritty Radddd #lovingit #randomness"

Ian Maclean   "[Glasgow] were eight down to Berwick but after a faltering start easily won by eleven on aggregate without putting Screen and Grieves in heat 15. There was some great racing with riders passing and repassing in some heats. Richard Sweetman even managed to win two races. He lacks bottle going into the first turn in lap one."

Blunsdon Blog   "Four of our finest, Keith Johnson, Dave Whiting, John Nobbs and Mark Price, loaded the 42 panels into a lorry on the Saturday morning and then travelled to the track (no names, no pack drill) with an expectation that maybe someone from the track would be there to help them erect said fence. Sad to say, they were disappointed, a disappointment that was enhanced when the only refreshment that they were offered while they put up the air fence on a hot day was a glass of water provided by a member of the greyhound staff who took pity on them as they struggled with the massive job of fixing the fence in place. They made the long journey home to Swindon no doubt buoyed by the fact that the Sunday could be no worse than the Saturday. Oh dear. Back at the track after the 2 hour drive on the Sunday morning, they had to make significant changes to the positioning of the air fence at the request of the hosts - what a shame these hadn't been pointed out on the Saturday when the fence was being put up. Once practice had been completed Keith observed to a member of the host track staff that the fence would need to be cleaned before actual meeting. What he didn't expect was to be shown the pressure washer and told, in so many words, that if he wanted it cleaned he should do it himself. Needless to say, he declined. At the end of a meeting at Swindon track staff stay behind and pull back the shale and make sure that any shale clinging to the fence or the kickboards is brushed or scrapped off. We like to think that we have sufficient goodwill to help out anyone else who is clearly in need of help. At the end of the meeting in question, despite being asked if they could help earlier, the home staff disappeared almost before the presentation was over leaving our intrepid foursome to dismantle over 40 air fence panels, most of them liberally coated with shale and therefore significantly heavier than they were before, and then load them into a lorry to take them back to Swindon."

25th July

Jason Attwood   "Kauko had been stopping with me since Thursday, and I promised him on the Sunday morning that we'd do him a full English – so my wife got up and did that for him, and when the fans heard about that they were asking if we could do it for all seven next week!"

Fredrik Lindgren*   "Here we go! Back to work at Wolves speedway Monmore Green 19:30 tonight! First I need to get there, on my way to Skavsta Airport"

Jan O Pedersen   "I have a dream and that is to become a professional speedway rider again, for how long I just don't know but I certainly feel good on the bike again."

Niels Kristian Iversen*   "Nice run this morning. Car has now gone for service. Time for a shower and spend the day with the missus."

Kenni Larsen*   "Sat at the airport in billund. Waiting to board"

Lewis Bridger* "at Southampton Central station , checking out the new MOTO mag.. :-) need to be home sharpish got Wolves tonight !"

Fredrik Lindgren* "Have meet up with PK at Stansted, going up the Midlands. He's just upgrading our car today from a Ford Focus to a Mercedes S 350! Why?!?"

Chris Holder* "Wish I was jet ski'n today! Not driving to Coventry!!"

Fredrik Lindgren* "Food at Ikea in Walsall today, it's meatballs time!"

Chris Neath* "Hearing good things about the track at rye. Some of the lads had a practice today and reckon it was pretty good with the new dirt."

Sam Masters* "Shit for me last night left me gating gloves home I reckon 0,3,1,2,2 atleast I got 1 win"

Kelvin Tatum "Sayfutdinov was almost facing the wrong way...he's almost going backwards"

Nigel Pearson "Nick Morris could ride for Great Britain if he decides in the future"

Kelvin Tatum "The front wheel washes out"

Kelvin Tatum "When you get off the bike, there isn't a lot of give in the track, I can assure you"

Neil Middleditch "[Doyle's] shoulder has been a big problem – he's popped it out five or six times this season"

Kelvin Tatum "He really hit hard against the ground, the track"

Nigel Pearson "I have to say that bit of the track is causing problems"

Kelvin Tatum "It is and they had a stock car meeting at the weekend"

Kelvin Tatum "He almost stops it inside out"

Chris Louis "Rosco described you as smooth and composed which aren't words you usually associate with Ryan Fisher"

Ryan Fisher "Hear that? It's a bomb ticking"

Nigel Pearson "Back in February March, there were doubts about Coventry being in the Elite League, in fact they were out of the Elite League"

Emil Sayfutdinov "Today is my first meeting when it's sunshine"

Nigel Pearson "And, of course, Sayfutdinov's English has improved significantly but Russians do have to take an English test to ride in the UK"

Nigel Pearson "I know a lot of it is instinct and a lot of it is skill as well"

Kelvin Tatum "If you can't tell your brain to put it down"

Nigel Pearson "Well, the medical vehicle is probably the busiest vehicle in the stadium tonight"

Kelvin Tatum "His arms and knees all sort of landed on the track"

David Watt "Something from the stockcars, the track flicked up and hit me foot"

Chris Holder "The track's absolutely fine"

Chris Holder "I'm the same as everyone else, I can't believe we're losing riders so much"

Chris Holder "With Emil behind you, you've got to be everywhere"

Paul Burbidge* "Carnage at Coventry. This is ridiculous. Poole's title bid could come crashing down at Brandon for the second year running"

Updates [heat 13 at Belle Vue] "Pedersen tried taking Schlein out but ended up in 3rd then teddies and dummies came out of pram as Nicki and Rory starting fisty cuffs with handbags at 10 paces"

Fredrik Lindgren* "Have to say that this Mercedes car that we've had today is pretty darn good! Back at Stansted can't wait for my bed, early flight tomorrow!"

Chris Holder* "Finally home! What a weird meeting tonight! We still nearly got a point! Haha sun back out tomorrow I hope"

Trevor Swales "We were totally let down by the middle order, there are two or three riders tonight who have lost the meeting for us. It doesn't take a genius to work out who they are."

26th July

Niels Kristian Iversen* "Dont enjoy getting up 2.30 in the morning. A sleep on the plane would be good. Piraterna - indianerna tonight"

> Rory Schlein* "So iv had night to sleep on it and to think if I over reacted about wat nikki did.. Fuck know Im sendin hi An invoice for a new foot rest"
> Nicolai Klindt* "remember the vat aswell haha"

> David Watt* "Running late for the plane today but I should still make it as I have my new scooterbag and will be cruisin to the gate ! Some Stansted staff want photos with me and my bag and then the fun police kicked me off already ! But I'm back on it !!"
> Darcy Ward "so problems already ??"
> David Watt* "nah just one guy that was a wanker. Everyone else loves it !! So pumped I got one !! And the bag fits perfectly in the overhead locker !!"
> Chris Holder* "hows she handle..."
> Nicolai Klindt* "that is so cool man! where do you get a thing like that?"

Mads Korneliussen* "I hate screaming children"

Fredrik Lindgren* "Love having spotify straight in my TV love my harman/kardon sound! Chillin listening to Winnerbäck at the moment"

Mads Korneliussen* "When I stop racing in 15 years time. I want to be that man driveing the bus at stansted longstay carpark #cooljob"

Lewis Bridger* "There is no I in Team"

Peter Johns* "PJR 'so when did it blow up?' mechanic 'the last time he used it' no shit!"

Kenni Larsen* "Athlete feet fuck off!!!"

Ludvig Lindgren* "what a day! first i nearly missed my flight because boarding ticket wouldent print! then i ran to the wrong gate and train! But made it!"

27th July

Dakota North* "breakfast not really filling!!"

Taylor Poole* "Wants instant healing magic"

Nicolai Klindt* "not bad for a fiver to get coffee and a breakfast roll with cheese and ham. flying out to sunny-england to make my bikes fast!"

David Watt* "Nice day in Sweden today. On the plane now and I hope it's like this when I get back to the UK !!"

Mike Bennett* "looking forward to Stars v Eastbourne at the Norfolk Arena tonight. Messages on here- best be careful with those tweets LBR???"

Lewis Bridger* "just at my mum's AVEDA salon, I have just had a massage and now feel ready for kings lynn tonight"

Niels Kristian Iversen* "Longstay at stansted has gone up to 12pounds pr day.. Pisstakers."

Mads Korneliussen* "Todays 5k run done, now just bring on tonight, lets get it sideways"

Lewis Bridger* "Going for a 40min cycle then a sauna then hitting the road for Kingslynn"

Mads Korneliussen* "Frankie & benny's meatballs, can't beat that for racefood"

Lewis Bridger* "Ended up going swimming instead of a cycle ride, now have to find some decent race food for tonight"

Niels Kristian Iversen* "Just had dinner. My home COOKED Rice and turkey :) Getting ready now to go to Kings lynn"

Lewis Bridger* "LBR , Woodwardski , Lahti in convoy from Eastbourne 2 Lynn #stylinguptheM25"

Lewis Bridger* "Was at the Dartford tunnel jammed wid boys, we turned of into LND a2 & picked up the a12 feel sorry 4 the rest of the boys #fullgastomakeit"

Cameron Woodward* "your a shit team rider mate"

Chris Holder* "Jus busted a guy stealing from HMV haha #fightingcrime"

Rory Schlein* "Seen Mr. Watt with his new scooter bag and I must say it's cool but not happy that he left me trailing"

David Watt* "Im already thinking about pimping my bag with new wheels !! "Pimp My Bag" business getting started now ! On my way to Peter Johns to collect engines for tonight and see if he can make my bag go as fast as his engines !!"

Troy Batchelor* "going to wash the car when I got home then drove past a hand car wash couldn't resist it"

Paul Burbidge* "They're dropping like flies on turn one at Wimborne Road. Track being graded now. Watt, Gafurov, Havelock and Bondarenko all struggling. Poole are carrying too many passengers. Lakeside beating them 23-16 after 7 races"

Fredrik Lindgren* "I Wanna make you sweat, just wanna make you sweat!"

CovbeesfanAli* "I'm sure you do love but don't tell everyone!!"

Kevin Long* "I've tried [reading tweets] at Ipswich and hasnt really taken off. . . plus I think Mike Bennett relies on it a little too much.. i like to balance things"

Lewis Bridger* "track was pritty narly ;-) but my motor was strong & had some good racing"

28th July

Chris Holder "It couldn't have been impossible because I am stood here talking about it, but it was a bit tight. I'm just stoked that I pulled it off and then me and Watty were able to ride the last race as though it was a final."

Lukas Dryml "From the back it looked like Bjarne was faster than Nermark and was going around him. It looked like Nermark was trying to take him out. That's how it looked. I'm not afraid to say these things. Nermark is a nice guy but sometimes these things happen. Bjarne is so lucky I didn't run him over. I looked into his scared eyes when he went down and I did everything I could to miss him. I put the bike on its side and I missed him but Bjarne's bike was in front of me and I couldn't miss the bike."

Rob Godfrey [on Glasgow] "Surprised me? It's shocked me! I don't even think they're a good team. Although the stats clearly prove otherwise."

Nigel Pearson "I know some people will say we could replace Jon Armstrong or Ashley Morris with Adam [Roynon] and keep Kyle [Hughes], but that would be a win at all costs attitude and that's not what this club is about."

Gary Irving "I've been in positions where I have felt that places for riders like myself have gone to foreign riders. I wasn't happy at the time and said so. But now I have this chance at Workington... I'm not making anything much in the National League but it's what you have to do to get noticed. As long as I keep getting chances in the Premier League and start making a bit of money, I can carry on."

29th July

Graham Drury "That was the sort of performance I expect week-in, week-out, and it beggars belief how Krzysztof can ride like he has in the last few home matches, and then nobody could get near him!"

Matt Ford "Thomas [H. Jonasson] has not fully committed to British speedway but I am really keen to have him at Poole. I came close to signing him a couple of seasons ago and have been keeping a watch on how he has been going. I have given Thomas a schedule of our fixtures and if we feel we need to make a change to our declared 1-7 then obviously he could come into the reckoning, but as things stand at present it is more to a view of 2012 that I am looking."

Rob Godfrey "We had a bigger crowd in for this [Glasgow] meeting and it was great that we could dig deep and win so well against strong opposition. It's a shame that our fans didn't get to see Screenie riding but they picked some outstanding guests and it was like facing an all-stars side."

Rory Schlein "I love coming back here [Edinburgh] and showing the people who gave me my first break in speedway how I've progressed. I've still got so many friends here."

Steve Shovlar "Swindon parking system is a huge bug bear to me. it is shoddy, badly organised and very, very irritating. You pay a quid, then r stuffed down a track which is roped off until you get to the bottom. Then you are guided (forced) into a spot you don't want. I wind the window down, tell them I don't want to park there but further up at the front. Reply is 'park where I tell you'. I tell them to shove it and to let me out. They then go on their radios and a military operation takes place to lower the rope and allow escape from the gestapo. I park at the top where I wanted to, and look back to see these clowns waiving their rms at me. they don't like it one bit. A complete and utter joke. Now look at Poole as a different example. You pay a quid and find a spot yourself. no cronies or jobsworths, no anger or finger pointing. Blunsdon needs someone to collect a quid with a counter (not needed this year by the sound of it) and let the drivers park where they want. Coventry is better. Free parking and no hassle (although cars do or certainly did get damaged there during meetings). Swindon need to sort this out as a matter of urgency."

Kim Nilsson "I am a bit of a thinker when I am riding"

Terry Daley "The bout of handbags at ten paces between Magnus Karlsson and start marshal Ken Petherick...has nothing to do with speedway"

30th July

Niels Kristian Iversen* "What a shitty meeting last night. Could not make it work my way. Going for practice this morning at the local track"

Fredrik Lindgren* "Tonight is the night! The night to show the world I can make great starts! Come on Freddie fight it out!"

David Watt* "Spain is great for many reasons. Sunshine & topless sunbathing are my favorites though !!!"

Scott Nicholls* "u love gettin ya boobs out!"

Dick Barrie "I am convinced a boy will learn more from a single NJL match – having to race with a partner against two others in a competitive situation – than in a dozen after-match, solo spin training sessions. Already this season we have introduced teenage talent such as Liam Carr and Brenton Barnwell to our Borderers, with more to come. Down at Buxton, the nomadic Halifax Dukes have stuck Connor Coles into their dressing room (with the two girls?) and Redcar have brought in Connor Lamb. Teenagers all. It is for these young riders, and other teens who will follow in future, we endorse and support the Northern Junior League. To learn about racing, they need opposition, and if that must come from enthusiastic amateurs of uncertain age, why not? The most-common reason given by other local circuits for not joining the Northern Junior League is that 'there aren't any riders around' – well, maybe not at their tracks. I wonder why?"

Alex Davies "I spoke to a few people about it, including my dad, who said that I should go out and enjoy the experience of racing. After all it's not a bad life being a speedway rider, I can think of a lot worse things I could be doing! I'm only 18 and here I am on the other side of the world from home, doing something I love, you can't ask for more than that, can you?"

Danny King "I'm more than happy to go on record and say there is an issue with team spirit at Birmingham...we seem to be fine one week and enjoying our racing and then the next we are riding against each other....A No.1 doesn't just bring points to be table, but he also lifts the rest of the team and we don't have a rider like that at Birmingham. I know that we have Krzysztof [Kasprzak] but how can explain the fact that he rides so badly for us and then goes on and wins the World Cup with Poland riding like a World Champion?...I don't want to sound too controversial, I'm just being honest with my feelings because right now I feel pretty down about it all."

Nigel Pearson* "water only for us. But after the meeting, who knows!!"

Paul Burbidge* "BA are delivering my lost suitcase to my hotel between 3pm and 4pm. I can finally change my underpants ahead of the Italian SGP!"

Paul Burbidge* "The numbskulls British Airways have finally delivered my suitcase. But can they can get it back to Gatwick tomorrow without losing it again?"

Nicolai Klindt* "coventry fans - i really enjoyed it last night! felt sorry to let you down in heat 13 but couldnt do anything els. defo come back if asked!"

Dave Tattum "I still work closely with Mike Corbett who is managing director of Corbettsports. We get on well and Mike is delighted to be sponsoring such a prestigious event [NL 4s] here at Loomer Road."

Nigel Pearson* "Will try and tweet during meeting but harder when doing world feed with no breaks"

Paul Burbidge* "Chris Harris has his smile back ahead of the Italian SGP. He's worth a few quid each way tonight"

Dick Barrie "Actually, there was a spill – two of the guys taking part in the 'Blast From The Past' race piled up. Great old codgers, these lads - more than 200 years between the four of them, and lovely noisy old JAP machines to race on! "

Mike Bennett* "looking forward to visiting Glasgow Speedway tomorrow as they take on the "Moan-archs". First visit of the season for me!"

Paul Burbidge* "Raining harder in Terenzano - this is a worry"

Paul Burbidge* "Looks the rain is easing in Terenzano ahead of the FIM Nice Italian SGP"

Jan Staechmann* "Getting close to starttime in Terenzano. We've had a shower but it's stopped now"

Nigel Pearson* "Rain has stopped and sun is shining here in Terenzano. Lasagne available in office, but still full from pizza!!"

Dick Barrie "Although not perfect, this season's system of an SPL-style 'split' to provide extra league matches was vastly preferable to the old idea of having a separate, average-adjusting, Premier Trophy in the early months before launching into proper league business. Just a bit of fine-tuning next year I submit, and we're sorted"

Niels Kristian Iversen* "Just been for a 42,5km ride ón my mountain bike. Now to watch GP. Meeting in Gorzow tomorrow"

Nicolai Klindt* "heading for wolvo now. big lost for swindon! not happy with ref excluding me - fish took me leg? bit unlucky in heat 14. 11p/6h 2,2,6,ex,1,0"

Mike Bennett* "Not the best GP so far? No Italian riders, crap track, poor racing so exactly why are they running a speedway GP here?"

Nigel Pearson* "This is wide open what do u think so far speedway fans?"

Mike Bennett* "Oh well, at least I'll see some real speedway at Glasgow tomorrow :-)"

Paul Burbidge* "Heat 14 should have been re-run in Terenzano. Tapes went up wonky. Holder and Harris had no chance. Holder was seething. Phone got trashed"

Lewis Bridger* "Had another Decent meeting tonight at eastie against swindon, 11pts/4h 1week off now it's a joke"

Nicolai Klindt* "for £7 you get bag of crisps, coke zero, bangers and mash plus a tray"

Maciej Janowski* "Greg Hancock no questions cingratulation and big whellies for Greg brooopppppppp"

Fredrik Lindgren* "Congratulating fellow swedes AJ & Antonio not forgetting Greg Hancock well done! I'm forgetting my own performance though, that was poor! Not looking forward for the long drive to Tarnow now! All night long!"

Scott Nicholls* "What a prick of a day.van arrived 10 mins before 1st race.touched tapes,then a crash,rode my balls off for a crap score. Better tomorrow"

Chris Holder* "Wat the f*%k!!!! Wat a shit night!!! Now only 14hour drive to Poland!"

Will Pottinger "Nights like this make everything worthwhile. It was very tense, but Ashley was brilliant to win it [NL 4s] for us in the last race. It was nice for us to celebrate with our fans, once again they were brilliant!"

John Anderson "In the past three seasons Berwick supporters and our visitors from Edinburgh in 2009, Newcastle in 2010 and now Glasgow in 2011 have swelled the Ben Fund by over £4,300 and it has simply left me breathless at their magnificent generosity."

Gary Patchett "We know it was a busy holiday weekend and traffic was heavy but several of our riders did not allow enough time. We have to question their commitment because it would not have happened for a major qualifier or main event."

John Louis "I'm enjoying the racing more than I have for the past few years. Entertainment at Premier League level has been very good and I like the commitment of the riders. It was the right move for us and I'm looking for a move back up the table."

31st July

Fredrik Lindgren* "Seriously hate my life at the moment!"

Chris Neath* "Well that was eventful last night. First bike wouldn't run so stole bits off 2nd bike and ended up with neither working!"

Linus Sundstrom* "Off to rybnik now for the last meeting in poland this season.. Far to early to finish the season in july over here!"

Nigel Pearson* "Just been ripped off by taxi driver taking Jan Staechmann and me back to Trieste Airport. Not happy. Just wanna be home now!"

Charlie Webster* "Doing a Reiki course today...very interesting, moving of energy, healing. Little bit wary at first, breaktime now time to peak at F1"

Ludvig Lindgren* "just chillin at home! and iam Naked atm! Sweet u cant see it but some how u already got a picture in ur head! SimSalaBim"

Fredrik Lindgren* "Very nice that after the match get into the shower and there was no hot water! We've not had any problems with hot water in Tarnow before"

Linus Sundstrom* "What a sh!et day.. 5hrs to a rain off and 5hrs back to the hotel!"

Hans Andersen* "Tough decision to be made about a possible UK come back"

Scott Nicholls* "Better day today. Had another crash,but all good. Paid 10 & team won,so some happy polish bunny's tonight.3am start,so shut eye for me!Night"

Chris Holder* "Was getting spat on by the zielona gora fans!!! Hahahaha look at the scoreboard guys we smoked use!"

Fredrik Lindgren*

"Finally at my hotel in Krakow, headed to same hotel as last week. Got a different room tonight and it don't have the same bed as me at home. Really looking forward to this shower now as the hot water in Tarnow mysteriously vanished after that home loss tonight"

Chris Holder* "we need to make a plan Freddie!"

Fredrik Lindgren* "Amen!"

Peter Johns* "beat the old fella then! can't buy experience"

Tony Jackson "I just cannot believe the run of injuries we are having at the moment, we seem to finish every match with one rider less than we started with. We should be known as the Workington 'Casualty' Comets at the moment"

Gordon Pairman "The speedway world is small and it is often sensible to think twice before speaking (or tweeting in the case of a Team GB rider!). A good case in point is with former Glasgow captain Shane Parker, who used to hate everything to do with Sheffield, promoters and track especially, but had to cosy up to them, firstly to get a team place anywhere this year and secondly so that he can get a farewell meeting there next year. A meeting which may well attract fewer Glasgow supporters than would otherwise have been the case, after his recent antics......Actually, I appreciate that some of the stuff being thrown towards us from South Yorkshire hasn't been solely from Shane and I find that all rather disappointing. Those of you who read these programme pieces know that I am a great believer that, if you want to be a member of a club, then you have to follow its rules. And if you want to sit on the committee that runs that club, then you have an even greater duty to ensure that you do not undermine the club, or its members, in public. Further, if you are given the role of mentor to a new club, you should use that for the good of the club and not for points scoring. Maybe I should write an ethical guideline for those that appear not to understand that a position of authority brings obligations as well as privileges."

1st August

Chris Holder* "Pissed off right now"

Lewis Bridger* "had a good weekend & have let my hair down, now back to the Speedway life tomorrow & some Mx training tuesday/Wednesday"

Fredrik Lindgren* "Bad weekend has come to an end, a new week awaits with more speedway around the globe. A better week for me I wish!"

Olly Allen* "4 years ago today I lost the most amazing woman in the world, she was an angel. Rest in peace mum #missyoualways"

Nigel Pearson* "Looking forward to having the National Fours Trophy in the lounge. Might cover up a pic of the mother-in-law, though"

Jim Lynch I know youngsters Kyle Howarth and Jason Garrity showed they were not out of place when we brought them into the side but [Lucasz] Jankowski is much more experienced and that's what we need on the run-in to the season."

Nicolai Klindt* "had a good weekend, been racing a lot, went alton towers and had a nice bbq with the other halfs family.. now some paper work and food!"

David Watt* "Only half way though and I'm so over this paperwork !! I need an assistant... and money !!! #ijustwanttoridemybike"

Nigel Pearson* "No Emil for Cov, Aces by 6"

David Watt* "WizzAir rocks ! RyanAir sucks !"

Nicolai Klindt* "never been this close missing my flight. thanks to traffic n loads of w*nkers on the road"

Nicolai Klindt* "but im in, safe"

Hans Andersen* Hmmmm sat watching Belle Vue Vs Coventry and is wondering WILL Emil ever ride enough meetings to get an average"

Mike Bennett* "Nick Morris doing his talking ON the track tonight. Better than talking on twitter eh? :-)"

Nigel Pearson* "Great night well done both Aces and Bees deserved some reward. I love my job!!!"

Peter Adams "Freddie [Lindgren] is in good spirits right now but doesn't know what day it is or who he is. He's taken a bad bang to the head and he is complaining of pains in his neck and back but has full movement which is good news."

Jim Lynch "We can say goodbye to a top four play-off place. Coventry rode as a team and we were disjointed. Our new signing Lukasz Jankowski made a great debut with six points and it was criminal he should give a performance like that and we only get a draw."

Rory Schlein* "Bye bye play offs"

Ludvig Lindgren* "Fredster is Ok. he dident have any broken bones but he took a big hit on the head and is going to stay at the hospital over the night"

2nd August

Graham Drury "I'm not talking about one or two riders here, I'm talking about clearing out almost half the team and bringing riders in. The difficulty I had in the end was it was like a pack of cards. If one deal failed then they were all off, and that's what happened by Monday lunchtime."

Nigel Pearson* "Hate it when riders I regard as mates get hurt. Part of the sport I guess, will update again tomorrow on Fast Freddie when Pete Adams calls"

Ludvig Lindgren* "just got 50 extra followers because of freddies crash how sad is that!"

Rory Schlein* "Just at stansted airport and want to know why every man and his dog is here? Just finished I nice Chinese at 6am mmmmmm"

David Watt* "On my way to Stansted and the M25 is so crap !! If it stays like this, I'm gonna ride my scooterbag to the airport !"

Chris Holder* "Jus layin down in the lounge at gdansk airport"

Chris Holder* "Never knew they had this room! Usually fly out from the other side of airport!"

Fredrik Lindgren* "Almost out of hospital, feel a lot better today but still in pain. Thanks to nurse Sharon who took care of me this night when I was in pain"

Mads Korneliussen* "Just thinking 75000km is = 750 hours and thats = 31,2 days fu€kkkkkk"

Lewis Bridger* "It's all about hitting up a few energy drinks when u go party, not the alcohol it does nothing for you being a sportsman"

David Watt* "Oh please!!!"

Lewis Bridger* "just activated my micro sim for my new iphone 4 in white bling,bling !! iPhone 4 is up & running can everybody with my number send me a txt plz missing number"

Mads Korneliussen* "how lucky am I. I am sitting beside two young children on the plane"

Nigel Pearson* "Need a holiday big-time"

Sir Gerald Kaufman MP "We are breathing new life into Belle Vue speedway, another local historic institution and I am happy to do whatever I can to help"

3rd August

Graham Drury "All our discussions with Greg, Antonio and Hans were very amicable and we actually spoke to Hans in the winter and he came and had a look around Perry Barr but decided to join Coventry. I think it's only fair to let our supporters know exactly what we have been trying to do and I'd like to thank the three riders named for the professional manner in which they held talks. I would like to think we could have the opportunity to talk to them again in the winter with a view to the 2012 season."

Fredrik Lindgren* "In the day I told myself I felt ok. In the night truth catches up, been in some pain. Why did I not get stronger painkillers I wonder now?"

Darcy Ward* "fucking hell dude cat-d right off"

Olly Allen* "Just cycled to bakery for my pre match ham salad sandwich, the woman in there in there says 'the usual sir'"

Olly Allen* "maybe I go there too much??"

Lewis Bridger* "If I could slide a diamond ring on anybody right now it would be taped to the front of my new iphone4"

Nigel Pearson* "Spending all day on Heathens speedway business - but it doesnt pay the bills! Priorities..."

Rory Schlein* "Walking through the terminal and was expecting to see 3 Poole riders on their scooter bags"

Chris Holder* "On way home after a week on the road!! Jetski tomorrow? I think so!!!"

Mads Korneliussen* "Run done, ready for tonight and I found 10 quid in the street when I was out running. Cool as"

Niels Kristian Iversen* "Mega rain shower in peterborough. Hope it wont make kings lynn for tonight. Swindon is in town. Go stars.."

Not Len Silver* "Been busy sorting out admiral nelson's poor performances this season, told that boy to take off his eye patch and he'll be mustard"

Hans Andersen* "My UK comeback have been delayed due to some missunderstanding with the BSPA so hopefully things will get sorted IF i'll be back 2012 4 sure"

Jo Lowry* "Heard [false rumour] Tai Woffinden tried to start a fight amongst Poole fans tonight. I had a feeling he wanted to be a Bee, but didn't realise how much! P.S although very funny, I do of course hope no poole fans were injured during this"

Jo Lowry* "Unless of course it was Shovlar"

Jo Lowry* "Oh no! Jeff Scott is following me now! Best watch what I tweet :p"

Mads Korneliussen* "pissed off about today. But win is a win"

Niels Kristian Iversen* "What a bastard meeting. 2 bikes packing up, 1st at startline and the other while leading. Guess it cost us all league points"

4th August

Ludvig Lindgren* "just got home from poole and what a meeting never done so many practise starts in my life and hopefully i never will again"

Dakota North* "20 today! I don't feel twenty that's for sure! oldman"

Nicolai Klindt* "can feel the body is pretty sore after crash in heat one last night. good meeting by the robins boys and what a star Maciej Janowski is?"

Niels Kristian Iversen* "Must be about a million people in Stansted airport just now. wanna get on that plane and sleep. Gorzow - Rzeszow 19.00"

Nigel Pearson* "Morning all day in voiceover studio ready to relive Greg Hancock extending SGP lead to 22 points! Surrey bound"

Linus Sundstrom* "Just boarded the ryanair boeing 737-800 to london stansted!"

Chris Neath* "Beautiful all week then the day I'm racing its hammering down. Please be nice mr weather god"

Niels Kristian Iversen* "Busy times atm, Gorzow tonight, DK tomo, poland playoff start this weekend, Wolves mon, Swe tue, KL wed"

Lewis Bridger* "How can the weather go from like being in marbs to this, it's shocking was loving life yesterday and today it's shit"

> **Linus Sundstrom*** "Arrived in the uk and its typical uk weather! I didnt come here for another rainoff"
>
> **Olly Allen*** "no chance buddy! You have definitely arrived for a rain off!!"

Nigel Pearson* "Lovin the tunes on Capital FM - a young person's station!! M25 nightmare tho"

Chris Holder* "Me an Darcy gotta go shoppin for some jet ski gear yeewwww"

Chris Neath* "Just spoke to my mate (15miles from Redcar) and he reckons its been pissing down all day. If I do £100 diesel for nothing, not goNna be happy"

Paul Burbidge* "Chris Holder says he had 'no energy whatsoever' after pulling out of Wolves guest booking tonight"

Nigel Pearson* "Just to confirm to all Heathens speedway followers I have just brought back Danny Stoneman to replace Adam Portwood. Welcome back Danny"

Paul Burbidge* "Can't wait for my first visit to Leicester for the PL Fours. In 8yrs of covering speedway, I've never done the Fours"

Chris Neath* "Awesome meeting tonight on a wicked [Redcar] race track. 11+1/5h and we got a draw. Worst ref decision ever seen cost us the match"

Chris Neath* "I want to know how we've been to Redcar quite a bit, have sat nav and yet still Noel goes the wrong way. Not once but TWICE!!!!"

5th August

Malcolm Simmons "At the end of every year [Tai Woffinden] talks about 'going home' for the winter to recharge his batteries, and home to him is Perth, Western Australia, so in my book he's an Aussie"

Chris Neath* "Straight to bed, busy day tomoz. Bike wash, change cracked back end and loads of other shit"

Hans Andersen* "Finally through passport at Luton, one of Them days were millions of poles decided to fly to England arrrrghh ! Oh way I'M here now"

Fredrik Lindgren* "Hate nights and specially mornings, freaking painful! Eat painkillers like candy"

Hans Andersen* "was hoping for elite league action BUT nothing on tonight bummer"

Fredrik Lindgren* "Lying down thinking, Smiling Gold-Brown Eyes!"

Rory Schlein* "Wow who needs the gym when ya got 2 girls that run ya into the ground at a play house"

Lewis Bridger* "These Motorways are a f&€king joke M4 now :-/ The M25 is stopped, ideal"

Fredrik Lindgren* "Been to do some Physio therapy with Steve Williams, another session again tomorrow"

David Watt* "I'm rockin out out with my boys Darcy & Chris love live music !!"

John Campbell "I have had concerns for some weeks now about the standard of racing we are presenting here. Last week we tried something a little different with the track and I think it produced a meeting with much more spectacle and far more opportunities to overtake. Those riders who were prepared to attack the track, and in particular Morris, Tully and Wolbert, did well but for others it proved more challenging. It is how I would like the track to be every week but our great British weather means that, with wind, rain and sunshine and generally on the same day, it is difficult to make the track the same week on week."

Rob Godfrey "To be honest, I think the grippier the better, because that's the way to produce good racing"

Nicola Sands* "congratulations [Julia Bradbury] from all of us at BSI Speedway / SGP. Enjoy Motherhood - Zephyr will have a wicked sense of humour! :-)"

Mike Hunter "[Glasgow] owed an immense amount to Nick Morris, who gave probably the best reserve's display ever at Armadale. To dominate the home reserves is one thing, but to run rings round several of the top five is quite another, and that's what Morris did. The track was deeper than usual and several riders found it difficult to ride. You would not have thought that watching Morris who revelled in it, with outstanding control and the ability to turn tight and pass coming out of the turns – the essence of a good speedway rider."

6th August

Hans Andersen* "In need of sleep, these early morning starts and no sleep are getting to mé, not feeling very well NO time for sickness now #onthegas"

Jason Lyons "Len Silver puts a lot of time and effort into the track and if all the other promoters did the same, then speedway would be a lot more enjoyable"

Darcy Ward* "Fuck has the worst ankle #donedamage"

Alun John Rossiter* "taxi for ward :-) stick to speedway it's less dangerous mate !"

Simon Lambert "I used to be a bit of a Jack-the-Lad but all that has changed now and I feel better in myself and about my racing. I have a new girlfriend and enjoy spending time with her and my family as opposed to partying. I guess it's about growing up and now I feel I am acting beyond my years and that is showing in a lot of ways."

Ricky Wells* "Plymouth bound to race Ludvig Lindgren #takehimtothefence"

Magnus Karlsson "[Beaumont Park] is a gater's paradise. There are a few passes, but it is very hard to pass around there. The corners are very tight."

Fredrik Lindgren* "Have to go back to New Cross hospital now with a few questions from my Physio"

Gary Patchett "First of all let me say that I rate the rider [Thomas H. Jonasson] very highly indeed. I did when he came to Swindon last year and I still do, but some of the things you sweep under the table affected our decision to keep the money in the bank rather than to finalise his signing from Edinburgh. We took him, knowing he had a one month ban after taking bad advice. We then had a series of missed flights, dental problems – and then of course another ban...some, even much of this, was known at the time so I am not engaged in dirty washing in public. I am simple re-stating the known problems we had during his short stay with us to explain to fans who are not happy about Poole's potential interest in Jonasson for the future."

Fredrik Lindgren* "Interesting question today, a photo I put on Twitter some time ago involving me & a hairdryer. A man want to use that for a book cover"

Chris Holder* "What a sick night with David watt & Darcy Ward!!!!!! We starting up a band"

Darcy Ward* "moshpit done me"

Fredrik Lindgren* "Looking at a picture of an awesome bottom. My favourite bottom!"

Cameron Woodward "Doing seven rides is not an inconvenience. I've got to take the rides. It's all income if I score points and it helps the team out."

Neil Machin "We haven't been officially told, but my understanding is that no action will be taken by the SCB apart from slapping Glasgow on the wrist. That's certainly not the outcome we wanted and we will say more if and when we get the official letter. We would have been confident of winning there in the original fixture but it now looks as though we will have to go to Ashfield and take the points if we want to stay on top of the table, although we haven't been offered a re-staging date yet."

Poole fan "Bloody Hefenbrock isn't riding, he's turned round and gone back!"

Jo Lowry* "Shamek has had his ipod on all night. I asked him what he was listening to. He puts the earphone in my ear, only for it to be Adele"

Jo Lowry* "Someone like you to be precise"

Jo Lowry* "not the motivational music I was expecting, but hey! If it does the job."

Scott Nicholls* "Think if Jennifer Aniston was the swindon boss we'd be un-beatable! Well no complaints anyway,Haha"

Ashley Wooller "The best quote I can think of is the headline in the German equivalent of the *Speedway Star* after Cam won the longtrack that said – in German – in big letters 'Who the fuck is Woodward?'"

Kevin Coombes "£24! That's a very good price"

Mick Bellerby "As you say, they are two fantastic meetings!"

Jo Lowry* "Fuck you Lakeside"

Lewis Bridger "It doesn't seem to have the mid-range torque with the silencers"

Nick Barber "Johnny [Barber] was saying that the best Play Off Final would be King's Lynn versus Eastbourne"

David Watt* "Well atleast we won the coin toss ! Gotta take the positives from it tonight ! I'd wanna be better tomorrow !!!"

Pirates of Poole "I have to feel for the fans that made the journey and paid to watch a team perform like that, Watty lost his voice and looked like he had a cold, said on the mic him Darcy and Chris did somthing last night [Pennywise concert in BoMo] that helped him lose his voice"

Ian Rae "This was one of the very best Bandits' team performances I've ever seen [36-57 at Plymouth] and that's over more than four decades!"

Edward Kennett "I couldn't ask for anything more really, my starting was good, the bike was working well on the track and I feel like I'm back to where I was a couple of months ago. What a great team performance as well, everyone dug deep and young Nick did a great job – he even had to jump on my bike in one race and he did the business, so I'm proud of all the boys tonight."

Dick Barrie "The [Plymouth] locals were pretty confident too, and I was repeatedly told how Ben Barker had won his last 31 races at the track, and was – to put it bluntly – an absolute God to the fans and just unbeatable. Well, that lasted all of 50.59 seconds of Heat 1, when Seb and Ludvig handed Mr God a 5-1!"

7th August

Fredrik Lindgren* "Need my energy!"

Mads Korneliussen* "Goooooddd night. Hotel van #loveit"

Scott Nicholls* "What a prick of a road system they have at Luton airport.clear all the way,then takes 25 mins to do about 1/2 a mile! Need some wings"

Nigel Pearson* "its a shambles on that approach road mate does my head in there"

Scott Nicholls* "it's shocking! Let's have an international airport with a farty little road off a roundabout. Good call!"

Chris Holder* "need a scooter bag ;-)"

Scott Nicholls* "maybe. Reckon I'd be pretty knackered by the time I got there from ipswich though! :-)"

Darcy Ward* "Just jumped the line at Luton airport #ruthless"

Chris Holder* "aren't u at Stansted? Hahahaha #dumbass"

Darcy Ward* "haha yeah I am. was bit tried ment Stansted"

Jo Lowry* "Speedway really is a fucked up sport. Shamek [Przemyslaw Pawlicki] did not look guilty. Nor was he worried when the protest was made. Just because he's polish doesn't mean he's guilty #racist Maybe the machine examiner should be sacked"

Jo Lowry* "clearly not doing his job properly checking all machines before the start of the meeting. Not saying anymore now. This place is turning into a bloody speedway forum! Too much rubbish from people who weren't there"

Lakeside The Lakeside Hammers have confirmed that they have made an official protest about three of the silencers used by the Coventry Bees at the Raceway on Saturday. The Complaint follows observations made by the SCB machine examiner and relayed to the Referee, Mr Allan, after Heat 7 of the meeting and passed on to the Bees Manager two heats later. As the referee was unwilling and unable to stop the meeting to address the complaint at that time the protest was consequently dealt with at the end of the meeting at which time the Bees too decided to make an official protest about the silencers of three of the Hammers. The Club will make no further statement on the matter at this time.

Philip Rising "There are lots of things we could include if the magazine had more pages, so it is always a balancing act that some think we get wrong and others who do not. For the record, an extra 16 pages in *Speedway Star* costs around £1,500 in printing costs alone and there are additional postal charges for subscription copies."

Steve Shovlar "Young Mr Dugard on his tractor even managed to outdo himself last night with his gate cheating. Holder got seriously wound up about it when talking to Middlo on the rerun of heat 13. This is of course nothing new at eastbourne and they have been cheating this way for donkeys years but last night took the buscuit. Ward arrived at the gate on gate 4 and demanded the start marshal scrape some shale together. It didn't make any difference as all the stuff had been dumped on the Eastbourne gates.....If Eastbourne do make it to the playoff Final, the BSPA or away team, whoever they may be, need to have someone standing at the starting gat with their own bucket of shale and rake. Otherwise their riders will arrive to a gate as bald as a gibbons back side. Regardless of that Poole were poor. Dugard certainly helped make sure Poole were left at the tapes but the team rode poorly and never loked like wining. Gafurov is now riding worse than King Artur ever did last season. He need to be gone. Matt was there last night and I am sure he won't let things just lie and is on the case. Luckily we probably have enough meetings in the bag to be in the playoffs, but we are probably not strong enough to win the title this year. With Coventry hitting form and with their extra 1.18 over every other team they are clear favourites to retain the title, which is a shame for the other fair minded clubs who played within the rules last winter."

BoMo1 "There was nothing wrong with the track!!! There were imo a couple of dubious first turn decisions by the referee, but you come to expect that from mr Gay at Eastbourne"

Fredrick Lindgren* "Have had to take the decision that I can't take part in the meeting at Wolves tomorrow, am very disappointed but my back still ain't good"

Darcy Ward* "its ok mate. Fuck I don't won't you there"

Ludvig Lindgren* "hiho cooking for my brother"

Fredrik Lindgren* "Looking forward to this sirloin steak with hasselback potatoes that my young bro Ludvig Lindgren is preparing and bearnaise sauce"

Paul Burbidge   Coventry star Edward Kennett has been stripped of the 15-point maximum he scored at Lakeside on Saturday after being found to have used a silencer that had been tampered with. The Team Great Britain international has also had his registration suspended by the Speedway Control Bureau for seven days from today. Kennett's team mate Nick Morris has also been stripped of three points he scored using the Sussex rider's bike in race 12. As a result, Coventry's 48-42 win at the Arena-Essex Raceway has been amended to a 42-30 victory to the Hammers, handing them three Elite League points instead of the Bees. And to make matters worse, Bees skipper Kennett could now face a fine or suspension if found guilty of tampering with the silencer. He is set for Disciplinary Court hearing after being charged with "non-compliance of the 2011 Speedway Regulations." A statement from the SCB read: "At last night's Elite meeting, a protest was made to the referee by the Lakeside team manager during the meeting, and another similar one was made by the Coventry team manager at the conclusion of the meeting. These protests concerned the validity of silencers being used during that meeting. At the conclusion of the meeting, six silencers were handed into the custody of a nominated SCB official, who this morning, in the presence of a representative of both Lakeside and Coventry had these examined by David King, the manufacturer of King Silencers. One silencer, that belonging to Edward Kennett, was found to have been tampered with and therefore used illegally."

Lakeside   The Lakeside Hammers wish to place on record their thanks to the SCB for the swift and forthright manner in which this weekend's events have been dealt with and to also thank the SCB Licenced Officers involved for their professionalism....we wish to record our thanks to the Management of Coventry Speedway for both their direct personal contact and commendable Official Statement. The two clubs have always enjoyed a warm relationship and we feel sure that this will continue.

Dakota North*   "At the fours this rain isn't looking good"

Paul Burbidge*   "Rain has stopped at Leicester and track looks in good condition. If we get a few dry hours, the PL Fours could go ahead"

Paul Burbidge*   "Rain is back at Leicester. I have a bad feeling"

Sam Masters*   "This rain is killen me could be at aoife's birthday but nooooo"

Ludvig Lindgren*   "watchin polish speedway with Freddie Lindgren thats how bored iam!"

Charlie Webster*   "Got a little bit carried away at gym,2 hrs,despite overpowering urge to run I behaved&didn't, plus did all my rehab exercises #hatebehaving"

Darcy Ward*   "WTF is wrong with you Hahah don't go to gym me #allnatural"

Chris Holder*   "hahahaha classic!"

Coventry   Following the SCB disciplinary hearing, the club will be taking its own internal action against Edward Kennett if necessary, and we can also confirm that the captaincy will pass to Ryan Fisher with immediate effect. Coventry Speedway has a long and proud history, and under no circumstances does the club condone cheating of any kind, whether that relates to race fixing or machine tampering. The club are shocked and disappointed by the actions of their captain, and would like to stress that no member of the Coventry management had any knowledge of Edward Kennett's silencer tampering. We would like to re-assure all speedway supporters that the management are as appalled by his actions as any fair-minded supporter would be. Coventry wish to express sincere apologies to British Speedway, its supporters, and in particular the supporters of Coventry and Lakeside who attended the meeting on Saturday, for this unacceptable misdemeanour. We would also like to thank the licenced officials at Lakeside for bringing the matter to the referee's attention, and for dealing with it in a professional manner.

Scott Nicholls*   "So then,I see riders have been caught cheating with the silencers in England. Let's hope the penalty is so strong it stops the other cheats!"

David Watt*   "So how many more illegal silencers are out there ???"

Peter Johns*   "I hear the sale of GM barrel bolts has gone up #toomuchnitro"

Scott Nicholls*   "Be interesting to see who has new silencers on now won't it!"

Olly Allen*   "really Cozmo? Fill me in! Who has been busted?"

Scott Nicholls* "I'm not naming mate,but u can easily see. I was shocked to be fair"

Rory Schlein* "Clean as a whistle here boys"

Ludvig Lindgren* "Any one got 2 new king silencers that i can buy for monday i really need them!!!!!"

Fredrik Lindgren* "The 2 I gave you not ok anymore?"

Ludvig Lindgren* "nah i gave them to another rider for the lakeside meeting!"

Nicolai Klindt* "just sorted my books out and business is looking good. now making some food and trying to watch polish league. does anyone have a link for some live stream polish league?"

Nigel Pearson* "As if Speedway, especially in the UK, needed any more crap"

Scott Nicholls* "best time to get it all clean then don't u think"

Nigel Pearson "All I am saying is that following the shambles of the winter the sport doesn't need this. Other sports are prospering"

Nigel Pearson* "Where exactly did I say it should have been covered up? And how would an independent body have changed this situation? Strange response"

Scott Nicholls* "Sorry I got on my high horse a bit.just hate cheating.Especially when I'm havin a tough season.To cheat would be an easy way out,but I won't"

Nigel Pearson* "Apologies to all darts and football fans for the nonsense regarding speedway on here tonight"

Jan Staechmann* "and a 7 day ban? That's a complete joke..."

Lewis Bridger* "SHOCKED If the likes of Kennett has the balls to cheat then there is defiantly loads of others in Speedway doing the same cheats"

Darcy Ward* "Fuck 7 days I'm doing it #moneyin"

Olly Allen* "Just read the Bspa news"

Olly Allen* "naughty edward if it's proven he is guilty!!"

Lewis Bridger* "hey make a decision about punishment in 7days, & It wouldn't surprise me if you ain't already ;-) Let's Keep all keep a eye on who's average drops by 2+"

Alun John Rossiter* "Thank god for carling heaven !!"

Lewis Bridger* "What's making me laugh is to catch someone out at Lakeside of all places !"

Steve Shovlar "Same old Coventry, always [redacted]. Am I suprised? no of course not ...They cheated with gaining a 1.18 advantage over every other team, they held the league to ransom and now we discover their team have been [redacted] allseason. What a suprise, who would have thought it? [some text redacted.] Enough said. But what about this then. Surely Kennett has been using this silencer all season. Therefore ALL the points he has scored this year SHOULD BE DEDUCTED FROM THE MEETINGS HE HAS RIDDEN IN AND THE RESULTS ADJUSTED ACCORDINGLY. Only fair way to do it. Coventry fans would surely back this 100% as they would not want to be thought of gaining an advantage over other clubs with illegal silencers, would they?"

Philip Rising "LET'S just say that if we printed that in *Speedway Star* the writs would be flying through the door. Posting such comments online is no defence and if I were SS I would consider posting an apology as soon as possible for what are quite obviously defamatory remarks"

Steve Shovlar "Oh for gods sake I post a windup and the forum goes into hyperdrive. Someone posted that it must be like a birthday and christmas rolled into one. No it's not because I actually like Eddie Kennett and think it's a real shame its him that has been caught. Would have been far better for it to have been one of the Poles/foriengers to be honest. Either way it's a Coventry rider who cheated, and that brings disrepute on that club. Perhaps I was a little over the top in my post and for that I apologise but at the end of the day club rivalries make it funny that Coventry are the ones who have been caught out. As for Eddie Kennett, as Nicholls has mentioned, there could be other riders who were also using illegal silencers and I am sure by now those have been dumped in the bin and they have tydied up their act. Well I hope so because I am sure this will bring around a lot more spot checks this season....Eddie will learn from this and after facing the consequences not do anything as silly again. Might hav to miss a while out but he will come back better for it"

Philip Rising   "BUT Steve, apart from anything else, you included the name of a respectable company in your tirade and if their lawyers get to see it I fear you might be in for a rude and potentially expensive awakening"

Nigel Pearson*   "Twitter is great but I need to sort out who I'm following because I've realised I don't give a toss about some people's views!"

Mike Bennett*   "any questions for Rosco on Wednesday night tweeps? Dedications could include 'silence `rs Golden?'"

Jo Lowry*   "Feel so angry that I spent so much time and effort on a rider that has put our club to shame. I'm not just a worker. I'm a fan. So disgusted & disappointed. Makes me so angry that its affected the team. All those fans that travelled yday. For nothing. I seriously hope he's not back in our team. Too much damage already been done. That would just make it worse. If that's even possible."

Philip Rising   "THE last time you had a cheap shot at Briggo I asked what your contribution to speedway was or is ... any chence off an answer this time? By PM will suffice"

Nigel Pearson*   "would be ironic if Leicester won when they only qualified as hosts! I agree you need home involvement, however"

Paul Burbidge*   "You need local interest and Leicester have pulled about 3,000 fans. If that's not good for the sport I don't know what is"

David Watt*   "And I wasn't feeling bad from the show the night before yesterday at Eastbourne, I just had a bad day. Sorry if that's not acceptable !!"

Niels Kristian Iversen*   "Gripped off in Leszno. Sucks.."

Dakota North*   "First day back and a meeting is rained off haha"

Chris Holder* [to Nicolai]   "lame is like not kool man! Haha I was expectin better then zero coke for relaxing after a tough week!"

David Watt*   "Would be cool to know who calls up the spares shops for new silencers tomorrow !!!"

Darcy Ward*   "ted said he's bring me mine tomorrow"

Paul Burbidge   "the most important thing Hemsley built when putting together an absolutely stunning speedway facility was a drainage system which looks like it could probably dry out the streets of Venice in no time."

Philip Rising   "It is frustrating that no matter what we do our circulation expectations will always be governed by the number of people attending speedway in the UK which is why we, like so many, are continually frustrated by its administration and regulations in this country"

Travis McGowan   "Everyone did a good job to put it [PL 4TT] on, and unfortunately the rain came back. There's nothing we can do about that, but there is a lot of cost involved in travelling and running the bikes. It could have been worked out a bit better. To be honest, it's probably costing me money to run in this meeting. I enjoy riding my motorcycle, but I think they did enough racing to get a clear result. Leicester could have had the win and World Championships have been decided on coin tosses before."

8th August
BBC Leicester
Leicester speedway cash stolen by masked gang

Masked men have stolen a large quantity of cash from Leicester Speedway after threatening a man and his teenage daughter. The 41-year-old victim [David Hemsley] was leaving the stadium late on Sunday when he was stopped by three men on Beaumont Way who threatened him with a metal bar. They made off with the cash towards Krefeld Way. Police said the man and his daughter were slightly injured and were left badly shaken by the incident. Det Con Paul Vincent said: "This was an extremely traumatic incident for the victim and his daughter and will no doubt leave a lasting effect on them. "There were a number of people in the area yesterday evening due to an event [PL 4TT] at Leicester Speedway and we are keen to speak to anyone who saw any suspicious activity prior to the incident." The stadium opened in April, bringing speedway back to the city after 28 years.

Kenni Larsen* "My fucking van has broke down in the middle of nowhere in Poland"

Fredrik Lindgren* "Hate it in the nights sometimes, the pain makes me wake up and it's a struggle to get to sleep again. I hate crashing!!"

Hans Andersen* "Cheating In our beloved sport is just a joke, i'd say people gettin court should be treated as where they doped, otherwise riders dont see the risk In doing so, people cheat In All sports but the amount is lowered if theres a risk of being suspended for a year or two !"

Gary Patchett* "7 days, laughable. Just encourages others. No deterrent. How many other results in question?"

Jan Staechmann* "I understand it is just 7 days, before the disciplinary hearing, which will determine action"

Daily Mail Speedway ace Kennett banned after using illegal silencer

Great Britain speedway star Edward Kennett has been banned for cheating in Coventry's Elite League win at Lakeside on Saturday. Coventry management last night cast doubts on his future after stripping him of the captaincy and vowing to take further action. The two-time British Under 21 champion will face a Speedway Control Bureau hearing after it was discovered he used an illegal silencer.

Philip Rising "WHEN was the last time the *Daily Mail* carried a headlined speedway story, especially on a busy Monday with soccer, rugby, cricket and golf vying for space? No prizes as to what was the subject matter."

BSPA At the conclusion of the Meeting, 6 Silencers were handed into the custody of a nominated SCB Official, who on Sunday morning, in the presence of a representative of both Lakeside and Coventry had these examined by David King, the manufacturer of King Silencers. One silencer, that belonging to Edward Kennett was found to have been tampered with and therefore used illegally. The points scored by Mr Kennett (15pts) and those scored by Nick Morris (3pts) when using Mr Kennett's motorbike in Heat 12 are deducted from the final score. The Revised score now reads: LAKESIDE 42 – COVENTRY 30 Mr Kennett has been charged with non-compliance of the 2011 Speedway Regulations and a date for a Disciplinary Court Hearing is being arranged. In accordance with the 2011 Speedway Regulations, Mr Kennett's SCB Registration is suspended for a period of 7 days as from yesterday."

Fredrik Lindgren* "Big thanks to Steve Williams helping out. I've done magnetic- elektro- & laser treatment as well as his hands have worked my problem areas"

Sam Masters* "Bought a new hot wash yesterday probably the 1st time I've been keen to wash my bike

Peter Johns* "remember the shaft & bearing I showed you last week!"

Sam Masters* "yeah boss ;)"

Chris Holder* "hahaha go easy sudden!"

Darcy Ward* "the keeness will not last long"

Sam Masters* "well guess what I haven't even started and I'm over it lol"

Mads Korneliussen* "how can I get my DEP exhaust to give more power, where do I drill a hole"

Mads Korneliussen* "Everyone is haveing a go at ED, but have everyone forgotten about Leon Madsen getting done last year, he only hat a fine. #whatajoke"

Fredrik Lindgren* "Agree with that when he only got a fine for that what a joke it was. I've not forgotten!"

Jo Lowry* "that's because there's clearly much more to it Mads. I'm 99% certain of it. Leon Madsen, wasn't he a Poole rider.....?"

Justin Sedgmen* "To true Mads there all kunts !!!"

Chris Neath* "Anyone got any of these new regulation silencers? Can't get one anywhere. Seems all suppliers have sold out today!"

Chris Holder* "Go karts with the boys yess please!"

Taylor Poole* "just tried to ride the pitbike… ouch its not looking gud :("

Edward Kennett "Having just arrived back from Poland I would like to make the following statement. I wish to state my deep regret and offer my sincere apologies to the fans, the management of Coventry speedway, the sponsors, and my team mates. On Saturday evening (6 August) I was unaware that I was using an 'illegal' silencer. It has been brought to my attention that someone within my team had taken upon themselves to tamper with the silencer without my knowledge believing their actions would give me an advantage. I am extremely sorry to my team mate Nick Morris who suffered as a consequence having used my bike in heat 12. I have taken swift action to resolve this matter and the person in question is no longer in my employ, however, I would like to thank them for their support and commitment over the years but I cannot condone cheating. This has been a most unfortunate and upsetting incident. I would like to finish by saying that I love speedway and have been proud to represent my country. Being part of the Coventry 2010 winning side has been one of the highlights of my career thus far and I hope this matter has not jeopardised my future in the sport."

Justin Sedgmen* "I can't Waite to see all these new silncers in the coming weeks… I would say there is a frew more out there that have been mess about with"

Darija Pavlic* "Banned FOREVER? whatever! What about riders with 600 cc engines, etc?! One silencer, it's not end of the world"

Paul Burbidge* "If Kennett didn't know, his punishment should reflect that. But I wouldn't trust whoever tampered with the silencer again"

Craig Richardson* "After being a mechanic for many years I find it a unreal that a rider would blame a mechanic for having illegal part on there bike"

Jo Lowry* "Clearly I need to block Kenni Larsen from twitter. Can't cope with having every tweet virtually spoken back to me at every meeting"

Jo Lowry* "Plus I must clearly not say anymore on the incident that happened this weekend"

Rory Schlein* "just had my muffler checked funny thing was that the ref didn't evan know what he was looking for"

Lewis Bridger* "If people believe kennetts story then pigs can fly that's all I'm saying"

Lewis Bridger* "kennett has been stealing unfair pts away from other riders including me that he may not of got without cheating"

Darcy Ward* "na he just beat you. Dude you need to stop writing about ted and do your own thing livelife"

Troy Batchelor* "agreed"

Luke Corbett* "agreed mads.. Have you ever tried to get a point across to Nicolai it's like talking to the workshop floor"

Nicolai Klindt* "im old enough now to sort out my own business"

Red5 "What a fantastic Caberet at Plymouth [v. Berwick] on saturday, no wonder you people down there say the meetings are always entertaining let alone the racing. Promoter fighting with his wife over the his bit on the side, promoter fighting with grandson after caught playing with bit on side, screaming and shouting over Family Fortunes. Bugger me will have to come again if its always like this!, East Enders and Corrie in one. Best £15 quid I ever spent, wish I could have got me a drink though. Racing wasnt bad either,and when is round 2? Breaking News Jeremy Kyle is scheduled for filming the next home match"

Kelvin Tatum "More policing of the silencers will come in"

Nigel Pearson "Well, tyres get given to the riders at every meeting so why not silencers?"

Kelvin Tatum "You're going to be building a complete motorbike when you get to the track if you don't look out"

Chris Louis "I've got Nigel Middleditch with me"

Chris Louis "While we're talking about Chris Holder, he's suffering a little bit of fatigue earlier in the season this season"

Nigel Pearson "Some information on the weather looking over the back of the stand"

Jason Doyle "If you can make a good start, you're not eating shit all the way through"

Chris Louis "Still only a coupla points in it"

Darcy Ward "Yeh? I wouldn't have a clue"

David Watt "Doyley has his own lines"

Chris Louis "Is that a polite way of saying he's erratic"

Kelvin Tatum "Fortunately Peter Karlsson was able to get out the throttle"

Tai Woffinden* "Big thanks to David Watt and Darcy Ward for gettin me online with all the tweeters"

Darcy Ward* "yeah welcome to the games fella"

George English "Considering Bowen was nearly a lap behind our riders, the most he could ever have hoped for was to finish and get a point, so it was an amazing decision and had it been one of our lads in the same situation, I would have been livid."

9th August

Fredrik Lindgren* "Have I been missing this early flight out to Sweden from London-Stansted Airport?

Fredrik Lindgren* Feels nice to be back in Sweden will feel even nicer when I'm all the way home would feel the nicest if I was fit to race tonight! Someday!"

Nicolai Klindt* "i love when your mechanic wakes you up an hour earlier than you was ment to, but brings you a nice cup of tea! good start to a new day"

Rory Schlein* "Got up went into get into the taxi and the driver 'wat u doing' I was getting into the driver seat ha ha ha need more sleep Ricky and Daniel found it funny as hell the driver didn't find it funny. I thought I was in Sweden"

Nicolai Klindt* "last night i decided colors and design for my 2012 bikes which is almost same as i had 10 yrs ago. sorted clubs and team out aswell!"

Fredrik Lindgren* "PK pulls a shocker with a Lady Gaga CD in his van then claim it's his daughters. 'This is PK' he says and bring forth Take That!"

Ludvig Lindgren* "wish i was in london or birmingham now i could really do with a new TV now!"

Fredrik Lindgren* "My bro Ludvig is so rotten! When he let out me & PK are very close to faint!"

Lewis Bridger* "Morning Manchester :-) 2 weeks of & there's alot of work going on behind scenes 2 come back stronger so we can rock these playoffs"

Dakota North* "Time to get into the work shop! This I have not missed!!!"

Rory Schlein* "release the guy from Norway they soon will shit themselves and go back indoors"

Nicolai Klindt* "can anyone please tell me what the riots am for? like why am people angry?"

Alun John Rossiter* "good call [Darcy wildcard] to many nobody's in the GP so it's not technically the best line up!"

Chris Holder* "Never thought I would get fucked over this bad!"

Niels Kristian Iversen* "Just seen a dude freak out cause hé is in the wrong airport. Hé wants the staff to call the other airport and delay his flight"

Lewis Bridger* "The Trafford centre in Manchester is amaze :-) had a cool day shopping here"

Tai Woffinden* "Kristof kasper can not ride today big holes in exausts haha tut tut...."

David Watt* "So EK and KK have been caught !! Who else ???"

Rory Schlein* "KK I new I should iv protested last night"

Hans Andersen* "well hé still rode so what happen there ?????"

Tai Woffinden* "i dono man"

Scott Nicholls* "yeah,I thought kk was quick all of a sudden in England too! Haha. Silly boys"

Darcy Ward* "fucking unbelievable"

David Watt* "Bloody throttle fell apart in 1st race, then got screwed in 1st corner in my next heat. Then pulled out of my next 2 !"

> **Fredrik Lindgren*** "How am ya thickalai? Lol"
> **Nicolai Klindt*** "yea ive got it now boys"
> **Nicolai Klindt*** "just take the piss around me! I can hack it, haha"
> **Fredrik Lindgren*** "you know we love you dude"

Fredrik Lindgren* "News, words, information yea everything spreads very fast today. A lot faster then the old jungle telegraph!"

Steve Shovlar "Kennett is not likely going to get the sack from Coventry. They feel that Kennett stood by them during the winter so they will do likewise. Stripping him of the captaincy is probably as far as they are going to go. It's as far as Coventry will go. Not as far as the higher authorities will go. I know that Coventry don't want him to be made a scapegoat as they feel others have also cheated but haven't yet been caught."

Lewis Bridger* "get me a team slut & I'll race & f&€k in sweden"

10th August

Alun John Rossiter* "Can't believe iam awake this early [07.00] long day ahead !!"

Darcy Ward* "waking up 40 mins late cause Troy Batchelor turned the alarm off twice"

> **David Watt*** "So that's 2 days running where someone has been caught for being naughty and got away with it !!!"
> **Darcy Ward*** "lets do it then"

Matt Ford "I am actively exploring team changes to take us through to the end of the season. I have been very disappointed with some performances of late and quite frankly I do not believe that our team is strong enough right now to bring the success we are seeking. If I can find the right combination then I will not hesitate in re-declaring the side, but that obviously will not be in time for these two big meetings [against Swindon] coming up."

Birmingham Speedway Birmingham Speedway are aware of reports from Sweden concerning Krzysztof Kasprzak and apparently illegal silencers. Kasprzak was reportedly found with the units prior to his meeting for Vargarna at Vetlanda, but he did subsequently take part in the match on legal machinery, scoring seven points from five rides. Brummies promoter Graham Drury said: "We as a club are awaiting official reports from the meeting in Sweden, and as soon as we receive that we will decide on what action to take. We need the full facts as there is plenty of hearsay at this stage, but clearly this is a major subject in the sport at present and once we have all the information we will make further comment."

Linus Sundstrom* "On the way to norrköping now for a meeting with masarna!Going with twitter man seb alden,he is everywere on here but we cant see him!"

Paul Burbidge* "Chris Harris doesn't want to rely on a wild card to stay in the SGP. But unless he picks up quickly, he may need one"

Chris Neath* "I swear the drive to Norwich is the most boring I've ever known"

David Watt* "Flight FR3645 skavsta to stanstead on the 10th of august 2011. I wont forget that flight for a while !!! A story for another day !! Just wish I had a photo to remember it....hmmm"

Chris Holder* "Gotta brand new bed for sale! Anyone need a double bed?"

Dakota North* "Anyone know of a mechanic that wants a job"

Jo Lowry* "I'm also very much looking forward to sending electricity through one of our riders knees later. #imevil #itsfortheirowngood"

Chris Neath* "Emil looking rapid at Kings Lynn now. Still bored out my mind! And people like to say Rye House is boring racing...whatever!"

Chris Neath* "Looks like Fisher is upsetting the apple cart. That's out of character!"

Jo Lowry* "Best comment of the night 'Don't get excluded for fuck sake!'"

Chris Neath* "There's more dust at lynn than rye house!"

Hans Andersen* "Nice to see Kasprzak's swedish club have suspended him this coming tuesday and cant he not prove his innocense he'll be sacked! Think others. Should follow and to say the least hé should be banned like other sports people caucht cheating ! fairplay the only way In our sport"

Jo Lowry* "Up The Bees! (Although some of the boys really do need to sort out the 'smelly feet' situation!)"

Linus Sundstrom* "Are you riding for us tomorrow?"

Dakota North* "don't think so mate the have never told me, not wanted anymore at Pboro Panthers"

Phil Chard "Ward audaciously pulled wheelies along the finish straight on laps' two, three and four during his easy Heat 11 triumph."

11th August

Stuart Towner "I do like the way Edward Kennett is riding now, much more stylish and has lost that 'rag doll' way of riding [Bridger take note] and most of the time as smooth as Simmo – well almost!"

Annette Maybach "Sadly domestic speedway also, at some venues, suffers from poor preparation of tracks. Many tracks are either poorly watered or have material on them that does not absorb water sufficiently. This results in a slick surface which generally does not produce good racing but also produces dust"

Charles McKay "It is a sad reflection of how the sport is run in Britain that two major changes, re-admission policy and Premier League second phase format, have been introduced via supplementary regulations due to the BSPA changing their minds and then failing to tell the SCB."

Edward Kennett "After the events of the last few days and with my Disciplinary Hearing coming up next Tuesday I feel that the least I can do to help repair some of the damage this incident has done to Coventry, my team mates and above all Coventry supporters, is to resign from the club with immediate effect. Coventry is in my blood and I would not wish to do any more to harm the club or the supporters that I love. I know that I will be punished on Tuesday and I am prepared to accept whatever that decision is for the good of British Speedway."

Jo Lowry* "Todays news is now making me find Mr Sandhu's daft grin yday even more annoying! Who's coming?! Someone tell me!"

Mikael Johnsson* "Krzysztof Kasparzak is banned by his Swedish club, Vargarna for suspected cheating with silencers"

Jan Staechmann* "So, Edward Kennett quits. Didn't see that one coming"

Scott Nicholls* "have they issued the penalty yet?"

Jan Staechmann* "no mate, hearin is not until Tuesday"

Fredrik Lindgren* "9 o clock tomorrow I will leave my home head for Målilla and the SGP Practice. Eat some hockeycandy and hope it will be ok, No pain No gain!"

Graham Drury "I have been touch with all of the governing bodies to establish the facts, and they have all said that Birmingham Speedway have no grounds to put any sanction on Krzysztof. I understand his Swedish club have now suspended him but that is their own issue and could be for any reason – it is a different situation compared to if it had come from SVEMO. The PZM hold Krzysztof's licence and they have received no reports from SVEMO that any of their riders have committed any offences. I would like to thank the SCB for their help in making thorough investigations and for clarifying the position for us, and Krzysztof will ride for us tonight."

Chris Holder* "Getting my shit sorted for this weekend!! Need a fucking win!!!!"

Nigel Pearson* "Emotional day, said I'd never do it, but just dumped 20-years worth of football and speedway programmes in the skip. A part of me gone! and I have kept all programmes from when I was a child. They are most important to me and will pass them down"

Nigel Pearson* "Wow can't believe the stick I'm getting for putting my programmes in the skip! It's dry, should I get them back out? Genuinely shocked! Programme controversy!! I have kept the ones that really are personal! Cradley/Hull speedway, wba and Fev Rovers rugby league in the loft!"

Charles McKay "Judging by Mr. Tatum's' other customer relations policies this season I would believe that it is a cock up rather then a conscious decision by the Stoke promotion."

John Chaplin "[Simmo says] 'they are not promoters now in the true sense of the word...they are mostly fans with money. Speedway meetings are their toys.' ....'If we lose Sky TV money the sport in this country would possibly have to go completely amateur. I really fear for speedway's future'."

   Troy Batchelor* "Kristof kasperzack has 2 new mufflers on tonight at birmingham , that shows he was cheating especially after the Swedish episode on Tuesday. What a cheater I hope he scores no points tonight. Maybe kasperzack lent his mufflers to his mates at the swc after the first races when we were smoking them!! Just had my mufflers checked, I'm clean"

   Hans Andersen* "In the pits at Birmingham and guess who's Got two ALL new silencer on his bike = Kasprzak ! Weird when his not cheating"

   Lewis Bridger* "unbelievable haha"

   Hans Andersen* "Think this proves the c... Does play all fair and should be banned"

   Chris Holder* "good point there batch!! That's why they started winnin by length of the straight! Cheeky dogs!"

   Lewis Bridger* "Atleast KK ain't sly about the matter haha, he has got caught out & now whacked x2 standard silencers on"

Tony McDonald "Not saying speedway is still anything but dangerous, it will always be to some extent. But there's a difference between charging round the wide line with an air fence to crash into and dicing with death inches from solid steel/wooden fences, with no 'give' in them, and playing Russian roulette at all the many old tracks surrounded by lethal metal lamp-posts. Bikes and tracks are much easier to ride today compared to Simmo's era"

Updates "Schlein's celebration wheelie didn't go to plan! - ended up flat on his face on the backstraight!"

   Rory Schlein* "from hero to zero ha ha oh well it happins to the best of us ant done that sence I was 17 ha ha"

   Peter Johns* "did you inspect the track after heat 15?"

   Nicolai Klindt* "im glad that you made a good show with a bit of a fist fight and then a wheelie that didnt really happen"

   David Watt* "I vote we ask to have every silencer checked at every meeting for the next month and then do random checks"

Scott Nicholls* "It's good they're doing checks,but how funny is this,2nd time now a ref [Dave Watters] has asked what he's supposed to be looking for! Haha,quality"

Chris Holder* "that's fukn great!"

Lewis Bridger* "that's unbelievable"

Scott Nicholls* "He's looking in both ends with no torch & I say,do u know what u're looking for...no, we had an email to check them. No idea"

Chris Holder* "unreal man!"

Lewis Bridger* "no way haha so how do u no they are not passing illegal silencers then ?? #justlookininthepipe #joke Ref can not stop the cheating, dave king has 2 cut them open cause it's easy 2 cut bigger holes around the 2nd plate without ref knowing"

Scott Nicholls* "like to think that won't happen,but I did laugh. Not a clue"

Lewis Bridger* "no way of checking the silencers with out a proper machine to go inside with a HD cam/torch like FIM have and look both ends !"

David Watt* "so get the right tools for the job. I spend alot of money on my kit so they should spend the money to check them !!"

Chris Neath* "same shit as always mate"

Lewis Bridger* "YES this is what I'm getting to Davey they got to have the correct kit also"

David Watt* "when they catch the cheats and fine them, they'll get the money back for the cameras !!"

Lewis Bridger* "couldn't agree more, until then passing all these silencers when no1 has a clue what they r trying to see is pointless"

Trevor Swales "I have made my feelings perfectly clear to the team and they know that that performance was simply unacceptable. We just weren't good enough all night and we were beaten by the better team. This form away can not continue because we are not going to get into the play-offs with the way we are riding away from home."

David Watters "An enjoyable affair with Swindon riders moving at the start all night long must have thought they needed an advantage some really great speedway to boot"

Graham Cooke "Most of the talk in the pits is inevitably about silencers. Rory Schlein, guesting for Poole in place of Chris Holder, tells me that this is third day running that he's had his silencers tested by the machine examiners. Rumours abound that suppliers of silencers have been over run by orders for new silencers in the last few days. You can make of that what you will but stories are already leaking out about silencers being carefully taken to pieces, the rivets being drilled out, baffle plates being removed or having holes drilled in them and then the whole lots being re-assembled and then re-chromed. Someone tells me that some plates inside the silencers have been fitted with small hinges so that they appear closed when prodded by a machine examiner but then open when the exhaust gasses push the flap open. Whatever is happening, it is a sad state of affairs. My mind inevitably goes back to a brief conversation with a very angry and frustrated Scott Nicholls earlier on in the season. Scott had just been passed by a number of riders that he would normally have been expected to beat. 'I don't understand it - I had the throttle wide open and they still went past me.' Perhaps he understands a little better now. Whatever the situation, inevitably we will all look back on some performances this season and wonder if it was skill or cunning that contributed. It all leaves a sour taste in the mouth."

12th August

Chris Neath* "Always nice crossing the Worcester border and getting that sweet smell of home. Fresh air, farm yards and Worcester sauce"

Chris Holder* "shithole Neathy"

Chris Neath* "haha! I love my city man! Fuck, what am I saying, I need to get out more! Get on the gas sat and pull some shapes for us"

Tomas Topinka "Rob [Lyon] said before the meeting 'make sure you have a good meeting' as we were riding rider replacement for Olly Allen. Unfortunately, I had a nightmare meeting. The first I heard about it was from my mechanic the next day, and later in the day the team manager got in touch. That was not the way it should be done."

Nicolai Klindt* "Poole was SO lucky to get the win, they need to thank the ref [David Watters] at least a 1000 times. Scott Nicholls clearly didn't touch tapes in heat 15"

Peter Johns* "If it won't go any louder, you're not trying hard enough! #kickoutthecheats"

Jon Cook It was with an extremely heavy heart that I handed over the £550 protest fee as even in my 15 seasons at Eastbourne I had never found myself in that position as I always felt it smacked of being a rather desperate act of a sour loser. Saturday night was different, had I not taken that action I would have been ignoring our officials and riders views and what they all said was compelling evidence....On a personal level Sunday was a desperate day, as of all the Bees it was really Edward's silencer that I hoped would be okay. We have known each other for years and I hope he sees the error of his ways and is back racing cleanly in future."

Mike Bowden "[Hayley Stadium] is very rough and bumpy. They've said they've done a lot of work on it, but I don't believe it's improved in the last five years."

Fredrik Lindgren* "Good breakfast done! All-Bran/SpecialK with sour milk, wholemeal bread with cottage cheese and turkey, glass of water"

Rory Schlein* "yeah last night had everthinh 2 fights good racing last heat decider and I dick who flipped it ha ha great nights entreatment"

Olly Allen* "2 fights??!! Fill me in schlong!"

Mike Bennett* "just had a facebook friend request from Emil Sayfutdinov!! Obviously that lad is a fine judge of character!! :-)))))"

Ludvig Lindgren* "on the airport coach on my way 2 västerås for a afternoon flight! sick of traveling now tho! oh wifi on the coach how rad!"

Linus Sundstrom* "Gonna be a good watch and learn weekend at målilla to see how the propper pro skidders is doing it SGP"

Ludvig Lindgren* "to follow Linus is a good watch and learn way to see how a proper ass kisser is doing it"

Lee Richardson* "been flat out racing! And got a busy couple of weeks.."

Ludvig Lindgren* "is thinking that it should be a law on tashes so every one at least try to grow one! Iam trying my best but i cant do it alone people!!!"

Cameron Woodward* "Waiting for my flight to gatwick to arrive here in Nice. It better be on time, I've gotta do battle for the Hammers tonight"

Dakota North* "Jetlag. Fuck!"

Troy Batchelor* "Rained off in outrup...the sun is out but the rain messed up electricity and called it off... Devoo..Off to Polska"

Lewis Bridger* "Going to do some strength conditioning at home"

Cameron Woodward* "On route to lakeside. Please m25 be kind to us. Cheers easyjet for being on time"

Nigel Pearson* "Landed in Gothenburg, staying here now and driving to Malilla in morning. Kelvin and me have found the English bar!!"

Taylor Poole* "In Ipswich till Monday bored"

Ludvig Lindgren* "This years mission try to get hold of a SGP grid girl suit and put it on! snap a pic and upload it on twitter"

Ludvig Lindgren* "challenge Accepted"

Dakota North* "made some start way too tense need to relax"

Jon Cook "For all the criticisms of our 'trick track', or is that now unique as coined by the hilarious Nigel Pearson on his "Spot the Cliché' Show on Sky on a Monday, we simply don't seem to have any discernable home advantage at times."

Ian Smalley "When Poole are here – and you only get it with Poole – and you get Darcy and Chris, you can hear them whooping after they finish. And when they won Heat 13, you could hear them screaming down the back straight. They are something special. Speedway riders are a unique breed."

13th August

David Watt* "Not bad last night but crashing sucks !! Feeling a little sore this morning and have a cracker of a headache still !"

Dick Barrie "We will be staging our final NJL mini-match of the year tonight, with plenty to race for and plenty to prove! The criticism of this promotion's efforts to locate and recruit young talent is baffling at times. Some of you just want success, total success – and you want it NOW. A young rider has a couple of low scores? Sack him! Bring in someone else, regardless of cost. Well, I'd prefer to see the club do things more slowly and within our limited budgets. Yes, there are times a speedway club – any club, in any league – has a bad spell as regards results. The ones that survive are those who have a store of youngsters, perhaps farmed out through a lower division, who can be called up to serve the cause when the time comes. Rich sponsors – or misguided new club owners (I hesitate to call them promoters) with more money than sense – have made it easier for clubs to paper over the cracks in their lack of forward planning with a quick fix of expensive, sometimes poached, foreign talent, but when the cash runs low the truth will out. To build your club for the long haul, build from the bottom, not the top."

Taylor Poole* "Excited for the journey to Berwick today"

Nigel Pearson* "Just enjoyed a traditional Swedish breakfast here in Gothenburg with Kelvin… Corn Flakes followed by egg on toast"

Dakota North* "On my way too Milton Keynes"

Jan Staechmann* "What a night last night! Let's forget that one in a hurry! Hope Matiej Janowski is ok after his monster crash. Will report any news"

Lee Richardson* "In Germany racing in Landshut tonight, then heading back to Poland in the van after the meeting"

Niels Kristian Iversen* "Still wants a team helikopter.. One Them large ones where the Van Can be inside. Oh yeah and a fuel sponsor"

Paul Burbidge* "Ole Olsen has just told me the Nordic SGP in Vojens on Sep 10 is 40 years to the day he won his first world title in Gothenburg in 1971"

Jon Cook "I think Eddie is a great kid, but I think people have over-exaggerated the amount of riders doing this. People have created this culture of 'everyone is at it' and that has created the problem for Edward. We all want to know the sport is clean and I've got to say that the reaction I've had from my own riders, and also a couple of riders from other clubs, is astonishing. It's astonishing how angry these people actually are and it leads me to believe that this isn't widespread. Certain people have been banging on about this for a long time and they're doing the sport a disservice because they're suggesting everyone is at it. Quite clearly they're not"

Peter Morrish "I'm a bit puzzled that many [NL] teams appear to have a lot of meetings left to fit in when the season started back in March or April. The top four teams will go into the play-offs but the cut-off point will be September 11."

Linus Sundstrom* "In målilla now and trying to kill some time! Wierd feeling when you dont know if you gonna ride (SGP) or not. Track looks awesome!"

Jan Staechmann* "Good luck tonight to the BSI SGP media team & of course Torben Olsen!"

Lewis Bridger* "Been out on the roads of Manchester Cycling, need to be as fit as I can be to finish the season on a high"

Dakota North* "do you live there now?"

Mike Moseley "Could I pass on my thanks to the many riders, promoters and supporters who have showered myself and my wife Jan with messages of condolences following the recent death of my Mum [Dorothy 'Dot' Moseley] at the age of 92. Mum was best remembered for her days on the Plough Lane terraces in the mid-fifties onwards, never missing a meeting in around 25 years, until circumstances prevented her going anymore. She introduced me to the sport in 1958, where like her, I became a staunch Dons fan, with Ron How being our favourite all-time rider. In those days, it was possible to visit a speedway track every night of the week in the London area….we seldom missed a Wimbledon away meeting either, travelling the length and breadth of the British Isles on the Supporters' Club coach for many years, quite often the riders travelled with us too. She never quite forgot the time we went on a Scottish tour with the likes of Jim Tebby and Olle Nygren having a pillow fight on the back seat of the bus, where she went and joined in."

Jo Lowry* "Don't understand speedway riders"

Jo Lowry* "always give it the big talk, yet do bugger all to look after themselves when its needed!! I'm aware its not ALL riders, but most do. Bloody annoying I tell ya!"

Lewis Bridger* "Anybody in need of a Apple MacBook Pro 13inc, like new £600 everything included, receipt price £1,000 bargain"

Lee Richardson* "u been looting in those riots lbr?"

Paul Burbidge* "The FIM checked every silencer on every bike at the Scandinavian SGP. All clean. Top boys setting an example"

Alun John Rossiter* "did you expect anything else ??"

Greg Hancock "The FIM makes these rules and they have to police it. None of us were really up for the silencer thing and it's just what we have to do for the environment… it's destroying our old methods. It's costing everybody more money and we have to service our engines more frequently.

The silencers are more expensive and everything is just going up and up. There are ways to beat the system and if they don't stop it early, then it's going to get out of control."

Rory Schlein* "Referee take a bow you ball bag and Emil over riding ya gonna hurt someone"

David Watt* "Well Emil has gotta be thinking that today is gonna be good !!! Take the luck when ya can !!"

Nicolai Klindt* "what do you think? i think it looked like jonasson got scared and put the bike down"

Rory Schlein* "ha ha r u for real"

Nicolai Klindt* "yea i am. he touched him i agreed, but he didn't knocked him off. thj got scared. Darcy Ward would defo have kept it on!"

Rory Schlein* "so ya think u would of stayed on"

Nicolai Klindt* "yep, u felt how strong i was on thursday haha"

Rory Schlein* "please explain...."

Paul Burbidge* "THJ was very unlucky to be excluded from heat four. Sayfutdinov went for a gap that wasn't there. Fans fuming"

Rory Schlein* "iv just figured it out ha ha yeah ya pretty strong"

Nicolai Klindt* "were on twitter, can't explain. where we stand when we watch the racing and u lost ur cap haha"

Rory Schlein* "hahahaha..... i should be a match ref!"

Jim Lynch "It's nobody's fault but the team hasn't been successful in the last three years....the ones you sign at the end are not necessarily who you want but they fit the points situation. But it means you can get five places in the team sorted out with riders who you really want."

Jan Staechmann "One problem is that we are so often 5-1 down after race one, and I don't know how to deal with it. I am aware that Scott Nicholls has raced through immense personal problems, I don't know what they all are and they are none of my, or anyone else's, business. But I do know he is a good lad, totally honest and committed, and he does always give you his best effort."

Jordan Frampton

"We're a southern team and we're being sent back to Berwick, Newcastle for the third time this year and Workington. People talk about cutting costs but I'm going from Poole to Berwick twice in a season? To be honest, I've been getting down about it as we haven't had many meetings because of the weather and now the price of diesel is killing me. You have to score at least three points at places like Edinburgh just to cover your fuel costs, that's without working on your bikes...what was wrong with the Premier Trophy riding against the southern teams? When you look at it even Somerset and Newport are a lot closer than Berwick. This must surely be costing the promoters money as well and leaving the fans wondering?...It's been a pretty good season in riding terms, but I'm not really enjoying it too much. I think you need a job to make speedway pay at this [PL] level. I don't have a trade as such and I'm beginning to think about things too much....maybe I think too much and I need to just take a few brain cells out and concentrate on riding"

Nigel Pearson* "Whats going wrong with Gollob folks? Can he get it right?"

Nicolai Klindt* "he's got a new silencer on mate"

Alun John Rossiter* "can't ride grippy tracks tonight has sorted the men from the boys !! tonight has proven the need for dirt the Italian gp was painful !!"

Robert Henry "Obviously Cameron [Heeps] has been brilliant. He just has to learn that thing which come hard for young talented riders, that you don't always need to get through on the first lap."

Stuart Parnaby "Lee Smethills is an experienced lad, so the lay off shouldn't affect him, he'll just sling his helmet on and go out and turn left."

Nick Mallett "On both occasions, the problem was started by members of the visiting sides and as such, we obviously had neither any idea it was going to happen or indeed control over it. It is crucial that people realise that speedway is an emotive sport and it would not be right of me to hide that fact that verbal and physical differences do happen from time to time. In the main, it normally happens away from the public. But on the two occasions at our ground recently, it has been in full gaze of everyone. We regret what has happened, obviously, and we are satisfied that appropriate action has and will be taken in an attempt to ensure it doesn't happen again. But I stress, none of this was in anyway the blame of Newport Speedway and we cannot emphasize just how safe watching speedway at our ground is."

Philip Rising "Norrie Allen, who managed Mark Loram, the last British rider to win the World title, in 2000, for 12 years has recently left the camp of Chris Harris after an internal disagreement"

Rory Schlein* "I'm sorry but some referees need their licence taken off them awful decisions but like always they neva get punished like the riders"

Nigel Pearson* "Starting tapes didnt go up properly in final of SGP but result stands - wow what a meeting well done Jarek hope u all enjoyed it!"

Kevin Long* "about time the starting gates were given a good service after the problems of previous round. Very poor prepartions for a GP!"

Fredrik Lindgren* "A painful night tonight! #Fastfreddyisnotbackyet I'm gonna go home!"

Nicolai Klindt* "what a final by hampel.... respect, full on respect! i'm gonna grab his track record next tuesday tho"

Charlie Gjedde "I still live in Swindon and I had my workshop there and it was a long drive to a [Berwick] track that didn't suit me. I didn't like the way the track was prepared and the wooden fence and brick wall behind it. It preyed on my mind a little bit. I know they are saying there's not been any serious injuries for years but I know there was a few in the past."

Taylor Poole* "Just found out that Pete Simmons had to share a double bed with Chris Louis"
Kevin Long* "gives a whole new meaning to the term 'Team Riding!'"

Fredrik Lindgren* "How poor was the referee tonight? Indirectly referee cost me a place in semi when Emil didn't get excluded when he took Jonasson down"
Chris Holder* "yeh was bullshit!"
Chris Holder* "Another tough SGP for me!! Fuk need more practice!"

Fredrik Lindgren* "Do you think practice is the answer mate? Wonder how much Gollob has practiced since Terenzano? Seems to work?!?"

Chris Neath* "Jordan and Jaryton just saw Van Persie at South Mimms services. Hope they stamped on that left foot of his!"

Lewis Bridger* "Need to get the coin in bad, not enough meetings, have to be in two leagues minimum next season, must find a decent polish club ;) #bullshit"
Lee Richardson* "you're age I was racing in 5 leagues!!! And still am...;)"
Sam Masters* "double down cheify"
Lewis Bridger* "it wont get the Coin in, will end up just paying my mechanic fuk loads and bending bikes left right and centre"

Fredrick Lindgren* "Wish I had someone beside me tonight not feeling the best, energise me!"
Sam Masters* "I like your style #nevergiveup"

Philip Rising "FIM Race Director Tony Olsson, along with his fellow Swedes, was able to present a racetrack [at Malilla] that made for a memorable event. Olsson has had more than his fair share of problems this year at Leszno, Prague and Terenzano in particular, proving that you cannot make an omelette without eggs."

14th August

Richard Hollingsworth   "The pundits at the beginning of the season had us down as finishing 12th whilst ironically, the Plymouth reporter, has us down to finish last. It is great to prove these people so very wrong and the more wrong they are the better it feels."

Tai Woffinden*   "Luton airport with Darcy Ward & Scott Nicholls polska bound hooray"

Rory Schlein*   "keep it zipped this time"

Lee Richardson*   "Road trip to Poland. Left Landshut at 8 this morning, should be in Zielona gora at 14.00"

Nicki Glanz*   "the awkward moment when you go to someones house thinking your in and finding out she gotta Boy friend"

Nicolai Klindt*   "i hope i'm getting a new silencer, a new carb and a new engine all oversized for christmas so i can be as fast as my heroes"

Scott Nicholls*   "Yeah,if u get caught before the meeting with them on,u're ok because u haven't actually used them according to rules!#Bullshit"

Nicolai Klindt*   "that's what i'm thinking. like leon in denmark 'i found out my silencer was illegal when i warmed my bike up' #bullshit"

Scott Nicholls*   "Haha,brilliant. And good old kk,got away with it twice now apparently!"

Nicolai Klindt*   "bless him for being smarter than bspa or who ever is pretty useless #sorryformycommentpleasedontbanme"

Scott Nicholls*   "I called heads of our sport Monday with suggestions to sort all this out.said they would call me back that afternoon.still waiting!"

Nicolai Klindt*   "they probably went on holiday and forgot you. it's not like it's anything important you asked them for? well, good question"

Scott Nicholls*   "maybe they'll send me a postcard with a response! :-)"

Fredrik Lindgren*   "My pain riding yesterday was worse then I expected. I've had to make the decision to pull out of Wolves meeting tomorrow. Sorry to let down!"

Linus Sundstrom*   "is dak attack back with us tomorrow?"

Dakota North*   "don't think so mate have not herd anything #notgood"

Fredrik Lindgren*   "Went to the grocery shop today wearing my onepiece! felt weird everyone looking, couldn't care, trivialities!"

Nicolai Klindt*   "that's one piece of sikk thing"

Andy Povey*   "Need a full-length photo of this for the Wolves website. LOL"

Tai Woffinden*   "get me a one peice like freds got! The 1 he posted on twitter ;)"

Niall Strudwick*   "had another good meeting 7+1 cant grumble at that, just sucks it was academy instead of NL but still had fun"

Scott Nicholls*   "Had an alcohol test in Poland today....0.00. Said I should probably go have a couple of vodka's! Haha,polish style"

Ludvig Lindgren*   "Lethal weapon 2 on ITV4 classic!!!"

Taylor Poole*   "I've had to resign from ATM after our loss today, very upsetting but I've been promised to be given a new position in the club shortly"

Hans Andersen*   "Arrrggggg bullshit have to apologize to Gorzow management and not at least the fans, Leszno just ain't my track for some reason :(#scared"

Lewis Bridger*   "need a KK silencer mate"

Ludvig Lindgren*   "oh how cold is it in this fricking house! hate the weater atm... thailand anyone?"

Tai Woffinden*   "Pumped with tonights 15 point haul fast as fuck see if i can have a good 1 in england tomoro"

Jack Lee   "After last year it's such a big disappointment to come down with a bump, but once you get to the top the only way up is down so we have just got to keep sticking at it."

15th August

Tai Woffinden*   "Nice early start to the day just what i want NOT haha plenty of hooray's flyin about :)"

Fredrik Lindgren*   "Aaaaaaahhh!! Hate my back can't sleep properly! Too much grief! What is happening got sick pain it's like going back to first couple of days after the crash"

Chris Holder*   "go back to the hospital get checked again!?"

Linus Sundstrom*   "Up for another week of speedway! Uk today, sweden tomorow, denmark wednesday & uk friday again!"

Mads Korneliussen*   "Landed in the UK and the sun is out, what's going on"

Scott Nicholls*   "Just left hospital to have leg checked.doc pleased with progress but still can't say if I will need a skin graft.2-3 week wait.hoping not!"

Rory Schlein*   "Not many meeting left now lucky I got sweden play off bound but the aces I think play offs is a bit of a big ask but...A win tonight and I'll call in a favour from Poole and ask if we can have all points when we race them ha ha ha can only ask"

Dakota North*   "Awesome weather today in Milton Keynes! But I'm not racing tonight!"

Mads Korneliussen*   "On the way to wolfs. Transit van power, got to love this van, team colors and everything"

Moira Perrott   "The SCB told the refs to check two riders silencers at random from each team but other than a diagram didn't tell them how to exactly check a silencer! The machine examiners refuse to help and you really need an extendable torch. Another problem is that there are other makes in addition to King! If it had been a foreign rider, they'd have had no hesitation in making an example of them but as it's a Brit we'll see. Six months, I reckon. With Madsen, that was held under international jurisdiction so since he got fined at the meeting that was that. You can't be tried twice for the same crime. It's interesting to hear that if you change the exhaust you have to change the engine set up so it's less believable that any rider wouldn't ask why the engine set up is different. The SCB are lucky Edward has pleaded guilty since if any outside lawyers were involved they might look at how the six silencers were shipped to Rye House in the boot of car before Dave King looked at them the next day. Any lawyer worth their salt would ask about the procedures taken to ensure that they were exactly the same as they had been when they left Lakeside. Nothing might have happened but it could have."

Chris Holder*   "Can't believe nothing has been mentioned about the tapes not goin up properly in the final in malilla #strange"

Darcy Ward*   "didn't even know"

Chris Holder*   "the went up slow as fuck on the inside! They were guna re run it but then they didn't"

Mads Korneliussen*   "There is just to many cars on the roads in this country. The roads needs 10 more lanes"

Fredrik Lindgren*   "Oh man my new TV is just fantastic! I love it!"

Lewis Bridger*   "it was a silencer I wrecked in crash, we cut it open 2months ago to see if it was possible 4 riders to modify #itsurewas"

Leszno Bulls   "The decision of club president Joseph Dworakowski is that Janusz Kolodziej is ineligible for the Swedish league this coming Tuesday. We want Janusz's mind devoted to preparing for Sunday's match."

Lewis Bridger*   "So I'm here cycling in the gym thinking upgrade the van pimp it up spend every penny on kit for UK & double down Premier leauge #coinin"

Nigel Pearson   "I'm not so sure if certain clubs asked them [Poole] they'd be so obliging"

Ulrich Ostergaard   "On a good day I can beat anyone and, on a bad day, anyone can beat me"

Nigel Pearson "It's great to see a city the size of Birmingham in speedway"

Sam Ermolenko "Are you asking my honest opinion? I don't think this [Birmingham] is the best track in the country"

Nigel Pearson "Ten teams is the perfect number for the Elite League: variety of fixtures, competitive teams and a battle for the play-offs"

Sam Ermolenko "There's no excuses, it's not raining at the moment is it?"

Dakota North* "Had a sweet few laps tonight wish I got to race on the track tho. Ohhh never mind!"

Ulrich Ostergaard* "Is wishing vissing would stop trying to touch my balls"

Ben Randall* [r/t by Nigel Pearson] "how far are you up darcy wards arse ever heard of impartial commentary"

Claudia Staechmann* "wow nigel i'm really impressed that you manage to fit up darcys arse. Well done my man, well done!"

Nigel Pearson* "Well done Brummies, hope to see them in Elite again next season. And I call it as I see it, end of story"

Nicolai Klindt* "learned that its stupid to make changes when ur winning heats. big mistake so ended up with two lasts. not a happy chap! and we got smocked"

Lewis Bridger* "I'm glad alot of you think that doubling down with a premier team is a good idea, I want to race my bike it's simple loadsaheats"

Jan Staechmann after Swindon lose 63-27 "Holy cow what a night! I'm speechless."

Scott Nicholls* "not a lot u can say mate. We were sh*t. They were just better tonight. Get it right Thursday"

Paul Burbidge* "How good is Rory Schlein this season?! Shame he didn't make the GP Challenge at Vetlanda this Saturday. He may well have got through"

Tai Woffinden* "sign said juntion 10 to 13 closed and i counted how many juntions it was with my fingers what a idiot! #classic"

Rory Schlein* "No play off this year for the aces I thought it was possible this year but aces got a new era to look forward to"

16th August

Rory Schlein* "Me and Darcy shared more than a room last night ha ha 3 ppl 2 bed do the math luckily no spooning"

Nicolai Klindt* "just seen a man at stansted with a homemade laptopcase. carboard and ducktape!"

Mads Korneliussen* "Stansted is busy this time a day, to many people, aarrrrrrrggg"

Nigel Pearson* "Big night for the Dudley Heathens boys against Belle Vue tonight. Hope we can pull it off, tough at the moment"

Moira Perrott "That little roller at the start is what gives them the biggest advantage – they all do it but no one talks about that as cheating"

Jo Lowry* "Is in need of polish lessons asap! preferably the ones which will help me get across what I'm trying to say to Piotr!"

David Watt* "Gonna kick my mechanics ass for the flat tyre in heat 1 last night !!"

Paul Burbidge* "Scott Nicholls calls for silencer cheats to cop a year's ban as Kennett faces the SCB at 2.30pm this afternoon"

Hans Andersen* "Cant agree more with Scott Nicholls cheats should get banned minimum a year otherwise i Think cheating is gonna become normal"

David Watt* "So Ed K is going to find out his speedway future today. It was stupid and I'm against what he did, but good luck Ted !"

Josh Gudgeon* "If Eddie's ban is 6 months, it should be 6 months of the season!"

Hans Andersen* "Think FIM and BSPA should take a long look at Them self, 6 months Ban (2 really as season finishes) HA would hardly Call it punishment"

Scott Nicholls* "6 months ban! What an absolute disgrace!! That's effectively 1 1/2 month ban as we have 4 1/2 months off in the winter! What a shambles!"

Hans Andersen* "couldnt agree more mate, but what Can we dó ?? Cheat ourself #bullshit Think we'll tried our best shouting out via media..."

Scott Nicholls* "total joke! I even spoke to the head of our sport & thought he agreed with my views. Clearly not! May as well all cheat!"

Alun John Rossiter* "way to go nige last nite doing a Rosco said it as it is woo !!"

Nigel Pearson* "I'm sick of being accused of sitting on the fence mate. I'm entitled to my opinion and will stick to it. makes me laugh when people say Kelvin is biased with some clubs. This is a man who has no feelings either way for any club!"

Nicolai Klindt* "can i ask what you said nigel my Oakley mate"

Nigel Pearson* "clubs should be allowed to sign 2 No 1 riders to share, riders moving at starts out of order, GP at Malilla a proper track"

Nicolai Klindt* "exactly my point of view aswell! Well said i think i would be the perfect man to be in the box with you cuz people would gonna hear the truth from my mouth"

Nigel Pearson* "knowing you Nic you would land yourself in trouble!! Always enjoy our chats, but guess that means I am Klindt-biased!!"

Nicolai Klindt* "maybe i would"

Nicolai Klindt* "i'll wait to my retirement comes up, then i will be in there. i enjoy our chats aswell, always a good laugh!"

Alun John Rossiter* "wasn't just the sharing number ones it was a few things he said last nite was bob on !"

Nigel Pearson* "and forget about Kelvin ever joining twitter. Says he has better things to do with his time. Reading some tweets last night, I'm with him!!"

Kenni Larsen* "Love my girlfriend"

Paul Burbidge* "Kennett decision will be announced at 9am tomorrow morning I've just been told. According to the Leszno president, Kennett has been given a 6-month ban."

Fredrik Lindgren* "Good match in Kumla today, score level going into the last heat, Pepe & Kylmis doing what's needed for a Indianerna win! Crowd over 5000!"

Nigel Pearson* "Sensational finish for Heathens, last gasp 46-44 win over Belle Vue. Well done boys and thanks to our fans, u were awesome!"

Moira Perrott "The air flow tests showed the advantage was negligble and the only real advantage was psychological"

17th August

Scott Nicholls* "Love to see peoples sense of achievement as they RAM their bag into the Ryan Air measure tool...only to discover they can't get it out!#Funny"

Paul Burbidge "Former Coventry star Edward Kennett has been hit with a six-month worldwide ban from racing after being caught using an illegal silencer at Lakeside on August 6. This means Team Great Britain international is free to start the 2012 season, but will miss the rest of the 2011 campaign. Kennett was handed a 12-month suspension by the Speedway Control Bureau Disciplinary Court on Tuesday afternoon, but the court opted to suspend the second six months for a year. The rider was also fined £2,500 and must pay costs of £700....According to an SCB statement, 24 holes were found to have been drilled in Kennett's silencer, ranging from 3mm to 6mm. This potentially would have allowed the exhaust gases to escape more effectively and improved the performance of his bike."

Nicolai Klindt* "really nice with a lie in, but didn't hear my alarm anyway at 7am... need a new pair of ear me! think i will try to do some work later"

Nicolai Klindt* "actually rate people tweeting about them self, telling other people how awkward, stupid or what ever they have been/done. makes me laugh!"

Nigel Pearson* "Boring day today putting finishing touches to accounts"

Scott Nicholls* "Right not going on about it anymore but have to state my absolute disgust at bspa/scb's decision. An absolute joke & no deterrent.... Only hope is that they at least step up the checks bigtime & learn from their big mistake!"

Venner spkv* r/t by Scott! "spit your dummy out and get in with it , Ed could beat you with he's eyes closed, you need to do something"

Lewis Bridger* "Funny that mate, I swear you was something like 6x British Champion & kennett how many times ?"

Scott Nicholls* "Haha,thought the same thing"

Dakota North* "what do you expect there clowns"

Lewis Bridger* "Silencer front I don't no what to say :/ a ban till the end of the season so they mean 1nhalf month ban & 2.5k ban bullshit"

Darcy Ward* "Tedward Kennet lucky mother ducker"

Newcastle speedway "It is with great regret that due to the unavailability of the intended [Plymouth] opposition, this Sunday's (August 21st) meeting at Newcastle Speedway has had to be postponed. Newcastle Speedway can only apologise for the lateness of the announcement but in the last few days they have received the full co-operation of 6 of their fellow Premier League clubs who have attempted to alleviate the problem by making every effort to bring their teams to Tyneside on Sunday only to be thwarted by a series of problems, mostly down to rider availability. The efforts of the likes of Neil Machin at Sheffield and Steve Mallett and Laurence Rogers of Newport only go to show the true nature of the overwhelming majority of Premier League promotions and we also thank the managements of Berwick, Ipswich, Redcar and Workington for their efforts."

Mike Bowden "The plus side is crowds have improved and the fans are sticking by us...the racing is 50 per cent quicker and we are getting proper teams every week, full teams coming down"

Troy Batchelor* "Scooter bag is here .. Whoop"

Scott Nicholls* "mate,I've seen u on darky's. U're a liability! :-)"

Ludvig Lindgren* "off to the hills running cuz my life is in danger nanana naaaaaaa na na aaanaaaa"

Nigel Pearson* "only left school in 86 mate... then went to college and knackered my A-Levels up through a love of ale"

Dakota North* "3 gm engines for sale, all fresh"

Troy Batchelor* "The inbetweeners movie out today ! Definitely keen to see that"

Rory Schlein* "Inbetweeners fucking brilliant a must see"

Michael Addison "There's only really six promoters in the country – who really promote speedway – the rest are just speedway operators"

Paul Burbidge* "Kasprzak has just knocked Jason Doyle into the fence at Poole. Pirates fans are giving the Pole some richly deserved stick. Dirty move."

Moira Perrott "The squad system benefits the continental based riders for sure and it means that the British riders will get even fewer rides. Plus you can get that all the squad will still want their signing on fees"

18th August

Fredrik Lindgren* "How much is the fish?"

Nigel Pearson* "Morning all heading to Farnham for SGP highlights show, can't wait to see the Greg Hancock show"

Nicki Glanz* "With All this tax iam paying there shouldnt be a resesion in DK"

Linus Sundstrom* "Sad news about the junior school rider who passed away after a crash at practice in gniezno yesterday :("

Rory Schlein* "All the rioters who got caught your sentencers were not enough and the family's and human rights ppl saying their hard done by Blow it out your ass don't do the crim if ya can't do the time"

Nicolai Klindt* "just arrived in lovely england, the most beloved country in the world! hopefully its gonna be a good and eventfull weekend"

Lewis Bridger* "How boring is Life when im not racing my bike :/ or riding my Mx bike :("

Kevin Long* "just read my Speedway Star and your schedule does appear a bit stop/start. Bad times"

Ludvig Lindgren* "oh what a crash i had today on the push bike! could have gone rly bad! hahaha ledgend!!!!!! how fukt is my family soon as i leave the door everyone starts looking after me! how bad is it!! Is that the reputation i got.. ledgendary!!"

Nigel Pearson* "Job done, awesome feature with Greg Hancock on SGP show great work guys"

Paul Burbidge* "Pretty shocked to see pictures of Bournemouth on the news - the town centre looks like Atlantis. So much for the Great British summer!"

Nicki Glanz* "That awkward moment when u left your wallet in Haderslev and need diesel in van to get back"

Dave Croucher "Most clubs are losing money – I expect Matt's making money as usual – so the fewer meetings you run, the less money you lose. Costs have got completely out of hand. Independently wealthy men like Sandhu and Frost don't care what the riders wages are they just want to win. That's why you've got Sayfutdinov and Pedersen – it's great for British speedway and the fans but will, eventually, force the weaker clubs out of business"

Evening Chronicle "[George] English was unable to elaborate on the reason why Plymouth have pulled out because of likely further investigation by the sport's authorities. However, he was intending to send a full report setting out Newcastle's case."

Terry Russell "The prospect of a nice new [Swindon] facility, new flood lights and soundsystem, can only be exciting for the public."

Troy Batchelor* "woffie call me mate pboro want u to guest or contact Trev Swales on facebook"

David Croucher "My time had come and it was time to move on. I was very privileged to do what I did in the sport and I got as high as I could have got, with my jobs as GB and England U21 and U23 Manager. I never expected, or felt I was suitable for, the senior GB / England Team Manager's job. I have always believed you have to be doing it in the Elite League every week as a manager to be on top of the game. Nothing against Boycey, I love him to bits, but Australia have had the strongest team in the world for the last two years but haven't won anything."

Chris Louis "We do find ourselves in a position where we are suffering costs with a series of away matches and no income coming in."

19th August

Linus Sundstrom* "My 3rd season in UK now and people still cant say my name! Everyone says Lajnus but it should be Linus pronounced like leenus, get it?"

Nicolai Klindt* "what about anus, thats easier haha.... got the same issue. im just nicholas klit instead!"

Chris Neath* "Weird how I can hang on to a bike that's trying to rip my arms out but I get arm pump using a pen after 5 minutes!"

Dakota North* "Iphone4. Sucks I'm lucky to get three quarters of a day out of it before it dies! faaarrrkkk"

Nicolai Klindt* "on route to lakeside speedway home of the hammers. guesting for swider tonight, so going for a big score. defo going for a big dinner before"

Chris Holder* "wicked mate when we all have time we will be sporting full wetsuits because of the cold. But I'm game"

Cameron Woodward* "chiropractor will be on standby"

Chris Holder* "well needed ouch"

Darcy Ward* "tomorrow then it's our gym"

Cameron Woodward* "I've gotta fly to Polska tomorrow sorry mate. Damn! Grrr. You boys flat out next week?"

Chris Holder* "wet suits a must bro hahaha"

Stuart Douglas "These are just my PERSONAL opinions, not those of the Club, or the BSPA. Edward Kennett got caught cheating; there is no getting away from that fact. He is not the only rider with dubious pipes, but he is the only one who got caught. The same with illegals carbs, and oversize engines, the riders rarely get caught, and that is the real issue here."

Jon Cook "On a day when the worst speedway team in the League were in town (Swindon not Lakeside – please note Mr Pearson) and the crowd level reflected that fact, the [SRBF collection] total raised was just short of £1000. Unbelievable, if it weren't for the fact I counted it all myself."

Stuart Douglas "Edward is a lovely lad, and an excellent speedway rider. He is also impressionable, and those that advised and encouraged him to embark on this fraudulent activity should hang their heads in shame….let him serve his time and then not alienate him further. This Country needs all the decent speedway riders it can keep."

Jon Cook "On the subject of Linda and George [Barclay], I have to again record my thanks to them, and now also to Russell Paine, for helping us to build the best training system of any club that does not own its own venue."

Dakota North* "Average night"

Niels Kristian Iversen* "Golf this morning, just had dinner with wife to be and now Cinema to watch the inbetweeners"

Paul Burbidge* "Lakeside 66-26 P'boro. Sounds like a farce. Time for the Elite League to introduce a squad system. Guest system isn't working. Squads would bring more top riders to the UK. It would also ensure clubs have good cover for injuries and when riders have FIM meetings. Clubs get blamed for cheating the public, but riders were absent for genuine reasons. It's the system that's wrong."

Chris Holder* "So tired after a big day of jetsking! 2 red bulls down! Now in bed to recharge and go again tomorrow"

Linus Sundstrom* "Sorry to all peterborough fans for that team performance tonight.. They smooooked us bigtime! Early flight home tomorrow"

Graeme Gammell* [r/t Nigel Pearson] "You complete stiff! You had Lakeside as relegation candidates on your elite league predictions in March, goina give us credit?"

Nigel Pearson* "if people are going to have a pop they should at least get their facts right - there is no relegation. Poor"

Trevor Swales "I just feel sorry for the fans that came and watched. It wasn't a loss, it was a humiliation. Congratulations to Lakeside but we were exceptionally poor – but for two riders we didn't take a point off the opposition all night."

Rob Godfrey "It was a good job Sheffield lent them [Plymouth] Ashley Birks because he scored nine and God knows how bad they would have been otherwise. To be honest, we didn't even treat it like a normal league match, it was just a training exercise really. The mandate was to give all our riders five rides each and we produced a slick track to give the likes of Steve Worrall a confidence boosting meeting, which was a big plus."

Byron Bekker "Gary [Havelock] said to me after my second ride I shouldn't pull silly moves like that on a wet track so in Heat 14 I thought 'okay, I'll pass him on the outside if he doesn't want me to go up his inside.'"

20th August

David Watt* "RyanAir says final call before priority que even starts and then you wait outside for another 15 mins !!"

Scott Nicholls "I'm having the worst season in Britain that I've had for probably 12 years. But the one thing I haven't done and the one thing I will never do is cheat. It frustrates and disappoints me. We all know there are cheats and it has come to light now. Sadly, Eddie has been picked out. We know for certain that he is not the only one...if you cheat, you're not only cheating yourself, but it's stealing. The points you score are taking money off the guys who aren't cheating."

Dakota North* "Worst sleep ever"

Shane Parker "To be honest I was hoping to finish my career at Foxhall this year. I would have loved that. I made my feelings known to the right people and to Ipswich director of speedway Chris Louis. Perhaps it was my age but the call never came, and it was a shame."

Linus Sundstrom* "Landed at skavsta and jumped on the bus to stockholm city terminal, doing it the hard way today!"

David Hemsley "I thought we might get 1500 on a regular basis but we have been getting more than that. Considering some of the dross turned out during June they have stayed with us and considering we are learning as we go along, it is just amazing."

Jo Lowry* "What the bloody hell happened last night?! I'm away for one meeting, and the whole thing goes tits up! Ironically the only other meeting I've missed this year was the Poole meeting. Yeah..the one we got battered in. But last night was worse!!"

Hans Andersen "I couldn't ride for them [Birmingham] for the amount of money they offered me. It would have more or less cost me to ride in Britain. I want to ride, but I don't want to pay to go to work. They made me an offer, but it was a lot less than I'd been on at Coventry and in previous years at Belle Vue. They came back again less than three weeks later and by then I had sold a vehicle, sacked my mechanic and everything."

Mads Korneliussen* "Walked the dog and cut the grass #speedwayprolife"

David Hemsley "The attitude of some speedway riders, they are so amateurish. Even though they are paid for their living, the way some don't commit to the team and the club...I'm stunned by some of the professional riders I've come across. That's one of the reasons I gave up the team managership really because I couldn't relate to the mentality. Perhaps it's the ones I picked!.... some riders appear lackadaisical, it doesn't matter this week. It's not just the winning thing, it's the whole mentality."

Mike Bowden "Obviously we weren't in the Premier League until late.....I wouldn't have gone for the older riders who had done well in the past. Someone like Jason Bunyan had come to our track with the Isle of Wight, broke the track record the first time he saw it. But I didn't take into consideration he'd been out all last year with injury. I'd also have gone for at least one Australian and American but I don't have a sponsors' licence to get a work permit which prevented me doing that. Certainly I'd have stayed with Mark Simmonds who is still a very good rider but as you get older you don't bounce as well and when you do get injured, it does take longer to recover. If I'd have known Lee Smart was going to get injured in the second match of the season I would have had Claes Nedermark down here, I could have had him, he'd already signed."

Lee Richardson* "Back garden done! Front garden next! Then sort out hot tub! Rico junior here helping! Then time for a BBQ me thinks!!!"

Hans Andersen* "So today is the day were i turn a hopeless season around by finishing top 3 and returns to the GP stage 2012"

Dakota North* "Nice Saturday drive to Newport after washing my bikes all morning!"

Dakota North* "Hav not moved in 1 hour"

Dakota North* "Moving now thank god"

Dakota North* "Don't think il be making Newport tonight #fuckihatetraffic"

Dakota North* "Tomtom says 2 hours to Newport don't think that allows for the traffic I'm sitting in #fuckyouM5"

Dakota North* "Fuck me I was stopes for 2 hours no I'm moving, the shut 3 lanes because I car is broken down in the left lane #dickheads"

Dakota North* "Tough night in wales"

Fredrik Lindgren* "GP Challenge today always tough to predict. I wouldn't be surprised if Peter Ljung or Jesper B qualify, good in Vetlanda"

David Watt* "It's hard to get excited about a meeting that I probably won't get to ride in !! Nevermind. Should be good to watch !!"

Paul Burbidge* "I'm tipping Protasiewicz, Kasprzak and Lindback to secure SGP spots for 2012 at the GP Challenge this afternoon"

Rory Schlein* "In the workshop and the misses is at the footy where did I go wrong"

Hans Andersen "At the end of the day, it's not like we are going to perform better if we put some drugs in our bodies as in other sports. Your body is the bike and when you tamper with that, it should be treated the same as if you were an athlete taking drugs. They get banned for up to two years."

Dick Barrie "Another successful (Northern Junior Speedway League) campaign completed -- these little leagues are easy to suggest and begin, but don't always come to any kind of conclusion -- my thanks to everyone who helped publicise and promote a mini-league which has this season introduced three 15-year-olds, two 16-year-olds and another two 18-year-olds to team racing for the first time."

Chris Holder* "At mx GP! Some huge jumps!!!! And sweet bikes too"

Paul Burbidge* "Three third places for Hans Andersen in Vetlanda. It looks like we won't be seeing him in the SGP series next year"

David Hemsley "In hindsight it's easy to say that perhaps in February or March I should have spent more time considering the team than my stadium"

Mike Bowden "I'm waiting for the council to make up their mind what to do with the land at Ernesettle, but I keep asking myself do I really need to build another speedway track? I've got a lease until 2015 but it's renewable"

Chris Neath* "Gutted speedway was cancelled. Kinda of strange sat here in the sunshine with Bert Werner but hey!"

Hans Andersen "Riding on the track unfairly is one thing, but when they go and tamper with their bike, there's no chance of beating people."

Mike Hunter "I think one of the main arguments for the defence, if you can call it a defence, is that it seems certain that many riders have been using illegal silencers. Kennett is guilty but unlucky to be the one caught. The problem for any rider who realises there is widespread cheating going on is - whether to join them if you can't beat them. By and large riders don't like reporting fellow riders."

Paul Burbidge* "Lindback wins GP Challenge after beating Bjarne Pedersen in run-off. Both qualify for SGP series 2012 along with Piotr Protasiewicz"

Troy Batchelor* "Looking forward to watching the gp next year some as exciting riders got through the race off haha not!"

David Watt* "Well that fun ! NOT !! I found it hard work wanting to race knowing I couldn't qualify but that's life. Congrats to Anton, Bjarne & Pepe"

Jan Staechmann* "You could qualify providing you had enough points. A reserves points count towards qualification in FIM meetings"

Talking Thumb* [r/t Nicolai Klindt] "Just what we need for 2012, more young riders? Bjarne Pedersen 33 yrs 39 dys today & Piotr Protasiewicz 36 yrs 207 dys today!"

Paul Burbidge* "Look on bright side. At least we have three riders who will be competitive. Vaculik is first reserve by my count too"

Steve Worrall "Rob [Godfrey] has been doing the track to make it grippier and grippier and I think that's maybe made it harder for me."

John Anderson "We made Charlie [Gjedde] feel very welcome at Berwick. We took him out for meals and the team manager [Ian Rae] also opened his home to him. We did everything we could to help him during his spell with us, but the simple truth was he just didn't perform on the track. I don't think he made himself the most popular guy round the pits either. It would be safe to say that we didn't part on the best of terms because there one or two things going on behind the scenes..... He said he didn't have the Newport deal lined up before he left us, but I think everyone knows that wasn't true."

Ricky Wells* "All the way to Workington for a rainoff"

Hans Andersen* "Never In my wildest fantasi would i have thought the setup needed today was the right one BUT bad day to get it wrong :("

Chris Neath "The new dirt is really good, it's bedding in week after week now. It's got grip without being heavy and for me personally that's what I like, I don't like big heavy tracks."

Steve Mallett "To have only 401 for a meeting with our nearest rivals was a huge disappointment and people must realise that we, and I include all my family, cannot go on losing any more money."

21st August

Niels Kristian Iversen* "Hate it when ryanair makes you stand outside the plane like a retard, for 15min before boarding. Specially in the mornings #plonkers"

Hans Andersen* "Well back to life again..... Just left for Gorzow where Leszno awaits In the second leg. Let's win some races today eh boy #fullthrottle"

Darcy Ward* "Gotta love a push in at airports"

Jon Cook "We can now reach a total of 46 League points with a win next week against the form side of the Elite League, Birmingham, and that's our aim. We will then have to sit back and see if we can be caught but we did ourselves a huge favour, race points wise, with the win by 40 points over Peterborough on Friday and with our four own riders showing great form we are confident we can hold our own against anyone once we return to full strength in ten days' time."

Fredrik Lindgren* "Hate my blocked nose, hate that my cold never let go! #Manflu"

Nigel Pearson* "Rare and much needed day off, Sunday lunch at the Bell with friends & a couple of beers. Won't be tweeting today"

Linus Sundstrom* "Not raining today so thats good! Gonna take a walk to the workshop now to see whats going on there. My body feels more like 61 then 21 !"

Nicki Glanz* "On my way to the steakhouse for lunch with some good company"

Fredrik Lindgren* "Had Subway today for the first time while in Poland, me like. Now waiting for my ride to Czestochowa with a Cappucino"

Nicolai Klindt* "its soooooo sunny in wolves! wrong day tho.... going carvery with luke and family! later lively drive to stansted"

Sam Masters* "I'm sooo bored what can I do?? England #dogshit"

Dakota North* "Feeling it today, old jd is a bad influence"

Nicki Glanz* "Head is hurting ! fuming"

Sam Masters* "Can't wait to get these angry boy DVDs might take up a bit of this time!!! bored can't wait to get home #longseason"

Paul Burbidge* "Brits should be allowed to compete in PL and EL. More signing on fees is a price worth paying to lose the farcical guest system. It's up to clubs to sign good non-GP riders to cover for SGP regulars. They can also be more flexible with fixture planning."

Ian Maclean "The real reason for the big win was that Workington were just not competitive - something has gone wrong there. James Wright nil from four rides at our place??"

Troy Batchelor* "Who's staying in Poznan tonight"

Fredrik Lindgren* "Tough night, blood taste in my mouth after every heat, exhausted! pain in my back! Scored 10p/5h just keep it going!"

Chris Holder* "One more follower to hit 4,000!! Cone on! Yeewww"

Randall Butt "Midway through the thriller however it looked as though Mildenhall....were going to be the victims of a new verb. They were in danger of being 'Worralled'."

Fredrik Lindgren* "Back in a hotel Krakow tonight, night night racing Wolves tomorrow! Be hard or go home! Funny thing I got a handicap room, did I really look that poor?"

22nd August

Gary Patchett* "Arctic Monkeys! Headline or flatline? Crap!!"

Niels Kristian Iversen* "Flat tyre.. Just what you dont want in the middle of the night. Quick change of wheel and we are back on track"

Niels Kristian Iversen* "Why does the german customs people always treat you like a criminal when they stop you 20km from the Danish border?? He ask "what are you gonna do in Denmark ?" While holding my danish passport in hes hand #cleverfoxnot"

Niall Strudwick* "had another good practise at mildenhall yesterday. Just want to keep riding now"

Tai Woffinden* "scooter bag race is on"

David Watt* "smoked ya through immigration !!!"

Peter Johns* "you lot go & have a sleep. See ya later"

Nicolai Klindt* "got a question for you matey? who decides where to go on a monday? is this the 10th time for poole to be on telly.."

Nigel Pearson* "hello mate it's a combination of Sky and GoSpeed who allocate meetings. And stadium availability too. Hope you're good"

Nicolai Klindt* "ok, just thought cuz swindon and lynn have only been on once this year i think"

Scott Nicholls* "Why haven't swindon been on again then?....oh that's right we're poo :-("

Nicolai Klindt* "we ain't that bad!"

Scott Nicholls* "Haha,just kidding. We're awesome"

Paul Burbidge* "Clubs can only pay riders what they can afford. But promoters must invest in their product. Keep cutting, it will die"

BSPA LEICESTER have released both of their reserves, John Oliver and Charles Wright, following their home defeat by Glasgow on Saturday. Both riders scored three points in the meeting but were overshadowed by the Tigers' Nick Morris who piled up a bumper 19-point haul. Oliver made 24 league and cup appearances for the Lions, and was one of three original members of the team who started the season for the club, who have made wholesale changes during the summer. Wright, meanwhile, was a loan signing from Workington in June, and the Lions will name the replacement riders following approval from the BSPA.

Chris Butterworth "There seems to have been a bit of unrest in the camp as well which absolutely kills team spirit. It seemed to start for me when Charles Wright was dropped. James' performances since then just haven't been the same culminating in four no scores yesterday at Glasgow."

Paul Burbidge* "If you see how many guests Coventry, Lakeside and Birmingham have used, it's ridiculous. Fans want to watch their own riders"

Nicki Glanz* "Never let someone borow your Van for 'an hour or so' its been 3 now"

Chris Holder* "Jus got sky installed"

Scott Nicholls* "is that free coz u're on there all the time!"

Chris Holder* "yeh but I'd rather not be on tv at belle vue!! Haha #notcool"

Scott Nicholls* "ah,come on. What more can u ask for,bit of water,berms,bomb holes,whoops... awesome. oh I'm thinking of mx. Unlucky! :-)"

Chris Holder* "truth hurts mate tracks shit! Worst in England! Hopefully get new stadium an it be the best in Uk!"

Paul Berry* "yep, when we get new stadium will be fine, but riders need to be more professional on here"

Chris Holder* "If u don't like wat u hear don't follow us!! Simple! #notrocketscience"

Paul Berry* "surely as a professional you should take responsibility for what you say??"

Chris Holder* "I don't tell u wat to do so don't tel me wat to do ?"

Scott Nicholls* "what have u started Mr Holder! Naughty boy"

Chris Neath* "Todays summary so far - trying to get a mortgage is nigh on impossible and solicitors cost a fortune. All pretty negative shit really!"

Chris Holder* "House be finished this week!! Bout fukn time! Big party comin up"

Cameron Woodward* "I'm up for getting rotten. Will it be finished for wavys meeting?"

Darcy Ward* "omg no way same"

Chris Holder* "you bloody better believe it!"

Nigel Pearson "I understand that Kildemand wants to stay at Coventry – that needs to be sorted for the good of the sport"

Chris Louis [to Charlie Gjedde] "Stuck on the M6, changing in the van – it's a glamorous life as a speedway rider"

Lee Richardson* "Bit of united vs spurs for me !!!"

Paul Burbidge* "In two and a half years, Craig Cook has gone from total novice to beating seasoned international riders. Great news for Team GB"

Lewis Bridger* "not total novice he was a awesome Mx rider that switched to Speedway the same as what i did at 14yr and was in the EL at 16yr"

Paul Burbidge* "Fair point. But I gather switching from mx to speedway is far from easy. You and Cook have both adapted very well"

Troy Batchelor* "Spark plug went in last race had to take second bike .... Damn it..12pts"

Darcy Ward* "Allways got excuses"

Fredrik Lindgren* "Did anyone see me flip the bike on a practice start then miraculous save it! #surreal"

Darcy Ward* "Well made it out of bellevue in one piece after living on the edge :)"

Fredrik Lindgren "Interesting night. Nicki tried to get over me but I didn't want to let him do it and he ended up in the fence. The second one I kind of got sandwiched between [Troy] Batchelor and Nicki and we all ended up in the fence. Heat one, as well, he tried to get over me even though we were level. What can I say? I won't back down to him. 'I wasn't feeling very good when I hit the fence,' he said. I could feel my back stretching to the limit. I'm not 100 per cent yet. It will take between four and six weeks before I don't feel any pain any more. I'm going to have to ride with the pain and raise the bar of what I can take."

Trevor Swales "Nicki's taken quite a heavy impact to his left leg. I rather fancy it's going to stiffen up quite heavily. I don't think there's anything broken. It could have been much worse, three of them all through [the fence] in the same place. It was a speedway incident, nobody's fault."

23rd August

Nigel Pearson* "Just want to say well done to The Aces on their cut-price admission. Speedway for a tenner, food for thought?"

Troy Batchelor* "Ssslleeeppp please! Not the airport"

Rory Schlein* "Last night was hard Darcy Ward and Chris Holder were on it"

Chris Holder* "gotta be on it with u round there! Wheeling all over the place"

Andy Irons* [r/t by Chris Holder] "i surf because Kelly Slater did it, for chicks, for the cool cars, for the hype, but it all became just stuff"

Linus Sundstrom* "Out in the workshop now to strip the bike and wash the parts zzzZZzz need more sleep"

Chris Holder* "Happy with the new neck pillow! Darcy good buy"

Olly Allen* "Weetabix....an oldy but a goody!!!"

Fredrik Lindgren* "Does the Ryanair pilots get their licence from the serial box? Hard landing felt like I compressed my back!"

Rory Schlein* "I herd that Freddie upset nikki last night is this true and not just once"

Kenni Larsen* "youre starting to slip mrs lowry! #parttimejob"

Jo Lowry* "u give me a % of your wages for those meetings and I'll be there...I've only missed 2 meetings this year. Not a bad effort!"

Ian Lane "Are you aware of the rule that - Elite team riders with less than 5 Elite meetings to go cannot sign for a Premier League team? This was 'invented' by the management committee in the last couple of days to stop Somerset signing Claus Vissing and also Workington who wanted to make changes. The rule is regarded as 'unwritten'."

Greg Hancock* "The new silencers cost at least 1/3 more, engine maintenance has more than doubled and only the riders suffer from it! Hmm! #laughsoyoudontcry More silencer issues & more expense to the riders. If your silencer is cracked, you're not allowed to repair it. Just toss it! #itsonlycash"

Hans Andersen* "Tell me WHY cant a rider WHO wants to ride In UK (but doesnt fit into any teams) at least be aloud to take GUEST bookings ? Think about it"

Scott Nicholls* "good point. I'm sure there's a good reason...or should I say a bad reason? I don't understand a lot of their decisions/rules"

Alun John Rossiter* "that's called squad systems mate !!"

Jan Staechmann* "I presume you mean "not be allowed" - he isn't, because in order to do guest bookings he must be in a declared 1 to 7"

Keith Denham "Our heat leaders produced four points from 12 rides on Sunday and after that performance I thought we have got to do something because the fans are demanding changes. I don't expect the performance I got from James [Wright] on Sunday who is the top paid rider and I expected him to be top of the Premier League averages at the start of the season. He has been letting us down in terms of our chances of success and our title chances went up in a cloud of dust on Sunday... I take the blame for not making changes sooner and I should have been more forceful because I have put off changes week on week and seeing what would happen next. I was embarrassed by the Glasgow performance and have never been as sick in my life as after that match. I didn't think Glasgow rode that well but they didn't need to – it was just that we were that poor and it was an embarrassment that Richard Lawson scored nearly half our points. I just thought these performances cannot continue or we will lose the fans."

Nicki Glanz* "Just been asked if i cud train little 50cc kids i was like only if they bring there moms :)"

Lewis Bridger* "Just going to Watch the *Inbetweeners* in Hastings odean"

Philip Rising "What struck me is the simple fact that in both Poland and Sweden once a rider's contract was concluded he became a free agent to go elsewhere. And how well that process worked in both countries. We all know that the British system of rider assets is illegal (Bosman and all that) but, of course, no one has ever bothered challenge it in the UK. So, the question is, would British speedway improve by having freedom of movement for riders once a contract had expired? Would speedway here benefit or would the rich (even that is subjective when applied to speedway) scoop the best talent? Could we introduce some sort of salary cap that would help spread available talent around all the clubs? Would it help to develop a squad system where tracks would have a pool of riders to chose from to help reduce the need for guests and rider replacement?"

Nicolai Klindt* "impressed with my self, did better than i thought i would do tbf. 10+2pts/5h against dackarna. good to be back on worlds best race track!"

Nigel Pearson* "Got my management hat on today - Dudley Heathens v Stoke at Monmore, tapes-up 7.30. Need a win, big meeting ahead, should be a good un "

Hayley Armstrong* "Well what a fantastic birthday present. 4 points to Stoke Speedway. Final score Dudley 27 Stoke 64"

Nigel Pearson* "Well our boys took a good ommering by Stoke, congrats to them. Less than 2 years ago we didn't even have a team"

Dakota North* "Why do all young men in uk hang out at mcdonalds car park with there Volkswagens"

Malcolm Vasey "We got our heads down and put in a thoroughly professional performance and achieved the outcome [27-63] that we deserved. I accept that losing both of your [Dudley] reserves as early as Heat 2 creates problems."

24th August

Leigh Adams* "Apologies for the Aussie racesuit auction being withdrawn. Sorting out some logistics issues at the moment but we will be back online soon"

George English "We're indebted to Neil Machin, the Sheffield promoter, who has moved heaven and earth to get a team to us for Sunday and help save the day and avoid a second blank Sunday at the height of summer, as we had to suffer last Sunday under the most frustrating of circumstances."

Backless "Surely the BSPA will have learned from the mistakes made during the last winter... & hoof this collective embarrassment out of the PL. How on earth are other promoters supposed to sell the impending visit of Plymouth - whether or not they turn up - to a recession hit public? They turned up at Workington with five riders & R/R because they seemingly couldn't find anybody to ride at reserve for Kyle Hughes - having been provided with Ashley Birks the night before at Scunthorpe."

Mike Bowden "In the National League a couple of teams arrived with five riders and I think Buxton turned up with four riders a couple of times and had to borrow some of our juniors....I don't regret stepping up at all, we could have stuck in the NL but would the crowd have stayed with us watching four or five man teams?"

Nicolai Klindt* "hard to wake up in the morning after being awake all night home from sweden. no Wolves speedway for me due to ludvigs not riding in Sweden"

Fredrik Lindgren* "You not racing with us tomorrow?"

Nicolai Klindt* "no because ludde is not on the team in sweden an available in uk, cvs can't use a guest. was soo ready tho!"

Sam Masters* "Waiting for Dakota North fucking starving hurry up"

Niels Kristian Iversen* "Now at stansted to find out my bag has not arrived.. Useless easyJet plonkers"

Rory Schlein* "my spelling ant as bad as Darcy Ward"

Darcy Ward* "blow me spelled that right"

Dakota North* "bored as at pool, me and masters trying to talk to my polish team #itaniteasy"

Nigel Pearson* "After all day on the phone on Dudley Heathens business, time to focus on Exeter v Liverpool"

Fredrik Lindgren* "Been taking care of some paperwork & bookings today!"

Jo Lowry* "Just seen that we're giving away free caps on monday. I want a cap! Can the physio have a cap please?!"

Paul Burbidge* "Still can't believe Poole are tracking THJ at reserve. Masterstroke by Matt Ford. He just flew under Bjerre while the Dane was on tactical"

Dakota North* "Engine was flying intill my 3 race #fuckednow going to cost me lots of coin! #Notsatisfied"

Ludwig Lindgren* "how boring is it!"

Sam Masters* "Mechanic for Dalota North tonight I was shit but he was on the gas, shit about his engine but #walletemptyout"

Lewis Bridger* "Just had a hot bath ;) feel exhausted after some hard sessions at Mx only 20min sessions :/ them 40min Moto must be so hard"

25th August

Linus Sundstrom* "Home now after a shit night at poole, always knew its gonna be a hard one but i was just rubbish tonight! New day tomorrow again Have to get my head right and show some fighting spirit tomorrow v wolves!"

Fredrik Lindgren* "Let's go wake up my brother Ludvig and drive to Stockholm Skavsta Airport, Nyköping in other words"

Paul Burbidge* "Don't you just love Stansted first thing in the morning? Can't stand the place. Wish BA went to Bydgoszcz from Heathrow"

Niels Kristian Iversen* "Few things to dó in the office today. Weather is shit so guess its no golf. Tomorrow its Danish league in Outrup"

Dakota North* "Over washing both bikes already! So much todo!"

Chris Holder* "Brando bday.... So me and Darcy had a couple... Know wat I'm saying"

Paul Burbidge* "Numbskulls at Ryanair won't let you read a newspaper in an exit row during takeoff and landing. How much harm can the *Daily Mail* do?"

Nicolai Klindt* "thanks fuck for being near the midlands where the sun is shining. stansted was too wet and dangerous as we almost had a crash"

Linus Sundstrom* "Not cool to spend nearly all day in the workshop.. Need some rest now so im sharp for tonight! #powernap"

Fredrik Lindgren* "So here we are at Peterborough heavy rain at Stansted when we landed didn't give good vibes but here it's clear! Panthers Vs Wolves"

Taylor Poole* "Finally get to have a race. Just like the give a HUGE thanks to JC for the weather #happyas"

Paul Burbidge* "Maciej Janowski has made way for Grzegorz Zengota at Swindon. Strange move. Wroclaw are out of play-offs, so Janowski can't be that busy"

Nicolai Klindt* "had my hair cut and again its looking good. gone shorter than before tho, see how it turns out with the other half"

Nicki Glanz* "Had another awesome session in the gym for 2nd time today #gettingthere"

Fredrik Lindgren* "That was a poor result for us at the showground. Now I'm off to Luton Airport, going Poland tomorrow for the Grand Prix in Torun"

Chris Neath* "Bad night at Ipswich. Pulled out after 2 rides feeling rough and dehydrated. Hate doing that so much. Sorry rocket fans"

Lewis Bridger* "Good night early morning jog for me then to the stadium when it dry's up for some laps on Karger motor with special cam"

  Linus Sundstrom* "The lindgren brothers had far too much spare time today"

  Ludvig Lindgren* "why give freddie any cred of that art work?!?! its time to come clean it was all done by me ludvig piccasooooo"

Dale Allitt "It was Lewis Kerr's first-ever maximum and I could have done with him doing that in Heat 14, but he said he wouldn't ride in that heat for £200 per point!"

Linus Sundstrom* "Decent night tonight! Panthers won and i scored 1,3,3,1',2':10+2 . Back home to sweden over the weekend trying to recharge the batteries!"

Ludvig Lindgren* [after paid 2 from 5 rides] "anyone got a gun?"

26th August

Fredrik Lindgren* "On the plane Luton-Gdansk seems to be a few speedway folks on here going for the Torun SGP"

Nigel Pearson* "Morning all, Stansted here we come. Back on speedway duty for Polish GP in Torun on Sky Sports on Saturday alongside BSI boys and girls"

Linus Sundstrom* "Back in sweden after a early start this morning! Looking forward to a well needed couple of days off from speedway"

Gary Patchett "When Zengi [G. Zengota] called us and said he was ready to ride we couldn't offer him a position without Magic [Janowski] stepping down. However, I spoke to Magic and offered him the opportunity to take a breather from what has been a frantic schedule for him this season. This will give him the opportunity to prepare for his World U21 finals which resume this weekend."

Nicolai Klindt* "sometimes i'd like to slap my self in the face, cuz fuck i'm daft sometimes"

Dakota North* "Feel so shit"

Pete Simmons* "spoken to Mike Bowden at Plymouth and still very much on- tweet Later if i hear any different"

Fredrik Lindgren* "Weather is great in Poland, summer is still here. Is nice!"

Chris Holder* "So hot in Polska! yeehaa"

Taylor Poole* "so cold in Plymouth!"

Ludvig Lindgren* "u all suckers in poland should know how cold it is in the uk and in Freddie Lindgren's house cuz u cant have any heating on!"

Lee Richardson* "switch on!!! He won't know!!"

Ludvig Lindgren* "i wish i could! got a big hole in the garden so the heating wont work! hahah f**king gas man!"

Linus Sundstrom* "Hate people that wakes me up when im sleeping,why cant the ticket man come before im falling asleep?The ryanair people are the worst though"

Nicolai Klindt* "first bus ride in uk, is propa excited!"

Lee Richardson* "Not linking this weather at all!!! Liking I meant!! Poxy I phone!!!"

Lewis Bridger* "annoying ay mate I keep doing it to and u read it back like WTF !!! ;)"

Nicki Glanz* "Sat in pubs beergarden looking at females"

Ludvig Lindgren* "just had a masturbation marathon! i won every time!"

Nigel Pearson* "Landed in Bydgoszcz boiling hot. Now eyes shut and in car with crazy driver on way to Torun. Big weekend ahead - if we make it!!"

Fredrik Lindgren* "Was no practice for me today, saving my body and the pain I get after riding. Full throttle tomorrow instead! Easy going in Torun!"

Lee Richardson* "It's taken me 3 hours from Hastings to dartford and I'm not at the tunnel yet!! Never seen it this busy"

Coventry THE management of the Coventry Bees would like to both apologise and explain why, last Friday against Belle Vue, the club was only able to track five riders. We also feel that supporters should know of the unsatisfactory circumstances that Coventry are operating under this season. We have refrained from issuing a statement earlier to allow the BSPA to reply to certain questions we raised and explain the reason why the sequence of events occurred as they did. As yet no explanation has been forthcoming and so we detail the sequence of events and our comments below because we believe that this episode highlights everything that is wrong with the manner in which speedway is run in this country: On Friday 12th as a result of the suspension of Eddie Kennett and the unproven fitness of Peter Kildemand who was due to ride that night and over the weekend for Workington we redeclared and included Piotr Pawlicki at reserve. On Monday 15th after speaking to Peter and him having proved his fitness over the weekend we resubmitted a further redeclaration including Peter Kildemand in our 1 - 7. We subsequently learned that using his privileged position as a Management Committee member thereby pre-empting any other club, Poole Promoter Matt Ford contacted Peter Kildemand on Saturday 13th after being made aware of our Friday 12th redeclaration and informed him that Coventry no longer wished to use him and he was to be included in Poole's 1 to 7. Peter informed Mr Ford that he did not wish to ride for Poole and wished to speak to Coventry on the following Monday (15th). If Coventry did not wish to use him he would speak to Poole again but he made it clear that he intended to remain with Coventry. Peter did no deal with Poole, no agreement was made and as a result he certainly did not consent to Mr Ford's illegal inclusion in Poole's 1-7. Scandalously Peter was informed that if he did not consent to ride for Poole he would be suspended for 28 days. Peter Kildemand then telephoned

Alun Rossiter on Monday morning (15th) and an amended redeclaration was made by Coventry at 12.09 pm on that Monday. It was confirmed to us verbally by the BSPA office that our Monday 1-7 would just need ratification by the Management Committee. We heard nothing more until 4.30 Wednesday afternoon August 17th at 4.30 pm effectively close of the office's business when we were told that we could not use Peter because he had been included in another unnamed team's 1-7 (Poole). That was the first we had learned of this and incredibly our redeclared 1-7 was not circulated until Friday 19th, 4 hours before the start of our meeting against Belle Vue. Why was there such a delay as any other club wishing to use Peter Kildemand would have been informed one week after Poole's Management Committee member and Vice Chairman, Matt Ford.

We believe this incident reflects the following:

1. Apparent abuse of his position by a Management Committee and BSPA Vice Chairman to gain an advantage over other clubs.
2. An inappropriate approach to our rider by the same MC member on Saturday August 13th.
3. An illegal submission of a 1-7 by the same club which prevented our legal 1-7 from being applied. Poole's illegal submission must have been before 12.09pm on Monday and we require substantiated proof of the time and date of this illegal submission.
4. A dilatory approach by the BSPA office in dealing with our 1-7 resulting in our rider unbelievably being included in another team's 1-7.
5. Further reasons why Promoters who have a vested interest in decision making should not be making key decisions on their competitors.
6. The unsatisfactory nature of the way the sport is run which Coventry and Peterborough sought to change last winter.
7. The unacceptable breach of the agreement made between the BSPA, Coventry and Peterborough on the latter two clubs return to the Elite League at the start of this season. We are now approaching September and there has been no Independent Appeals Panel set up neither have there been any move towards setting one up, of which we are aware.
8. Since Coventry's and Peterborough's return to the Elite league there has been no General Council meeting or convened meeting of Elite League clubs. We believe this to be unacceptable or worse in the extreme.

Peter Kildemand was in the pits ready to race against Belle Vue on Friday 19th August but because of what we believe to be machinations on the part of certain parties we were prevented from using him and as a result we had only five legal riders to use. Nick Morris was unavailable and Josh Auty broke down on the motorway en-route. We therefore believe that the match should be re-run as a result of our being prevented from using Peter Kildemand due to the ratification and enforcement of Poole's illegal 1-7. If our 1-7 had been approved before the Belle Vue meeting we could have used Peter in place of Nick Morris but as it was we could not use Peter effectively guesting in place of the non-show Josh Auty because Peter's average was higher than Josh's. During the winter we took a stance together with Peterborough to eradicate many dubious and discredited actions which favoured certain clubs against others. After receiving the BSPA's assurance that effectively tainted procedures would be "cleaned up" we alongside Peterborough returned. We returned on the clear understanding that goodwill would be forthcoming from both sides for the betterment of British speedway. So far we have seen little of the promised goodwill. We feel we have met obstruction, obfuscation and inactivity some of which we believe has been designed to frustrate the level playing field we were promised. Possibly we should just return the Elite League trophy to the BSPA office for them to hold on Poole Pirates behalf indefinitely and thereby avoid the necessity to run meetings and incur the resulting financial losses only to ensure that Poole win the trophy anyway. The key to our return was the promise that the ruling body would introduce an Independent Appeals Panel. Immediately the season started an unsatisfactory situation occurred involving Poole's Dennis Andersson when previously applied rules were ignored and he came into Poole's pre-season 1-7 on an advantageous 4 points instead of the expected 5 points. So far we have seen absolutely no sign of this and we can only assume that certain favoured promoters, for their own reasons, do not wish to see a diluting of their control and this coupled with the absence of any meetings imply a desire to retain the discredited status quo. The purpose of the IAP is to rule on disputed matters from the rule book. It would never be involved in the running of speedway despite the distorted misinformation put about by those people who would not benefit from a fair and democratically run sport. The IAP would rule on matters such as this and many many other disputes that appear to be settled unsatisfactorily.

Steve Shovlar "Hilarious rant full of misinformation and innacuracies. love the bit about Andersson. Someone in Coventry needs to learn the rules."

Nigel Pearson* "Reading Coventry's statement, perhaps speedway fans will now realise why I was urging promoters to work together during last week's show.

Marmite "Was that between the times he was trying to influence the meeting he was supposed to commentate on? Pearson also said that a 10 team league was the perfect number, again, utter tosh and rubbish from the man"

Nigel Pearson* "And as a follow-up, there are two sides to every story folks. Dont care who is at faultn just sort it"

Paul Burbidge* "Just seen the Coventry statement. This is going to get ugly. I'll have to speak to all parties before running any stories for legal reasons. Until someone without a vested interest governs British speedway, there will always be suspicion from rival promoters - rightly or wrongly."

Philip Rising "Surely, the point is that serious allegations have been made (yet again) and either the BSPA or Matt Ford should at least answer them, with whatever documented evidence they have in their possession, to prove to us all who is telling the truth. Is that too much to ask?"

Steve Shovlar "Doubt you will get a reply out of Matt. He more than likely would never reply to such an embarressing rant. Time for the 'here today gone tomorrow' promotion at Brandon to go. The are outsiders and allways will be no matter who is on the MC"

Jo Lowry* "Wow. Don't you just love being a speedway fan people?! Nothing is ever simple in our sport. Nothing"

Alison Chalmers [after Glasgow 39-54 at Armadale] "Wonderful, brilliant, magic, amazing, stuff of dreams, superb . . . Just got in from one of the best night's ever. Pinch me I am dreaming. 1-10 after 2 heats and the banter on the 1st bend was as good as our team. Only downside was poor Christian out for the season thanks to Byron Bekker attempting to ride beyond and above his capabilities. One FINGER on the league title I will concede!"

Alison Chalmers "As far as speedway racing goes, it was non-existent. I cannot recall when I last saw a track like that and I am not saying that because it was at Armadump. When we arrived just before 7, they were dumping loads of shale onto the track and not doing much else with it. We knew before the tapes went up on heat 1 that there were going to be problems. Of course when we reached heat 2 and no Monarch had crossed the finish line and we were leading 10 - 1, the appalling track conditions were playing into our hands. If you had seen Joe Screen ride round in heat 1, you would have wondered why the referee was allowing the meeting to go ahead. Everyone was expecting someone to get hurt and I was watching Nick (Morris) bouncing about through my fingers but, once again, it was Christian Henry who was the innocent victim in heat 7. It took forever for an ambulance to arrive and during the delay, they started scraping the pre-meeting dirt back off the track! You couldn't make it up. It was a few minutes to 9pm when the meeting resumed with the rerun of heat 7 and there were all sorts of mutterings amongst the red and white hordes that Edinburgh were deliberately stalling to get the meeting abandoned due to the curfew! Stewart Dickson was seen several times walking along to the ref's box and standing below it remonstrating with Mr. McGregor. More fuel for the Tigers faithful, of course! Nick Morris was so good but sometimes hairy to watch. It is actually scary how a 17 year old can master that track and that is twice in 3 weeks in tricky conditions. It will be interesting to see how far he goes in the sport?"

Alan Bridgett "On Friday the biggest problem was that it was very cloudy, not a breath of wind, and misty. We had a lot of rain on Thursday. The downpour came about three and there was absolutely no drying power in it. By about half past five I said – worst case scenario we'll get it on, and if there is any drying power. I can get it good. But that never happened, I never got to finish properly. Then we just had to get it the best we could, because people would not appreciate when it isn't raining, why we're not going to run."

27th August

Terry Russell "We weren't prepared to put that on for our public given the free dates we have ruminating"

Scott Nicholls "Bear in mind all the bad press speedway got in the winter over Coventry and Peterborough, this was a great time for them to really stamp their authority on it and say 'we're a professional outfit, we don't tolerate cheats, we're doing this, this and this', they could have redeemed themselves a bit."

Neil Middleditch "He has been punished and the amount of money he's going to lose is huge. I don't know what point money Eddie is on, but it is certainly a lot of money."

Jim Lynch "We want to be the Poole of the North within the next five years."

Piotr Protasiewicz "This winter I started with a very good lady in Zielona Gora, who helped me make my head stronger when the pressure gets very high. This has been my problem before in the GP, but I hope this problem is gone and now I'm born again!"

Matt Ford "Renat [Gafurov] sat down with me a week or so ago and said that he didn't want to be the reason why Poole could lose out on the title this season and if someone else could be fitted in that could do a better job than him he would be willing to stand down."

Renat Gafurov "I like the promoter at Poole very much and I understand that winning at Poole is important. I'm unhappy I've lost my team place but the most important thing is what is best for the Poole team. If this is what they feel is best, then so be it."

David Watt "Renat was great. As quiet as he was, he was always a great part of our team. We're not going to forget the work he did earlier in the year. But he felt his time had come to an end. He felt he wasn't going as good as he could. Very nobly he stood down and that says a huge amount about his character. Certainly we're not going to forget what he's done."

Scott Nicholls "We're not arguing over one cc here or there, you're talking 10ccs and more....I can understand it if you're a rider and you've got a meeting the next day, you don't want to have your engine taken out, then sealed up and taken away. If it's sealed up there's still a doubt about corruption, has it been sealed properly?"

Neil Middleditch "Now they're ripping off silencers at every meeting and it's all after the horse has bolted."

Scott Nicholls "It's not a problem with Ed at all, I like Ed, but I do not like cheating, it's that simple."

Graham Drury "We haven't had a single rain-off this season which is amazing and I've been in this sport a long time. Back in 2009 we had 11 rain-offs and that crippled us."

John Davis "Someone should stick up for Ed a little bit. Riders have tampered with silencers from the first day they were introduced, we've all tampered with them, that is fact. Speedway is renowned for people pulling strokes. Everybody is competitive and if you can get an edge over anyone by doing it, you will. Ed's not a junkie, he doesn't do drugs, he doesn't drink, he simply drilled a few holes, and that gets him sent down for 12 months. He's the only decent thing in British speedway right now, he's a decent kid, a good kid, who lives and dies for speedway. he's the best thing British speedway's got going for it. It's very sad, and very unnecessary......As I said, I'm not condoning cheating, I'm just saying every man and his dog has done it. I think 75 per cent of silencers have been tampered with, and you'll probably find 10 per cent of riders are on illegal engines. The punishment does not fit the crime. If Ed did turn his back on speedway, can you justify that?"

Rory Schlein* "Just read a story in the *speedway star* saying every man and his dog has cheated and 75% have tampered silencers. Wat a load of shit!!!!"

Cameron Woodward* "bahaha. What cock wrote that"

Lewis Bridger* "well I'm the 15% then & would surprise any1 haha ;) #cheatsneverprosper"

Rory Schlein* "If he thinks other riders are cheating put up the £550 and protest against the 75% who he thinks are cheating"

Niles Kristian Iversen* "who is saying that ?? I havent Got #*speedwaystar*"

Jan Staechmann* "yes I read that too mate. "whatever it takes to win?" I suppose he had to, so he is obviously speaking for himself"

Jason Attwood "Speedway is a results business and we have looked at things over the last month – this isn't just a knee-jerk reaction to Nick Morris scoring 19 against us for Glasgow. John [Oliver] and Charles [Wright] have both become friends of mine and I know they are fans' favourites, so it was with a very heavy heart that I made the 'phone calls to them.....I'm on trial here as manager, I realise that, and I want that job for 2012. We need to start winning meetings"

Scott Nicholls "I don't want to look like I'm getting on my high horse, I'm not perfect, I've made mistakes, but I'm having the worst season in I don't know how long, and I haven't cheated, and I won't cheat."

Jan Molyneux "Hopefully the new [Swindon] stadium will be built before the old one is demolished so there won't be any disruption, and they can transfer from one to the other. The [Abbey] stadium is quite old and it doesn't really meet anyone's expectations of a modern stadium."

Sam Masters* "Faaaark m5 is getting as bad as m25"

Nicolai Klindt* "bikes from this year for sale! complete for £3500 and £2000 for rolling (without engine). contact on here or nklindt@live.dk"

Paul Burbidge* "I've just met Torun's club chaplin Piotr. Very nice man. He's overseeing Ryan Sullivan's wedding in October"

David Watt* "Has mixed emotions ! Pumped for SGP with the boys tonight but pissed off at the same time !! It's just not my day today !!"

Steve Shovlar "Coventry ditched a rider, and hoped no one would notice. Now that's a fact. They hoped to re-sign him on Monday. Another fact. Matt Ford beat them to it. Yet another fact. Coventry were simply naive. They had a decent team capable of walking into the playoffs but tried to be clever. Their cunning plan was to strengthen, but the wheels came off the moment they released Kildermand. Not expecting a professional Speedway promoter (It's what Matt Ford does for a living, not a side line) to not notice was frankly naive in the extreme."

Nigel Pearson* "I make editorial decisions in every commentary - and Heat 12 shows why I 'big up' Darcy Ward folks. No bias, just fact"

Lee Richardson* "What a shame Darcy Ward isn't English!!! That boy is pretty special!!! Awesome"

Paul Burbidge* "What's going on for Chris Harris? No points from four rides in Torun. Not on the pace"

Fredrik Lindgren* "Seriously what's going on with my racing at the moment? Am I this poor?!? Confidence level down at 0!"

Mike Bennett* "Oh dear - a few problems with the audio feed from the speedway GP tonight!"

Lewis Bridger* "me thinks Mr BOMBBBER Harris needs some new kit"

Mike Bennett* "What a speedway GP debut for Darky? I'm sure I predicted this on the mic at Kings Lynn a couple of seasons ago? #mysticmike"

Lewis Bridger* "Maybe some Peter Johns power but not Aussie they get all priority kit unless ya names RICO with all the $$$$$"
Lee Richardson* "what u like lbr.."

Nigel Pearson* "Well done AJ and a great night for Jarek and Darcy. But track very slick, slightly disappointing. 17 pt lead for Herbie"

Nicolai Klindt* "well done Darcy - loved your fucking pass on gollob and greggy"

Nigel Pearson* "Just a quick word, abuse won't be tolerated. Have one go with abusive language and you are blocked, your choice"
Lee Richardson* "what's going on mate??"
Nigel Pearson* "just some followers lowering themselves to the depths of a speedway forum just coz they disagree mate"
Mike Bennett* "aint that the truth- just another bunch of forum jockeys! You're doing the job and they're not so stuff 'em!:-)"

Bjarne Pedersen "Since they [new silencers] came into it there's really not a long way between the bottom and the top. Everyone can win races and everyone can lose races. I think the GP is open now, I think it's so level."

28th August

Nigel Pearson* "Just sorted Kelvin Tatum out on Blackberry Messenger... Next stop twitter! #hasntgotaclue"

Moira Perrott "Have seen the crazy rant from Sandhu on the Bees website absolutely mad as a hatter. Matt Ford must be laughing like Alex Ferguson when he knows he has finally got Arsene Wenger wound up. Sandhu is not a promoter so is voiceless and has no part in the sport apart from being a stadium owner that rents to the named promoter Colin Pratt. Clearly Ford has been playing his tricks and mind games, but in the end two questions from me. 1. Where was Nick Norris on August 19th rather than saying he was "unavailable" as that was the total root cause of what happened that night? 2. Peter Kildemand was unfit and had to pull out of all his rides at Glasgow two days later and because if this was dropped by Workington but he rode at Outrup Friday night and could ride due to his shoulder injury suffered in the GP qualifier six weeks ago. If he had ridden he would have pulled up like at Glasgow. Coventry failed to protest on the night. They have zero chance of the match being restaged as they forgot to protest and that is the protocol. They only thing they have highlighted is that Matt Ford has been effectively "insider dealing" with information getting passed by the BSPA office. There will be no response from Matt or the BSPA as there is no need to."

Ian Rae "When King's Lynn installed their polyfoam barrier this season – after having it fully-tested at MIRA (the Motor Industry Research Association) and fully-approved for all FIM speedway meetings – we felt this might be the way forward. It is a big move, a huge investment, by the A & J Scott Bandits – but as in all walks of life, health and safety is a natural requirement, and we want this speedway to be the safest, as well as the fastest, in the land!"

Paul Burbidge* "an absolute scrum to get on Ryanair flight at Bydgoszcz"

Dakota North* "Subway in Aussie shits all over uk subway #australianquality"

Nigel Pearson* [to BSI SGP team] "A truly fantastic weekend in great company"

Paul Burbidge* "Screaming kids, baby vomit and a bouncy landing. Thank you for flying Ryanair!"

Press release Available on the night is the Phil Morris Story DVD. This features a 3-hour extensive interview on Phil's career and also includes lots of racing action highlights. This exclusive item comes complete with a second DVD featuring all the action from Phil's original Testimonial Meeting staged at Reading's Smallmead Stadium back in July 2000. This specially produced double-DVD package costs just £4.

Swindon fan "Bad news – Scott Nicholls is riding"

Cameron Saveall "Depends on what Coventry do – they have seven meetings left but only five before the cut off"

Michelle Saveall "It would be nice just to get to the play-off final to stick two fingers up to an unnamed Sky presenter who has it in for Lakeside"

Mike Bellerby & Trevor Geer "We were sorry to learn recently that the visits of corporate guests to the centre-green has inadvertently led to seated patrons on the back-straight having their view obstructed on odd occasions. Chris Mac is aware and will be trying out a different plan at future meetings."

Kevin Coombes "It's Sunday afternoon with our traditional 3.30 start time"

Simon Stead [before 4 points from 4 rides] "As you know you get paid for your performance"

Cameron Woodward "We can't let this slip, this team [Swindon] are a good side"

John Hazelden "That Zengota rides like Lahti"

Kevin Coombes [on Lewis B] "Bexhill's finest"

Nick Barber "Scott Nicholls doesn't cheat. You could see that when he was in the GPs. He can't cheat he's Britain's number one and his dad is a tuner"

Nick Barber "If they ran the World Cup at Eastbourne, Poland wouldn't win but with 30,000 fans there, the money means they're going to aren't they?"

Kevin Coombes "We've got to get through 40 heats next Saturday. Just a reminder the price is £24 – that's very good value: half a meeting free!"

Kevin Coombes "Coventry and Peterborough – two teams making headlines for all the wrong reasons over the winter"

Nick Barber "They need proper testing and I mean proper testing"

Kevin Coombes "Nicolai doing a head stand at 30 mph coming out of bend number two"

Lewis Bridger "I don't mind running the odd second at home if it's a fair race – he [Nicolai Klindt] read it just right"

Nick Barber "The smaller teams have to put up with all the time but when it happens to one of the bigger teams they really moan"

Lewis Bridger "From when I started in the Elite League aged 16, I always thought I was too good for the Premier League but you are never too good for any league..I need some more saddle time"

Ludwig Lindgren* "just at Ian's house with edberg and kozza! Seb is out in the garden washing his bike! bwaaaahahaha sucker raining aswell"

Nick Barber "What about last season when Coventry got Bridger on a false average? It helped them and they didn't complain then"

Philip Rising "YOU [Speedibee] seem to be obsessed by knocking Briggo at every opportunity but how you can manage to get dirt-deflectors into this thread is amazing. And just for the record: the ILLEGAL dirt-deflectors that have forged Briggo's name and FIM homologation number on them are not equal to the original and have been manufactured from inferior, sub-standard and potential dangerous materials. If they are as good as the Briggo why not get them properly homologated instead of mounting a fraudulent operation that is conning riders into buying something that is certainly not what it says on the tin."

Gary Patchett* "Referees aren't just crap in football"

Barbara Horley "I suspect that what he is referring to is that he believes I should have also disqualified Lewis Bridger in the race in which I disqualified Cameron Woodward because he would argue that he wasn't under power when the red lights were on. To be honest, I was more concerned with Cameron Woodward as he seemed to have totally disappeared from view after crashing. Football refs make mistakes and so do I but I'm sure that I'm not the only referee to have ever made a mistake - he obviously expects his referees to be perfect!"

Jan Staechmann* "Being a referee is a thankless task. If the job is done properly, noone will know she(/he) was even there"

Nicolai Klindt* "on the way home from sunny eastbourne. great place, but ended with two lasts AGAIN! gate 4 aint the best round there... got a sore arm tho!"

Lewis Bridger* "Not a bad Meeting with a new Special cam in making some rippers ;) Nicolai & me had a great race, hard but fair"

Nicolai Klindt* "defo hard but fair, best race ive had in a long time. what speedway all about!"

Steve Shovlar "Coventry have absolutely no claim whatsoever on Peter Kildermand. He was dumped by them so they have nothing to argue about, regardless of what you are reading on here. They ditched him, and in doing so now have no say whatsoever in where he will end up. IMO Coventrys rant (press release) was simply blowing off steam because they had dropped a howler. But like Bom01 said earlier, Coventry, in putting out that press release, could find themselves being charged with bringing the sport into disrepute."

Backless "So the rest of the Premier League has to suffer? In the last couple of weeks [Plymouth] have rocked up at Scunthorpe, Workington & Sheffield with 5 riders - or maybe it's just a coincidence that Sheffield Saints / Sheffield Prowlers have coughed up a guest for Kyle Hughes? And a Team Manager at Sheffield."

Dakota North* "where are you fella?"

Linus Sundstrom* "up in the air in a minute mate! Landing at stansted 11oclock. What have you been up to?"

Dakota North* "oh I'm at the [Peterborough] Marriott I though you might be staying here?"

Nicolai Klindt* "HEART FM is killing it tonight"

Nicki Glanz* "Need to be get back to hard training again this week after a unhealthy weekend"

David Watt* "What a weekend !! Great time again in Torun. That place rocks and so do the people !! #alwaysoptimistic"

Linus Sundstrom* "Finaly in bed after too many hours of travelling! Also a great thanks to stansted airport for a 45min long passport que, made my evening!"

29th August

Lewis Bridger* "Big prob can not sleep went in fence hard in heat14 tonight & hit my handlebars into my chest really tight hard to breath #fingerscrossed"

Nigel Pearson* "If clubs were allowed to share two No.1 riders, Cov could for example use Hans Andersen instead of Emil in two meetings today. Simple!"

Kevin Long* "and, given that this is British Speedway we are talking about, you think your simple scheme would actually be that easy?"

Nigel Pearson* "Anyway, my information is that there are far deeper issues which need resolving this winter before we can even think of 2012"

Gary Patchett* "But are their 20 of them of equal ability that are all willing to ride in GB and at 24 hours notice? #notworkable"

Nigel Pearson* "not saying every club should do it mate, just bring in a rule to give clubs the option?"

Matt Ford "He was taken out of the Coventry one-to-seven and was a doubling-up rider with Travis McGowan. They asked for an urgent management committee decision and the other members and I replied to say what they were doing was perfectly okay, to contract Piotr Pawlicki. I contacted Keith Denham, the owner and promoter of Workington, for permission to speak to Peter Kildemand. That was granted and I got a number to contact him on from the Workington team manager. I spoke to Peter by telephone and text messages are still on my phone and have been sent as proof to show he agreed to the fixture on August 24 and agreed to join Poole and would be in the second doubling-up position alongside Jason Doyle. What has happened since then is very unfortunate as Coventry tried to reinstate the rider in a different position and move one of their other riders, Josh Auty, out of the team. If at the time of bringing in Pawlicki they had requested Kildemand come in for Auty, that would have been agreed. What is not acceptable is that two days after they tried to reinstate the rider in a different position (doubling up with Nick Morris). I have the total support of the (BSPA) management committee because I acted in the interests of speedway. However, I don't want to pursue a rider who isn't sure what he wants to do and at this point in time, he is injured anyway."

Jo Lowry* "Chuffin' cold at the showground today! August my arse!!"

Jo Lowry* "Sorry guys, I can't tell you how Rory is, I'm not allowed to check on one of my riders here. Great. Just great."

Nicki Glanz* "Watching Eastenders b4 heading down to the gym for some #bloodsweatandtears"

Jo Lowry* "Only Nicki P would fence his own rider...twice. Its a shame 'Norbi' doesn't grow a pair and stand up to him though"

Charlie Webster* "this evening, Coventry v Peterborough...Bees injury woes, full of guest riders and R/R"

Charlie Webster* "Coventry bound shortly... Hope it's closer then the reverse fixture at P'boro"

Charlie Webster* " currently. P'Boro 40 - 28 Coventry after 11 heats!" uh oh!"

Jo Lowry* "Woah. What's happened to Rory?! He just came from last....to first....on a tactical (extra pressure) this isn't the Rory we're used to...."

Dakota North* "okay meeting paid 6 have no idea why I got taken out of my last ride strange"

Nicolai Klindt* "been at the dogs and thick as i was i didnt wanit to bet cuz of the que. then the dog i wanit to bet on won the last race #ineverlearn"

Nicolai Klindt* "man its cold. someone give me a blanket and a brew"

Alun John Rossiter* "TGIs mate way to go now mate in cov !!"

Lewis Bridger* "Thank you everybody for such positive tweets recently, it really does make me love what I do onwards & upwards"

Chris Neath* "Fucked up shit on the M25. This literally just happened 10secs before we got there. Now a dog has escaped out the lorry and running down the middle of the motorway. We followed it for bout 2 miles before someone caught it!"

Josh Gudgeon* "If Pawlicki rides in Sweden tomorrow he won't ride for Coventry again this season, according to Rosco"

Paul Burbidge* "Can't see Coventry loaning out Rory Schlein next year. The guy always turns up, gives his all and his career is only going one way"

Mads Korneliussen* "Hat a nice walk/run with the dog today, he is getting old, he can't keep up"

Dakota North* "Track went slick I went shit!! farrrrrkkk Engine choice tonight was not good!revs?? Nope!!!"

Paul Burbidge* "Farce at Coventry. How complicated do they have to make heat 15? Let team managers pick anyone. If there's an exclusion, reserve comes in"

Hans Andersen* "Hmmm getting fed up with watching Elite league speedway on telly, when teams are full of guest. Whats happen to the days where teams maximum Had one guest (for a short term injuried rider) is riders taking the piss or just not bothered ?? Seems wrong when riders WHO are fully Committed to British speedway cant even get a ride…"

Paul Burbidge* "According to my results input page on speedwaygp.com, Coventry have used 31 different riders in the Elite League this season"

Mike Bennett* "just heard the news about John Oliver. Broken both ankles and a bone in his back. Wishing him a full and speed recovery"

Nicolai Klindt* "what a performance by Tai & Freddie tonight at monmore green - really enjoyed that! now enjoying a chinese"

Lewis Bridger* "Not a bad meeting for me around Monmore green stadium tonight 9+1 Tai Woffinden was on the gas smoked me tonight !!!"

Tai Woffinden* "Havent tweeted much coz im thick and havent worked out how to use the hole twitter thing gettin there tho ;)"

Jo Lowry* "Just to make sure he listen's..Rory Schlein -Hospital in morning! No excuses! Consequences of broken bones not healing properly are bad!"

Tai Woffinden* "Best feeling roling up to the tapes of gate 4 dont even a dig and getting to the curb a bike length infrount"

Linus Sundstrom* "Home from a long day!Got 18+2 from the 2 meetings so pleased with that. Not happy with not scoring the points when the team need it the most Like in heat 14 tonight.. Did my best though but it wasnt good enough in that race! Time to sleep, early flight tomorrow"

Nigel Pearson* "please note Kelvin Tatum has nothing to do with this (unfunny sppof) twitter account. Many thanks"

Peter Collins "I was enjoying the match, Belle Vue had got a good crowd and the track was good. But, unfortunately, Chris Louis and Kelvin Tatum were having a big influence on the result of the match, and I think they cost Belle Vue the win in the end. They kept whingeing all night that the Belle Vue riders were rolling at the start, or moving when the tapes went up."

Chris Louis "I can't believe I influenced a team manager with the experience Middlo has got as a rider, and a national and club team manager. But, if I did, then of course even I feel that's not on…. If I influenced it, okay well I've made a mistake in one meeting out of however many I've done, but I won't lose sleep over it. I only do my best to let the fans at home understand what is happening."

Jim Lynch "We have got to stop the way our referees are being handled. We are fortunate that our referees are the best in the world and we ought to be treating them with more respect than this. Both Belle Vue speedway and myself as team manager cannot understand why our referees seem to have become a target for criticism in this way."

George English "Once Rye House realised we were coping very well with track conditions that included bringing the water cart out after almost every race, they stopped doing so and it turned into the old Hoddesdon dust bowl again"

30th August

Rory Schlein* "Just woke up the hand is like a balloon god knows how I'm gonna ride in Sweden today"

Mads Korneliussen* "3rd cup of coffee today, it's needed, long day ahead. Speedway is to must work for the money we get payed plonkers"

David Watt* "Sitting in Stansted airport with so much on my mind ! Just want to go to sleep and forget it all !!"

Sam Masters* Loving the fact I'm sitting here doing nothing while Dakota North is in my workshop washing his bikes"

Fredrik Lindgren* "Rain-off in Motala what's going on?!? Have not seen anything but sunshine since arriving in Sweden! I blame Stefan Andersson, yea!"

Chris Holder* "Pissin down in vetlanda"

Chris Holder* "Should be fun tonight!!! Stoked I got here without a passport! Good to have it back now tho!!"

Mads Korneliussen* "Train is the best way to travel,, NOT #hateit"

Paul Burbidge* "Even MI5 wouldn't be able to get to the bottom of why Peter Kildemand couldn't ride for Coventry on August 19. I've tried and failed"

Nicki Glanz* "Good boxing session at gym today now off for a 5km run b4 bed :-)"

Darcy Ward* "Party at chris holder new pad wednesday night 31/08/11 so tomorrow ask for details it's after #daveywatttestimonial"

Linus Sundstrom* "Nearly back at skavsta now. What a waste this day have been.. Will sleep before my head hits the pillow at the hotel!"

Lee Richardson* "What a funny day...broke down, then got excluded on a first corner...lucky won the last 2 heats, but we lost at home :("

George English "With the whole [Hoddeson] stadium expecting Derek to be awarded second place and Boxall disqualified, it was unbelievable the referee [Chris Gay] ignored what everybody else had seen and gave Boxall two points and disqualified Derek for causing the stoppage. The Rye House riders could not believe their good fortune. A very fussy and incompetent referee ruined a good meeting."

Darcy Ward* "Might go go karting in the wet"

Sam Masters* "oi man me and Dak went go karting in Milton keynes yesterday and the were 2 stroke karts haha we need to go ;)"

Chris Holder* "oh yeh thanks for the invite Sam....prick haha"

David Watt* "What's bloody going on here ?No invites huh so me and CH need to have a lil chat with you !!"

Sam Masters* "okay David you invite me to things but not these other 2 haha!! We seriously need to sort a kart sesh there it's nuts ;)"

31st August

Paul Burbidge* "Kasprzak is banned from riding for Birmingham by Tarnow for the second time this year"

Olly Allen* "What's the weather like in kings Lynn anyone? It's not great in Norwich at the mo"

Rory Schlein* "I best make a comment about last night shit happens either like it or don't I don't give a shit I'd do it again but land a few more on him [Grigory Laguta]"

Olly Allen* "classic Schlein I call that! Love it :)"

Ray Blackwell "It was a massive over reaction and the line that Laguta took to the finishing line was his to take, he was clearly in front and also did not change his line at all, I don't even think Greg knew that Schlein was there. Additionally Rory did indeed begin the hard riding with his lap 2 move. Not the first time that Rory has massively over reacted this season."

Lewis Bridger* "My Fax machine is taking my stress levels to another stage haha useless"

Lee Richardson* "fax machine...scan it and email it. #comeonson"

David Watt* "Davey Watt Testimonial has finally arrived. Im really looking forward to tonight but been stressful. I'll be in the bar after the meeting !"

Peter Johns* "good luck with the meeting tonight. Thought I would stay away cos I new I would get dragged to the party #worktomorrow"

Paul Burbidge* "The Pawlicki brothers face a 28-day suspension in Britain for withholding their services from Coventry"

Alun John Rossiter "It's a great shame we have to take this action because they are two great lads, but we simply can't have this lack of commitment. It's not fair to the club or the supporters. We've been told they are practising for the Polish Final, but there is no reason why they can't be at Swindon on Thursday and then back in Poland the following morning. We are trying to reach the play-offs here, and it's not acceptable....I could just about accept Piotr missing Monday as he did have a crash on Sunday and we had two meetings in a day which was a tough schedule, but what they forget is that there were English officials at that meeting who saw what was going on. I can only apologise to the supporters, because we have looked after the riders throughout and we don't expect to be repaid in this way. We have no alternative but to request a 28-day facility for riders withholding their services. We are doing all we can to get a competitive side together for the three meetings in three days coming up, although it's not easy."

Chris Neath* "Seen the video of Boxall gettin excluded at Redcar and its an even worse decision than I first thought"

Sam Masters* "1st meeting at Poole and I think I like that track keen for another crack around there ;)"

David Watt "I salute each and every one of you [fans], for without your support I would probably be back home in Aussie just kicking my heels."

Terry Daley "Gjedde's new winning time [57.34] wasn't the only historic note because this was the first time Newport had hosted a midweek fixture since 1976, while it's believed team managers Laurence and Gareth Rogers became the first brothers in British speedway history to hold the positions in the same meeting."

....

1st September

Hans Andersen* "Too early [05.30] for mé. Great to see a big turn out for Watty last Night enjoyed riding In UK again but Will be even more enjoyable on own kit"

Nigel Pearson* "Early start for another trip to Farnham for SGP highlights show followed by Isle of Wight with Dudley Heathens"

Linus Sundstrom* "Wished i could stay in bed all day today, but im gonna clean the bike and make everything ready for tonight on my own!!"

Jan Staechmann* "Swindon v Coventry tonight. Seems ages since last home meet. Hope we get a decent ref"

Rory Schlein* "Great news no breaks but 3 dislocations in 2 fingers 2 of them back in will pit the other In myself ha"

Lewis Bridger* "Ladies & gentlemen get your backside trackside for the legend Phill Morris ;) raaadd"

Kelly Ingalls "I always seem to ride better when I am under pressure and I think on Saturday I will just go for it. The shoulder is getting better all the time and I am doing all I can to get it right and we will give it a go at the weekend. I was thinking about having a spin at Birmingham tonight but I might not because the shoulder is still not feeling strong enough. Keith [Denham] really wants me to be back on the pace so I don't really have a choice about whether I can race or not because the team has had so much bad luck it has to be done. I think if I had another week there would be no problem but it has got to the point where they need me in the team."

Chris Holder* "Jet skiing was crazy today!!! Big waves =big crashes!! Darcy goin big"

Darcy Ward* "unreal man so crazy hectic"

Philip Rising "IT is a suggestion that Carl (Blomfeldt) and others hope to put before the FIM and for homologated silencers to have two small holes to allow the heat to escape. I didn't mean to give the impression that it is being done illegally. As for Ashley Holloway... he lives in Bydgoszcz and still tunes engines for Sayfutdinov amongst others but admits he gets to nervous being around Emil at GPs. Remember his antics at Cardiff following the incident involving Scott Nicholls? I believe he is about to get married"

Nicolai Klindt* "what a night, what a loss! had 3 wins where two was cracking heats, a touch tape and last one where fish closed the door on me watsgoinon"

Lewis Bridger* "Barker win of me on the line, me & barker chucking bike at each other crumpy 3rd, Rico 4th"

Nicolai Klindt* "good one mate! was it JRM power or GM this time?"

Lewis Bridger* "no JRM mate saving it for cov tomorrow"

Kenni Larsen* "having a discussion in the van. How old is Jan?"

Nicolai Klindt* "i think he is nearly 59 aint he?"

Claudia Staechmann* "he is 28. But really he is a young looking 45"

Claudia Staechmann* "Nico u cheeky twat!!!"

Kenni Larsen* "he looks 59 like! #likeclaudiadoes"

Nigel Pearson "This news is a relief to us all, although Kyle [Newman] feels like he's done 20 rounds with Mike Tyson! The crash was awful and it was on one of the fastest parts of the track. There was a hush around the stadium, that's how shocking it was."

Jan Staechmann "I am not a man who gets angry often, but I did feel anger"

Bryn Williams "The stadium fell silent the instant the collision [Kyle Newman & Nick Simmons] happened, and the medics raced to the stricken duo whilst track staff surveyed the damage to the safety fence, which included damaged fence posts and a torn-off red stop light leaving exposed electricity cables, and that damage led to the match being abandoned with the result standing."

2nd September

Jan Staechmann* "Exciting news for Swindon Robins fans as we have signed Copenhagen SGP wildcard Mikkel B Jensen. He will make his debut on Thursday"

Nicki Glanz* "14 hours sleep over 3 days just isn't enough for me"

Cameron Woodward* "Does anyone have cove comps number. Need some shpeedway rubber for weekend. Prague road trip"

Lee Richardson* "he might have an old Dunlop!!! Or some clutch plates for 3 spring jawa clutch!!! Lol"

Cameron Woodward* "You don't have any softened, i mean old rubber laying around at yours?"

Lee Richardson* "no I haven't mate sorry...buy some out there...they will have tyres there"

Cameron Woodward* "might do. Just though I would let mechanic do it over here in comfort. No dramas. Cheers mate. Is Prague a good track??"

Lee Richardson* "yeah it's not too bad..normally a bit patchy to start with then goes slick as starts normally really slick gate 4 by the fence ;)"

Cameron Woodward* "cheers mate. Jrm engine is up for grabs the the gloves are coming off. Its on like donkey kong. Haha"

<u>**Lewis Bridger***</u> "there is no comp, im taking the skoda of the centre green"

<u>**Cameron Woodward***</u> "If I do ya I promise to sell it to you cheap"

<u>**Olly Allen***</u> "Woh! Impressed by the toilets at the services in Germany, the toilet seats wipe themselves!! Need one of those at home!!"

<u>**Chris Neath***</u> "flatout in the workshop to get ready for Plymouth. Cracked rear section slowing down proceedings"

<u>**Dakota North***</u> "I thought a sunny day was dew soon after all the rain offs we have had #smilesallround"

<u>**Coventry**</u> It is now Friday 2nd September, 7 days after our press release and 16 days since we last spoke to the officials at the BSPA, exposing the Peter Kildemand situation and true to form we have heard absolutely nothing from the BSPA office, Management Committee or the BSPA Chairman. The outrageous abuse of his position by Matt Ford and BSPA office apparent connivance has potentially ruined Coventry's season and cheated our fans. Yet even now over two weeks after these disgraceful events no-one in authority has the stature or cares enough about British speedway to enquire into what typifies everything that is wrong with the Poole promotion's way of doing things and the help he receives from certain official sources. All we require at Coventry is transparent, fair and honest decision making. This requirement affects all other clubs in the Elite League. If one club gets treated in a favourable and illegal manner then that is to the disadvantage of all the others. What does it profit a club to win the league by consistently bending the Rules? What is the point of sport if all competitors don't start on a level playing field?

More facts have subsequently come to light since our last press release and these are as follows:

FACT: On Friday 12th August at 11.30 we redeclared. According to the BSPA office Matt Ford through his privileged position claims to have sent a fax to the BSPA office that same day (Friday) redeclaring with Peter Kildemand in Poole's 1-7. This remember was before he had spoken to Peter. Even by his own admission Mr Ford did not speak to Peter until Saturday morning 10am. So he redeclared a new 1-7 without speaking to the rider and that 1-7 was conveniently sent by fax by him and not received by the office. It will become apparent why Mr Ford needs to claim it was sent by fax later on. We require a sight of Mr Ford's telephone records to establish the number and time the alleged fax was sent to the BSPA's fax number.

FACT: Poole then redeclared the same team on Sunday 14th August this time by email and again including Peter Kildemand who last Wednesday spoken to Mr Sandhu and confirmed that he did not agree to leave Coventry and ride for Poole. Peter's own words confirm Mr Ford that you **have been very economical with the truth**. Produce Peter's text message for us Mr Ford so that we can establish the source of that text message. Peter says he never sent the text message and that he told you he wished to stay with Coventry if we wanted him and he would speak to us on Monday morning 15th August. This he did and we confirmed he was still our rider.

FACT: The office sidelined Coventry's legal 1-7 in favour of Poole's illegal 1-7. We sent our team in on Monday 12.09pm and the office confirmed our request 12.12pm.

FACT: Refusal of Coventry's redeclared 1-7 was withheld until Wednesday 17th August at 4.32pm. Knowing this would disadvantage us why would the office do this? Who is running the Office?

FACT: Why, knowing that two clubs had included the same rider in their team didn't the office or Management Committee simply speak to Peter and confirm which team he wanted to ride for?

FACT: Two clubs sent in 1-7's, Poole and Coventry, Coventry's was legal and Poole's was illegal yet the office and Management Committee chose to support Poole's illegal redeclaration why?

FACT: At every turn the Management Committee and the office followed a procedure that was against both the spirit and the rules of speedway. Coventry want to know why? Why bend and break rules just to favour Matt Ford and Poole to the disadvantage of the rest of us. When the Vice Chairman of the BSPA is involved in benefitting from a decision not only does the right and honest procedure have to be followed but it has to be seen to be followed. This is quite clearly not been the case in this and other instances we are aware of.

FACT: It is a fact that a 1-7 NEVER comes into effect until that side takes to the track and in fact teams have the right to cancel their submitted 1-7 at any time and in that circumstance the old 1-7 would be reverted to. On that basis Peter Kildemand was still a Coventry rider throughout this episode quite apart from anything else.

FACT: We require the Coventry V Belle Vue match to be replayed because we were illegally prevented from tracking a full side. If the match is not replayed we reserve the right to take whatever action we consider fit.

Dakota North* "Spoke way too soon! Traffic jam on m5. Fuck you! #smilesnowgone"

Linus Sundstrom* "Very happy that a busy week is over, quiet happy with paid 38 from 4 meetings in uk this week! Not many meetings left now #cantwait"

> **Chris Neath*** "maybe its eddies special secret for a rye house engine tuning do I get commission if Boxy buys your engine as I told len?!!"
>
> **Linus Sundstrom*** "He already bought it, using it tonight i think. I let you win when we meet at the ace of hearts as a thanks ;)"

David Watt* "Have been driving for nearly 3 hours and am just getting on the M25 from a very busy M3. Thinking I might be in a bit of trouble"

Steve Shovlar "For all the "facts" (a word used incorrectly) thrown at Poole by Coventry, one fact remains. And it is the most imprtant "fact". Fact. Coventry released Kildermand. Now if they did, they have absolutely no comeback whatsoever. None. Zip. Nada. Because if he was ditched he is no longer their rider, no matter who many tantrums of hugely embarrassing press releases Coventry shove out. They were caught out trying to ditch him and then re-sign him, except it just didn't work and there was a more intelligent promoter out there who swooped. It's as simple as that IMO. No ammount of screming and toys out of the pram throwing will change that. And to be blunt the press releases coming ut of Brandon are frankly highly embarassing and doing serious damage to the sport. There is a procedure to follow through the SCB yet we get someone posting these press releases and acting like some type of screaming banshee. Its beyond bad and I would be amazed if any promoter (especially Matt Ford) would consider for a nano second making some type of reply to them. They dropped Kildermand. They suffer the consequencies. The rest is superfluous."

Chris Neath* "What a shit night for me, blown engine before heat 1, had to borrow bikes cos I have no engines left and then I bend boxys gettin took out. To make it worse I only got the engine back last night with new rod, piston etc #twograndand4practicestarts"

Dakota North* "Somerset what a joke Not happy with the club, eastbourne tomorrow for Coventry, double header and we race second tough. lets get some points"

Lewis Bridger* "A absolutely shocking night for me tonight at Coventry the second time I have been there & just can't get round #mudnotshale"

Scott Nicholls* "Thanks for all the nice tweets.had prick of a season so glad I could score some points & help cov win.nice to have a nice reception2.thank u"

Chris Neath* "Cruising back home with pops and he's more gutted than me poor old fella. Don't think I've heard him say sorry so much #nobodysperfect. "

> **Chris Neath*** "Is that you with the full beams on Sam Masters?!!"
>
> **Sam Masters*** "that's me man haha #fuckem"

Lewis Bridger* "Can't believe I have 1 bad meeting, of a run of brilliant meetings, and get so much negative tweets^ from inconsiderate fans. unbelievable"

Cameron Woodward* "dude have you not worked put how to block them. I don't know how to but stuff em. You back to Hastings yet ;)"

Lewis Bridger* "yea man I keep blocking the wasteman fans & just seems to be more pop up yea ur right can't plz every1 & nah bro not yet ;)"

^1 "just face it Bridge your a small/tight track rider and always will be, just not quite good enough to mix it with the big boys!!" ^2 "you've been shocking for awhile though mate, no offence like. All the potential in the world!"

Sam Masters* "It's killing me this angry boys DVD ain't working on my play station #notgood"

Mike Bowden "It was a tremendous psychological boost to get off bottom place in the table and the meeting was a brilliant advertisement for British speedway."

David Rowe "With Chris Harris and Scott last night and a big crowd going home happy, it was just like old times"

3rd September

Lewis Bridger* "The positive tweets tonight have definitely over powered the two so called supporters swipe at knocking me whilst I'm down thanks everyone. It's great when you feel you have friends & support in the sport you love makes it so much more enjoyable #slideforpride"

BSPA website THE British Speedway Promoters' Association is aware of critical statements made by Coventry Speedway recently. The Association is disappointed that Coventry have chosen to go down this route rather than use the mechanisms in place for the pursuit of grievances. We have no intention of making any public comment on Coventry's accusations but instead have referred the matter to the Speedway Control Bureau.

Steve Shovlar "Just goes to show how it should be done. The fact that the bspa put this out (everyone bar Coventry) shows how far away the Coventry promotion are from every other club. Those two press releases have probably done damage that will never be repeared. The fact that the bspa have reffrdd the matter to the scb rather than Coventry themselves is quite iroinic. Perhaps Coventry really didn't want to go that route after all."

Debbie Hancock "One of the risks of the second phase idea is..all three of the Friday night tracks, Edinburgh, Scunthorpe and ourselves, have ended up in the same group....as a promotion, one problem with a double header meeting is that you have twice the outlay with regards to rider costs and other overheads, but you only have one crowd from which to draw your income source"

Tony Jackson "I did receive a 'phone call from Matt Ford but a 28-day ban was never mentioned at all. Unfortunately Peter's grasp of English is not as good as it can be....I must emphasise that a 28-day ban was never mentioned by Matt Ford to me and I never mentioned a 28-day ban to Peter [Kildemand]."

Chris Neath* "Went to get off the M50 and the junctions closed. Now got a 20mile detour #pissedoff I asked dad why he's driving in both lanes and apparently he likes it cos it makes him feel like a pilot coming into land! Has he lost it?"

David Gordon "I think a lot of promoters would like to see Elite League speedway as a £10-£12 ticket but the level of wages, insurance and stadium rental against turnstile and sponsorship income makes it unsustainable. It was great to see so many people at the Poole match but reducing prices on a permanent basis is not the answer."

David Watt* "You know your traveling lots when some of the staff at luton airport remember you !! #justsayin"

John Anderson "In the past we have had incidents involving the likes of Scott Smith and Paul Fry, Gino Franchetti, Andreas Bergstrom, and of course, just recently, Alex Edberg. The incident involving Alex virtually forced our hand, because after that I sat down with some of my fellow [Berwick] directors and said it was about time we looked into installing a new safety barrier. At the end of the day the riders are going out there and risking injury – even their lives – so safety has to be paramount."

Dakota North* "Hate getting up this early [07.30] to wash bikes"

Jon Cook "I think the racing has definitely improved because of the silencers and if you look at the Grand Prix series, we've got most of the exciting riders from that series racing over here. It's only the ones that are perhaps coming to the ends of their careers that are giving Britain a miss."

Dick Barrie "My belief, my firm conviction, is that we nearly got it right this season – just a little fine-tuning and next year's Premier League will be great! I've said this before – what we should have is the second phase first, on a north/south split. We would race off the local league fixtures in the early weeks and then around May launch into the full campaign against everybody else, including the other northern clubs again. No Premier Trophy (which might allow the unsavoury practice of average manipulation by teams who were prepared to cheat their paying public by attempting to restructure a squad to be ready just as the actual league was kicking off) but a split which would give all member-clubs not one but two, lucrative, meaningful official fixtures with locally-based rivals. But get this clear – what will be decided will be determined at the BSPA's AGM by all the clubs voting on how to set out the year's fixtures. It isn't something just foisted upon the league's member-clubs. We should remember that rules and regulations, and changes thereto, are made by the full body of the BSPA – meaning every club, in every League – on a one-club-one-vote democratic principle. Changes, whether or not we personally agree with them, are not made at the whim of an evil dictator, sitting on a remote island stroking his cat. They are decided, discussed and voted upon by the same clubs who constitute the BSPA. Once made, these changes must be accepted by all concerned. It is called democracy. Live with it."

Tony Jackson "Things have been so bad at Workington, even our nine-year-old mascot Kyle Bickley was injured in a training track crash at Northside"

Jan Staechmann* "Just letting everyone know that Kelvin Tatum is NOT on Twitter. The one on here is an imposter"

Kevin Long* "even the Kelvin Tatum we see on Sky speedway sometimes leads you to believe he has been taken over by aliens ! ;)"

Nigel Pearson* "how do we stop this Paul..."

Paul Burbidge* "I've just reported the account as spam, but what good that will do, I don't know. They should have a way of reporting fakes"

David Watt* "what kind of goose makes out they're someone else !! So when is Big Kelv getting on the twitter train ??

Lee Richardson* "Theres some twats around!!!"

Nigel Pearson* "says he's not interested mate. I've tried!! How do we stop fake accounts..."

David Watt* "your profile pics look similar too !! He can stop it by getting on here and proving there's only one KT !!"

Nigel Pearson* "Just a clarify, someone is tweeting in the name of Kelvin Tatum - this is NOT Kelvin. What kind of idiot does this? #getalife #sad"

Lee Richardson* "some stupid twat with no life...#getajob"

David Watt* "force his hand mate. You've got to have some dirt on him by now to bribe him with !!#gettherealkelvintatumontwitter"

Nigel Pearson* "well he looked a bit out of shape on the dance floor in Poland last Friday night!!"

Scott Nicholls* "bet this fake Kelvin tatum wish he'd thought twice now! Getting slated"

Lee Richardson* "Awesome last night to grab all the points...got a bit too close though..."

David Watt* "funny watching Cooky stress though !!"

Lee Richardson* "he was stressing a bit...;)"

Nicki Glanz* "Bouncing down the motorway in the Van listing to 80s hits"

David Watt* "Arrived in Gdansk and got my wallet back !! It's hard living without your wallet for a week !!"

Nigel Pearson* "put your hand in it then and get the beers in!!"

Nicki Glanz* "Shit day today 2,0,0,1 + seized Engine and didnt beat Mads Korneliussen #unhappydays"

Dakota North* "At Roscos mad house, about to leave and go to Eastbourne"

Niels Kristian Iversen* "Busy last few days with Racing every day since tuesday. Was good fun ride 1.div today in Holsted and very usefull as well. Now on the plane back home to my mrs's. Looking forward to a Nice evening with her winning Didnt make the shower after the meeting cause i had to catch the plane. good thing is that i Got more room cause noone sit nxt to mé dirty"

Mike Bennett* "Really not impressed with people just adding me to groups on Facebook without asking me first? #notbignotclever"

David Watters "The racing is excellent at Newport at the moment! If they win their cup match, they get to race Glasgow five times in October"

David Rowe "We're not taking King's Lynn for granted but with those three points we need two more points to be sure because of Lakeside's points difference from their big win"

Cameron Woodward "It's something new, two in a row – let's go good!"

Tim Hamblin "Trevor [Geer] gave Cameron six rides [against Wolves]. I don't know why – he didn't need to – he'll be needed for seven rides here [versus Coventry]. I think Trevor just uses a template."

David Watters "I have this down to finish at 11.57 in the sweepstake"

Tim Hamblin "Pete Adams was saying both riders should have gone off 15 but the ref told him there was an unwritten rule that they couldn't – not that it would have made any difference. Haines was excluded twice in the same heat [12]"

Tim Hamblin "Bob's grading was flagrant"

Dakota North* "sorry Coventry, tough night. fucking so annoyed, how hard can riding in circles be?"

> **Alun John Rossiter*** "Know wonder team mangers get wound up with awful decisions like that tonight even worse when every one is laughing"
>
> **Gary Patchett*** "Who did you have? Ours had a nightmare there last week"
>
> **Jeff Scott*** "if 1 disputed decision is a "nightmare", are 2 a catastrophe and 3 armageddon?"

Jay Herne "I've had a pretty rubbish year and I haven't ridden in two weeks, so to get (NLRC) third is a good result."

4th September

Chris Holder* "Off to Sweden"

Chris Holder* "Gotta full row to myself #goodtimes"

Tony Mole "Birmingham Speedway is available for sale on financially favourable terms. It will be the intention of the vendors that the Speedway Club stays in the Elite League in the 2012 season. I hope this will reassure our fans."

Dakota North* "Fuck I hate the next morning after a fucking shit night #justsaying"

Jo Lowry* "Would like to apologise to Kenni Larsen & the rest of the Bees representatives last night. Because I weren't there, we lost. Fact. Every meeting I've missed, its all gone tits up!"

> **Alun John Rossiter***
> "Mick Bates normally very reliable. cam hit the air fence came back in and caught fishers rear wheel and fell off right in front of him"
>
> **Gary Patchett***
> "Twitter has just suggested I follow me!! Don't think I'll bother as I don't have much to say"
>
> **Alun Jon Rossiter***
> "even worse when all the easties riders laughing that's how bad it was any way let's move on #justsaying"
>
> **Jan Staechmann***
> "Pot, Kettle etc. #justsaying"
>
> **Alun John Rossiter***
> "wot do you mean jan?"
>
> **Jan Staechmann***
> "You, last Thursday"
>
> **Alun John Rossiter***
> "you have lost me"
>
> **Jan Staechmann***
> "ha ha, just a little jibe mate, ref. laughing at others' misfortune"
>
> **Alun John Rossiter***
> "I was going to say there was no incident on Thursday just a roller coaster meeting"

David Watt* "I'm in pain !! Currently have 2 parts of my anatomy in my stomach that shouldn't be there !! Rough track today !! Ouch !!! #lemmesleep"

Scott Nicholls* "Not a good day in polska! Roughest track I've raced for a long time. Crash,tapes exclusion & then 5pts from 3. Look forward to my bed"

Olly Allen* "track was rough, scotty hit a hole in front of me and looped it, I had nowhere to go but straight into him! #concussion"

Nicolai Klindt* "auch.... not good, saw davey said it was bad. it's not the best of places to go to when it's like that. hope you'll be ok!"

Olly Allen* "Would like to point out that Scotts crash was all about the track, nothing he could do to save it. I just couldn't miss him #nowheretogo"

Scott Nicholls* "I kinda did u a favour in a way....the track was dogsh*t! Sorry mate"

Olly Allen* "oh thanks Cozmo! Very thoughtful of you teamwork"

Scott Nicholls* "well,think about it.It's your way in the team next week..I won my first race good,then Scott cleaned me up!I Felt good"

Olly Allen* "are you saying i got a max? I like that story! I'm gonna roll with it"

Scott Nicholls* "if that makes u feel better,u stick with it! :-)"

Kenni Larsen* "Nice to be back in Denmark for a few days off chilling winning"

Tai Woffinden* "Good day today 15 plus 1 pumped on the way to poznan for a nice bed shame i wont be in it long #skiddingforaliving"

Dakota North* "Just lowering my average iwish #slicktrackslickass"

Kevin Long* "what a great Sunday. . . my Witches won and my Fen Tigers won. . . Happy Days for Suffolk speedway"

Michael Lee "I'm proud of all the boys, including Newport, who went out and gave it a go despite the tricky conditions. Referee Chris Gay also deserves praise for being patient and allowing us the time needed to get the track ready, and the fans were superb as well, showing incredible patience while we sorted things out. It'll be interesting to see who we end up facing. It looks like Stoke will be able to pick their opposition, but I truthfully don't envy them that decision, as anyone who finishes in the top four is capable of winning the play-offs."

Dakota North* "I'm just happy to finish the meeting at sCUNThrope I fucking hate that place not intrested, #FactsAboutMe"

Jitendra Duffill "The track was 'tricky' and a lot of our riders felt it was dangerous. There was quite a big hole developing going into turn one and even some of the Glasgow riders were struggling."

Alan Dick "We extend our best wishes to Jason Lyons, a man who started his career at Glasgow, and it would be very cruel to think that he might have ended it at Glasgow too, but it will be a tough assignment for him to come back from that at 41."

Eric Thornton "Statistical oddity – there wasn't a re-run, an unsatisfactory start, a faller, an engine failure or any kind of retirement in the entire [Newcastle v Ipswich] match"

5th September

Dakota North* "Oh pacific!"

Lewis Bridger* "On route to Prague with Cameron Woodward in the party bus with ash & lenus it's going to be sick to race here tonight after watching GP here."

Sam Masters* "Wow man my van is making some suss noises. Keen to get back to Australia and hopefully see some superX"

David Watt* "go to bed !! You bees to be sharp tonight !! NEED to be sharp ! Sorry, can't type well this early. Just woke up and on my way to airport. #lemmesleep"

Tai Woffinen* "hows it goin num nuts haha classic"

David Watt* "feelin ok this morning in that department !! I wouldn't wish that pain on my worst enemy !"

Tai Woffinden* "Why the hell they have a flight this early i do no know #shootmenow"

Scott Nicholls* "Luton airport = congestion! If it's not the road,it's passport control! Normally both actually,chaos"

Nigel Pearson* "First Monday night off for ages with no Sky Sports Speedway. Back on Wed for King's Lynn v Birmingham. At Sky Sports"

Mads Korneliussen* "Cleaning bikes is the one thing i love about my job #speedwaylife #shootmenow"

Fredrik Lindgren* "Swedish Prime Minister Fredrik Reinfeldt will visit my sponsor Stensåkra on Wednesday! Guess he wants to know the secret about #speedwaykorv!"

Cameron Woodward* "Lewis Bridger, the crew and I have driven through some mega rain. But so far she is dry in Prague. Please hang on. We want to skid."

David Howe* "nandlstadt again lol?"

Cameron Woodward* "not even funny. Damn. We are getting messy on red wine if it happens again"

David Howe* "with the points u scored u can afford it mate #rainsucks"

Lewis Bridger* "Me & Cameron been heavy rain all the way through Germany but it's looking bright now ;) coming for ya Greg Hancock"

Nicolai Klindt* "just been for some acupuncture, lovely! 8 needles in left and 3 in right ear"

Nicolai Klindt* "now waiting for some take-away lunch at aunt betty."

Rory Schlein* "I hear the weather shit down at Poole I hope we don't get there and then they call it off"

Dakota North* "Just finished a long day in the workshop , need to stop this shit form #badtimes"

Paul Burbidge* "Chris Harris pays tribute to his long-standing mechanic Ted Midgley, who resigned from the team on Sunday"

Hans Andersen* "Finally :) looking forward to join Linus Michael Dakota Troy in panthers colours. Weeiiii"

Paul Burbidge* "Belle Vue won one of the meetings of the season 48-45 at Poole. But given that Pirates were 14pts down after heat 8, the hosts did well"

Rory Schlein* "Good win tonight track was a bit wet and we had luck on our side. Still struggling with my fingers can't work the clutch"

Sam Masters* "Is in some pain right now big crash tangled up with Rory Schlein and hit fence cut me balls opened nobabys who wants to pay fir bent bike?"

Peter Johns* "Now taking new engine orders for 2012 season #don'tleaveittoolate"

David Watt* "ooooooh yes please !!"

Tai Woffinden* "1 ofset 1 normal for england am i firts order? ;)"

Chris Holder* "ya JRM's seem to be ok wuffy? #aintbrokedontfixit"

Tai Woffinden* "yeah man just fancy a change i think bit unsure what to do"

Chris Holder* [at 23.30] "Can't wait to wake up at 2:15am to go to Sweden!!!"

Greg Hancock* "Tied on 14 points with NP tonight in Prague. Rain soaked track was no fun from the start but we managed for the cause. Tomicek Memorial"

Lewis Bridger* "Not bad meeting for me & Cam & Rico 8pt/5h with a exclusion :-/ cam also scored 8pt/5h with a Eagles team ride heat2"

6th September

Rory Schlein* "On the plane at stansted with Fredrik Lindgren, Chris Holder, Tai Woffinden, Darcy Ward, Hans Andersen, David Watt & Lee Richardson"

Chris Holder* "lucky u ay schleiny"

Fredrik Lindgren* "Landed in Sweden, Judgement Day! Local derby Dackarna Vs Vetlanda! We need heroes! Fight for our life! elitserien speedway"

Philip Rising "THE BSPA refused to grant Trump a licence unless he apologised for remarks made during the winter...something he has refused to do. Rossiter's bid to be granted a licence was due to be heard by the SCB today."

Rick Frost "Nicki [Pedersen] is just below the cut-off for automatic qualification for the 2012 GP series and like everyone currently out of the top eight he has to make sure he gives absolutely everything to securing his GP future without having to rely on a permanent wild card selection."

Nicolai Klindt* "sweden tonight.. 4 teams can drop out of the league which will be decided in 3 different meetings!"

Dakota North* "Off to crumpys to sort out engines #changesmustbemade"

Lewis Bridger* "Fish & chips on a rainy Tuesday in Hastings with the Cameron Woodward racing team #yewwwgottalovespeedway"

  Nicolai Klindt* "don't have to look twice. it is the no. 1 racejacket believe it or not!"
  Fredrik Lindgren* "No 1 (heat leader) in Danish league? Well done Nicolai I applaud you"
  Nicolai Klindt* "thanks fred! never thought i would try and wear the number 1, but my dream came true"

Tai Woffinden* "Walkin track with lee and i think there is goin to be a fue problems today carnage"

Sam Masters* "Been in bed all day struggling to move and a rotten headache, must get up tomorrow wash bikes and fixed bent bike needhelp carnage Hoping to feel better tomorrow this sucks #badtimes #death"

Dakota North* "Another long day in the work shop! Everything should be fasssssst for tomorrow!! #gettracksidefollowers"

Ian Smalley "I think of speedway as the extreme team sport for all the family"

Sam Masters* "Where's this Swedish speedway suppose to be on premier sports! sort ya shit out #PremierSportsTV #notgood"

  Kenni Larsen* "fattybumbum :-)"
  Jo Lowry* "excuse me whilst I go and cry. Can't believe you've just called me fat :(that's so mean. I've never been mean to you :("
  Kenni Larsen* "who said you were fat? I didn't. Just thought it was a funny word"
  Jo Lowry* "fattybumbum means fat! :(#cryingmyselftosleep"
  Kenni Larsen* "shut up u tart. Any way I don't think your fat."
  Jo Lowry* "and now you think I'm a tart! This is too much abuse for one Sports Therapist to handle. I may have to resign..."

Tai Woffinden* "Fuck man cant work out sweden and it chewin ma head!"

Linus Sundstrom* "Piraterna lost to hammarby today, but i topscored with 8+2 and beat gollob from behind to destroy his maximan! #goodshit"

Peter Johns* "at last the dyno is working again, RFI has a lot to answer for! #resistorplugs"

Nigel Pearson* "Good win for Dudley boys tonight in tough conditions, now for birthday meal with Gary Patchett (50 tomorrow!!)"

Stuart Douglas "We are on course, fingers crossed, for a fine financial performance - I would have a guess at probably the 2nd best performing club in the Elite League. Given the circumstances of our hugely competitive location in terms of leisure spending, that is huge testament to how well everyone has contributed to make a real team effort into turning this Club from a speedway club at death's door, crippled by spiraling costs and unable to get off the foot of the table, to a club with an outstanding rider asset list, a balance sheet that is the envy of the majority of our league, and we are still in a Play Off position, with the KO Cup around the corner."

7th September

Ludvig Lindgren* "3 yrs with Tina F**k me well done to her putting up with me 4 3 yrs should get a medal 4 that or a necklace a pearl necklace ;)"

Lewis Bridger* "Really happy with my pace in Prague on some new kit, can't wait to strip some Kg's & be even faster. #whosaidicantracebigracetracks #fastasfuck"

David Watt* "Feeling pretty sore this morning. Feel like I got run over... oh yeh, I did !! #lemmesleep"

Ludvig Lindgren* "ive sent you a email with the logos fella! and quit your jibby jabba u aint hurt fool!"

Lewis Bridger* "New suit for the playoffs"

Dakota North* "Somerset tonight Swindon thursday Edinburgh Friday glasgow Sunday peterbro maybe Monday? Let's get some form back Maybe an hour total racing tine and about 40 hours doing bikes and driving time maaaaatttttttteeeee"

Cameron Woodward* "awesome dude I'm jealous. Only have three or so more weeks of racing so lap it up. Yeeha"

Tai Woffinden* "Well i woke up 1h ago [13.30] boys have washed all the bikes and bout to drive to polska 500km to the ferry"

Paul Burbidge "Harris refuses to give up on his sgp dreams and still feels he is the man to represent Britain on the world stage"

Dakota North* "Love the weather in Somerset"

Hans Andersen* "Hey man just looked at your suit and looks like you got 4 arms bloke haha"

Dakota North* "I gotta hold on with as many as I can ride these 650s with Kk silencers"

Mike Bennett* "had to get changed in the hire car- don't ask! Ah the glamour of being a high flying executive and superstar speedway presenter eh? :-)"

Nicki Glanz* "Old peeps birthdays are boring sneeky G&T for NG"

Mike Bennett* "Landed ! speedway at Norfolk Arena here we come :-)"

David Howe* "in 30 years 6 months I'll be 60, can I get a RT?"

Cameron Woodward* "your bloody mental. Does that make your birthday 6th of march. Man you must have fuck all meetings on thinking up that shit"

David Howe* "close 1st march but I couldn't figure that out haha. Hey what front pipes do you use longtrack?"

Cameron Woodward* "Joe Hughes stainless one mate"

Gary Pinchin "At the risk of sounding like Jeff Scott (the man behind the quite brilliant, but very quirky collection of annual speedway road trip books), I thought I'd offer some observations."

Jo Lowry* "As much as I DETEST Graeme Drury, I reeeaaallly want Birmingham to win tonight!"

Taylor Poole* "I petty the fool that goes to a rock concert without ripped jeans"

Jo Lowry* "Kenneth Bjerre...the most boring guy in speedway... Actually no, scrap that...most boring guy EVER!"

Jo Lowry* "The fact that they've not replayed that [Kozza] crash once, is worrying me"

Jo Lowry* "But I want to see it! (I know that sounds terrible) but I can't help but be curious as I didn't really see what happened"

Taylor Poole* "best wishes koz. P.S richie you have red hair!"

Kevin Long* "Doesn't Cameron Heeps look good in that Ipswich speedway coat in the King's Lynn pits?"

Julian Sumner* "Can everybody please RT this so hopefully Nigel can understand: - it's pronounced LASS-A not LASS-E"

Kevin Long* "Ermolenkos commentary like Eric Morecombe quote 'all the right words, not necessarily in the right order!'"

Rory Schlein* "Can I just say sky make such a deal of rolling at the start, watch some old school speedway u could touch the tapes bk in the day"

Jo Lowry* "Well...that's it then! We need a win monday and thursday. Anything less and there's no point. But, we can do it. Come on the Bees!!"

Dakota North* "Better night! Good night for the team rebels. Thanks for turning up followers even tho the weather didn't look good"

Nigel Pearson* "well done King's Lynn on reaching the play-offs. Good achievement in 1st season back in EL"

Johnny Barber "When Kozza came in before the meeting I said 'you've had a fantastic season and haven't had an injury' – so it's all my fault"

Amy Allen* "Oh great Olly Allen is drunk after one bottle of beer #lightweight"

Nicki Pedersen "I'm as shocked as [Peterborough] fans and other people are because I didn't see it coming like this. There is only a maximum of six or eight meetings left, so it didn't have to happen. As you can see, I'm fifth on the Elite League average list and I have done a decent job lately. So I don't think it's anything to do with my job. I haven't spoken to them. I just got this e-mail and I don't think it has been done in a very professional way. But if that's the way they think it should be, then that's the way it is. I think they want to try out other riders and juniors, and I don't know if my average was too high. But it doesn't matter to me. It would have hurt more if it was an Andreas Jonsson or Jason Crump replacing me."

Steve Saint* "poor show by any management. Decisions should always be done face to face. Where's the backbone in an email"

8th September

Paul Burbidge* "Feeling human now after a [07.15] McBacon roll at Gatwick. Flying to Billund shortly for the Nordic sgp at Vojens"

Olly Allen* "Watching last nights sky match with my son....damn we did good! I think my boy is secretly proud of his old man :)"

Chris Moss "If I were a dog, I'd have sniffed the adrenalin and the lad-sweat beneath the nose-stinging methanol fumes."

Johnny Barber "I haven't seen Mike Bennett for a few weeks. Last night he was too busy helping Sky or speaking a different voice to normal to get noticed"

Nicolai Klindt* "school-kids on today's flight, they better be quiet. gotta treat my self with a new passport so i don't get people moaning over my picture!"

Jeff Scott "I love the smell of methanol in the evening"

Lewis Bridger* "Just looked at the weather what crap it is everywhere in uk for next 5days #watajoke"

David Howe* "Is twit of the week on sgp website and proud"

Lee Richardson* "Already stressed out and it's only 10 am!! Peter Johns rescue mission!!"

Niels Kristian Iversen* "no rain in pboro boys. Not sure about swindon though"

Chris Moss "Speedway is a simple sport. It's exciting, skilful, spectacular, but it's straight-up – no fouls, no fakery, and no robbed penalties."

Niels Kristian Iversen* "Hope Kozza Will be okay after last nights crash. Was a nasty one"

Alun John Rossiter* "That's cheered me up just had a call from Leigh Adams he's working flat out on rehab sounded in good form :-) !!"

Johnny Barber "For some reason, no one from Sky ever seems to want to mention that Emil's British Speedway average is 7.80?"

Lewis Bridger* "Got to keep scoring big points to pay bills & progress at skidding to the highest level #finishtheseasonstrong"

Alun John Rossiter* "Woo ha just hit 1000 on here :-)"

Paul Burbidge* Tai Woffinden has ruled himself out of the running for a 2012 sgp wild card."

Dakota North* "Swindon bound"

Lewis Bridger* [to *Speedway Star Twitter identity*] "hey mate I want to put a bike for sale in a ad in the mag how do I go about doing this ?"

David Watt* "Just booked the flights to Aussie !! Can't wait ! Woohoo you little bloody dancer !!! #letthefunbegin"

Paul Burbidge* "Just had a tour of Ole Olsen's beautiful house. Trophy cabinet was huge. Don't think Cash my Gold have an envelope big enough for that lot. And if the people of Vojens are wondering where the local deer population has gone, they're all on the wall in Ole's hunting room"

Nicolai Klindt* "finally out of that one on junc 6 m5. small KA rolled over the fence! auch...."

Mads Korneliussen* "Ryanair delayed what the hell is going on #nothappy"

Niels Kristian Iversen* "Another sick gym session. 4th This week. Gotta keep fit for the playoffs in PL, SWE and UK"

Kelvin Lapworth "I have just read on the BSPA website that Dudley are giving an outing to a 43 year old (Mark Robinson) who is making a comeback. Can I say that I think this is an absolute joke, yes its sentimental that a former Heathens favourite is ridng again but I thought the whole idea of the National "development" league was to give up and coming youngsters a chance and not to give old has beens a jolly (I don't mean any personal offence on you Mark). As coordinator of the Midland League I have been on the phone to nearly every NL team manager until my face turns blue trying to get the better riders the chance that they deserve. If only Messers Pottinger and Pearson would open their eyes they would see talent in the likes of Conor Dwyer, Lee Geary, Tom Woolley and Conor Coles all of whom have all beaten national league level riders in the Midland league this year. What do these guys have to do to get an opportunity? I wish all the best to Mark but in all fairness The NL should be used to bring on raw British talent - isn't that what Nigel Pearson preaches to us every week on SKY?"

    Sam Masters* "Sick of this working on bikes it's all I do #fulltimemechanic"

    David Howe* "arrr boo hoo #moaningaussie"

    Sam Masters* "oooh don't you start gayvid you've done your fair share of winging in your time #wingingpoms"

    David Howe* "sure have, I can take winging to a new level #youwillnevermoanasgoodasme"

David Howe* "Just read in star and I'm meant to be at Redcar tonight, no-one asked me!! #disgusting"

Lewis Bridger* "Radio 1 is heavy right about now heavy"

Terry Russell "My eight seasons here [Swindon] have been extremely enjoyable; it really is a great club. I'm sure that I'll be remembered for finishing bottom in my final season, but obviously I would prefer people to focus on the good times I've had here, and the 4 Play-off seasons in a row incorporating two finals in the process!....I certainly won't be a stranger to the place either, and whenever the cameras are in town I'm sure I'll be here in a Commercial capacity giving good opportunities to catch up with people."

Dakota North* "Had a rough first 2 races then came a bit better in the end"

Hans Andersen* "Oh well First meeting out of the way... Tried a lot og things bike/engines wise today so we know a little what Will work & what doesnt !"

Chris Neath* "Snapped forks, dodgy box and a blown engine. Is anything else gonna go wrong this week???"

Nicolai Klindt* "thanks to all the swindon fans for backing us up through the hole of a disaster 2011 season!"

Scott Nicholls "It has been a terrible, terrible season for me, not the one I planned at all. It has been totally frustrating and sometimes the more you try and search for solutions, the more you struggle and I tried not to do that. No one has been more frustrated or disappointed than me for sure. I agree 100 per cent that I have not done the job Swindon expected of me or what I demand from myself. For the last twelve seasons any score less than ten points in a match in Britain I've always personally regarded as a disaster. I don't read forums but there has been criticism, and I agree with that right of free speech. The only thing I will say is that I have never stopped trying. To me it's my job, my livelihood and reputation on the line. Hand on heart, I have always done my best."

Nigel Pearson* "Need to remember to check in online for my flight to Denmark tomorrow. In fact, I'll do it now rather than tweeting!! Not a big Ryanair fan"

Arnie Gibbons "It [Elite League] has very little credibility as a result of last winter's shenanigans. As a neutral I have felt little interest in the outcome, certainly considerably less than in previous years"

> **Hans Andersen*** "Dont know why people give shit! If a attacker ain't shooting balls HOW dó you expect him to score goals? Need time to settle & with silencer"
>
> **Nicolai Klindt*** "don't think about what people is saying, think about your self and what you could do to make it better!"
>
> **Nigel Pearson*** "i agree with Nic - good luck Hans and take no notice!!! Welcome back to England skidding"

Dakota North* "Big drive tomorrow to scotland then Glasgow Sunday peterbro Monday #goodluckdakota"

Dakota North* "Just arrived home an tried to get out of the van and I'm #fckingsore ouch! Can't wait for tomorrow now #nopainnogame?"

9th September

Chris Neath* "Love how time flies when I get on the internet in the van"

Derek Barclay "Though i know Spedeworth's unhappiness about the shale track was a factor I've never heard this allegation before about them threatening to leave... And I was close to those promoting in 2002-05"

Tim Hamblin "Pros and cons. Ten [Elite League] teams helps, Lynn and the Brummies have given variation (and good race tracks, especially Lynn), some of the bigger names have participated. The play-off system, like it or not (and in general I don't), has kept the season alive despite one team being well clear at the top. The rule changes appear to have kept more teams involved in the hunt for longer. Fixture variations have been a nightmare, overall standards don't appear to have improved (sign of a deeper malaise) and the repercussions from last winter clearly haven't played out fully yet.

If we have 10 at the tapes next year I'll be surprised (but very pleased)."

Hans Andersen* "Hate early mornings probably coz i ain't use to them at the moment..."

Jan Staechamnn* "Chlling with Mrs Staechmann in the BA lounge at Manchester, before flight to Billund to see the folks. Nordic GP weekend w BSI crew awesome"

Stewart Dickson "The beauty of this is that [David Bellego] comes in with absolutely no pressure on him, and all we ask of him is that he settles in well and gets a grasp of the sport in this country."

Chris Neath* "Problem is were gettin over the hill ourselves now! #oldbirdsneedloveto"

Paul Burbidge* "Just in case anyone in Vojens is hungry, my iPhone's McDonalds finder says the nearest one is in Great Yarmouth. Better start swimming!"

Dakota North* "On my way north! north?"

Fredrik Lindgren* "Hate it in Poland when I talk in English and they chatter back in Polish! Realised today that they did same in Sweden to my mechanic! #bad Difficult in Denmark to know speak Swedish or English with the Danes start speak Swedish they get it & answer in Danish I don't get a thing!"

Sam Masters* "Nice way to start the trip to Scotland with a flat tyre in the van better get better #shitstart #speedwaylife"

David Howe* "could be worse you could be going scunny #sunnyscunny"

Fredrik Lindgren* "theawkwardmoment When talking to Nicolai Klindt and realise he hasn't the fastest moped on the dock!"

Nicolai Klindt* "are we on about that again? haha. the awkward moment is when you tell something funny and people don't get it"

David Howe* "Bloody glad I decided not to do gp quali now that poland only have 1 gp rider, clubs will be flocking after me now #onlykidding #slowassnail"

Troy Batchelor* "It's funny how some people have 30 followers but tweet flat out, it's like a tree falling In the jungle no one hears it!"

Chris Holder* "not everyones as kool as u batch!"

Tai Woffinden* "what a nice day had a layin. chillin in the sport pub having lunch tunes pumpin suns out might go for a practice"

Dakota North* "What a cccc of a drive"

Paul Burbidge* "In a frank and honest interview, Crump admits he hasn't been confident in his machinery this year"

Dakota North* "Cramping up in this van! 3 in the front isn't ideal! Pretty sore from lastnights little events"

Lewis Bridger* "hair cut #feelingfresh"

Jonathan Chapman "We've asked Poole if we can race them to fuck their minds up a bit"

Rory Schlein* "I'm gonna have a guess practice rained off at the GP ha ha ha ha"

Chris Holder* "nah bro she was on! Dry as a bone to ! Crazy"

Paul Burbidge* "Just spoken to Holta, his hand is getting worse. This man badly needs the end of the season. Vojens is smooth. He'll feel less pain here"

Nigel Pearson* "Freddie are u back to England on Sunday mate? I'm on early Billund - Stansted so can take you to Wolves if needed. See u tomorrow"

Fredrik Lindgren* "Thanks for the offer but I have to head straight to Polska for more speedway action"

Chris Holder* "Ping pong battle royal …. 1 hour"

Alun John Rossiter* "be there in ten noddy!"

Paul Burbidge* "Never knew Vojens could be so much fun. Just had a superb karting session with the BSI crew. There is life in this place after all!"

Nicola Sands* "Go Karting in Vojens brilliant. Didn't make the podium but beat Paul Burbidge on his performance he'll never get to drive the hire car!"

Nicola Sands* "Sky Sports 4 red button. [SGP] Repeat on Sunday."

Charlie Webster* "The v lovely Christopher Biggins and myself "

Tai Woffinden* "had a practice today 0.43 of track record felt good"

Fredrik Lindgren* "Thinking to myself got to make the most of this night at hotel Scandic because tomorrow night it's the rolling hotel Sprinter! ZzZzzz"

10th September

Paul Burbidge* "For my British followers, Nordic sgp from Vojens can be viewed via the red button on Sky Sports 4 at 6pm. RT and spread the word"

Tomasz Suskiewicz "I think it [the EL play-offs] clashes with the Russian league. I know Emil's flying to Coventry's meeting on September 12. But after that it clashes very often with the Russian meetings, the trips to Russia and the trips to the Grand Prix. So I think Rosco will have some hard work to do to get everything right."

Rob Godfrey "Stuart [Parnaby] went to see him [John Oliver] on the Tuesday night and he was sickened by what he saw. He had an operation on his ankle, but in his other ankle there is no enough bone there to repair it yet. On hearing that, I was alarmed. Then I got a call from the Speedway Riders' Benevolent Fund and Paul Ackroyd (president). He had a call from Shane Parker, who said John Oliver was 6,000 miles away from home with a young family and was basically skint. They had no money and were wondering how they were going to feed the family or get home. That set alarm bells in my head and I thought we had to do something. Straight away the SRBF deposited £1,000, via King's Lynn, into Mrs. Oliver's account. On top of that, we have raised £950 and the Leicester promotion are also doing good things to ease the burden on him because the last thing he needs when he is recuperating is to be worrying about his family. I am very pleased to say the SRBF have also said if he struggles, because we believe he hasn't got a plane ticket home. They will get him, and his family, home."

Dick Barrie "I've had a query (that Banditfone's got a lot to answer for) about why, on a night when rain is threatening, we still hold a parade instead of cracking on with racing. Fair question, but on this one I can offer a fair answer – our planning restrictions preclude our starting the first race until seven o'clock."

Speedway Star "Should SGP series organisers BSI Speedway and the FIM opt against giving Harris a sixth straight season in the competition, Woffinden would appear the only genuine British candidate to replace him."

Graham Drury "Birmingham Speedway has been run on a very tight budget this season and we are on target not to lose any money, which not all clubs can say in this day and age...[Tony Mole] is not an individual who uses the sport as a toy just to enjoy himself and throw silly money at it to win at all costs, he does it properly and there is a lot to be said for that."

Hans Andersen "Panthers are probably thinking ahead to the future by bringing me back."

Trevor Geer "If a rider is struggling, most teams will get rid of them and find someone else. We don't do that. We persevere with them, try and help them and find out what is wrong."

Dick Barrie "I also like riders to look smart on parade, each in his club's race-jacket. Only one rider in the entire league has regularly declined to take off his anorak for our parade, but even although Shane Parker has this annoying trait I will be sorry to see him go, as he has told us emphatically he will, after this season ends."

Kevin Harris "Also of interest that night [September 3rd] was Nicki Pedersen's hygiene. Does anyone else take the tissue they have just used to blow their nose and proceed to wipe it all over their face and head?"

Dakota North* "ffff I'm sore today!!!"

Paul Burbidge* "Krzysztof Cegielski says Kolodziej is over his kidney problems and hopes he can recapture his 2010 form"

Nicki Glanz* "3,1,EF,1 for NG today blew another Engine today in 2nd heat thanks to Risager for lending mé a bike, now 5km run then VojensSGP with gang !"

Fredrik Lindgren* "spotted Greg Hancock & his hangarounds sneaking in a Italian buffet bar!"

Olly Allen* "Does anyone know what channel the speedway gp is on tonight?? #confused"
Nicolai Klindt* "how do you work this red bottom thing? can't find the gp when i press it"
Gary Patchett* "U won't find it til programme time fella"

Ludvig Lindgren* "Fredrik Lindgren needs his tash back! no man without a tash!"

David Watt* Thinkin that Chris Holder is gonna smoke em all tonight. He's in the groove and ready for a win. Climb that table man !!"

Darcy Ward* "who's licking who's ass here ?"

Ludvig Lindgren* "oon the train now! loving life atm just got 3hrs of traveling left! f*ck me its fat to berwick from stansted!"

Paul Burbidge* "Weather is unusually clear in Vojens for the Nordic sgp and there is even a sniff of shale on the track. We're in for a good one! Huge congrats to Ole Olsen, who won his first world title 40 years ago today. His contribution to speedway since then has been immense"

Nicolai Klindt* "just want to tell everyone i'm sorry i couldnt be in tonights gp as a wildcard. i had more important things to do! hope you will enjoy it"

Sam Masters* "You know ur desperate to watch the GP when u watching it in the bookies"

Rory Schlein* "What excuse will nikki have for that ha ha"

Linus Sundstrom* "bjarne turned left on him, did you miss that?"

Rory Schlein* "you miss him don't you"

Paul Burbidge* "Horrendous move by Nicki Pedersen. Fenced Bjarne in heat 2. Cynical move on his fellow countryman"

Derek Banks "Rude swear word ************ ** I get my Sky Sports courtesy of Virgin Media where there is no red button facility."

Gary Patchett* "Has NICKI still got Readypower on the covers? #sackedbyemail"

Tai Woffinden* "B.Pederson better get used to a bit of close racing now he is in the GP #nofuckingabout"

Lee Richardson* "your so sexy lbr..."

Tai Woffinden* "whos gonna be in the GP for next year for england"

Gary Patchett* "Signal on red button is crap!"

Nigel Pearson* "Question for you speedway fans - does the sgp need a GB rider in next year's series? Who would u pick?"

Brian Owen* "SGP needs to have riders who qualify on merit more than it needs any substandard Brits. british final winner goes to Cardiff"

Scott Nicholls* "great 4 UK speedway to have one,but think gp's should be for the best riders,not a spread of nations.Not performing is worse"

Peter Johns* "3 x PJR in final!" [Hancock, Lindgren, Holder]

Andy Povey* "Well done to Greg Hancock, showing the Reading Bulldog spirit. Nearly there buddy!"

Keith Huewin* "Greg Hancock's achievement tonight is epic - pole position for a second sgp title at 41 and at the toughest time in speedway"

Fredrik Lindgren* "Prince Fredrik! Bronze medal in the Nordic GP in Vojens!"

Dakota North* "What's the weather doing tomorrow in Glasgow? Will we be racing or not? #fingerscrossed"

Fredrik Lindgren* "Funny thing, security tried kick me out of the pits! Where is your pitpass? he asks. Don't have it but got this trophy, I replied. I stayed!"

Tai Woffinden* "will be to females walkin around at wolves on monday giving out woffiden 108 stickes"

Fredrik Lindgren* "So it's rolling hotel MB Sprinter tonight just after a quick stop at the McD not ideal but here we go!"

11th September

Darcy Ward* "Way way way to early [05.00] for my flight excited or just dumb"

Nigel Pearson* "Early start back from Billund to Stansted still buzzing after awesome display by Greg Hancock well done buddy!"

Lee Richardson* "Running this morning at home in my gym"

Fredrik Lindgren* "Our 10+ hour drive throughout the night is almost done. Heading for a real good Polish lunch soon! Polish food rocks!"

Sam Masters* "We got rained off but it's sunny here in glasgow??? #dontgetit"

Paul Burbidge* "At Billund Airport in Denmark with the BSI crew - Paddy, Gemma and Nicola Sands waiting for the Cimber noddy plane to take us back to Gatwick"

Dakota North* "Craving a pizza from this little Italian place I know in aus #cantcompare"

Paul Burbidge* "That plane was barrelling all over the shop on the way into Gatwick, but we still didn't get a Ryanair landing. Love Cimber Sterling"

> **Darcy Ward*** "on a track walk with Tai Woffinden"
> **Chris Holder*** "who cares?"

Paul Burbidge* "Was he [Rosco] discussing his strategy to deny Poole another Elite League title? #specialone"

Mark Lemon* "Heading back to the toon again today, it's been a while since I've heard 'wy i man, away the lads'."

David Watt* "Not a good day today. Got 9 from 5 including touching tapes in heat 15. My brain and left hand aren't connected sometimes !!"

> **Fredrik Lindgren*** "There is no I in team! I want to pay tribute to all my mechanics who are working very hard all the time. In good times & in bad!"
> **Ludwig Lindgren*** "lier!"

12th September

Scott Nicholls* "This is a load of ballhang,I should still be tucked up in bed [03.30],not going to an airport! Ok day yesterday,11,but we lost.fans not happy!"

Nigel Pearson* "Back on Sky Sports duty tonight for Elite League speedway Eastbourne v Coventry - Bees need two points or the play-off dream is over!"

Alun John Rossiter* "on the slippery slope been to spec savers got reading glasses oh no !!"

Nigel Pearson* "Just a reminder Kelvin Tatum is a false account and is handled by a sad loser in life - suggest you block him"

> **Alun John Rossiter*** "I was always told you are as old as the woman you feel I felt 25 this weekend !"
> **Nicola Sands*** "wasn't anywhere near you! #whoisdisillusionednow"

Niels Kristian Iversen* "Wanna go cycling today but its not really fun when there is a hurricane outside"

Nigel Pearson* "Hectic morning with office work, now for Eastbourne. 210 miles to go"

Dakota North* "Bikes done washing done off to crumpys to do some adjustment to my engine and then ready for Pbro tonight!"

Ludvig Lindgren* "Wolves vs Bellevue 2night with Chris "frodo" Harris and Rory "slugger" Schlein and also fellow swede Ricky Kling! c'mon wolves!!!"

Michael Whawell "I did say that our season might be elongated due to weather - I'm rarely right about anything - but 55mph gusts at the EoE sent tiles from the bar/hospitality suite flying on to the track. So, match orff. Elf 'n safety rules"

Troy Batchelor* "Haha we are winded off tonight that's a first #lazyday"

Hans Andersen* "i've tried a lot of things throughout My carrier BUT Wind OFF is the First crazy world"

Linus Sundstrom* "wind off tonight!"

Nicolai Klindt* "winded off, no more clean boxers and a sore toe. what more can you ask for? on the way to holiday inn as radisson is 2 expensive! #lowbudget"

Ulrich Ostergaard* "low budget is The airport floor with a jacket and a small pillow:-)"

Jo Lowry* "Charlie Webster do me a big favour and tell kenni to speak to the st johns ambulance guys for ice for his wrist! Be much appreciated!"

Lewis Bridger* "At the gym doing some planks and abs training before tonight's meeting because I can ;) #bangtidy"

Brian Owen* "no Kylmakorpi on Sat for Eagles due to longtrack. In comes Lee Richardson"

Rory Schlein* "Anyone got a kite?"

Nicolai Klindt* "i want to buy a dog. any for sale?"

Eastbourne fan "The meeting has been delayed til 8 cos of a smash on the M23 and two of their riders [Pawlicki brothers] aren't here"

Phil Hilton "If I turned up late to my work, they wouldn't say okay we'll wait they'd send me home"

Bev Barber "Are they waiting for the rain?"

Lee Richardson* "Gonna watch Peter andre sorry I meant Lewis Bridger #getyourabsoutforcharlie #lbrshow #theresonly1lbr"

Nicolai Klindt* "hahahaha, that is funny!"

Lewis Bridger* "ur a funny Fu£&er just read ya tweet ;)"

Jo Lowry* "I'm sorry but a team with a home crowd THAT low (even on sky) does not deserve to win the league (or tonights meeting for that matter)"

Jeff Scott* "er, loud sound of barrel being scraped! Or sour grapes pressed? is there eva a big crowd on Sky? v.few Bees fans there"

Jordan Hazelden "How can Max Clegg break the tapes in the [U15 500cc] final and win the rerun from the tapes?"

Sinead "I'm a Facebook friend with Nick [Morris]"

Nicolai Klindt* "arrived to holiday inn at stansted, but very disappointed that joanna wasnt here so i could get my normal rate. going for some dinner soon!"

Shaun "That Morris is a lively kid, they say"

Mike Bennett* "Oh dear- not the best speedway so far. Guess our meeting at Kings Lynn last week was a hard act to follow?? Lakeside must be enjoying this! Got to love watching Nick Morris- a fine performance from the Tigger!"

Jo Lowry* "Nice to know that kenni broke his scaphoid....I did ask, but it was Kelvin who I found out from! This being the same bone that I prodded lots #confused"

Mike Bennett* "I'll have a word about young Mr Morris coming to Kings Lynn next season when I next visit the Tiggers! :-) Future speedway champion!"

Shaun "Fing hell, he's a crazy-boy in he?"

Kevin Coombes "You know what it is – he's [Timo Laht] just had a haircut. That [race win] was pretty pretty amazing"

Jo Lowry* "Maybe its a good job I didn't go now I've just seen who's there"

Alun John Rossiter "Eddie's here – what's happened has happened. He'll be coming back to Coventry no problem"

Kevin Coombes "Fresh pair of pants for Lewis Bridger"

Jo Lowry* "So Lahti has taken down 3 bees riders in 2 heats. And its not his fault....BULLSHIT"

Alun John Rossiter "Hindsight is a wonderful thing on the terraces in speedway – they're not in the pits when it's going full throttle"

Mads Korneliussen* "Rosco what's up with the glasses, are you getting old, never #foreveryoung #skysports"

Claudia Staechmann* "Nigel Pearson have you been practising your danish surname pronunciation? Sounding very good Mr P! My husband is impressed! X"

Alun John Rossiter "young boys are the future. Like Piotr [Pawlicki], the trouble is being so young there's so many championships in Poland"

Mike Bennett* "speedway play off teams confirmed so bring it on! Come to the Norfolk Arena Pirates . . . . a warm welcome awaits!!! What do you reckon??"

  Mads Korneliussen* "Is thinking who will pick us for the play-offs #kingslynntowin"

  Nicolai Klindt* "poole vs lakeside - eastbourne vs kingslynn"

  Gary Patchett* "Doubt Poole will pick Lakeside"

  Brian Owen* "the feeling in the Eagles camp seems to be they will get the Lakeside Hammers in the play off semi"

  Mads Korneliussen* "I don't think Eagles want us as we won there but they did beat us at home too. Bring on poole"

  Gary Patchett* "Poole will pick the best racetrack. U got that mate"

  Mads Korneliussen* "yea but to be fair not all of them go well there, if we can get kenneth to get so points at poole for once we are ok"

Nigel Pearson* "Seemed like a long night at Eastbourne, bad luck Bees, good effort. Hope Emil does a full season 2012. Bring on the play-offs"

  Charlie Webster* "I'm thinking Poole v Kings Lynn...Eastbourne v Lakeside...Poole v Eastbourne Final"

  Olly Allen* "no way charlie!! as captain of kings lynn i have to disagree"

  Charlie Webster* "ha ha fair play... it would be a great story if you reached the final...good luck! Who do you think you'll get semi's?"

  Olly Allen* "after speaking to holder a few weeks ago i think we will face poole"

  Chris Holder* "fukn easy buddy"

  Olly Allen* "how cool would a win for kl be though! id love it"

  Chris Holder* "We might let use off... Team meeting tomorrow hahaha #tactics"

13th September

Lee Richardson* "At heathrow, forgot how far away the long stay car parks are!! Too used to flying out of stansted...;)"

Rory Schlein* "At Frankies and Bennys with the bomber well needed breaky"

Fredrik Lindgren* "Eating a bowl of porridge from Pret at Stansted Airport at 5 o clock in the morning! My highlight of the day!"

Nicolai Klindt* "funny enough... 3 guys decided to walk to midstay to take the bus from their instead of the holiday inn one which is £2!"

Lee Richardson* "Great news about the play offs, great achievement from everybody....wonder who it will be against though"

Niels Kristian Iversen* "On the roads to Hammarby. Tough meeting is coming up tonight with indianerna. Its time to sort myself out on that track"

Hans Andersen* "Just left Newborough Will meet up with Danny King around huntingdon as both ride for the Mighty Dackarna"

Fredrik Lindgren* "Two monkey kids next to me on this flight & a mom that can't keep em steady! Destroyed my flight today, I'll never have kids like that!"

Hans Andersen* "Hmmm nothing beats a bit of YamYam (chili chicken)"

Dakota North* "This weather is starting to annoy me more than normal #2meetingsoff maybe3?"

Olly Allen* "Now sitting in a speed awareness class for getting busted speeding, feels like being back at school"

Olly Allen* "bored already!!"

Tai Woffinden* "Just had nandos ;)"

Linus Sundstrom* "On the way down to vetlanda with 40th birthday boy and teammanager stefan "ando" andersson !"

Alun John Rossiter* "Woo hoo night in with a bottle of red and cheese happy times #goodtimes"

Chris Holder* "that's sad Rosco!! Tell me thats not wat excites u these days!!"

Alun John Rossiter* "how about ping pong !! Chris you know wot excites me mate!!"

Freddie Gorgeous aka Chlo*

"never spoke t him sept at the party, he stopped & said hello at monmore to me before tho"

Lewis Bridger* "That is wrong in so many ways like Cameron Woodward said last night deffo came in to Hot #ifindoutflatout"

Fredrik Lindgren* "Horrible meeting for me, didn't have a clue what to do, still scratching my head. I feel awful! Back to the drawing board"

14th September

Hans Andersen* "Last nights ref was a right shocker, excluded me for turning left too early In My first race (made a clean start from four across everyone)"

Niels Kristian Iversen* "On the plane now to UK. Coventry tomorrow and then a few days off before going Poland Sunday"

Avtar Sandhu "Yesterday we went to meet with the Chairman and BSPA Management Committee to discuss the recent events surrounding the line up of our team and the consequences of the decisions taken by them. We do not agree with the version of events that was presented to us, we were not happy with the decisions that were taken and we still find the entire situation as totally unacceptable however we have decided to draw a line under the matter. We have not reached the play off's which is a disappointment to all of us and made harder to accept as this was due to off the track influences rather than on track performance. Our team had some bad luck this year however we had great attendances, a roller coaster of season and some World Class additions to our team. We would like to thank all our fans for the huge support you have given us, our growing list of sponsors and of course the riders both in the full squad and those that helped us sometimes at short notice. I would like to congratulate all the teams who have made the play off's including Poole but in particular I would like to single out Kings Lynn who managed to reach the upper level in its first Elite League season."

BSI There has been speculation in sections of the media [wtf!! where?] over the last few days regarding the staging of an FIM Speedway Grand Prix event in New Zealand. It is no secret that BSI Speedway is in negotiations to stage a Grand Prix in New Zealand. As with the staging of any new event, negotiations take time and at present there is no signed contract or official staging date. These discussions are still ongoing and BSI Speedway urge fans not to make travel arrangements until contracts have been signed and the event has been officially confirmed by BSI Speedway. As in previous years, the calendar for the forthcoming FIM Speedway World Championships will be announced at the FIM Congress in October.

Niels Kristian Iversen* "I hear we are up against Poole in the playoff semi. Its going to be a tough one but if anyone Can dó it, its the Stars"

Nigel Pearson* "Heading to London for important meeting... Could get interesting!! #watchthisspace"

Scott Nicholls* "I reckon U'll make a good prime minister. Good luck! :-)"

Nigel Pearson* "with Clarkie as my press advisor!"

Lee Richardson* "Had to go from stansted into London, to go and get my van from heathrow...#longday"

Nigel Pearson* "Dirty smelly man just got on train, real bad hygiene. Are these people oblivious?"

Chris Holder* "Can the rain please F%#k off thanks"

Lewis Bridger* "fuck we don't want that :-/ do summing CH #stoptherain"

Dakota North* "Just found out 8oclock start tonight whyyyyyyy! Did we leave this early"

Hans Andersen* "Just sat of towards Belle vue and thx to Dakota North i've just Found out we're way too early as 8 o'clock start tonight"

Rene Bach* "this weather is taking the piss now! #hatedanishweather"

Lewis Bridger* "On my way down to poole for the Knockout cup, hopefully the whole eaglits team will style it up"

Rory Schlein* "What shit few days iv had"

Dakota North* "faaaarrrrrkkk! Got a parking ticket!"

Nigel Pearson* "Cheshire cheese, Fleet Street, great pub. Sam Smiths Stout, very smooth and tasty. Time to go home!"

Lewis Bridger* "Sun is out in Poole it's going to be a tough meeting against the Pirates, but me & Cameron Woodward and the boys are up for it. Traffic getting into Poole is hard work :-/"

Dakota North* "where are you batch?"

Troy Batchelor* "oi are we racing today ? I'm still home"

Dakota North* "il let you know what the tracks like we are walking it now"

Paul Burbidge* "Dennis Andersson has missed the parade at Poole tonight because his bike caught fire. Looks like his spare one is doing 7 rides tonight"

Hans Andersen* "Full credit to the Mighty aces for their 10 win tomorrow is a new day and i fully believe In My team sorry for not making it happen of 1"

David Watt* "I'm in mega pain !!! Dang this hurts I'm hopeing for a nice nurse !"

Dakota North* "Tough night in manchester tonigh. Okay for first meeting there I guess"

Lewis Bridger* "What a mare of a night at Poole, I was out in front in 1st race broke down, on a 5-1 in next heat broke down, still ended up with 5+2/4h"

Paul Burbidge* "Nightmare for Poole. Watt, THJ, Andersson carrying injuries, Doyle's season said to be over, guests at reserve. Fancy a double Eastbourne?"

Chris Holder* "Not a good night for our team!! But at least we got the win!"

Jim Lynch "I don't want to see riding like that in speedway. It was really unnecessary and I am very upset about it."

Troy Batchelor "It was hard, but I didn't touch him [Rory Schlein] and he didn't fall off."

15th September

Mads Korneliussen* "tonight it's time to Tango, all the way into the airfence #kingslynntowin"

David Watt* "Am really hurtin this morning. Can't lay down, can't move my arm, can't do anything !! This sucks !!"

Niels Kristian Iversen* "Oats for breakie. Going to the gym now. Coventry away tonight against Kenni Larsen"

Mads Korneliussen* "What if the plane falls down, and i miss tonights meeting, will i get 28 day ban by BSPA #justasking"

David Watt* "There seems to be alot of people standing around doing nothing in this hospital ! I just want an X-Ray and an answer ! Let's go #justasking"

Rory Schlein* "Damage to my ratio cuff in my shoulder possible and soft tissue damage also they got to the bottom of my finger issue tendon damage. So ant at Peterborough tonight hope the boys can kick ass big thanks to Chris Morton for helping me out last night"

Olly Allen* "Away match at my former club Coventry tonight, be good to see many old friends and faces #goodtimes"

Mads Korneliussen* "Travel by train, Superstar lifestyle #loveit #justsaying"

Dakota North* "Bikes doooooonnnnneeee! Getting hungry now!!"

Hans Andersen* "sorry mate, wont be able to eat before meeting as stranded at Johnsy waiting for engine to be ready for a biggen laters…"

Dakota North* "haha it's okay fella! Il just have my steak with out you! #yourloss"

Lewis Bridger* "Subway it up that's king ;) chicken teriyaki wrap + oat meal rasin cookie + tropicana ;) racefood"

Dakota North* "maybe that's where I'm going wrong man! #lewis'shealthtips"

Lewis Bridger* "Nutri grain bar strawberry for breakfast, standard lunch + protein shake at 15:30 gym at 5pm dinner at 7-8pm #thewayimrolling"

Dakota North* "haha this is why we rant in the play offs!"

Lewis Bridger* "quite possibly man"

Fredrik Lindgren* "it's my 26th birthday"

Nigel Pearson* "happy birthday old boy!!"

Lewis Bridger* "Have a good feeling 4 the end of the season hold it together boys and will be hollywood in Spain before u no it #eaglestowin"

SCB "Lemon? Bvs double uppers are Gjedde/Frampton, Cook/Risager. (NB, no declarations allowed after 12th September, so them teams are now final). Nobody is guesting for Gjedde because BV are quite legitimatly using the other double upper Frampton. That means Cook/Risager are missing (both riding PL) so BV need a facility for them. As Risager is the lower averaged rider then he is the one the facility is for. Risagers 3.70 is lower than Klings(3.84) so Risgaer is number 7. The ONLY facility for a number 7 is your number 8 (Kyle Howarth) but he's not available, he's riding PL for Edinburgh so it's a Pl guest with a converted averages up to 3.17 (PL 5.28). So how the hell is Hall (PL 7.49) replacing Risager?"

Lewis Bridger* "Wtf chicks with Tattoos on chest in Bexhill today, sorry if I have offended anyone but it doesn't do it for me #notladylike"

Chris Holder* "Nice day to watch someone wash ur car"

Dakota North* "reading about the incident last night with troy and rory haha there was no contact and nobody fell off! So what was wrong with it? Bell vue manger said it was dirty and doesn't want to ever see racing like that? I don't understand? So he doesn't wants to see contact and rory to be put threw the fence? confused because that's the opposite to what happen last night"

David Watt* "Shoulder is ok even though I can't move it yet. Separated some bones in my thumb but it ok. Physio ASAP please !! #canseethelight"

Rory Schlein* "Phyiso Saturday hope to get to the bottom to my knuckle and finger prob and get some more movement back in the shoulder"

Rory Schlein "Loaned bomber an engine tonight wrap it on mate and good luck boys"

David Watt* "trying to link twitter and facebook ! its not working !!"

Tai Woffinden* "its easy man i dono how i did it tho"

David Watt* "is loosin it ! Ok. If this doesn't work then I'm getting someone else to have a crack at it !! #overit"

Darcy Ward* "Thinks David Watt has a twitter problem"

Chris Holder* "2nd that! #toomuchtweeting"

Rory Schlein* "Great start boys that kick up the ass I gave Ricky must of worked. No guys not there at home resting but watching live updates"

Lewis Bridger* "Problem after problem last night, nothing my mechanic could of done, just problem with carby needle jet #allfixed #happydays #playoffs"

Ken Burnett "Derek [Barclay], you seem to have plenty to say about the NL, but we haven't seen much of you at the meetings cheering on the Hawks, for that matter sadly we haven't see many others either and that is the reason why it is not working, fans simply are not coming and supporting these youngsters, if we are honest not many are coming to other meetings either and crowds are dwindling at most tracks. maybe just one day things will change, but all the time people say "I used to go" rather than actually going and are not being replaced, our sport is going to struggle"

Hans Andersen* "Oh dear oh dear :(never easy when First bike stop ! Sorry to the fans BUT need at least a few laps to sort setup...."

Dakota North* "Points have not come too me easy like they were before my injury tough. Tomorrows a new day! I think a maximum will help in many ways"

Olly Allen* "Very happy to leave Coventry stadium In one piece, worst track conditions I've ever ridden on! Shame as it's normally good"

Linus Sundstrom* "Shocked to be honest!Lost at home and didnt go trough...Not good at all! Ashame we didnt keep our unbeaten homerecord whole season:/"

Peterborough Panthers* "All we can say is sorry tonight guys. It wasn't our night but we gave it everything, and we will be back. Thanks for the support!"

Michael Whawell "Somewhat surprisingly Panfs reserves - 1, Aces reserves 15 + 2 Panfs machine failures 4. Aces ditto – nil. That was about it, really."

16th September

Troy Batchelor* "Just looking through top words and I see #holdergrowamo and im thinking #holdergrowamo do it son"

Chris Holder* "it's some new craze.... I thinking bout it.. Look pretty badass with a mow"

Troy Batchelor* "you would probably look like borat"

Chris Holder* "now that's wat im talking bout yeeew"

Linus Sundsrtom* [at 04.00] "Up we are and off to the airport we are! This time is more night than morning tbh.. swwdish U21 final tonight! #bringemon"

Hans Andersen* "What a shame Gatwick is so fare Away otherwise i would be In and out of there All the time, so easy and smooth through everything"

David Howe* [at 07.00] "bikes to wash"

Steve Mallett "We have been advised time and again that speedway fans will only turn up en-mass to follow a winning side, so we dug deep into our financial pot and produced one which has won 13 and drawn another in its last 17 league and cup fixtures. But crowd sizes remain below what they should be and we really have reached the stage now that it's make or break for local speedway followers. I really am urging fans who occasionally to come to watch to unite in a show of strength for Saturday night, without doubt the biggest meeting in our time here."

Moira Perrott "They say it's £8 or £9k to run a Premier League meeting at Newport so with crowds of 400 or less, you're gonna be driving home every week knowing you've lost at least three or four grand. It can't be good"

Fredrik Lindgren* "Thinking that my back might be able to take a running session soon, maybe try next week! Today I went with a Powerwalk"

Darcy Ward* "not me bud"

Taylor Poole* "Kebab Land ←···3 amazing #bestever"

Dakota North* "Bikes done for tonight I don't enjoy doing them after a shit night!"

Ray Blackwell "That's typical [Holta incident] of the Bratchelor. And so is the dummy spitting if he doesn't get things his own way. He will end up with a very big lesson I think."

Lewis Bridger* "At the gym pushing my self hard #bringiton"

Paul Burbidge* "Harris admits the new silencers have flummoxed him as he bids to get back into the sgp series' top-eight"

Darcy ward* "he liked them last year n wanted them lol"

Peter Johns* ":) :) do you have a problem? You probably do, but It's not the silencers!!!! :) :)"

Troy Batchelor* "yeah classic and now what"

Linus Sundstrom* "Long story short: second is the first loser! goodnight"

Dakota North* "Couldn't work out why I was so slow last night! Engine is dew for service so flat couldn't get it to work last/tonight A big thanks to Sam Masters to lend me his bike after we worked out mine was farrrrrrked #topbloke"

Dakota North* "At least I finished with a win on Sam's bike! #onlyasgoodasyourlastrace"

Bob Tasker "Scunthorpe v Leicester: well, didn't cover this meeting. Four & a half hours to reach Wetherby due to road carnage was enough for me before turning back home, shortly before the scheduled start time. Of course at that stage, no one knew that it would rain the meeting would eventually start 90 minutes late, just as I arrived home. Guess what? Despite my not being there, this morning the world is still turning, apparently in spite of at least one message I received. Thanks for your support."

17th September

Egon Muller "I look around the [SGP] pits and nowadays the boys have one woman and four bikes. I liked one bike and four women."

Linus Sundstrom* "Wanted that #goldmedal badly last night.."

Matt Ford "There'll be no Thomas [Jonasson] or Dennis [Andersson] at Arlington because they're in the Swedish Final. Unfortunately we'll have to travel with a very strange-looking Poole team with Kevin [Wolbert] making his debut and us using two guests and rider replacement."

Alan Dick "The Sheffield promotion have come out and said a lot of bad things about us but we have decided to let our riders do the talking."

David Howe* "#saturdaybikewashclub open"

Lewis Bridger* "Had a strange past 24hrs but I'm hoping to make up for it tonight"

Lewis Bridger* "Got to keep a straight head & all I must no is to WIN"

Darcy Ward* "just me and holder tonight"

Lewis Bridger* "x2 of ya yea haha no1 else ?? Pissing down at moment anyways bro #whygodwhy"

Dick Barrie "Speedway can be a cruel business at times – which brings me to the subject of the polyfoam fence. In order to have the TPBS installed in time for next season, certain arrangements and funding have to be put in place right now. As we have put on record, the total installation cost to the club will be £50,000. Money we don't have lying around. A deposit of £10,000 was required and has been paid to get the deal rolling. Over the next six months we will be announcing fund-raising ventures to raise the rest of the dough. Obviously, sponsorship will be a huge help – each of the panels can carry a fully-coloured banner, and I know, Julie, Phil and the rest of the promotion's commercial team will be actively working to have such paid-for displays in place by the time the fence arrives. As for the rest – well, if you want a safer speedway, we'll be happy to hear of any fund-raising ideas you might be able to come up with!"

Niels Kristian Iversen* "Good thing i Got the garden sorted this morning as its mega raining now. Was thinkin golf before, now im thinkin Shit weather.."

Olly Allen* "Just finished a 10 mile run with the guys from sportlink, really enjoyed it!"

Jack Steggles "With reference to the latest spat between Coventry and Poole, I was amazed to see that Matt Ford was able to act both as Poole promoter and the BSPA management committee member dealing with the same subject, and then state that he 'acted in the interests of speedway'."

Fredrik Lindgren* "Think I still hold the track record at the little track in Kumla from 1999 so my name still haunt the youths of today!"

David Mason "It's [special diet] hard on my wife and the children as well. She has to cook two meals for me every night – one to eat then and the other for the following lunchtime – as well as cook for the kids and herself."

Rory Schlein* "Good news about my shoulder from the physio no ligament damage just muscle damage and my collarbone joint had popped out my"

Christian Hefenbrock "I don't know why we've had so many injuries this year. It has been unbelievable. Look at any team and there has been one or two riders injured. I don't know if it's down to the new exhausts or what it is."

Tai Woffinden* "would like to no if I'm racing in sweden on tuesday? they won't answer my calls?????"

Marc Owen "The biggest thing we need right now to take my game forward is having someone with us on race-nights who knows what they're doing."

Julie Newton "We are moving speedway here [Berwick] into new markets all the time, and being honoured by New Holland – a global brand, manufacturing their wide range of agricultural equipment and marketing it in 150 countries worldwide – is another big leap forward."

Nicolai Klindt* "can't wait to get this season over with..#makingmesick"
Dakota North* "so true!"

Darcy Ward* "is it still raining ?"
Lewis Bridger* "it's just shitty mate no rain drizzle maybe"

Sam Masters* "2011 the year of rain offs and traffic jams :/ #overit #england"

Dakota North* "this rain is fffffed"

Linus Sundstrom* "Had a decent weekend, 7th in the swedish final and 2nd in the U21 . Could have been better though, as always! #dontletgoodenoughbeenough"

David Watt* "Is frustrated to be on the lounge when I should be racing !! I hope everything gets rained off !! #backskiddinrealsoon"

Tai Woffinden* "On the way to luton airport poland tomoro :D Wolves monday... Not in the team tuesday!!"

Mike Bellerby & Trevor Geer "Our website has received a few rather mischievous and at times, possibly libellous, e-mails from supporters of other teams who are pretending to be Eagles fans! Obviously this is not what the site is for"

John Hazelden [as Poole team pass on parade tuck] "Hard luck lads!"

Chris Holder "It's a shame the weather comes like this and ruins a good track, it'll get worse before it gets better"

Simon Gustafsson "The meeting is cancelled"
Kevin Coombes "Shush Mister Gustafsson"

Kevin Coombes "You'll be 24 next weekend"
Chris Holder "I'd like to have the win for me birthday that'd be great! Croatia isn't a bad track"

Chris Holder "I like King's Lynn. I think the rest of our team can do better at King's Lynn than Lakeside"

Mark Hazelden "I think Jordan's a bit down after his first meeting back but I told him 'you can always get another bike!'"

John Hazelden [after heat 4]   "Ah, come on, this is where it all goes tits up!"

Kevin Coombes [after heat 6]   "And a long way back in third place – Bjarne Pedersen"

Nick Barber   "Harris can't ride it [Belle Vue] at home but he scores everywhere away. They all ride well away. At Peterborough they were without Gjedde, Schlein and Cook and had Frampton and Hall yet won – what's that about?"

Alan Boniface   "I know Bjarne doesn't like the wet but come on! What's he gonna do when it's wet at the GPs? Before the Poole fans were telling me how pleased they were that the track was wet cos we don't like the wet"

Mark Hazelden   "I tell you what – Darcy Ward will win more world championships than Tony Rickardsson"

Kevin Coombes   "Respect where respect is due, they're not at full strength but they're through to the KO Cup final"

David Watt*   "The boys did an amazing job down at Eastbourne !! Well done to the mighty Pirates !!! Super proud #PiratePride"

Chris Holder*   "Wat can I say...? Fukn wat a win!!!!"

Darcy Ward*   "Well was not expecting that ! #PiratePride wolbert good goin"

Paul Burbidge*   "Cannot believe that Poole are still on for an Elite League double. Incredible performance with a team full of guests at Eastbourne tonight"

Rob Peasley   "Well, SCB has been proved right, Poole haven't been able to win at Eastbourne with their own riders, but they can with other people's riders. Surely the current guest rules are a nonsense - teams should not be able to strengthen up when using guests?"

18th September

Darcy Ward*   "Best team spirit of the season last night #topnotch"

Matt Ford   "I thought I had run out of miracles but the lads did us extremely proud and I cannot thank our three guests enough for the efforts they put in"

David Watt*   "you haven't been able see the team spirit while your head has been stuck up your own ass !!"

Darcy Ward*   "hook line and sinker dumbass"

Davey Watt*   "Same stoops ! Was hopeing you'd sit on the plane without being able to reply !!"

Darcy Watt*   "na na na don't go back tracking now"

David Watt*   "doubt it ! Your not that smart dopey ! Hahaha"

Chris Holder*   "Must win by 17points against last years champs, No pressure put on us by the club.. Haha jus the whole city said we must win.. #justgottadothis"

Dakota North*   "#lastnightsucked Too muddy!"

Nigel Pearson*   "Three short of 5000 followers - would have been less but blocked two idiots yesterday. Who will be No 5000? Exciting Sunday!!"

David Watt*   "I high sided at Poole on Wednesday. Hurt my shoulder and separated bones in my thumb #mustgoto final"

Paul Burbidge*   "What a mess in Poland. Leszno have reached the Ekstraliga play-off final, but have been given a stadium ban"

George English   "tragically soon after that we lost Matej [Ferjan] when he was taken from us after a blood clot in his leg brought a premature end to his life"

19th September

Tai Woffinden*   "Gotta hate it when that [04.00] alarm goes of and gotta go to the airport"

Fredrik Lindgren*   "Have to stop crashing my body certainly don't like it!"

Linus Sundstrom*   "Van broke down yesterday and the car dont start this morning #nothappy"

Scott Nicholls* "Sorry for jumping line at passport control today at Luton! Naughty boy I know. Queues there are redonkulas"

Nigel Pearson* "I have the same problem every time at Luton mate. Lack of staff, shambles. I normally get early Sun flight and it's chaos"

Scott Nicholls* "mate,it's mental! Not good. Still feel a bit guilty about jumping line though coz I get the hump when it's done to me :-)"

Nicolai Klindt* "ain't happy with my self... was actually up at 8, but somehow i fell back to sleep!"

David Watt* "Is bored ! Can't wait to go to KL tonight and see the patched up Pirates win !! #fightlikehell"

Nigel Pearson* "OK Lynn to beat Poole by 8 and Lakeside to beat Eastbn by 6"

Niels Kristian Iversen* "Is getting ready for my race meal. Then its the biggest meeting for the stars so far This year"

Lewis Bridger* "Ladies & Gentlemen, boys & girls of all ages get your self to Lakeside Hammers stadium tonight for some big heats & 1st turns"

Nicki Glanz* "Keeps getting eyed up by a oldwoman on the ferry would rather have her doughter"

Jo Lowry* "What a poor crowd - for both meetings! Coventry really are the best supported team in the EL. No doubt about it"

Nigel Pearson [after heat 1 of Lakeside v Eagles] "It's the type of riding you see in a world cup meeting, it really is brilliant"

Jo Lowry* "Oh god! Has Tony Millard not given up yet?!! Certainly not missed listening to his rubbish!"

Charlie Webster "The atmosphere is fantastic down here [the pits] – lots of tension"

Jo Lowry* "Next year, Bees WILL be in the Play-offs, and we WILL win the league. No excuses"

Sam Ermolenko "He [Iversen] couldn't be cruel but he did just enough to put him [Ward] off"

Nigel Pearson "I just wonder if it will take 60 heats to deice both finalists?"

Taylor Poole* "I drive tractors for a living ;)"

Neil Middleditch "Darcy and Chris can't win meetings on their own"

Sam Ermolenko "Chris Holder really enjoying the [KL] track here, I can tell by the style he had right to the end"

Nigel Pearson "Lee Richardson – the former Great Britain international"

Paul Burbidge* "Bjarne Pedersen has picked a terrible moment to go off the boil. His gating has been useless of late"

Kelvin Tatum "Lewis Bridger has certainly come good when the pressure was on"

Tony Millard "We saw the Pirates flag flying defiantly there"

Trevor Geer "His footrest snapped and several bits fell off Cameron's bike during the race but it's had a full service so should be alright now"

Nigel Pearson "Darcy Ward's race won't take place without you being able to see it"

Jo Lowry* "Does anyone else find themselves muttering the words 'fall off fall off fall off' when Darcy is out"

Jo Lowry* "feelingguilty...kind of... ;/ OBVIOUSLY I don't want him to be injured, but, y'know, I'm a Bees gal, he's a dirty pirate, its to be expected really"

Trevor Geer "It's a question of trying to motivate them that's all you can do really"

Paul Burbidge* "I didn't know they had two Bears in the King's Lynn team. Sounds like Poole have also signed a guy called Johansson. Interesting [Tony Millard] commentary"

Kelvin Tatum "I tell you what I'm convinced they'll be questions about how they lined up at the start there"

Nigel Pearson "They're rubbing arms that can't be right"

Paul Burbidge* "What was the Lakeside start marshall doing there? Bridger and Richardson should have been moved apart. Ref should have noticed"

David Watt "The latest is I'm getting old and not repairing as well as I should be"

Jo Lowry* "Seeing as I'm very nearly asleep, I will leave with the following comment - Come on Kings Lynn! Do us all a favour and DESTROY Poole!"

Sam Ermolenko "Look at Chris [Holder] look over his shoulder"

Chris Holder "I was just trying to keep Iversen, Sam – whichever one – behind us"

Kelvin Tatum "He's gone down on his own, he's [Stuart Robson] got to go mate"

Tony Millard "We've got a tight one here but not as tight as yours"

Paul Burbidge* "Robson didn't get knocked, but he couldn't turn the bike. He had no room. I think he was unlucky to be excluded"

Tony Millard "Wolbert is flying, Wolbert is almost in the fence"

Neil Vatcher "It's tough to be honest with ya"

Kelvin Tatum "Whoo – Lee Richardson like a knife through butter"

Tony Millard "Digging for victory – dare I say it?"

Tony Millard "I should remind you that nobody has won from heat one tonight"

Neil Vatcher "Eastbourne have been solid throughout and we've been a bit top heavy to be honest with ya"

Neil Middleditch "Chris and Darcy – I'm so so proud to be their manager"

Chris Louis "Davey Watt is running up and down the pits and he's supposed to be injured!"

Darcy Ward "I did the old – little bit dirty – left turn"

Nigel Pearso [on Ward & Holder] "They're the new Hancock & Hamill"

Lee Richardson "Do we take Stuart out [at Eastbourne]? I dunno. We've got a rider replacement facility – that works if your reserves are firing but not if they don't"

Paul Burbidge* "Great comeback from Eastbourne at Lakeside. But after what happened to them against Poole on Saturday, the tie isn't over"

David Watt* "Praise the Lord !!"

Mike Bennett* "What a night! Capped by abuse from one of our own fans for taking about Chris Holder and Darky!! Hey ho - hope it made him feel better!"

Jeff Scott* "surely any regular is used to you brown-nosing all the stars? Thankfully the tv viewers only heard Tony Millard all night"

Mike Bennett* "Hmmm very brave on here and your rip off books Jeff but how about you say that to my face?!! Trust you have a good lawyer????"

Tai Woffinden* "15 points takin the trophy home again swwweeeeeeeettttt!!!!!!!!!!!!"

Lee Richardson* "That was a tough night against a good Eastbourne team! Not over yet #webetterbeon #themoneynextweek"

Olly Allen* "Tough match tonight Chris Holder & Darcy Ward were on it! The team fought well though

Lee Richardson* "Better get some sleep! Got to be up in 4 hours for more play off action in Sweden tom"

Nigel Pearson* "at services on way home from Lakeside dude. M1 full of roadworks!!"

Niels Kristian Iversen* "Poor score from mé tonight. Dissapointed but fair play to the poole boys. They made it hard work. BUT its not over yet"

Lewis Bridger* "Gd result for Eagles at Lakeside, against a solid team, the whole team done there bit & we are looking good to Be in the final"

Lewis Bridger* "Shocked so many lakeside fans on the back straight swearing & shouting abuse every time I went in or out on track :-/ #whathappenedtotheuk?"

Nigel Pearson* "Enjoyed tonight's show, looks good for Poole v Eastbourne play-off final. Chris Holder & Darcy Ward the new Hamill and Hancock!"

Lewis Bridger* "Makes me laugh these people follow me to knock me down so what do I do ? Block them thank you Twitter for that option"

Nigel Pearson* "Lets hope cllubs are allowed more than one rider over 8-pts next year!"

Nigel Pearson* "Had a panic attack during show, wife rang and I thought she was in labour!! Told her never to ring me at work! #falsealarm"

20th September

Jon Cook "Eastbourne have it all to lose but we are determined to rise to the occasion and give them an uncomfortable night next week at their Arlington Stadium. They showed why they are the only team to have won at our Raceway this season when they beat us back on Good Friday and we need to take a leaf out of their book and keep last places to an absolute minimum. We can look at a few heats and blame misfortune for not holding a better lead or we can knuckle down and put on a real show, and it's the latter that we will do next Monday."

Fredrik Lindgren* "Sometimes you just have to take things in your own hands?!?"

Paul Burbidge* "Darcy, I need a quick chat. Please can you give me a call, or tweet back when you're free if you don't have the number"

Mads Korneliussen* "A win is a win. I do think we King's Lynn Stars can go to the final, big job ahead at poole but we can do it"

Nicolai Klindt* "all right to look through your followers once in a while. some very interesting people coming up"

David Watt* "Darcy Ward Most people only use 10% of their brain, & you use 10% of that"

Dakota North* "Miserable day"

Chris Durno "The refs collect more than anyone else for the SRBF through the fines"

Lee Richardson* "Tough day today. Burnt out 2 clutches! Problems with springs but hey story of my season! At least we made it through ;) some tough racing!!"

Scott Nicholls* "Seems that Kelvin's back! Well the cockhead pretending to be him. Block this sad individual people"

21st September

Nicolai Klindt* "stopped at ricky klings house last night and just woke up. will the breakfast table be ready in a bit? i hope so! #putthecoffeeon"

Olly Allen* "Now planning for Birmingham Thursday, Grudziadz Sunday, and Poole Monday. By my standards this year that's a busy week!! #loveit"

Scott Nicholls* "Just had a lady at stansted tell me I look like someone they know,I was a tad confused,then she said he's hot.made my day....then she said.. But he is old! Went from sky high to devoed in a flash!"

Lewis Bridger* "Who's is keen to come to Croation GP with me ;) come on everybody is waiting, & I would love to get some rays fri-sun #spectatorforliving"

Coventry speedway It is with great regret that Coventry Speedway wish to announce that they will not be operating speedway in 2012 under the current management. Coventry Racing Club cannot condone the manner in which the sport is run and as a result it feels that it is in the best interests of all parties if the club seeks a new owner to take Coventry Speedway forward into the future. The club now invites interested parties on a full acquisition of Coventry speedway or a season by season lease to contact Allen Trump or Jeremy Heaver to take the matter further.

Mark Lemon* "Ham, cheese & tomato toasted sandwich. Totally under-rated... mmm"

Alun John Rossiter* "Coventry Speedway up for sale!!"
Chris Holder* "ha ha who wants them?"

Moira Perrott "With Birmingham and Swindon already up for sale who's going to want to buy Coventry, especially when Sandhu remains the stadium landlord? They've had a year's grace but it's been a crappy team with riders not turning up and everything. They say to buy Birmingham it's £170,000. You'd have to be a very rich man to think about doing that"

Steve Shovlar "We don't need clubs to vanish we want more clubs in the sport. I certainly wldn't want clubs like Coventry to be turned into a housing estate. A feeder PL club for Poole perhaps but certainly not close"

Philip Rising "Trump has no financial stake in Coventry. Sandhu owns both the stadium and the speedway rights and is willing to sell the latter. As stated on the BSF previously, Trump is the mouthpiece for Sandhu but does not pull the strings"

Paul Burbidge* "Chris Holder admits a more organised approach to his racing this year has made a huge difference"

Nicki Glanz* "Nearly at Vojens shite weather"

David Watt* "Dang !! Gollob nearly flipped it while trying to kick Pepe and went from first to last !! Hahaha #dirty"

Paul Burbidge* "Jan O Pedersen made Danish league comeback for Vojens scoring 1 from 3 rides. He's set for 2012 contract"

Dakota North* "Broken collar bone"
Sam Masters* "been trying to ring you man wanna come see ya?? Call me when I get a chance"
Dakota North* "no service bro!"
Sam Masters* "faaark man angry Track not fun tonight needs sorting and seeing 2 team mates Dakota North & Cory Gathercole get injured bad night for us!!"

22nd September

Nicki Glanz* "Going to doctors today!!!"

Cory Gathercole* "Luckily all in one piece after last night nothing broken we don't think just a very sore back and leg"

Niels Kristian Iversen* "Just Got out of bed. Hate the feeling next day after a shit meeting. Going for a long ride on the Trek now to clear the head"

Dakota North* "Collarbone and shoulder are pretty average This morning"

David Watt* "What a great day ! speedwaylife BOOM! and my twitter is full of thongThursday"
Chris Holder* "wat u all excited about!? Am I missing something here..??"

Paul Burbidge* "Trundling through Hungarian countryside en route to Gorican for Croatian sgp. Gorgeous weather. Let's hope it stays that way this year!"

Nigel Pearson* "Great news for speedway fans - Sky Sports showing Croation sgp FREE this Saturday. HD4 from 6pm then on red button at 7pm. All FREE!"
Nicolai Klindt* "isn't it always free if you got sky or am i thick here?"

David Watt* "Everyone wants something more. WTF ??"

Jonathan Barber "Personally I thought your tweet to Mike Bennett was a little harsh. We all know what he's like but for fans to abuse him for bigging up Holder and Darcy - he is an ex-King's Lynn rider - who won three quarters of the races between them, is wrong. I disagree with Bennett on so many things but, at the end of the day, he is very professional with the job he does. In your books, you take the mickey but it's subtle and funny – this wasn't. You should apologise."

Paul Burbidge* "Bored! Been plodding through Hungary for three hours in minibus and we're still 15km from Croatia"

Nicki Glanz* "Going to take my Van for a service now"

Tai Woffinden* "Get the keys to ma new crib next week #hooray"

Chris Holder* "yewwww"

Jo Lowry* "feels strange to not be going tonight...... Damn you Graeme Drury!"

Chris Holder* "I rate gatwick shits on Stansted and Luton"

Cameron Woodward* "totally agree man. Hey have a great one Saturday mate"

Avtar Sandhu "Further to the numerous e-mails I have received since yesterday regarding my decision to sell the Coventry Bees I felt it only right to clarify my position.

I have had a fantastic time owning the Coventry Bees it has become an all consuming passion to do what is best for the club and that will continue long after my decision to sell or lease the promoting rights. The simple truth is that I can no longer work with the administrators at the BSPA as communication has broken down and this has made the running of the club almost impossible to do for this reason I felt it is in the best interests of all parties if the club seeks a new promoter/owner to take Coventry Speedway forward into the future. Coventry Bees needs and deserves an owner who will continue to strive for trophies and league championships which needs good communication and relationships to be in place. With no prospect of these improving my focus has turned to finding the right person or persons to make that happen so I can start to enjoy watching the Bees rather than being filled with dread as to what others will do next. As far as I am concerned all the talk of the club closing its doors to speedway is not correct all I wish to do is sell the club so it can continue to grow & prosper. In fact the statement has been made now to give maximum amount of time for potential buyers to come forward and to stop speculation about what I may or may not do with the team. We have received several enquires already and rest assured these will be looked at in detail to see if they are suitable to own the club over and above commercial concerns as the club needs a passionate owner if it is to keep lifting trophies. Please continue to keep the faith as you should know after all this time that I will do the best I can for the Club and I like you want to watch speedway at Coventry Stadium next year but as a fan rather than owner."

Nicolai Klindt* "not bad with free wifi at the ukraine border"

Cameron Woodward* "quality. How long did you have to sit there and how man euros did they have off ya?"

Nicolai Klindt* "one and a half hour so wasn't that bad. ricky showed of with a bit of russian so we got through like we was superstars"

Steve Shovlar "You seem to think that the BSPA have had it in for Coventry for years. That is just not true. Other clubs play by the rules and accept decisions made at the AGM. Coventry with their current promotion don't, and its the cause of most of the problems. A fresh new promotion at Coventry would work wonders. Looks what Poole had to put up with a few years ago. Rule changes made mid season to make sure they couldn't make the playoffs, by reducing the amount of teams participating in them."

Tai Woffinden* "10 tonight happy with that fram smashed my night nut so dident do the last race haha in pain!!!!"

Rory Schlein* "yeah bit fun some pocket money but I'd like the [Swindon] track widening if possible as we were a little to wide in that last one"

Scott Nicholls* "yeah u can only go as far as the fence! Kinda get in trouble if u try to go any wider!"

Rory Schlein* "I no I did get into a little bit of trouble for a split second"

Scott Nicholls* "that's what makes it fun. Just not for ya good lady when she goes to wash ya pants!"

Rory Schlein* "well we both have a thing to fight with the Russians"

23rd September

David Parker "In regards to the information on the Polish web site, i can 100% confirm that 99% is in fact not true. As one of Leigh and Kylies good friends, i can confirm the following : Leigh never broke an arm or leg, yes he had numerous broken ribs and a broken scapula (shoulder) but they have mended quite well and in fact, his older injury that he got from racing Speedway gave him more trouble, but that too has been fixed thru physio. He has movement very well in his left leg, but his right is a little lazy, but that is how his left one was about 6 weeks ago. He has sat for and got his drivers licence and i will be delivering his new car to him tomorrow. Leigh and Kylie, as all of us, are very positive and every day he is improving along the long road to recovery. He went to watch a junior Speedway meeting two weeks ago in his home town Mildura, some 5 hours away and went to a motorcross meeting at Gillman last weekend. So in saying all that, please do not take too much notice of the article printed on the Polish web site. In fact, do not take any notice of it. Leigh is Leigh and besides in a wheelchair for a little while longer, you would not know he has anything wrong with him. Keep the 'hope is LARge' going"

Charlie Webster* "Late night film wide awake...watched 'attack the block' definitely recommend funny, gripping but meaning behind comes through strong"

Lewis Bridger* "In bed now need some ZZZZ got a big few days coming up with the SGP in croatia where I will be on top form ;) 9pt/4h with a ef at Swindon"

Mads Korneliussen* "Is up and about [07.00], need to clean 6 filters"

Alun John Rossiter* "Up early [07.20] feeling better this morning missed brum last night good job done by the boys !!"

David Howe* "#fridaywashclub open [07.20]"

Nicki Glanz* "Is in the workshop [07.30] Guns and Roses flat out"

Olly Allen* "where was my old pal last night? I excepted less money coz I thought I'd be under your wing again!"

Alun John Rossiter* "sorry mate under the whether you did ok thou ?"

Olly Allen* "yeah it wasn't too bad...pulled out a couple of traps!"

Alun John Rossiter* "still good pocket money thou"

BSPA SUPPORTERS are in for a treat this weekend as they will be able to watch the Croatian Grand Prix on Sky Sports free-of-charge. The action gets underway on Sky Sports HD4 at 6pm and will go on the red button at 7pm - and it's all free-to-air for non Sky Sports subscribers.

Flagrag "I am very sorry to say that all the coverage is being downscaled to SD as there are no HD studios available to use can't wait until all the new HD studios are handed over for use so can finally do away with SD coverage due to lack studio capacity. With free weekend offer on and both Real Madrid and Barcelona playing Saturday night Speedway was always going get pushed to red button and SD coverage"

Nigel Pearson* "And so today's journey begins - Manchester - Frankfurt - Zagreb for Croatian sgp"

Rory Schlein* "Great to see the Lib Dems working hard on what wrong with this country banning page 3. You tossers bring back maggi"

Lewis Bridger* "Loved it at Swindon last night, man I was on the gassss enjoying my time on track so much !! #suchagreatfeeling"

Nicolai Klindt* "finally in ukraine. it's pretty cool it's £1 to 10 ruples or what the money are called"

Kenni Larsen* "The money is called Hrivna"

Alan Boon "Heard some talk in the last week that the BSPA intend to "sell off" Team GB next season, absolving responsibility, and giving commercial rights, to a 3rd party, such as GoSpeed or BSI. Is this something you'd support? Personally I consider a national representative side above such commercial concerns, and the reluctance to support it may speak volumes about the state of British speedway. I can see positives, too, don't get me wrong, but if the BSPA wants to run speedway in this country, it needs to run ALL of it..."

Arnie Gibbons "Surely this is nothing to do with the BSPA. Unless I've missed something the ACU remains the controlling body for British involvement in international speedway. The BSPA runs speedway in Britain at its member tracks. I do not see how the BSPA can decide not to enter the World Cup as it is the ACU that make the nominations."

Linus Sundstrom* "Next meeting for me is next sunday, so have more then 1 week off! Still flatout with everything outside speedway #loveit #lovemylife"

Nigel Pearson* "Delayed flight from Manchester so we miss connection in Frankfurt. Not happy. Jan Staechamnn looks a man not to argue with!! Long day ahead"

Lewis Bridger* "Take off.. here we goo Easyjet Bang ! SGP Croatia"

Nigel Pearson* "Fair play to Jan Staechmann used his card to get us in business lounge in Frankurt"

Nigel Pearson* "How very posh! (But no Guinness!)"

Ulrich Ostergaard* "Sitting eating chocolate weetabix :-) it's fun to sit and watch the mechanic do all the work"

Derek Barclay "For in doing progs for a couple of the 'away' tracks I've been mindful all year of following this protocol set - let us remember - by the new clubs concerned.. In my personal opinion it would've been far more sensible to call the team Scunthorpe/Sheffield (or, er, Sheffield/ Scunthorpe) from the outset, but it was their own decision not anyone elses and they have that right...: it's their 'buiness(es)...I guess the logic then follows this into the play-offs where as the semi home leg's at Owlerton the away leg is branded as vs. Sheffield and then if they make the Final a similar approach would be taken; but surely at this juncture common sense (sadly lacking all year so far...) should prevail and they need to go with Sheffield/Scunthorpe (or vice versa). Next year how about trying a 'neutral' name to avoid this...?"

Nicolai Klindt* "sitting at blues jazz bar and restaurant in rivne or rowne. don't know what the place is called tbh. waiting for food!"

Tai Woffinden* "On the way to cov big thanks to josh auty for giving me a lift"

Rory Schlein* "Live band at Brandon tonight there going out with a bang ha ha if you don't like heavy metal don't think u will like them"

Nigel Pearson* "Finally arrived in Gorican after 6 hours in Frankfurt. This sgp better be good!! Stek and Nicki P raving about iphone 5... Out of my league"

Carl Wilkinson "Heat 13 was the same, I made a bit of a ripper at the start but he pulled it back and unfortunately it's the same old thing, you can never do it twice and I ended up at the back in that one behind two very experienced heat leaders."

Mike Hunter "Edinburgh's gating is often poor but in this match it plumbed the depths – or maybe the Rebels gated like rockets."

24th September

Dick Barrie "Firstly Newport, when we will discover if a certain gentleman is truly unable to ride around Shielfield Park effectively (or if he is merely a liar and a cheat)"

Chris Louis "[Malcolm Vasey] appears to be suggesting that some young Aussie riders' averages have been assessed way below their true value, and that it is affecting the integrity of the NL. Whether he'd admit it or not he can only be referring to Mildenhall and Cameron Heeps. Of course everyone, including officials like Mr. Vasey, are entitled to their opinion. I just don't think a public forum [the BSF] is the right place for a licensed club official to express those views. Some would say that having an established Premier League standard rider like Simon Lambert as your No. 1 in the National League is questionable if we are talking about league integrity. So maybe that should be looked at as well."

David Watt* "Let's start this big rig up WizzAir and get moving. I'm bored already and want to go ride my bike. I'm having withdrawals !!!"

Dick Barrie "The speech made by Alex Harkess last week regarding the Premier League's, and the whole BSPA's willingness to rally around clubs who are acting positively in addressing safety concerns was a crystal-clear warning to those who believe speedway can run on and on without changes"

Nigel Pearson* "Can't believe we're almost at the end of the sgp season. Flown by"

Jason Lyons "I've had a few breaks and sprains in my career but this one is really painful. I'm on pain-killers all the time. I've done a few collarbones and fingers and toes and broke my back twice, once in Australia and once in Birmingham – that's more of a burning sensation that slowly goes away and you can live with it – but this leg is really crippling."

Nicki Glanz* "Bee Gees flat out in workshop while packing van for Big derby today #UniaOutrup"

Dick Barrie "The 'rolling averages' as they are called, creating a calculated average score for every rider – and thus allowing team line-ups to be constructed and, when required, changed – were a good idea. A very good idea. Gone at a stroke were the possibilities which allowed cynical clubs to manipulate their riders' scores over a single match (eg: Glasgow at Edinburgh, June 4th, 2010 – a date which will live in infamy)"

Rory Schlein* "15 points for the bees last night and the midland cup track was very slick but we seem to get it dialled in"

Jason Lyons "I've no worries about racing again – my bikes are ready to go. I hobble out to the shed and look at the bikes and am just gutted because I can't ride the damn things! As soon as I'm fit, I'll be up and running, no problems!"

Tai Woffinden* "4 points last night just wasent feeling it!"

Rory Schlein* "slick as shit and was surprised with ya exclusion ha ha #wired"

Dick Barrie "The other major change in our league was the dropping of the old early-season Premier Trophy in favour of a full league programme – but unfortunately, with fourteen teams this meant the now-much-maligned 'phase two' fixtures after a late summer SPL-style split. Good idea, but with hindsight badly administered"

Fredrik Lindgren* "Checking out of our hotel in Croatia going to the track!"

Rory Schlein* "Got a week off now will get the motors looked at before the KOP. Also would like to say sorry to the people at Berwick speedway that I can't ride there tonight 3 meetings on the trot is to much for the Shoulder and hand hope ya get a good turn out it for a food cause a air fence somthing all speedway tracks should have EL,PL,NL"

Nigel Pearson* "Glorious sunshine here in Croatia and a good forecast. Can Greg Hancock take the world title tonight? Won here last year! Needs 18-pts"

Adam Roynon* "Hope the weather in Leicester is better than in Cumbria.. It's pissin down!"

Nigel Pearson* "its boiling hot in Croatia if that's any use pal! Goodniiiiiiight #ommerumroynon"

Adam Roynon* "Thanks, very helpful! Havvy and me are going to watch the action tonight in the pits on my phone! Goodniight"

Lewis Bridger* "gd night last night see some faces I haven't seen in a while just had a huge pizza and OJ should sought me out then of to SGP #bangtidy"

Tai Woffinden* "just got a house in sheffield so got a project to do"

Dakota North* "Wouldn't mind being home I see the weather is bad ass!"

Dick Barrie "My ideal concept would be that we somehow increase the Premier League with two more teams. Remember there would have been sixteen teams this year if the Elite League hadn't commandeered/lured/bribed King's Lynn and Birmingham across the divide at a time they were running scared of Coventry and Peterborough's eventually-proved-to-be-empty threats to withdraw."

Dakota North* "Going to the office"

Alun John Rossiter* "few beers on the card tonight mate BOOM"

Greg Hancock* "The heart is racing, the blood is pumping and this is The Story of My Life!! Let's go racing!! #letsdothisthing"

Rory Schlein* "This GP is hard to pick Greg with an injury gollob off the pace crumpy up and down but I'm gonna say a win For holder gating well lately"

Paul Burbidge* "Lame attempt to get a re-run there by Nicki Pedersen in heat 6. Rightly excluded by referee Craig Ackroyd"

Rory Schlein* "My little girl roxy loves Chris Holder and wanted to know why he didn't win she only 3"

Nicolai Klindt* "want to get out of here asap just after we have had this meal here at bbq sports bar. a tough meeting for me 7pts/9plc #whatabummer"

Dakota North*   "Having a few stella's at the office watching the gp #stopit"

Andy Povey*   "Briiliant Greg Hancock 2011 World Champion - well deserved!!"

Lewis Bridger*   "Final time :))) come on Harris get stuck in #makeithappen"

David Watt*   "Stoked for Greg Hancock to now be called the world champ ! Again ! Congrats man. I'm sure everyone in the speedway world is happy for you"

Robert Bamford   "I reckon I'm just about at the end of the road now with my speedway career. My mind is made up, Jeff, I need to get away from the sport. Sorry to sound so defeatist, but speedway has increasingly become an absolute joke in recent years (as you know). I've had it with speedway, mate. It has gotten increasingly worse for a number of years now. I can remember taking Dave Wall to speedway in Scotland in the mid-90s and we agreed at the time that it could only go on for another 5 years. We were both wrong, but it hasn't exactly covered itself in glory - more lurched along from crisis to crisis!"

Nigel Pearson*   "Further sgp thoughts: Freddie and Bomber put themselves in frame for 2012 spots, AJ v Jarek for silver. Greg a remarkable story!"

  Sam Masters*   "need boots ;)"

  Niels Kristian Iversen*   "how many man ??"

  Sam Masters*   "just 1 for each foot haha, how many you got bro?? And how much??"

  Niels Kristian Iversen*   "i will tjek what i got thats not to fucked. About fifty quid. Well done yesterday man, thats was brilliant"

  Dakota North*   "some one should buy them boots thats a bargain guys! these sort of deals just dont last"

Derek Turner   "The [Stoke v Newport] meeting started nearly an hour late after some of the riders, officials and the paramedic were delayed after a serious accident on the northbound M6"

Nicky Mallett   "I wasn't at the meeting [at Stoke], but I am told young Lloyd [Barrett] did okay and his family can be proud of him. Making your club debut can be the most daunting of experiences and one which I am sure Lloyd is glad is now out of the way."

25th September

Greg Hancock*   "Thanks to everyone for all the freakin great messages before and after the event. Oh what a feelin. Gotta sleep on the Sprinter hotel now"

Nigel Pearson*   "On the dead heat question - yes of course you can call a dead heat, but there is an unwritten rule that you shouldn't! Laptops dont like it"

Paul Burbidge*   "It would have been quicker to walk to Budapest than take the minibus ride we had to ensure. Off to bed now. Airport at 6.30am. Joke"

Olly Allen*   "At stansted waiting for flight to poland...it's a little early for my liking redeye"

Paul Burbidge*   "You know you fly too much when you start recognising British Airways cabin crew"

Nicki Glanz* [at 09.00]   "Watching eastenders drama"

Nigel Pearson*   "Landed in Amsterdam, time for a quick Starbucks with Jan Staechmann and then Manchester bound. Poole tomorrow!"

Fredrik Lindgren*   "On my way to Örebro in my van am somewhere in Germany, Gorican-Örebro it's a long way! Was in huge pain this night, it's up & down my back"

Nigel Pearson*   "Won't be at Sheffield for PLRC as I need to spend time with family later. Good luck to all the riders - a great occasion at a top venue"

BSPA   GREG Hancock (41) has become the oldest World Champion in speedway history after clinching the title with fourth place in Saturday's Croatian Grand Prix

Jan Staechmann*   "Thanks to Greg Hancock for once again, proving that nice guys do win. Awesome bro, happy for you. World Champ 2011"

Niels Kristian Iversen*   "Congrats Greg Hancock on the WC. Deep respect man, You're a true inspiration. When im getting old, i wanna be just Like you haha ;) ;)"

Lewis Bridger* "Awesome weather today in Croatia on my way to Zagreb for food then airport"

Paul Burbidge* "Just found a huge gash in the side of my suitcase on arrival at Heathrow. Had a polite word with BA and it looks like they're replacing it"

Alun John Rossiter* "hey dak good fun light weight laugh"

Dakota North* "Think I over did it last night #soreshoulder"

Alun John Rossiter* "ha ha dak you are funny !!"

Rene Bach* "Good luck tonight mate! Get that bike out in that dirt!!"

Mark Lemon* "Cheers Bro, will be letting it hang out even if it means getting a nose bleed! Hope your leg is getting stronger & taking it easy"

Ludvig Lindgren* "anyone wanna take me to stansted from wolves? :D"

Bob Tasker* "Working on a feature entitled 'Parks at the PLRC'... c'mon, let's have the right ending, y'know it makes sense ;-)"

Hans Andersen* "What the F... Is going on #notfeelinggood #nothappy #notcool spent lots and is getting mé nowhere ahhhhhrrrrr angry"

Mads Korneliussen* "The man at passport control said, where have i seen you before??? I said maybe here???? #famous"

Tail Woffinden* "where u at today bro?"

Darcy Ward* "wattys joint bra shit hole #rough"

Rory Schlein* "your the best in the PL a the man"

Sam Masters* "thanks brother"

Mads Korneliussen* "you are the man.. Well done, so happy for you"

Chris Holder* "premier league riders champ! Good stuff bro yeewwww"

Adam Roynon* "Well Done bro! Awesome Job!!! #hero #hooray"

Sam Masters* "cannot believe it PLRC winning"

Phil Morris "Anybody who thinks we don't have talent in the British ranks needs to think again when you consider that the top three riders in the 500cc [British Youth Championship] were faster than over half of the National League meeting times the night before at the same [Stoke] venue."

Fredrik Lindgren* "Wow, how nice does it feel to come home after a 24h drive? #verynice"

Malcolm Vasey "Things boiled over at one stage in what was a very tense first leg"

Scott Nicholls* "got an idea from the sweedway man.if all my followers sponsored me £10 I'd have £36k to set up for 2012!Think better get a papal set up!... I could also then donate like £1500 every year to a charity of my Twitter followers choice. Looks like I best get this papal set up! Already some very worthy charities mentioned"

Gary Patchett* "sweedway!! Papal?? Looking for divine intervention Scotty?"

Nigel Pearson* "So it looks like the FTSEE 100 could dip below 5000 tomorrow - bad news. Not just Greece's fault #lookclosertohome"

Mads Korneliussen* "In the plane I was sitting next to a girl with a FAKE hand. WTF"

26th September

Sam Masters* "Junction to my house closed!! Faaaark nothing worse than half hour on the trip this time at night!! roadworks"

Niels Kristian Iversen* "Got pretty small eyes right now.. Not a fan of 6am flights #grumpy"

Nicolai Klindt* "just arrived to sweden. now off to a maccy breakfast #earlymornings speedway life"

David Howe* "Longtrack GP rider 2012 get in!"

Scott Nicholls* "Lovely day in Luton.....NOT!"

Nigel Pearson* "Poole by 12, Eastbourne by 10"

Niels Kristian Iversen* "In a taxi from Luton to Stansted to pick up my car. Thats what you get for travel with an engine what ryanair wont alou on their planes"

Mark Lemon* "Think I might start from a fresh page today!"

Fredrik Lindgren* "Going to my Physio Therapist again today which seems to be needed as my back has gone worse again! #NoPainNoGain #livingthe life"

Hans Andersen* "well done champ done yourself proud this season boy #onthegas"

Sam Masters* "thanks heaps man you wouldn't believe it 1st meeting with your bike ;) #needanotherone cheers mate"

Hans Andersen* "really..... No worries i've Got two sat In uk just need to ride Them friday 7th"

Hans Andersen* "Sat In Gdansk waiting to get our passports back (visa) Russia bound next week :) Will be interesting but good fun"

Lewis Bridger* "Yo man wats happening ?my air filters have all falling apart with new oil for foam filters what do you use on them ? Red isn't it ?"

Nicolai Klindt* "fallen apart? that's strange man. i use twin air filter oil and mix it with a bit of fuel"

Lewis Bridger* "yea it's new swaff rock oil product the twin layer just fallen apart :-/ like no-toil ill go buy some oil spray down to x2 filters"

Nicolai Klindt* "that's propa strange! i have used pj1 filter spray that's good"

David Watt* "Sorry Poole speedway fans but after 2 races yesterday I knew it wasn't good. I really want to race but my shoulder isn't as determined as me"

Mads Korneliussen* [en route to Poole] "Now the road is closed,, thinking is this Matt fords work"

Jo Lowry* "Think I speak for most of the speedway community when I say best of luck to King's Lynn Stars tonight"

Niels Kristian Iversen* "Just woke up in my car on a services somewhere on M3. Its time to get going and make things happen. Tough night ahead"

Sam Masters* "Brand new JRM complete bike for sale #fastasfuck"

Nigel Pearson* "Another day, another hotel - nice sea view in Bournemouth, perfect chillout for Poole tonight! #letsdothis"

Charlie Webster* "Davey Watt not riding tonight, 2 rides last night in Poland 4 points ... R/R for Poole. Does this give Stars a better chance? Not so sure"

David Watt* "no chance !!"

Charlie Webster* "Just had a nice little chat with the most famous person here [Poole] tonight ... Gordon the Tramp ... and the sun is shining"

Linus Sundstrom* "When its less speedway im more busy, strange! Swedish tv is sending playoff semi from uk tonight, wish i was in it racing. Maybe next year!"

Tony Thompson "I think he's aged about three or four hours this year! He needs to get a fukn brain and he'll be alright"

Fredrik Lindgren* "Didn't know Swedish TV10 are showing UK Elite League semifinals live tonight starts in 15 min! Shame I can't watch it"

Nick Barber "Steve Girdwood's got all four [EL] play-off tracks so he don't care who wins. I even saw him smile earlier"

Mike Bennett* "Racing not the best from either track so far? speedway play offs should be better than this!"

Paul Burbidge* "Sam Masters is flying for King's Lynn, but otherwise it's a procession for the Pirates. THJ and Andersson look great despite injuries"

Nigel Pearson* "Ward and Masters, superb! #lovingit"

Jo Lowry* "Safe to say King's Lynn Stars were clearly beaten before they got to the track. Poor attitude by SOME of their riders tonight #givinguptooeasy"

Nigel Pearson* "How did Holder and Andersson do that? Made NKI look ordinary!!"

Nicolai Klindt* "NKI IS ONLY ORDINARY!"

Nigel Pearson* "Get out of here Nic!!!"

Nicolai Klindt* "I'm on my way. people don't like me taking the piss on this site. you should work instead of being on twitter tho!"

Mike Bennett* "There are occasions when its best to say nothing - this is one of those occasions! speedway season heading to a close :-("

Nigel Pearson* "Wonderful Ward does it again!! What a rider!"

Mike Bennett* "This would be slightly more bearable if the racing was any good. Crap track preparation at both meetings ! Boring speedway play offs"

Nigel Pearson* "As always, Kelv and I call it as we see it. Ward 3 wins out of 3, enough said!"

Mike Bennett* "FF SAKE MILLARD make your mind up Yung or Lung?? Its pronounced Young- when in doubt ask the team manager and yes, I could do better!"

Jo Lowry* "Tonight's speedway = BORING"

Nigel Pearson "Ward is looking over his shoulder with great maturity"

Kevin Long* "Please Kelvin, don't use the phrase 'Bucks himself off!'. Its just one slip of the tongue from commentary disaster!"

Nigel Pearson* "Pirates awesome here, fair play Lakeside having a real go at Eastbourne! Poole look unstoppable to me!"

David Howe* "If ward was shepherding the German home does that make him a German shepherd?"

Rory Schlein* "Mear and masters riders of the night for me showed some bottle and fight"

Mike Bennett* "Darky and Chris Holder- simply awesome ! No doubt I'll be slated for saying that but its true! Only one 8 point plus rider per team in 2012?"

Nigel Pearson* "Well, Ward/Holder/Poole haters - reaction to Heat 13?"

Mike Bennett* "Totally agree with Rob Lyon about great season for the Stars back in the Elite League. Fans should be proud - even after tonight"

Fredrik Lindgren* "Watched the last heats of the EL playoffs. EL speedway is a great product great spectacle to watch! should be more spectators at the arenas!"

Mike Bennett* "OK peeps, that's the end of my speedway season for 2011. I kept the next 2 Mondays clear- just in case! :-) No plans for 2012 at this stage!"

Fredrik Lindgren* "And Sky Sports put on a very professional show when they produce the Elite League speedway!"

Nick Barber "If there's not a big crowd here [Arlington] next week for the [EL] final, speedway wants to worry!"

Lee Richardson* "That was a tough day! Pushed the eagles but not enough! Good luck in the final to all at Eastbourne speedway! Also a big Thankyou goes out to all the lakeside supporters who came tonight! And got behind us! Now to focus on the koc Friday ;)"

Lewis Bridger* "Didnt even feel it tonight & I killed it braaappppp #playoffsfinal fakkkkkyeaaaaaa"

Nigel Pearson* "Enjoyed the banter tonight, that's why we love the sport! Agree or disagree, that's what sport it all about - opinion. Thanks to you all!"

Steve Shovlar "One thing we need to do next Monday is get ur gating heads on. Track will be slick and the budgies will be set up to get out of the starts, with the added help of Uncle Bob and his tractor. We can win this. Have the faith. Woodward is a massive trump card at reserve but we have fire power elsewhere."

Trevor Geer "Bjarne [Pedersen] tried another bike out in Heat 15 and he looked really quick in that, so I hope that will do the business."

Alison Chalmers "At the pre-meeting parade, some of the Glasgow fans wore sunglasses and put up umbrellas."

27th September

Olly Allen* "just out of curiosity has Darcy learnt anymore big words?"

Chris Holder* "dude that's every week!!! Seen it so many times!!! Good experience for new comer's..."

Olly Allen* "I liked the amount of shit that watty got! Darky was on top form"

Chris Holder* "I'm was waiting for watty to flog him! Ding ding it's on!"

Nigel Pearson* "were we live in Sweden tonight guys? Loving it!"

Fredrik Lindgren* "Yea Scoop your voice could be heard live on Swedish TV tonight!"

Nigel Pearson* "so they didn't use Swedish commentary? I need an agent...!"

Charlie Webster* "Great action speedway Darcy's class looking forward to final. Eastbourne going to have to do some serious work home to have chance at Poole"

Nigel Pearson* "agree matey... Big night ahead at Eastbourne next Monday... Take it easy and see you there!"

Olly Allen* "you forgot to mention my excellent motivational skills!"

Tai Woffinden* "heat 13 fuckin killa aye yeeoooowwwwww"

Nicolai Klindt* "breakie at the hotel and then watching last part of 'loose change' - watxh it on youtube and see what really happened on 9/11 #insidejob"

Charlie Webster* "Morning skype phono to Asia TV,didn't realise I would be in vision bed head,wide eyed stare to look awake and Tony Cottee pops up on screen"

Fredrik Lindgren* "Why is Burger King called Hungry Jacks in Australia?"

David Watt* "and it's called 'Holden' in Aussie !! Dunno why. Stop asking weird questions and focus for tonight !!"

Nigel Pearson* "Two days off... And boy, do I need it"

Fredrik Lindgren* "Why is Opel called Vauxhall in UK?"

Fredrik Lindgren* "I'm going to do a Q&A session for 30 min! If you have a question for me I'll try and answer. Starting now!"

Nicolai Klindt* "how much will dackarna lose by tonight?"

Fredrik Lindgren* "I can't look into the future but if I was to do a qualified guess. Dackarna will beat Västervik tonight & Lindgren will beat Klindt"

Fredrik Lindgren* "At the moment I'm all Wolves but you can never say never & that new stadium is great news for Belle Vue & UK speedway"

Fredrik Lindgren* "I don't know but I would guess Poole Pirates"

Fredrik Lindgren* "I finished Swedish "Gymnasium" (Senior High School). At the age of 19 then became a pro speedway rider"

Fredrik Lindgren* "while racing speedway you do not need brakes that's why we do not have it"

Fredrik Lindgren* "At the moment I'd say no [to leaving Wolves] but you can never say never"

Fredrik Lindgren* "My Q&A time is over but I'll try and answer the questions that's already posted. I tried to answer the questions as good and fast as possible. If it was appreciated maybe I can do it again someday in the future."

Nicki Glanz* "Just stuffing a mcdonalds for the first Time in ages #feelbad"

Nicolai Klindt* "dont lie"

Nicki Glanz* "kfc man me"

David Howe* "Tough meeting for King's Lynn Stars shame they couldn't pull it off. Enjoyed my short stint there hope there's room for me next year"

Troy Batchelor* "Getting organised for Russia. Should I write my will now or not ? #awkward"

Paul Burbidge* "Harris thanked fellow Cornishman Mark Simmonds for lending the engine which powered him to second in Gorican"

David Watt* "Having a hard time dealing with incompetent people today ! Do your job ! Is that too much to ask ? #pleasehelpmeout"

Dakota North* "pretty hungry guys, driven to south port and back today"

Nigel Pearson* "Amazing, Saturday I was accused of biased Greg Hancock commentary and last night biased Darcy Ward - Truth? I love everyone!"

Alun John Rossiter* "Nigel heat 13 u couldn't be anything else top draw by the kray twins #fastasfuck"

Greg Hancock* "Why are you so biased toward everyone then?? Come on Scoop! You did buy the wife a new car too!"

Alun John Rossiter* "your a shit commentator i am a crap manger good job are bosses like us"

Nigel Pearson* "like it boy.... alriiiight!"

Linus Sundstrom* "After next week im going from #skiddingforaliving to #workingseventofiveforaliving! Prefer the skidding"

28th September

Darcy Ward* "your my hero herbie"

Darcy Ward* "shit I've been off twitter to long to reply to all but love xxx"

Greg Hancock* "Atta boy, its all about the love"

Alun John Rossiter* "hood to see you feeling the love at your young age"

Ludvig Lindgren* "thats why i might move up here Greg Hancock 1st and 2nd in the world atm is living up here so it must be something with the water! haha :D"

Greg Hancock* "You got it man but it's not the water! It's the chicks! #TOPNOTCH"

Dakota North* "Radio 1 is so shit!!"

Nicki Glanz* "Working hard unlike Luke Corbett fart arsing about in Sweden"

Nigel Pearson* "Ok I'm having car serviced, waiting in showroom so let's go for it - Q and A until 10.15am, anything"

Dakota North* "Think I woke up in a Different country the suns out?"

Chris Holder* "Business is done it's play time! Now where's that jetski... Oh there it is"

Dakota North* "Dont enjoy seeing holders tweets about having a jet ski, I'm stuck in side with a broken shoulder"

Rory Schlein* "I herd Darcy broke it"

BSPA BERWICK'S Bordernapolis handicap event on Saturday will feature Milen Manev – the first Bulgarian rider to appear at the venue

Lewis Bridger* "Looks like my Mechanic can't make Friday at Somerset :-/ looks like we need a sub in quick haha practice in the morning then"

Dakota North* "I bought a jawa engine haha never thought the day would come"

Nigel Pearson* "the shorts are on... now there's a treat for the ladies!"

Fredrik Lindgren* "At my dear old friends place in Västervik. Preparing lunch, moose killed by himself are going to be yummy #wildlunch"

Ulrich Ostergaard* "Nice swim with The kids This morning .Van now loaded and soon off to Grindsted for our last Danish meeting.. :-)"

Rory Schlein* "Workshop clean and tidy"

Troy Batchelor* "Bye bye uk hello Russia #russianplanesbadtrackrecord"

Hans Andersen* "Last meeting in sweden 2011 hope tonight Will have an happy ending so i Can recharge over the winter"

Chris Holder* "Awesome day on the water!!!!"

Mads Korneliussen* "just killed 82 mosquitoes, and for those who do not know, that is a lot of mosquitoes #hardwork"

Nigel Pearson* "Spent a few quid last week on winter clothes from North Face. Today I'm wearing shorts and flip-flops! #bizarreweather"

Fredrik Lindgren* "Sounds like bizarre in a good way?"

Nigel Pearson* "oh yes mate it's brilliant! See you in Gorzow pal #skiddingforaliving"

Paul Burbidge "Hancock would probably rather clean his bikes with his own toothbrush than sit and answer the endless procession of questions about how on earth he became the oldest world champion in speedway history at 41 years and 113 days old. But it is a talking point."

Niall Strudwick* "seems to be no commintor for the Swedish league tonight on prem sports :/"

Rene Bach* "Better get the van check before tomorrows long trip #rememberoil"

Lewis Bridger* "Bexhill gym is about to feel for force of the duo me & drew r going to be killing it #rippingitup"

Paul Burbidge "The reason the Piraterna star is still in fashion is because he sets the trends. After last Friday's practice session, he was talking helmet cams with BSI's TV gurus Steve Saint and Nik Merrutia. Herbie has one of his own. He uses it to assess what he is doing with the bike at certain times and whether he is taking the right lines on the track. No-one else has taken this step. He's even leading the way off the track. Hancock joined Twitter nine months before any of his SGP rivals. His account, @GregHancock45, has attracted a massive 5,300-plus followers."

Fredrik Lindgren* "Very good job by everybody in Dackarna over these last two playout meetings. Am very happy we can leave this nightmare season in a good way!"

Linus Sundstrom* "To busy for twitter nowdays, im absolutely flat out! Working at the tyre center tomorrow & Friday goodnight"

Fredrik Lindgren* "Me & AJ split and shared a Cloetta 'Kexchoklad' today after heat 10 to celebrate the secured Elitserien spot for 2012! #happydays"

29th September

Taylor Poole* "They chemical symbol for Potassium is 'K' #veryinteresting"

Nigel Pearson* "Early start today... sgp highlights show to be done in Farnham for IMG/ BSI - with Sudden Sam. Should be a belter!"

Tai Woffinden* "checked in to london luton airport"

Nigel Pearson* "where u heading to kidder? Niggle"

Tai Woffinden* "poland mate the driving to check for friday and back to polska sunday!"

Nigel Pearson* "have a good un see u at the Olympique"

Tai Woffinden* "sweet man thanks!"

Nigel Pearson* "Not a McDonalds fan but that sausage and egg Mcmuffin just hit the spot! #didthejob"

Mark Lemon* "Lets gets the shorts back out of the cupboard! #sunshine"

Troy Batchelor* "Just had the don't look for your team partner just win speech from the russians ha #highspeedskidding"

David Howe* "Sunny Redcar tonight, scunny fri, dry house sunday, kings lynn wed, and I thought season was slowing down"

Chris Holder* "Jus finished another session on the water! #gottaloveit"

Adam Roynon* "Cruising up the A1 listing to CapitalFM!"

Chris Holder* "Poole is really crankin up the heat this last few days!! That's why we live here! #smokinnnn"

Scott Nicholls* "Finally got round to giving blood for the first time! Hope many more do the same"

Nigel Pearson* "Another top sgp highlights show done and dusted"

Dakota North* "When the sun comes out here you see some shit tattoos on people"

Nicki Glanz* "Should i keep my sideburns ??? LetMeKnow"

Rory Schlein* "Down at the pub having a meal with the family can't belive the weather it's september and it's 30 deg WTF"

Lewis Bridger* "Practice went well 9 practice starts on all new clutches, cables etc.. Everything serviced :) #playoffs"

Troy Batchelor* "12 points in Russia . Now straight to airport 4 hours drive an straight to the plane nice!"

Tai Woffinden* "How good must it feel for Greg Hancock to put #GHWC2011 at the end of a tweet"

Niels Kristian Iversen* "Just had 2 hours of struggle in the Gym. #keepfit"

Tai Woffinden* "Just burnt my tounge on sum soup devo!!!"

Peter Johns* "End of season? No way, still tuning :)"

Cory Gathercole* "Just hit the course up today after a few weeks break. Still can't putt to save myself but the driver shoot straight"

David Watt* "Just found my headphones in the pocket if my shorts after they have been washed and they still work !! #dumbbutlucky I love continuous progress"

Nigel Pearson* "had a gentle reminder today about the industry I'm in - be very careful! Just when you think you know certain people....#knifeinback"

Tai Woffinden* "sounds like speedway"

Nigel Pearson* "absolutely correct young man! Got it in one!! More to the point, BRITISH Speedway!! #nomorerespect"

Tai Woffinden* "the sport is goin down hill in the uk shame to say"

Fredrik Lindgren* "Transformers doesn't disappoint, keep delivering. First Megan Fox now they shake up Rosie Huntingdon-Whiteley! Beautiful!"

Adam Roynon* "Got to the changing rooms to find this happened to my shoes.. Nice team mates! Lol. wankers #goodtimes"

Charlie Webster* "Ok I think I need to go home and have hot lemon...apologies for my bungedupness on SSN... was desperately trying to talk and breathe!"

Chris Holder* "yeh wat the Fuk Charlie!!?"

Charlie Webster* "eh watch it you...I blame you lot...started sneezing in the pits at Poole, was fine until then!"

Chris Holder* "oh bulsht!!! Hahaha! Don't blame it on me!"

30th September

Taylor Poole* "Everyone follow Jack Fulton Smith ! If we can get him to 250 followers, I will shave my hair off at the Ipswich 16 Lapper for Charity! :)"

Fredrik Lindgren* "I'm freaking amazing in bed! I can do it for hours and hours.. thats right... sleep! Or?!?"

Adam Roynon* "Oh yea.. Enjoyed tonight! Track was sic!! ..but pissed I blew another motor"

Darcy Ward* "Just found out Greg Hancock don't follow me feelin like I'm not in the wolfpack"

Rory Schlein* "you don't follow me either ya doosh bag"

Nigel Pearson* "wishing my Dad all the best for his eye op today. Not that he reads twitter but I know some of you know him"

Mark Lemon* "Birthday BBQ for wife, who would of thought!"

Rory Schlein* "But I got to say jordan Frampton said a classic this year. Track was loose as and he said 'you must be fucking joking' his face was classic"

Nicolai Klindt* "soup time #gottaloveit"

Rene Bach* "Sun is out in uk today!! Shades on, good tunes playing!! not a bad start!"

Alun John Rossiter* "People on this m6 clue less no wonder there's always crashes"

David Watt* "paying credit card bill hurts!! #gutted"

Fredrik Lindgren* "2nd place in most followers in my hometown Örebro"

Nicki Glanz* "On my way home from Copenhagen with Guns &Roses on full blast #bangtidy"

Fredrik Lindgren* "On my way to Stockholm were I'll spend the evening today as I fly out from Arlanda to Czech Republic tomorrow morning Golden Helmet"

Mark Lemon* "wish it could be like this all the time, it's mental!"

Lewis Bridger* "On my way down to Somerset all I'm saying is this is going to be funny stuff #mechanichasnoidea"

David Watt* "Workin up a sweat today on the BMX with my kids !! #lovemylittlemonkeys"

Taylor Poole* "Every1 UNFoLLoW Jack Fulton Smith. His a creep. I repeat UNFoLLoW him!#hescaresme"

Linus Sundstrom* "Just finished work, tired after only 2 days of "normal life" work"

Rory Schlein* "Sitting in the van sweating my ass off and every londener is going home go backto work still got half an hour left you doll bludgers"

Taylor Poole* "Wish I had super powers"

Nicki Glanz "Why dont Women drink beer Like us men All these fanzy drinks is killing mé"

Lewis Bridger* "Can't believe this traffic been on the road since 1pm Mrs Garmin reckons TOA 7:01 & we are stuck still on the M5"

Dakota North* "ha ha your running late"

Lewis Bridger* "fukkkkkkkkk bad times bro.. Bad times !! :-/"

Dakota North* "if you make it good luck boss! Get that 57 on and braaaaap"

Lewis Bridger* "cheers man nothing more we can do mechanic broke every speed limit & bus lane rule etc"

Lewis Bridger* "got 57 on her peach :)"

Adam Roynon* "On the way to the Bears mid/end of season dinner dance!"

Taylor Poole* "At KFC. Very few skinny ppl. #whatsthisworldcome2"

Lewis Bridger* "Had fun at the oak tree arena tonight :) 14pt/5h 1st. Fisher, 2nd. LBR 3rd. Bjarne, roll on the playoff finals"

Cory Gathercole* "Steady night at Somerset tonight bit off the pace but track was alot better so bonus there"

Jason Lyons "It was great to be voted [Bear of the Year] by the fans, especially as at the start of the year I could feel the knife in my back at times, but I must have won them over. I know I was close to getting the chop and if I had, I know I would have deserved it because I wasn't doing my job."

Richard Hollingsworth "I must say there is a feel good feeling around the place over the last few months. I think crowds have been a bit better over the second half of the season and maybe that is because confidence is building in the team. I know the weather has been a bit better and Julie Harrowven (Marketing Manager) is doing a great job attracting new supporters but we're now in the top half of the league and holding our own. That has only happened once before in the history of Scunthorpe Speedway at this level but with Rob (Godfrey, promoter) at the helm we are planning on it happening more and more. Sometimes things don't go to plan but we are building little by little for the future and although it's hard work it's also exciting to think how far we can get."

1st October

Tai Woffinden* "ESKA radio playin a bit of dance at 2am on a friday woop woop"

Adam Roynon* "Parmo power at 4am! That's the way forward :p"

David Watt* "Stuck in traffic on the way to Gatwick at 4:45 in the morning !! What is going on ?? I thought traffic was only for peak hours ??"

Jeff Scott* "ideal time to get out the wheelie bag?"

David Watt* "I'll be very surprised if I make this flight !! Ain't traffic a biatch !!! My scooterbag wheels will be on fire when I get to Gatwick !!!"

Jeff Scott* "time for wings on the scooterbag too?"

Hans Andersen* "Zzzz... Already ón the move, going to England for a bit to check ón mé house :) still standing Then its Russia ón Monday"

David Watt* "I'm sure this flight stewardess used to work as a prison guard !! #justnasty"

Fredrik Lindgren* "Meatballs with beetroot-jumble sandwich for breakfast #yummy"

Darcy Ward* "Under /21 today Gunna be hot hot hot !!! See how we go hopefully be good for a party afterwards"

Len Silver "I was astonished to read in your letters column of last week's issue a tirade from Stuart and Sue Towner, Friends of Speedway, Chessington who allege that promoters do not invest money into the junior riders of our sport and further suggest that 'the authorities' ignore this aspect of things."

Dakota North* "can't wait to get back to Aussie, not long now"

Sam Masters* "when's your flight bruzz?"

Dakota North* "31st but going to change it to next weekend I think i gotta get home ;)"

Taylor Poole* "BEWARE!!! Scott Nicholls dog has got flees. Dave is on the case to get rid of them ;)"

Scott Nicholls* "oh no! They can keep her for longer if they want :-)"

Gary Patchett We knew at the very start it was going to be an uphill battle when we got hit with injuries to Zengi and Simon plus the Polish silencer problems"

Gordon Pairman "Matt [Ford] has a knowledge of speedway that is second to none and what sometimes seems to others as maximising his advantages is simply knowing the rules better than anyone else around."

John Chaplin "You may scarcely believe this, but there used to be a time when England suffered – pardon me, enjoyed – an embarrassment of young talent. Now we are hard-pushed to assemble a World Cup side that will not embarrass Queen and country when matched against the rest of the speedway world"

Len Silver "While I, and other like minded promoters, will stage events for, and to help, youngsters, the great British public will not pay to watch them in large enough numbers for them to grow and prosper."

Olly Allen* "Just before I order at Starbucks, I practice what I'm going to say in my head so I sound like a pro"

Sam Masters* "Can't believe this weather loving it, be good for England dry the country out a bit"

Nicki Glanz* "At a 30th birthday party, and allready been on dancefloor #80sMuzakIsMyThing"

Hans Andersen* "Cant believe the weather in uk felt a bit stupid turning up this morning with My winter jacket but eh i need it in russia for sure..."

Gordon Pairman "I do have concerns about what seems to be an increasing lack of respect amongst promoters, and that can lead to anarchy."

Tyson Nelson "I was a bit wild at the start of the year but now I think I've got a bit better at team riding and looking for my team-mates."

John Campbell   "Up until the end of August our crowds were running at acceptable levels, higher than 2010, and not producing any real financial concerns for us. However, our attendance on September 2 was our lowest of the season and created a loss of approximately £4000. Last week, the attendance lifted a little but it did mean that three of our five lowest crowds of the season have been experienced in our last three meetings…maybe there is not sufficient interest in speedway here at Armadale. And that is the factor that is causing us most concern"

Rene Bach*   "Fuuck Berwick is a bit cold today!!!"

Fredrik Lindgren*   "'The Mullet' still going strong in Czecho! Never out of fashion!"

Alun John Rossiter*   "On Poole quay looking forward to a meal in the oriel garlic prawns"

Gordon Pairman   "People should realise British speedway without Matt [Ford] would be a much poorer place."

Sam Masters*   "Late notice guest booking at turbojet on way to workshop to put engine in at 12:30am"

Gordon Pairman   "Ah, the [independent body] cure all! This crops up as the answer to everything, but the definition is woolly."

Jason Attwood   "The news I got from the ambulance when they took [Jason Garrity] off the track was that he wanted to know if he was in Heat 14!"

Matthew Wethers   "I've been through the fence and it's not much fun."

Keith Denham   "I haven't been impressed with the attendances but this year has been unfortunate. I thought we had a dream team to start the season but it hasn't worked out that way and I have made some bad decisions which have come home to roost. I know people are disappointed with some of the things that have happened this year but I can't keep using the money I have to carry it on. There are a lot of really good people who have supported the club since 1999 but I can't just keep it going at my own cost."

Malcolm Simmons   "I can't see how they can call it the 'Elite' League because there are only a handful of good riders. The Swedish league puts it to shame and every Grand Prix rider rides in Sweden. It makes our league look silly. I know it was a different era, but we always had a solid one to seven. In terms of team strength, it is for the worse now. Some of the meetings are boring because some of the riders at the bottom end are totally outclassed. But the play-offs have been good and the GPs are absolutely brilliant. Poole are going to walk it and I don't think Eastbourne have got a chance. They are one those teams that are just not strong enough all the way through. As much as he is a good rider, Bjarne Pedersen is not in the same class as Darcy Ward or Chris Holder. He basically left Poole as a third heat leader and that is what he will come back as next week. They will walk all over him. They have got the world long track champion [Kylmakorpi] but that is where he is best. He is not a superb speedway rider. Lewis Bridger is just all talk and he doesn't ever put it to use. He might win a race but he will run three lasts to back it up."

2nd October

Taylor Poole*   "We like to follow Taylor cause Taylor is our mate. He has a massive Twitter account and wants to make it great. RT this"

Chris Holder*   "go back to bed TP"

Sam Masters*   "Roger that this kid does my head in!!"

Casper Wortmann*   "Leaving Prag airport now. On my way to Pardubice"

Fredrik Lindgren*   "Amazing weather in Pardubice again today. Yesterday I saw the helmet today I want to bring it home!"

Dakota North*   "Arm is stinging like a bitch"

David Watt*   "So one of the hardest things to do today will be to pick the winner of the best mullet !! Difficult task as so many to choose from !! #1982"

Nicki Glanz*   "Busy doing nothing #SunOut"

Jerran Hart*   "Farrrrk this weather is on another level not feeling it at all ! Bring the winter back quickkkk !!"

Steve Shovlar "Most Poole fans drive themselves as households down here have their own cars"

Cory Gathercole* "Just finished a mad session on the pit bikes . Awsome fun . Stuck in traffic on the m4 . Sucks!"

Fredrik Lindgren* "It all went to hell today! Knocked out already in the QuarterFinals! #Nothappy #GoldenHelmet"

Nicki Glanz* "Online poker #letswinsomemoney"

David Watt* "Had a decent day. Feelin sore but will be all good for tomorrow. Pumped for the finals #budgiebashingtime"

Scott Nicholls* "Well that was a mixed day! 6 races,2 bike failures,10 points & broke the track record,but felt slow! Had it all today"

Timo Lahti "Other guys started [National Service] on Monday but I called them and told them I had to be in England [for EL Grand Final]. I got into a sports group in the army, where you have all the top sports boys from Finland."

Chris Holder* "jus seen the big right [Batchelor] leg into the side of dudek!!! #lovingit hahaha"
Scott Nicholls* "yeah like that. He's been watching too many gollob dvd's!"

Tai Woffinden* "Can we make 200 on spot pub page Damy rade 200 klikniec lubie to dla sport pub"

Nigel Pearson* "Back home from Bolton about to settle down for the night before journey to Eastbourne. Just filled car up, £90 - madness!! #ripoffbritain"

Fredrik Lindgren* "Brawo Falubaz Mistrz Polski! Gratulacje! ekstraliga"

Gary Havelock* "Jayne is being a bitch again!!! Made me fetch my own beer from the fridge"

Nicolai Klindt* "what a weekend this have been... hope it all changes from tomorrow! #cantlivelikethis"

Derek Barclay "No I'm NOT going to rise to the bait! I was going to, but due to the curfew coming up later I need to move onto the next thread!!!"

Derek Barclay "Look it's 100% clear that play-offs are box office but that doesn't make them right - from a sporting point of view it's equally 100% the case that they are not right. Alright, actually I'd admit that I've long advocated Speedway adopting a more crowd-friendly approach and the old-style hamming-it-up style of promotion etc. Having Play offs meets that mould. But then I see what happened last winter and the enormous amount of time and energy so many gave to a row about the tiny minutiae of the rules on team composition etc. and how they were applied - with two major EL clubs threatening to withdraw; and to me that shows for many the sport matters more than being popular.."

Lewis Bridger* "Bought some new Phf double Choc cookie whey protein with lots of extra goodness & I'm stoked with it yummmyyyyyy #killingit"

Rob Godfrey "It was crazy, I have no idea what the referee [Paul Carrington] was thinking to let the race go on. From where we were standing, Richard [Hall] was quite clearly knocked off because Hawkins took his leg away, but for the race to continue, I just don't know what was going on there."

Ritchie Hawkins "I didn't know he'd fallen off until the race had finished. It was heavily watered during the break so got a bit tricky. I only saw the bike in the fence after the race but it really wasn't anything to do with me."

Richard Hollingsworth "Richard was adamant his leg was taken from him and if Hawkins had been excluded, then it would have been an 8-1 and we surely would have won the match."

Randall Butt "After the stunning fightback victory in the away leg, another huge West Row crowd settled down to applaud Mildenhall's triumphal march into the play-off final. Imagine their surprise then, when instead of a classy, confident cavalcade along came the speedway version of the clown car at a circus, backfiring, on three wheels, with the doors hanging off."

3rd October

Fredrik Lindgren*   "If I'd won the Golden Helmet today I'd sat down naked with a beer only wearing the helmet and put a picture on twitter your loss!"

Associated Press   Motorcycle speedway fans attacked police with stones overnight in Poland, violence that began after a fan was accidentally run over and killed by an unmarked police vehicle. The violence broke out in the early hours of Monday in Zielona Gora, a city in western Poland. The speedway fans broke shop windows, demolished a fuel station and wrecked several police cars.

Lewis Bridger*   "Just watched the 2 semi final back on sky+ for a fresh memory !! #gottamakeithappen"

Jan Staechmann*   "Shoulder surgery today. Let's hope they can fix it this time! It's only 6 yrs since accident! Mrs Staechmann taling me to hospital now"

Rob Godfrey   "It is difficult to bring together a decent field at the end of the season when you don't know when the [Kenny Smith Memorial] meeting will be run. So rather than devalue it and run it as a second half we have agreed with Stockton Van Hire to open next season, and probably every season thereafter, with the meeting in honour of Kenny. We already know the date and we have plenty of time over the winter to plan the field. We're pretty sure it will be easier to get riders to take part in March and hopefully the meeting now has a regular place in the fixture list".

Eastbourne website   Eastbourne Speedway expects to host their biggest crowd for nearly a decade at the Arlington Stadium on Monday night (October 3)....Club officials have been told to expect around 1,000 supporters to make their way along the south coast from Dorset to support the visitors.

Gary Havelock*   "Youngest daughter off school today. Teacher training my arse....why can't they do it in the school holidays. They get enough of them"

David Watt*   "Back in sunny UK. Haven't said that often but happy about it !! And I'm feeling good !! Last bit sounds better when you sing it !! #Muse"

Yahoo speedway forum   "Just to let speedway fans throughout the world know that Australian Speedway veteran Neil Street is gravely ill and has returned to his home in Melbourne Australia to spend his last days. Neil Street has three children Carole, Graham and Andrew who are all with him now. Neil is the grand-father of triple world champion Jason Crump. Neil was awarded an OAM in 2002 for his services to speedway."

Charlie Webster*   "Grand Final 1st leg tonight speedway Eastbourne v Poole what do we all reckon? Eastbourne need to win by more than 10 to have chance?"

David Watt*   "We're coming in swinging !! Gonna be a good night !!!"

Pete Ballinger*   "Eagles to win by just 2 or 4 I reckon"

Paul Watson*   "The Elite Eagles team is ready. The weather in Sussex is glorious. There's going to be a big crowd and a big (hoping) home win"

Gary Havelock*   "Goalie gloves for our five a side team £3. How does Mike Ashley do it?"

Nigel Pearson*   "Right, good day in office, now time for drive to Eastbourne for speedway grand final 1st leg. Fancy Eagles by 4, Poole to win it next week"

Lewis Kerr*   "The joys of roofing in south Lynn classy"

Rory Schlein*   "Match race between me and bomber at the earlsdon cycle speedway in Coventry on the 13th oct oh yes bring it on"

Hans Andersen*   "Sat in Moscow having food before flying futher into Russia"

Nigel Pearson*   "What a night for sports fans – darts on HD1 (World GP) and speedway on HD2 (Grand Final)Sky Sports"

Gary Havelock*   "Playing five a side at 6-30 then watch the pirates spank the eagles. Sorry eagles fans but you did SACK me after half a season!!!!"

Nigel Pearson*   "On the outskirts of Brighton, so tempted to head to the beach. Oh well, work to be done!"

Lewis Bridger*   "God damn Nervous but watch me turn it into adrenaline Skysports2 HD #killingit"

<u>**Nicki Glanz***</u> "Going to England thursday to sort next year out !"

<u>**Paul Burbidge***</u> "I think Eastbourne will win on the night by no more than 6. This will be tight"

<u>**Olly Allen***</u> "My guess is a close score tonight, followed by a comfy win by Poole next week"

<u>**Paul Burbidge***</u> "The Aussie Pirates just got viciously booed by the Eastbourne fans. Atmosphere is great at Arlington"

<u>**Rory Schlein***</u> "key men for me woodward and wolbert eastbourne need 8-10 lead to put the pressure on poole"

<u>**Dakota North***</u> "Lewis Bridger to get a max, he will do something loose tonight"

<u>**Rory Schlein***</u> "no doubt joonas will get stick for that but it like footballers diving everyone dose it"

<u>**Paul Burbidge***</u> "Chris Holder is the fastest man on show at Arlington tonight. Two lightening quick times"

<u>**Jo Lowry***</u> "Come on Eagles"

<u>**Paul Burbidge***</u> "Haven't seen replays but there appeared to be contact between Ward and Bjarne. Eagles fans aren't happy but all 4 looked right call"

<u>**Jo Lowry***</u> "Love how I get moaned at for not wanting Poole to win, yet the majority of my timeline is anti Poole! Says a lot really"

<u>**Paul Burbidge***</u> "Darcy Ward just received harsh lesson in how to ride Eastbourne. You can't just bomb around the fence. Superb move by Gustafsson"

<u>**Rory Schlein***</u> "Change of bike for Darcy"

<u>**Paul Burbidge***</u> "Superb race from Woodward and Gustafsson. Those who thought Poole would walk this final may be sorely mistaken"

<u>**Lewis Kerr***</u> "Back from gym #Tysonlewis"

<u>**Scott Nicholls***</u> "Welcome to Russia..not so sure about the ingredients in the Apple juice!"

<u>**Rory Schlein***</u> "Chris Holder & Darcy Ward sort the zips out on them suits boys"

<u>**Darcy Ward***</u> "I know fuckin does me head in"

<u>**Nigel Pearson***</u> "whats the story with the zips boys? Thought you were letting air in ha ha - need to know!"

<u>**Chris Holder***</u> "don't make zippers like they used to!!!"

<u>**David Howe***</u> "Cameron well done high lift or should I say cam shaft"

<u>**Cameron Woodward***</u> "thanks bud. Win or lose next week where gunna party like we won tonight. Yeeha"

<u>**Gary Havelock***</u> "Kath46 blue. I like your style. Tatum rocks. Not."

<u>**Nigel Pearson***</u> "Nights like tonight make me feel very lucky to be doing my job. Top speedway from Eastbn and Poole and great working with Kelv as always. Good result for Eastbn but still fancy Poole to finish the job by Heat 13 in return leg. Should be a great night next Monday. Dont mind admitting I'm not a fan of the Eastbn track shape but that was great speedway racing tonight. Love it when I get tweets saying people are watching for the first time. Speedway is a good sport for the whole family."

<u>**Cameron Woodward***</u> "8 point lead. We will see hey. Where partying like we won anyway. Fuck it hey"

<u>**David Watt***</u> "Well that was good fun ! Feeling bloody sore but I'll be ready for next week. Pumped for my team tonight. All da boys did well #piratepride"

<u>**Gary Havelock***</u> "Pirates to win by 25 points next Monday!!!"

<u>**David Watt***</u> "come down for it man. Be cool to see ya there if you can make it"

<u>**Gary Havelock***</u> "F**k that for a game of soldiers!!! I did 320 miles one way for four and a half years to race!!! Will watch you win on sky!!"

Nigel Pearson* "Kelv and me did plenty of shouting and screaming so I guess it was good!! Must watch it back tomorrow! Top effort."

Chris Holder* "Good night tonight! 8 points is ok… We can do it! Pirate pride Monday is gonna go off domination"

Ludvig Lindgren* "how u doin? chillaxing in UK! gunna be here another 2 weeks minimum!"

Lewis Bridger* "No gd tonight but oh well I'm enjoying the drinks wid the boys tonight anyways & let fate take it's way next Monday #herewego"

Bjarne Pedersen "I don't want to shout back. People [Malcolm Simmons] who do that have their own problems to sort out themselves. If you look at the whole season, I have beaten heat leaders all through the league. I showed tonight I can still do it. I just focus on myself. Whatever people say about me, I don't care."

4th October

Chris Holder* "So happy to see my king size bed right now !!!! #socomfy"

Ludvig Lindgren* [at 06.30] "goooooooodmorning UK! lets go back to sleep again!"

Mike Bennett* "another day- another Norwich Airport adventure!"

Mads Korneliussen* "Taken the day off, lazy day, have to rest my arm, it's not cool to have one black arm"

Mike Bennett* "Very impressed with choice of food at Edinburgh Airport. Smoked salmon and scrambled egg definitely an improvement on usual offerings!"

Vernon Kay* "I'm slowly getting into speedway!"

Mads Korneliussen* "Thank fxck for vanish, that stuff just saved my new t-shirt #kaboom"

Dakota North* "Pretty bored guys"

Nicki Glanz* "Just spent about a years wages on iTunes #gotcarriedaway"

Chris Holder* "Goin to watch the famous bournemouth cherries tonight! U boys better win!"

Jonathan Chapman "The Pride Of the East meeting scheduled to take place at King's Lynn Speedway on Friday 14th October, has unfortunately been cancelled for the second consecutive season. The club has been struggling to assemble a competitive line up for various reasons and have decided to cancel the meeting rather than run a substandard product 'decisions like this are hard but in all honesty it was getting harder by the day to put the event together, I don't blame the riders, they just simply have a busy schedule and the ones that are available are not prepared to ride for the money that is on offer. We could run a Premier League standard meeting, but we did that last week with the International Top Gun meeting which to be honest wasn't very well supported"

Michael Whawell "Sad news about 'Streety' - a nice family all-round. Phil always affable. Jason too, now. I know that his old Exeter team-mate Jack Geran will be greatly upset. He told me some amazing stories about what they used to get up to in the days before speedway riders spent half of their lives sat on 'planes (well apart from spending half their lives in their cars with a bike strapped to the back). Neil changed the face of speedway with his pioneering 4-valve. And with us for a little while yet, I hope."

Ludvig Lindgren* "In UK chilling.. bored to tears! yeah u know the drill! anyone wanna do something? :D"

Mads Korneliussen* "I want a pair off bose headphones, but it cost a lot, #mustwait"

Nicki Glanz* "Sat enjoying a Fanta at pub"

Niels Kristian Iversen* "the good old days. Standing like i shit meself"

Chris Holder* "Wat a great game all over it!!!"

Gary Havelock* "Wow. That fish curry really hit the spot!!!"

Adam Roynon* "Where's the rest of it!!????"

Gary Havelock* "Jayne ate the rest. Be no good for you like cause you couldn't eat it like a pizza!!!!!!!"

5th October

David Howe* "One more long track bike to wash! Then day off"

Rene Bach* "Some one come and load this van for me please! #wannagobacktobed"

Mads Korneliussen* "Sorting out the new workshop, we start painting soon not fun but it will be so cool when it's done"

David Watt* "The first 5 minutes of 'Game Ready' ice treatment is horrible. The next 25 aren't great either !! #worstpartofspeedway"

Hans Andersen* "Looks like i Might be riding in the russian league this year"

Lee Richardson* "long way mate! I went there [Vladivostok] on my own and did a league meeting! And got stuck for 12 hours as plane was f***ed"

Cameron Woodward* "holy shit man. That's nearly the same plain trip as Aussie. But I bet their paying the bills. I will be ya spanner man #cheap"

Fredrik Lindgren* "I love Kalles Kaviar but I hate Vegemite! Think you either love or hate it #justsaying"

Dakota North* "man up lindgren! Vegemite is the jack Daniels of things to have on toast!"

Jitendra Duffill* "whats with the # before words, whats all that about i dont get it"

Gary Havelock* "I thought you were intelligent"

Charlie Webster* "Sky Sports News this evening live at 7pm ...we got some Johnstone's Paint Trophy action"

Chris Holder* "bournemouth killed it last night"

Charlie Webster* "and so did you I hear ;-)"

Chris Holder* "we had the fanclub there last night Davey, Darcy and co... And look at the result! JPT trophy I feel it comin"

Rene Bach* "Going to see my first 3D movie tonight! Looking forward to see what the movie is like"

Nigel Pearson* "Bought some Bose headphones from HMV today. Amazing, I remember when i only ever bought a TDK C90 and Now 4 LP from there"

Lewis Bridger* "Got all new BadBreed MMA training kit earlier can't wait to get training once season is over & roll on a fight mid winter"

Dakota North* "a fight?"

Lewis Bridger* "yea mate, a cage fight MMA ;)"

Dakota North* "faaark your the man! respect"

Sam Masters* "not a fan of left turns"

Kevin Long* "just heard that the speedway presenter at King's Lynn tonight used my 'We've only just begun it's heat number 1!' as his first race intro!"

Sam Masters* "is the ref trying to blow their engines up"

Dakota North* "Sad night, rip mate going to miss you so much! will never forget you mate or everything you tought/and did for me, so lucky I got a chance to see you this year when I got injured, Until we meet again mate :("

Nigel Pearson* "Not only has cricket lost a legend today, so has the great sport of speedway. Neil Street, a true gent, has passed away. #saddayforthesport Only met Neil 3/4 times but always a warm handshake. Also got to know Drew very well in last 2 yrs, top man. Thoughts with them all incl JC. Neil Street was a guy I thought would just live forever and ever. A bit like Bobby Robson #sportinglegends"

David Watt* "Just heard the horrible news about Streety. RIP mate. I wish your family and many friends all the best at this tough time. Nicest bloke ever"

Gary Havelock* "RIP Streety. One of a kind! Our thoughts are with his family and friends at this sad time"

Mike Bennett* "just heard the sad news about Neil Street passing away. He was a great rider and a true gentleman. Thinking of all his family at this time"

Mads Korneliussen* "Neil Street RIP, he took me under his wing at newport 2004 and learned me so must, and always so happy, i will miss him around. #legend"

Nicki Glanz* "Just heard about Streety, very sad day for speedway World, great bloke RIP"

Lee Richardson* "Saw the news about Neil street...very sad day. He helped me alot a Poole in the early days. All my thoughts got to him and his family..."

Adam Roynon* "R.I.P Streety! Such a legend and always a big help to me.. Going to be missed. God bless"

Scott Nicholls* "Very saddened to hear of the passing of Neil Street. A genuine nice & very helpful man. Will be very missed. My thoughts r with jc & family"

Chris Neath* "Gutted to hear about Streety. A true gentleman who's helped so many of us throughout our careers. RIP Bill #foreverwithus"

Jo Lowry* "RIP Neil Street x"

Rory Schlein* "Streetty you will be missed Mate still using sum of the things he tort me wen I was under 21 RIP mate"

Ian Adam* "Sorry to hear about the passing of Neil Street one of speedways pure gents RIP Neil"

Paul Burbidge* "Tributes are pouring in for former Aussie team boss Neil Street, who has died aged 80 in Melbourne"

Chris Holder* "Rip Streety... Great bloke helped jus every Aussie rider over here! Guna be missed big time"

Sam Masters* "RIP streety your the man always will be, never seen the bloke without a smile on his face, #legend"

Greg Hancock* "RIP Neil Street! Streety to all in Speedway. He was a pillar in our sport & will be missed! Condolences to the Street & Crump Families"

Alun John Rossiter* "Rip Billy Street theres a lot of people that have a lot to thank you for I am one sleep well pal x"

Speedway Star* "Sad to hear of the passing of Neil Street, a lovely man and a true gentleman. Thoughts are with the Crump family. R.I.P. Neil"

Taylor Poole* "RIP Streety :'(you helped alot when I was a junior along with I think every other Australian. #willbemissed"

Mark Lemon* "Two very inspirational people have departed my life this week, sad,sad,sad but they made my life very happy! Thank you Grandma & Bill, RIP."

Jerran Hart* "RIP streety :(thanks for all your help at newport buddy thoughts are with you #windthemflywheelsup"

Chris Durno "In speedway terms, he really was a legend and a hero. He rode and then remained deeply involved with engines and helped so many Australian riders. Nevermind what he'd done in speedway, he was also a real gentleman"

Peter Woodhouse "In Heat 8 Rocco Scopellite came in for Tuff McBride and fell on the second bend of the final lap for an awarded race."

Ludvig Lindgren* "me and proctor is dying of hunger any 1 wanna bring food or tell us were we can get food in rugeley!"

6th October

Linus Sundstrom* "What a night!!! Thanks to all people & fans involved in piraterna speedway, you all deserve the gold!! Time for some zleEep "

Nicki Glanz* "On my way to luvly England in a sec"

Paul Burbidge* "At Luton ready to fly to Poznan. Then driving on the right for first time in my life, hopefully only venturing to left for passing moves"

Nigel Pearson* "are u on the 6.15am flight back on Sunday Burb?"

Rob Godfrey* "Seven years ago we had a grass field, six years ago we were an average Conference League team, four years ago we made the big jump into the Premier League and two years ago we made it into three competition semi-finals. This year has been our best yet and we are still growing as a club."

Steve Mallett "We have done our bit in producing a side capable of winning ten successive home meetings and then picking up silverware. But what we don't want now is for fans to say to themselves, 'that's it, we did our bit by turning up for the Cup Final. We really do, and I can't stress this enough, want them all to return for our final few fixtures. The stark reality is if they don't, then the very existence of this great club is in doubt."

David Watt* "Bored with all this ice treatment. Want to get going !!"

Adam Roynon* "Bloody hell it's cold in Cumbria today!!! #freezing"

Sam Masters* "Can't believe it!!"

Taylor Poole* "I've got 2 pickles today hayhay"

Darcy Ward* "Feelin a jetski sesh coming along with Chris Holder"

Chris Holder* "I've jus felt it to... I can see alot of this goin on"

Nigel Pearson* "Thinking about all the lads and lasses I know on BBC 'Local' Radio today - hope it works out for you guys! #bbcjobcuts"

Nicki Glanz* "RyanAir must have some strong planes with the hard landings they dó, iam 40cm shorter now"

Paul Burbidge* "It's okay. I'm alive. Just drove from Poznan Airport to Gorzow - first time driving on the right and lived. My sat nav was a godsend"

Gary Havelock* "All ready to rock for the invasion of the American Dream Team at Redcar tonight. Be interesting to see how the track is after last week!!!!!"

Rory Schlein* "Now it feels like October"

Ludvig Lindgren* "watching movies with the doctor proctor! cillaxing in rugeley!"

Dakota North* "Thirsty Thursday"

Mads Korneliussen* "Just booked a trip to London for me & louise. Is so looking forward to it. so must to see. Big Ben and the rest"

Gary Havelock* "Blew another engine up tonight. What a bummer. But hey worse things happen in this crazy world we live in #atleastidonefisheruptwice"

Pete Simmons* "just back from ips hospital - Mat Tresarrieu been released but has mild concussion that rules him out for 7 days."

Sam Masters* "This wind is crazy nearly getting blown off the road"

Stuart Parnaby "At this time of the season, you've got to be prepared to ride in the wet. If you're not going to ride in wet conditions, then you're not going to be a speedway rider."

Keith McGhie "A cold and blustery wind would have done little to entice the largely Californian contingent into adding Teesside (or East Anglia) to their list of possible holiday hotspots."

7th October

Ludvig Lindgren* at 02.30 "well bed it is!!!"

Nigel Pearson* "bumped into Rosco at Luton Airport oh dear.."

Bornagainlion "Chris [Popple] has got better and to me the odd mistake has made him feel far more likeable than the Smashie and Nicey type at Brandon. His outburst the other week was full of passion and emotion, obviously peoples attitudes and constant sniping had got to him, maybe it wasn't professional but he came out and apologised so really time to move on. I dare say the same people who slaughtered Wayne Rooney for his remarks when the English fans team were booing the players will be the same people chanting his name if he scores a goal tonight that helps the national team qualify for the euros. If people can forgive that surely Chris deserves some slack"

Ian Rae "Regardless of Mr Gjedde's performance, Newport are a solid side who will give us a pretty fair trial."

Chris Holder* "Next stop Poznan....then we gotta try find our way to gorzow!? #dangerous"

Darcy Ward* [to banned Sam Masters] "hard done by #whatajoke"

Hans Andersen* [also to Sam Masters] "what you been doin, causing trouble?"

Gary Havelock* "Kids breky. School run. 2 dirty bikes. Engine to change. And then the joy of riding at scunny #yougottalovespeedway"

Nicki Glanz* "Got a hard ón that a cat couldnt scratch #justsaying"

Nigel Pearson* "Landed in Poznan, one of my fave Polish destinations in the summer. Sadly it's October!!"

Mads Korneliussen* "Weekend oh yes thank you #goodstuff"

Adam Roynon* "On route to scunny mudwith Robert Branford! A Bears win tonight it's what it's all about!!!"

Paul Burbidge* "Delighted to see New Zealand added to the SGP calendar. Contracts were signed last night. What a way to start 2012!"

Gary Patchett* "No consideration given to British season by BSI in a year when we have Olympics to contend with as well as WTC it sucks"

Debbie Hancock "Apart from the weather, one other thing that has remained consistent from that first meeting is the fact that Steve Bishop is still part of the Somerset set-up. Bish won the first race at the Oak Tree Arena, and here we are, 299 matches on from then and he is still with the Rebels in his role as team manager."

Dakota North* "Everyone get there self to Somerset tonight! Should be a close meeting! Il be there making my last appearance for the year! So come on down"

Paul Burbidge* "To all those asking about next year's SGP calendar, I'm led to believe it could be revealed in full as early as next week. No guarantees"

Adam Roynon* "Rocking out in the umbro trackies!!! What a way to mechanic!"

Nigel Pearson* "Non-speedway fans look away now – speedway fans name as many NZ riders as poss. Starter? David Bargh"

Nigel Pearson* "Move over Mauger, it seems Mitch Shirra is one of the most popular NZ riders"

Nigel Pearson* "Here's one - Ricky Wells??!!"

Nigel Pearson* "Geoff Mardon with thanks to James Easter"

Rory Schlein* "Don't no what to think of the GP in New Zealand I hear the bikes are big there and a lot of talent coming through there to. And I'm sure the GP boys are well please with the date to"

Dakota North* "How's Peterborough doing? Wish I could have made it tonight. No good! Come on boys!!!"

Rory Schlein* "Theres a photo in this weeks *speedway star* of Chris Holder and I'm nominating it for shape of the year respect crispy"

Sam Masters* "It's hard not riding and only watching!! #notfun harsh"

Brian Havelock "Everyone went to sleep, we couldn't blame any individual rider, all of them just totally switched off. To be honest, even I probably got the black and white helmets in the wrong places but that's always a gamble."

Mike Hunter "It was hard to believe Edinburgh lost this match after building up a 12-point lead. This was partly due to the excellence of Charlie Gjedde and the persistence of his team-mates, but in reality owed more to the blundering of the home riders."

8th October

Sam Masters* "Yeah everyone banned for 30 days for saying something in personal message on Facebook!! Yep I don't understand but it's true. It's starting to really sink in how lame this is no1 believes it!! #harsh #wannaride"

Taylor Poole* "that's bullshit man! wtf"

Niels Kristian Iversen* "who is banned man ??"

Cameron Woodward* "your banned from riding for 30 days?? What the f@&k"

David Howe* "Well its a bit rich, Sam Masters gets a ban for having a laugh yet I just had a message on facebook calling me a dirty little bastard"

Shawn Moran* [to Greg Hancock] "DAM, u sure finished n Style. F`n Good 1 buddy. U da man. Have a great nite, long 2 im sure. So Happy 4 ya Grinster. ABALULLY"

Jon Cook "Our fans showed their support last night and I would like to say we took a big step towards putting in a full team into the National League in 2012, subject to our landlord's continued help and approval at the National League AGM."

Paul Bellamy "Taking the SGP series out of Europe has always been a huge goal for us, so we are delighted to be bringing the sport's biggest names to New Zealand......I hope that bringing the stars of today to Western Springs will inspire a generation of young riders in New Zealand and encourage them to follow in the footsteps of past Kiwi world champions."

Darcy Ward "To be honest if you're not in the [SGP] top four, you lose money. You get more money racing at Eastbourne on a Monday than you do in the Grand Prix. It's so overrated in terms of prizes, unless you're winning of course. Poland is where you earn your money to pay your mechanics and have all your gear. Maybe a couple of the older guys will drop out and concentrate on Poland. I really don't know."

Chris Holder "I think with his riding ability – no problem. [Darcy] could be in the GP easily. It's not his riding that could let him down. It's all the other stuff. It's a lot of organisation. You have run a full-blown team with three guys. You need ferries and hotels and then you have Poland the next day. It's a big thing"

Linus Sundstrom* "2011 is over! Thanks to my sponsors,family,fans,mechanics,clubpeople,team mates &teammanagers! Been a great year with good memories. #happydays Taking a trip down to talon today to pick some bitz up for 2012 , the planning has already started!

Dakota North* "Waiting for a train, not a fan!"

Gary Havelock* "Can't wait for the last SGP tonight. Good luck and a safe ride to all the boys, with a special big up for Bomber. Pride of Britain!!!"

Paul Burbidge* "Raining in Gorzow. Let's hope it blows over for the Grand Prix tonight. I'm meant to be in Gniezno tomorrow!"

John Chaplin "[Bruce Mackenzie's] pranks got him banned by hotels, airlines and shipping companies."

Dakota North* "Had one 2 many lemonades last night and ended up in Swindon, and now I'm on a train back home, How does this happen? #notideal"

Sam Masters* "where u goin?? #idiot"

Dakota North* "Taunton"

Chris Holder* "Fukn freezing and here in gorzow!!"

Nicolai Klindt* "doing nothing at Hans Andersen's house. waiting for wash-boy to get done. #feelingsecondhand"

Mads Korneliussen* "Garden work done, hateit but has to be done"

Lewis Kerr* "1 Hour from Newport.. Last meeting of 2011"

Fredrik Lindgren* "Now it is time... It it time to unleash hell! #speedwayGP"

Rene Bach* "Mixed grill, gokart in the rain Newcastle toon after with the boys! #gohardorgohome #makeithappen"

Lee Richardson "Good day for Landshut, German champions! Helped them with 15 points! God did it rain though! #trackwasasroughas"

Kasper Wortmann* "watching GP with Nicolai Klindt & Hans Andersen"

Gary Havelock* "Is holta jade Mudgway in disguise!!!!"

Paul Burbidge* "Sad to see Holta struggling. The guy simply cannot hold on to his bike in these conditions. No strength in his hands"

Lewis Bridger* "Laguta man up I have £5 on u stop looking around & pinit"

Nigel Pearson* "Darcy does it again wow! Awesome! #sgp"

Gary Patchett* "Silent on the NZ issue Paul?"

Paul Burbidge* "The BSPA were consulted. Why do you need to run meetings in March? Still too many fixtures and clubs losing money"

Gary Patchett* "No they weren't. Had that conf by member of MC. Will delay start of EL by a month and will mean we miss out Easter fixtures"

Paul Burbidge* "The riders will be back in time for the Easter weekend. They fly out the Monday after the GP and will be back by Wednesday"

Gary Patchett* "And no jet lag or pre season practice. You have all the answers. #dreamworld"

Paul Burbidge* "They can practice before they go to NZ and while they're out there, but I can't argue about your jet lag comment"

Gary Patchett* "the Aussies won't even be here beforehand"

Nigel Pearson*

"Meeting abandoned result stands, Greg Hancock wins with 11. Right decision"

Lewis Kerr* "12 points at Newport tonight! F**king awesome night! Heat 15 best race of my life with jayHearn!"

Paul Burbidge* "Just left the Edward Jancarz Stadium in Gorzow and Greg Hancock is still holding court in the press tent. Who says nice guys finish last?"

Nigel Pearson* "I've seen many great sporting displays down the years, but Greg's world title is one of the most impressive. Great achievement"

9th October

David Howe* "Up at half four in morning to leave for Glasgow crazy Tedster on board #gpmechanic"

Fredrik Lindgren* "Checked in at my hotel in Berlin, flight back to Sweden in the morning. Going to try one brew before I fall a sleep!"

Nicki Glanz* "Hotel jumper as misus has kicked me out"

Nigel Pearson* "Early start. Silly early. Poznan – Luton"

Mads Korneliussen* "Think i have to start sorting out where to ride next year #noidea"

Paul Burbidge* "Few clouds over Gniezno, but today's World U21 should be fine. Nice press box - great view of an ambulance. Seeing start line would be nice. They're just about to drive a tank on to the track in Gniezno. That's going to make a mess!"

Nigel Pearson* "Back from Polska on early flight, given my boy a bath and cooked lunch for us all. I bet every woman wishes she had a husband like me, eh?!"

Fredrik Lindgren* "Wish I had a woman like you"

Dakota North* "annoyed that Darcy Ward didn't make it 3 in a row, unlucky! Was watching the stream, kid was on fire!"

Gary Patchett* "Like I said this has been imposed on us without any consideration of the impact"

Paul Burbidge* "They're trying to take the sport into new territories. Brit promoters seem to think the Elite League is the be all and end all"

Gary Patchett* "True, I don't have to sign any. Neither does any other club. That your preference then?"

Paul Burbidge* "I'd love more GP boys in the Elite. But the way to do that is reduce fix list and work around international calendar"

Gary Patchett* "Without a domestic calendar there wouldn't be an international one. Unless that's part of the master plan!

Ian Adam* "After his crash Alex davies is unsure where he is !!!!!!!!"

Alison Chalmers "Glasgow Tigers 2011 Premier League Champions. How good it is to type that. Yes, we are league champions and it feels so good after 17 long years. I finally cracked open the Moet after heat 10 and we all raised our glasses to our team. 6 hours at the speedway and worth every second! Drove down my street with the Tigers scarf out of the car window and tooting. It was my son's turn to be embarrassed this time as he was at home!"

Chris Neath* "Really winds me up when nob heads block a fuel pump at a rammed petrol station to just go for a piss and wander round."

Gary Havelock* "Pobol y cwm has now got subtitles. Class I actually know what's going on now"

David Howe* "M6 traffic jam grrrrr #gridlocked"

Eric Thornton "Exactly which part of Newman's bike tore through his kevlars and straight into his left groin area puncturing the femoral artery is unclear, though it might have been the clutch lever."

Martin Vaculik "I can't wait to do the senior championship now. Tony Rickardsson was never World Under-21 Champion, so I hope it will be the same story for me."

10th October

Matt Ford "To fit in with the health and safety criteria we had to shut the gates just after 7.30pm a year ago. We don't want anyone to be disappointed this year."

Joe Screen "I have achieved a lot in the sport, and this is well up there in terms of the best moments of my career. I joined Glasgow to win things and I always felt that this season had so much promise, but until we had the points in the bag I was not for celebrating anything."

Paul Burbidge* "Flying from Poznan Holder, Ward, Watt, Andersson, Gustafsson, Shane Parker. How do they do this schedule?"

Lewis Bridger* "It's official it's the Final today & nothing else matters.. It's time to get loose & risk everything.. Let the best team win"

Lee Richardson* "is cam up for that meeting mate?"

Lewis Bridger* "he said get them to get in contact with us about money etc.. what club blabla & if it's worth doing he is owed 9,000€ in Hun :-/"

Lee Richardson* "ok, I'm not sure what club it is to be honest, but with Nagy involved u will get your money"

Cameron Woodward* "g'day RICO. What track is it mate. Miskolc owe me to much money"

Paul Burbidge* "Darcy Ward stormed around the outside on his scooterbag on the way to Luton passport control. When is he not on 2 wheels?"

Chris Neath* "Man I've woken up with a stiff neck. And this dull weather isn't making bike washing anymore appealing."

Cameron Woodward* "hey batch are you doing Russia-Vladivostok Saturday??"

Troy Batchelor* "flying tomorrow for it"

Cameron Woodward* "can you give me a bell mate. Jk is doing same meeting"

Nigel Pearson* "Buzzing about tonight's Poole v Eagles clash but also sad it's my last meeting of the season"

Fredrik Lindgren* "Just seen that I've got the most bonuspoints in Swedish Elitserien in 2011! Interesting statistics"

Lewis Bridger* "Thanks guys for all the positive tweets really going to try & zone in tonight & do my best for Eagles"

Chris Holder* "It's onnn tonight!"

Ludvig Lindgren* [at 15.30] "oh i hate mornings! and now ive just seen Nicolai Klindt's penis as he is walking around the house naked! WTF!!!"

Paul Burbidge* "Chris Holder is keen to make the most of what could be his last play-off final with Darcy Ward in Poole colours"

Nicolai Klindt* "man..... i could catch a flight to sydney an back and still have to wait for luddechenko #showertimes"

Dakota North* "Wasn't the best year due to injury, but thanks everyone and hope to see you both again for next season!"

Jayne Moss "It gets harder and harder to compete with the 'rich' clubs every year and something really needs to be done about the costs involved to everyone, promoters and riders alike. The sad fact is that there is not enough riders around of the required standard and you cannot expect supporters to pay £10+ for an inferior product. It will be an interesting winter again that is for sure."

Sam Masters* "Just took Dakota North to airport and now on way home, this time next week that will be me #imcominghome"

Ulrich Ostergaard* "Hate changing dipers with one hand!!!!! #disasterwaitingtohappen #hardwork"

David Watt* "Poole traffic is nuts getting to the stadium !! This place is gonna be rockin. Let's get it on bitches !!!"

Nicolai Klindt* "had a haircut at wow and now waiting for a dominos pizza. but anyone know a pub they show the speedway at tonight in wolves?"

Gary Havelock* "Just off to play 5 a side then back in time for speedway on the telly. Come on you #piratepride"

Jayne Moss "As for saying the riders need more than £10 per point then that is fine but what happens if you havent got the funds to do that? I know several riders who were promised more than that and are outstanding wages from their respective clubs and it seems to happen every year. Buxton could agree to pay riders £30 per point but it wouldn't last long and the club would soon be bankrupt as there is not sufficient income to sustain high wages. Saying that though the problem has always existed in the third tier and I guess it will do long after we are not here. The costs are too high for everyone riders included especially as next year sees the new silencers as compulsary in the NL."

Nigel Pearson "sadly there are some people who've had to be turned away!...5000 packed into Wimborne Road"

Gary Havelock* "You know you know you know"

Kelvin Tatum "You can't believe the speed of that man [Ward] out in front – he's dynamite!"

Gary Havelock* "You gotta take your hat off to darky ward!! and only 19. I can't remember that far back"

Nigel Pearson "Eight heats to decide the whereabouts of the Elite League – don't go anywhere!"

Jonathan Barber* "Cam threw a brush.......he is sooooooooooo rock'n'roll"

Jonathan Barber* "Kelvin said he is gonna take his hat off to Greg Hancock.....but he is not wearing a hat....how can that be"

Lewis Bridger* [from pits before finishing last in heat 12] "Here we go last chance of doing anything !!"

Nicolai Klindt* "bridger man.... why the fuck are you tweeting while ur racing? u should be concentrating on doing the business.."

Gary Havelock* "what a knob"

Lewis Bridger* "tried to get pumped up for it but clearly didn't work shit happens !!"

Gary Havelock* "Tweeting while riding makes you a knob"

Chris Louis "you just confused him, he (Watt) didn't know where to attack you from"

Cameron Woodward "I'll take that mate"

Lewis Bridger* "Game over :-(f£&kkkkkk "

Darcy Ward "we hang out all the time so we know we've got each others backs"

Kelvin Tatum "He's gone into the side of him"

Nigel Pearson "But Woodward was ahead"

David Watt "We are a team in every sense of the word – we don't believe that anyone has done anything that has stood out more than the team"

Neil Middleditch "woo, Chris [hugs a startled Chris Louis]"

Jonathan Barber* "would have won it with Lukas..robbed"

Glen Campbell Kelvin the gerbil & Roland rat - the Brokeback Mountain boys - are quality on Sky Sports tonight"

Trevor Geer "Cameron wrote off two bikes tonight"

Trevor Geer "Some of them were too busy concentrating on where the Poole riders were rather than getting their heads down and riding"

Nigel Pearson "One of the best Elite League seasons for quite some time"

Nicolai Klindt* "it was luck for Poole speedway they didn't meet Swindon Robins haha #takingthepissbeforeyousayanything"

Jitendra Duffill* "Cam woodward, fair play that was total commitment 2nite, ucan #holdurheadhigh"

Manchester Paul "THANK YOU VERY MUCH SKY. Stepping aside from the much discussed topics of fans preferences and dislikes when it comes to the commentators, pits and studio teams, i think Sky have once again done the sport proud. It has been a season with some excellent racing at times. Too see the sport covered from so many camera angles is truly fantastic."

Lewis Bridger* "Really don't need the negative tweets right now, I no there is so many pissed fans but no rider goes out onto the track to fail #gutted"

Dakota North* "boarding"

Nigel Pearson* "Well done Poole, best team all season. Can't believe some of the tweets Ive just read, bitter and twisted!!"

Gary Havelock* "'what's the ruling on mobile phones in the pits Gary?' illegal"

Nigel Pearson* "One man cannot put two clubs out of business. AGM decisions were voted by majority i believe"

Peter Johns* "how many riders will lose there jobs unless the rules are changed. Don't dilute the league even more!"

Nigel Pearson* "That's it for 2011. Thanks to all my colleagues on sky sports speedway we have had a blast! And the winter will be great thanks to tweets!"

11th October

Chris Holder* "yeeeeeeewwwww"

Jan Staechmann "This sort of thing [European Super 8] has been proposed many times before, and pardon for being cynical but I'd be very surprised if it makes it past the concept stage. IMHO it lacks credibility. The UEM run a similar competition, the Champions Cup, which is a make-shift side mickey mouse affair. The above is purely an opinion based on experience."

Nigel Pearson* "Enjoy good debate on here as long as it's reasonable. Any foul language and/or personal abuse and the block button is pressed!"

Jo Lowry* "Ahhhhhh, that's better! Poole Speedway = unfollowed! I called it last night but my blackberry wasn't working! Far too many RT's from them!"

Paul Burbidge* "Congrats to EL champs Poole. After seeing Chris Holder's, Darcy Ward's and David Watt's distraught faces last year, this means a lot"

Jayne Moss "This years crowds aren't particularly down on last year but the sad fact is costs keep increasing but the crowd base doesn't increase in line with the costs. We have never had average crowds of 300 (even in 2010 when we won everything!!!), if we did we wouldn't have any worries"

Jim Lynch "Lukasz [Janowski] informed us that he couldn't ride on Wednesday because he had a meeting to attend in Poland. Then he told us he was taking his gear home as well. We are waiting for confirmation that we can use a guest."

Chris Holder* "Jet ski time with the boys! #killerstyle"

Roman Chyla "Robert Dowhan, chairman of newly crowned Polish EkstraLiga champions Zielona Gora, and recently elected member of the Polish Senate (upper chamber of the parliament) is not giving up in his fight to get the controversial rule of one GP rider for one EkstraLiga club overruled. He has on his books world no. 1 and no.2 (Hancock and Jonsson) plus Piotr Protasiewicz who won eligibility for SGP through this season's eliminating rounds. Mr Dowhan has apparently gained a powerful ally in his struggle - the BSI. The organizers of the speedway GP are said to be taking legal action against EkstraLiga rule which - as they see it - is ruining their business - reports sportowefakty.pl"

Philip Rising "OFFICIAL [wild card] announcement 8am tomorrow along with the 2012 SGP calendar"

Derek Barclay "Er, well as we're (meant to be...) talking about a brand-new [Sittingbourne] Speedway track here, in a superb stadium btw, then yes I'd say let's indeed be positive (aka in your perspective, wear rose tinted specs..!). To some of us this is VERY important, so keep the cynicism for somewhere else please..."

Troy Batchelor* "Siting in Moscow waiting for this big bird to get me to Vladivostok"

Nicki Glanz* "Fuck me Hotel rooms are boring on your own"

Nigel Pearson* "Think the 4 riders mentioned in the Danish media MAY have been asked if they would take a wildcard for sgp. Nothing confirmed"

Nicki Glanz* "Uhhhh Dillema plymouth dinner and Dance eller Outrup klubfest"

Nigel Pearson* "Got to the bottom of the sgp wildcard picks and if you have the iphone app you have the news first it seems"

Nicki Glanz* "Kan hear two people shagging in room next door #glassonwall hotel"

Tai Woffinden* "Wow i haven been on twitter since i lost my phone a week ago missed out on so much shit IM BACK hooray"

Nigel Pearson* "Had a great night of GB U21 46-44 USA at Monmore tonight. Great crowd. But must admit, I'm done with speedway till March. Bring on winter"

12th October

Linus Sundstrom* "working today #loveit"

Nigel Pearson* "Speedway GP wildcards now confirmed! Freddie, Nicki, Bomber and Darcy."

Lewis Kerr* "N.E.B GPV complete clutch for sale. Complete with countershaft Plates everything! Inbox me for details"

Olly Allen* "My kings Lynn race suit is up for sale, inbox me for details"

Speedway Star* "Scunthorpe are to apply to become an FIM-licensed track. It has been nominated to host one of next years World U21 Team Cup semi-finals"

Rory Schlein* "Sorry guys I ant tweeted for a while I went off the radar for a bit. Big news soon so stay tweeted"

Sam Masters* "Bike and bits packed ready to be send home #letsgetoutahere"

Roman Chyla "Crowds in Poland still think in the old way. They want in their team riders from their own town, or neighbourhood. Somebody with whom they can identify. Somebody whom they meet at street in local supermarket, and not 5 minutes before match presentation. That said, what they want most is their team to win, at any price. To achieve that they need top stars (foreign or from other Polish clubs). What they don't want is barriers, limits, CMA, riders replacement, jokers (not exactly in that order). Clubs Chairmen on the other hand are beginning to think in new ways. They also want to win at all costs, to satisfy their sponsors, to cover themselves with glory etc., They are slowly beginning to realize that the money supply (sponsors) to cover ever so increasing cost is about to dry out, if not completely then surely is to be decreased. Hence introduction, or rather re-introduction of CMA, employment of more home grown riders who suppose to be cheaper. Team building CMA limits, etc. And now they came up with an idea that by employing only one GP riders per one team they will save money. I personally don't believe that."

Ludvig Lindgren* "still in UK! lets do sum food shopping so me and Nicolai can eat later! after luddchenko the master chef have cooked something up!"

Ludvig Lindgren* "waiting for Nicolai damn he is slow!"

Nicki Glanz* "Must be sat in the shittyest hotel in the World.... Looks like a American motel ! Just no hookers"

Nigel Pearson* "One more speedway show to do - Thursday morning, sgp highlights show, Round 11, Gorzow. Heading for Farnham for final time this season"

Nicki Glanz* "My life is so sureal sometimes weird and wonderfull things"

Steve Shovlar [ruminates on Peter Adams' invite to Poole Dinner Dance] "Just possibly, perhaps, there might be the thought that actually Matt Ford is very highly regarded amoungst the majority of club promoters who try to emulate his success."

Lewis Bridger* "5hrs I'll be leaving with Cameron for California babyyyyyyy let the fun & games begin !!"

Nicolai Klindt* "Troy Batchelor pulls out of the Elite League riders championship and he is replaced by Nicolai Klindt"

Jan Staechmann* "Apparently Joonas Kylmakorpi has also pulled out of the ELRC. No news on replacement just yet"

Nicolai Klindt* "why is people pulling out of ELRC?"

Alun John Rossiter* "got too much money #anyexcuse"

Nicolai Klindt* "bet they do"

Chris Holder* "who is out?"

Nicolai Klindt* "there was four that pulled out yesterday and two more today. but dunno who!"

Sam Masters* "I'll do it, oh shit that's right I'm banned #badtimes"

The Aces* "Just to clarify that Ryan Fisher is guesting for Swiderski & it's R/R for Davidsson"

Nigel Pearson* "thanks, couldn't find any team news or info on Lakeside Hammers website today #keepthefansinthedark"

Gary Patchett* "Woe betide anyone not making relevant press releases #potsandkettles"

Gary Patchett* "Apparently it's very unprofessional. #peopleinglasshousesshouldntthrowstones"

Nigel Pearson* "when I hit the 10,000 followers mark I may offer further comment. End of statement"

Gary Patchett* "Please follow Nigel Pearson as he has some important news to share with us but won't do so until he has 10k followers. #breakingnews"

Paul Burbidge* "Thought I'd try the honey vodka that was given to us in Leszno this year. Goes superbly with lemonade. Great for sore throat. #spoton"

Greyhoundp "Before the last race 'Porky' mikeman was leading the Mexican Wave by running down the home straight, BUT,BUT he didnt jump high enough to clear the Tapes, went straight through them, and fell head first on his Belly, some WAG said it was like an earthquake, needed a lorry load of shale to fill the Hole"

Jon Cook "It was a tough night for both teams in Manchester on the wettest track I think I have ever seen a meeting start on."

13th October

Flagrag "I have not had a chance to fully have a look at viewing figures year on year but in general they have been down a bit which is to be expected as has been going head to head with MNF premiership football on Sky sports 1 but the audience share has remained good all year and Speedway still out performs a number of other more well known and supported sports and events"

Dakota North* "Lovely day"

Fredrik Lindgren* "Don't know what is going on with me woke up 5am & couldn't get back to sleep. Now I sit here wondering what to do? Not good for my system!"

Shawn Moran* "Ur not alone Freddie. Been up since 3 an on the comp since 4. Its not a bad thing, just ur mind wants 2 think, not dream"

Linus Sundstrom* "oap warning fred!"

Nicki Glanz* "How can it be so hard to check out of a hotel"

Nigel Pearson* "Early start today, heading for Farnham for last sgp highlights show of the season with Kelv. Should be a good one!"

Dakota North* "So tired! Jet lag"

Scott Nicholls "The Elite League is still a very hard league with some of the best riders in the world. You have to be at your best to beat them consistently, and that means having everything in place mechanically too."

Olly Allen* "Ok so I need a new website made...anyone out there wanting the job?"

Peter Oakes "Unfortunately I am not in a position to be able to give as much time and effort as I would like to my role with the Panthers. I actually resigned at the beginning of August, but agreed to continue doing some work until the end of the season at the request of the owners. It would be unfair on both Pam and the club for me to continue. Rick and Julie did ask me to continue in another capacity, but I do not feel I am in a position to do so. I'd also like to express my gratitude to all the fans who have asked about Pam's progress. She continues to make a remarkable recovery."

Chris Holder "There is going to be a lot of stuff going down at the [BSPA] meeting because they are jealous of how good Poole are and how successful we are. But I really don't know what to say. It is pretty bad what is probably going to happen but, fingers crossed, it all works out."

Paul Watson "How much these two signings [Wolbert & Jonasson] cost Ford, one can only guess. However, it is likely to have been a pretty penny because the riders would know how keen Poole were to win the title and would no doubt have adjusted their demands accordingly."

Darcy Ward* "Who has pulled out of the elrc ?? What's the new line up ?"

Nicolai Klindt* "fuck know man... dont even know whos riding and whos not from first line up"

BSPA advert strapline "They don't come much bigger than this"

Nigel Pearson* "season over speedway"

Adam Roynon* "Not quite Nige!!!"

Nigel Pearson* "it is for me kid - I've had enough! See u Nov 4 - at the bar. Your round #sessionon"

Gary Havelock* "thatsmybirthday"

Nigel Pearson* "Havvy to celebrate birthday in Cradley Heath then?!!"

Nicolai Klindt* "in a dilemma…. forgot my macbook charger at home. the mac is dead and only need it for 10 minutes. buy a new one or not?"

Jan Staechmann* "it's 65 quid… so I've heard, LOL"

Nicolai Klindt* "fuck that…. i aint buying a charger if thats the pricerate. i find someone who got on i can borrow!"

Olly Allen* "if you're willing to drive to Norwich you can use mine…however the fuel to get here will cost more than the charger!"

Nicolai Klindt* "thanks bud! i'm sure train will do it"

Mads Korneliussen* "Have hat a very good day with my dk team manager steven. I think he has to get his ass on twitter soon"

Rory Schlein* "What can I say about last night WET, WET, WET but we r into the final so bring on"

Chris Holder* "where bringing it schleiny"

Lewis Bridger* "Loving the Rays right now in CA America me & Cameron are just of to the track to check it out makeshithappen"

Rory Schlein* "At cycle speedway I thought my chances were good against bomber but now I'm up against robbo think I'll be struggling"

Taylor Poole* "the robots aint made of steel so why's it called real steel?"

Lewis Kerr* "Productive day.. Van is looking siiick"

Bjarne Pedersen "I'm disappointed with myself. I think the other guys in the team were really fighting but the four points I scored was very poor. I apologise for that. I just hope I can come back and do a better job for Eastbourne next year. I would like to say thanks to all the supporters at Eastbourne. It has been a fantastic season for me down there. I felt very welcome. A lot of things will happen in the winter and it's not all down to me so I can't promise I'll be back but I enjoyed it."

Gary Havelock* "Another season over. Unbelievable!!!! I have lost count now"

Keith Denham "The stupid and unhelpful way the league has been set up has cost us a lot of money. Travelling to places like Plymouth has played havoc with our finances. We've been hit big time by the new format and it's not right. One race in Plymouth has cost us £1,000, which is bad enough, but then think they bring next to no fans to Derwent Park and we've been stung again. We cannot continue like this because it's killing speedway in Workington. Everyone at the management meeting agreed with the points and made similar opposition to the current league format. Something has to be done or the sport, as well as Workington Comets, faces a bleak future."

Greg Hancock* "Heading to Torun, Poland on Sunday for Poland vs The World! I am also doing a Monster autograph signing in front of the Stadium at 3:00pm!"

Friday 14th October

Ludvig Lindgren* "chillaxing in bed!"

Nicolai Klindt* "ive just put a £10 bet on luddechenko aka Ludvig Lindgren for tomorrows meeting #prideofthemidlands trowing money in the sea!"

Mike Bowden "It's a different team from the one we had at the beginning of the season. If we'd had this team then, I think we would have been higher up the league than we are at the moment."

Rory Schlein* "So after calling my retirement to cycle speedway undefeated I was told I rode some good lines and was pretty fast to"

Fredrik Lindgren* "My name is Fredrik Lindgren #justsaying"

Mads Korneliussen* "Tour de Aalborg, here we goo #mumsfood"

Fredrik Lindgren* "ELRC tomorrow at Swindon, last year one! rider pulled out of it as he was retiring. I was proud to win last year, want to retain the title"

Nigel Pearson* "good luck mate. May see you at the Olympique if I make it there"

Taylor Poole* "After a good morning at FIFA12 I'm now on my way to Workington speedway with Pete Simmons. Just stopped at 'ok diner' for lunch #notbad"

Mads Korneliussen* "Our dog in the frontseat, so i have to sit in the back #notfair"

David Howe* "Gonna turn this around, not too late"

Nicki Glanz* "Is gunna make my Idol Mads Korneliussen praud next year #NewGlanzi2012"

Mads Korneliussen* "as always, you are a living legend #teammatesforlife"

Nicki Glanz* "you taking mé under your wing #1oma8s4life"

Dakota North* "Sick of waking up a 3am every morning wtf"

David Hemsley "People have asked about the name of the event, because I know the Golden Gauntlets was the traditional individual event name at Leicester. I just felt that the name came from a moment in time which we need to move on from now"

Philip Rising "I HEAR what you guys are saying but your comments would carry more credence if the current system [one eight point rider per EL team] worked. It doesn't. There will always be teams at the top and teams at the bottom. But I simply cannot see the sense in trying to bring every team down to the lowest level rather than encouraging them to aspire to something better. A higher limit would provide greater flexibility, especially at the lower level. Just look what Eastbourne achieved with Woodward at reserve, they actually weren't that far away from beating Poole over two legs. If Woodward had stayed on his bike more often, if Pedersen had ridden to his potential... if, if, if, I know, but it could have happened. It wasn't that long ago that an eight point rider wouldn't have been considered a true number one. The bar has been lowered. Would it not be better to try and get a better balance throughout the teams rather than have situations when riders are signed simply because of a number and not their ability? Hey, it's only an opinion but if everything in the garden was rosey we wouldn't be having the conversation."

Steve Shovlar "If a team is successful it will always be split up by the points limit. Poole 2012 will look different to Poole 2011 simply by the 2012 set points limit. Holder and Ward both live in the Poole area, both want to ride for Poole and have major local sponsorship. They are also extremely popular with the Poole fans. When the points limit is set, these two would probably take up almost half of the available points. Surely it is up to Poole to decided whether using so many points on two riders is the way to go?"

Iris123 "But that wasn't ok for Coventry last year when they seemingly had riders set to ride for them within the points limit,but had to let one go because of another limit within the limit.It would be very unjust if one of the instigators of this rule "for the benefit of speedway" then wants to get rid of the rule because it suits his team.Surely the rule must stay for another season,but plans for it to be dropped in 2013 put in place"

Steve Shovlar "The difference is perhaps that Coventry were bringing in riders. Poole already have them in the team. You don't know if Matt Ford voted for the one over eight or not. He could have been ardently against it for all we know."

Steve Shovlar "There comes a time when some promotions need to get off their back side and promote. Teams who are short of a top man need to get on the phone and talk to some of the GP riders out there. No number one, plenty of good 7-8 point riders out there to pack a team with."

Seb the Snail "I don't know why people are even debating this - Holder and Ward will both be back at Poole next season. Sad times for British speedway, but it was never likely to be any different with Ford on the Management Committee. Do you seriously think that he gives a stuff about the health of the sport in this country as long as he can pack Wimborne Road with his misguided disciples?"

G the Bee "Steve Shovlar, on 18 January 2011 - 11:42 AM, said: 'Interesting that some still think having two top riders in a team is perfectly OK, even though at this current time it would mean that two other clubs would be without a number one if the two renegades came back.' You weren't telling these clubs to go out and promote then. And that was a good two months before the start of the season when clubs still had plenty of time to sign riders. How opinions change when it is our own club which is threatened."

Tai Woffinden* "Ash birks was on it tonight broke my track record round scunny! ELRC tomoro cant wait…"

Sam Masters* "So glad I'm going home on Tuesday this joints turning to ice freezing"

Cory Gathercole* "Another dry dusty track at Somerset tonight . Can't wait for the last meeting "

  Nigel Pearson* "but do you really need to be at the meeting??"
  Alun John Rossiter* "sorry nige can't do that Swindon bristol thing nah #fact"

Nicolai Klindt* "man i feel like a complete twat missing out on a podium finish tonight at leicester. my own fault tho! hip felt decent so it was good"

Nicolai Klindt* "if i make the flyers i did tonight from the gate, i will be in for the win tomorrow at swindon…. and i will! #Bringiton #ELRC"

Alun John Rossiter* "that would be cool #ELRC"

Ludvig Lindgren* "Just in bed after todays meeting… Man did i cock that up or what! Well atleast ive ridden à new track!"

15th October

Dakota North* "Just updated the phone to ios5"

Rory Schlein* "It's to early for this shit and far to cold that mean season should be over"

Fredrik Lindgren* "Who do I bump into at Skavsta Airport if not PK, he's on his way to Poland. Myself heading to the UK for ELRC at Swindon"

Shawn Moran* "Good Luck 2nite at Swindon. Guess its a Last Chance Glory Season ender, kick some ass dude. They fear U, so get up"

  Nicki Glanz* "On my way to sign contract for Danish club, but WHO ? guess"
  Mads Korneliussen* "outrup, must be"

Steve Mallett "Here we are in mid-October and with only two weeks left of the season and this club still has seven Premier League meetings to fit in. That is a ludicrous state of affairs and one of the reasons we find ourselves in this mess is that other clubs have been highly uncooperative over dates and it was not so very long ago that we had successive weekends minus a home meeting. I said a few weeks ago that the two-phase fixture list had not worked as it had been planned and there are now many people agreeing with that thought."

Matt Ford "I hope that people are sensible enough to know it might benefit one person by taking away a rider or two, but it isn't going to benefit my business. I've always been fair to other promoters at AGMs and I will be again."

Neil Machin "I think everyone realises that we could have gone on and won the league this year with more consistency away from home."

Ludvig Lindgren* "Oh man i hate mornings! But need to clean a bike and then its off to Berwick!! Well guess its time to leave the bed! Geeeeeeeranimooo"

Rene Bach* "Need to get next year sorted! Have no contracks sorted yet and i have no idea where to ride! #bringiton #liveitup"

Lee Richardson* "Do not accept any direct messages or links from me!! Someone hacked my account"

Ken Middleditch "Streetie was a great racer, one of those riders who just never gave up. He had a great style. He was a very fair rider. He wouldn't do anything nasty or dirty. He was a real gentleman. I don't think anyone you speak to would have a bad word to say about him. His one ambition was to go and see the Dalai Lama. He was great believer in the faith of the Dalai Lama. He was a great believer in health food and that sort of thing."

Steve Mallett "The word legend is often mis-used and in many cases can easily be taken with a complete pinch of salt. However, in the case of Neil Street, I can't really come up with a more suitable descriptive word to emphasize just what he means to Newport Speedway other than legendary."

Joe Screen "I don't feel safe on the bike and I have to get it sorted for next season as quickly as possible."

Brian Havelock "[Jason Lyons] seems to be in good spirits and is probably going back home in November, so once he gets some sun on his back that should help. He intends to work as soon as he can when he gets home…if he says in January that he's not going to be ready then we've got a problem but hopefully, before then, he'll have got rid of his stick and be running on the leg and being well on the way to being fit."

Mike Hunter "As the season has worn on though, there have been an increasing number of nights of struggle. [Craig Cook's] body-language on these nights is not encouraging and supporters never like to see a ride pull out of a race at the back, as he has sometimes done….some downbeat comments in the local press showed the extent to which his head has gone down."

Nigel Pearson "The reason we are laying down plans for a third season is simple – our supporters. Right now we have no firm news on the search for a suitable site for a new stadium, but we have people in the background who are working on things and hopefully we will eventually realise our dream."

Gary Spiller "If it wasn't for bad luck, we'd have had no luck at all. Our injuries have made an already tough season in the Premier even tougher."

Chris Van Straaten "It's been a fine season in the Elite League and it just shows the rule changes which caused so much controversy during the winter have worked because Eastbourne have had a good season too. The league table proves the rule changes have worked and are good for the sport. The Elite League has been a success this year and long may it continue."

Hans Andersen* "Have to say I'm glad to an end to a nightmare 2011 after today's ELRC at Swindon #FinishOnAHigh"

Chris Holder* "ELRC today at Swindon.. Hope the track is good! then we can get loose out there! #godspeed"

Mark Lemon* "Just scratched & pulled out my so called dissolvable stitch protruding out through shoulder skin from 4 months ago. Arhhh, instant relief"

David Watt* "Gonna bend over, grit my teeth, hold on tight and feel some pain !! But later it will be good !"
David Watt* "Don't think naughty, I'm getting tattooed !"
Chris Holder* "where ya gettin the tattoo? On ur ass?"

Nicolai Klindt* "a rodney from food n' sauces will do the trick i recon.. now a shower, relax and then off to Swindon"

Fredrik Lindgren* "Back in the UK again was a long time since I've been here. Weather is nice so it feels good. Sunny England!"

Adam Roynon* "Just heard the weather update on the radio and it said to dig out the winter coats as there is chance of snow this weekend!"

Nicki Glanz* "Deals done in England and Denmark All befor end of october gunna make my Idol Mads Korneliussen so praud next season"

Chris Louis "I find it hard to believe that after more than 10 years of [air fences] being mandatory at the top level, it has not come down the leagues and that it's not encouraged."

Mike Hunter "The first question the other [Edinburgh] directors have to answer is whether the team will come to the tapes next March, and that has not been confirmed yet. As at most clubs there is a gap between turnstile income and expenditure which for years has had to be bridged by fundraising activities. Monarchs are probably amongst the most successful at this with upwards of £40,000 raised. But the question now is whether even that is sufficient for the club to continue."

Fredrik Lindgren* "Just been interviewed by ReRun wohoo! Weather great, here we go! ELRC at Swindon"

Chris Neath* "En route to eddie bulls to get my rye house puppy for tomoz then a night watchin the boxing"

Lee Richardson* "Can't believe the ignition probs I have had the last 5 weeks!!! Need to sort it, can't keep breaking down! Same as b vue 2 bikes with probs!"

Chris Neath* "What a dumb ass! I just assumed Eddie would be home, he wasn't! 2 hours later I've finally got my motor"

Gary Havelock* "Does anyone have a spare Stanley blade!!! I can't take no more 'S' factor. What a load of rigged shite!!!!"

Nicki Glanz* "Single again now, good times A's iam out with the lads, Ladies form a orderly que ! #ClubbingForALiving"

Chris Neath* "If 3 blokes sat on the M42 smoking and drinking tea constitutes to 'workforce in road' can I get a job please"

Darcy Ward* "can't wait to get home. Uk is frezzing"

Fredrik Lindgren* "They run out of water at Swindon tonight so at the moment I'm Stinky Fred! Not very nice!"

Chris Holder* "Shit night! To slick for my liking! well done schlong Rory, Scott & Fredrik too fast boys!!!!!!"

Scott Nicholls* "Thanks for the cuddle in the pit turn airfence!:"

Chris Holder* "I swear I headbutted ur ass!!!! couldn't half see that coming! Bomber bombed allrite"

Scott Nicholls* "I wondered where those teeth marks came from! Oh,he bombed us alright :-)"

Chris Holder* "yeh never nice goin on ur ass at that speed with 2 other guys!! Catchya Wednesday ;-) have a jack for me!"

Rory Schlein* "fella I'm glad ya lot weren't hurt in the semi looked narlley as"

Chris Holder* "yeh sorry bout that I had my eyes shut!!!"

Nicolai Klindt* "man.... i did fuck my starts up tonight, so that's what you get out of that when people going for a title"

Kevin Long* "dont beat yourself up Nic,like I said to you,it was a tough meeting with a load of visiting No. 1'sSo long as your ok after crash"

Rory Schlein* "Wow wat a nite thanks everyone for the msg to many ppl to thank u no who u r"

Fredrik Lindgren* "Back at my place in Rugeley & guess what I'm going to do? That's right a shower!! Will smell very nice soon.."

Kevin Long* "Run out of water? How bizarre is that!! Well done on another good night, plenty of entertainment from you!!"

Gary Havelock* "I remember winning the elrc at Swindon. Got booed to f*#k before the final cause I was British. Did crump,Adams and Hamill up like a kipper"

Marc Lyons "Often this [ELRC] meeting is judged by the number of withdrawals and both Troy Batchelor and Joonas Kylmakorpi were unable to get back from a Russian meeting in Vladivostok on the Pacific coast. So what is the difference between their absences and those of Polish riders who have suffered bans?"

Scott Nicholls
"After the race there was a part of me that said why did I leave Rory enough room to squeeze past? I know other who would have fenced him. But although I think I am a hard rider, very hard sometimes, it is just not me to intentionally do that and ride real dirty."

Bob Tasker* "Hats off to ref Willie Dishington for presenting Pepe Franc with a kids' bucket & spade to help with his gate gardening! #refwithhumour!!"

Fizzy "Richardson. have you ever read his twitter posts?? the man does nothing but moan. About the saddest things. like kids pressing the bell on buses"

Nicolai Klindt* "I really wished I would of stayed home, because I was an embarrassment to watch, I rode like a junior and my starts looked like the first time I was on the bike."

16th October

Nigel Pearson* "Well, what a day that was. New little man arrived at 9.10pm. #prouddad thanks for the fantastic messages. Jake Pearson's arrival means I won't be at the Hawthorns"

Hans Andersen* "You know what the saying is don't ya you only as good as your last ride (I'd be happy with that) just need more laps and I'll be fine"

Ludvig Lindgren* "im a size 8 in shoes but can anyone lend me a size 11 right foot one? seriously ive never seen my foot this big! #crashking #woodfence"

Dakota North* "I picked up a flu on my travels home! Happens every year! It's fffed! #crookas"

Scott Nicholls* "Is feeling a tad stiff this morning & no it's not morning glory! :-) Polska bound today"

Lewis Bridger* "Off out in CA with Cameron here we goooo !! ;)))"

Niels Kristian Iversen* "So 2011 season came to an end last Night. Looking back with mixed emotions, but most is good. Alot of work is waiting ahead of 2012. The new season starts with abit of testing next week if weather is ok #hardwork 2012 #bringiton"

Mark Lemon* "Bummed about the Rugby but I still like Flight of the Conchords.."

Paul Burbidge* "I'd love to be in Torun to watch Poland take on Rest of the World. Never get challenges like this in Britain"

Ludvig Lindgren* "just had a sweet English breakfast! And also happy that Fredrik Lindgren big bro is here to sort out the life!"

Paul Burbidge* "Congrats to Ales Dryml and Artem Laguta on winning the Czech and Russian titles respectively"

Chris Neath* "Fairplay to Ipswich, they out trapped and out rode us all day. On my way to A+E now to get my ankle checked. Really hope nothings broke.."

Rory Schlein* "seb larssons free kick was brilliant best iv seen for a while"

Chris Neath* "Amidst all the doom and gloom of today I did notice a man dressed as a women wearing a Poole Pirates coat, which was rather strange!!"

Jeff Povey* "That will be 'Victoria' - featured in *Poole Daily Echo*, for being banned from using female toilets at Wimborne Road"

Scott Nicholls* "Last one in Poland for 2011.so close,lost out on promotion by 2 points,gutted!Not such a bad day for me.bad start but good finish.getting... Cold in Poland now.better turn the heating on in the van..oh we can't,it's broken!Wrap up & shiver it is then,oh,no jacket either!Good times. There's a draft,feet r frickin freezin & nose's running!think I need to sort a better van next year.grateful for this one,just bloody cold!"

Nicolai Klindt* "feel sorry for you... i'm sitting infront of the fire cuz i'm frigging cold aswell"

Scott Nicholls* "thanks. Man,I'm in a fridge on wheels!"

Linus Sundstrom* "Back to work tomorrow again,been a busy weekend!Dont know what to tweet about when its no speedway.. all i do is #working,sleeping&eating!"

Chris Neath* "They just told me its a 3 hour wait, f@#k that, I'm coming back in the morning!!!"

Nicolai Klindt* "indian chicken jalfrezi, egg fried rice and cheese naanbread it is then.... man i'm hungry! #Needtostopeating"

Lee Richardson* "A big thanku goes out to all lakeside Hammers fans for all their support during this season! Been fantastic!!! Thankyou!! #Greatpeople"

Nigel Pearson* "nice words mate. They are a great bunch"

Dakota North* "Finally had an okay sleep for once! Didn't wake up at 3am. Off to work now for my old man!"

Lewis Kerr* "Thanks for everyone supporting my racing in 2011 and for the fans voting me for there rider of the season :) #happydays"

Nicolai Klindt* "g-o-o-d n-i-g-h-t e-v-e-r-y-o-n-e"

17th October

Scott Nicholls* "Good morning. Ah,wonderful,it's only -3. Lovely"

Nicolai Klindt* "g-o-o-d-m-o-r-n-i-n-g-!"

Scott Nicholls* "That was fun. Waited 10 minutes on the bus,then it travelled all of about 50metres to the plane! Well worth the wait"

Niels Kristian Iversen* "let me have a guess.. Poznan airport. Think i had the shortest busdrive of my life there a few weeks back"

Scott Nicholls* "this was katowice,it was stupid short!"

Hans Andersen* "Another early morning airport run Zzzz…"

Hans Andersen* "Just drove by a freak accident, a lorry had come through the barrier into oncoming lane nasty"

David Watt* "Racing is a beautiful thing that brings so many people together, yet is so ugly when it goes wrong. It went wrong today. Very wrong. RIP Dan (Wheldon)"

Chris Neath* "Let's hope the que at the hospital is better this morning"

Dakota North* "Havent been home a week and I'm sun burnt"

Nicki Glanz* "Working my ass off in sunny copenhagen, but still Got time to whistle at the girls walking past :)"

Adam Roynon* "No breaks! Pheww!! Doc said 'it's just had a big wallop!' fewdaysrest"

Chris Neath* "Good news is no breaks but I have damaged the ligaments around my ankle. Doc says 4 weeks, I say sunday. Lens giving me till sat to decide.."

Adam Roynon* "Glad your alright Neathy! I hurt my ankle yesterday too,carried on and was legtrailing and majorly sketchy DISGUSTING! #ShakenBake"

Chris Neath* "rubbish ay mate but we love it! Where were u yesterday? Were u giving Hally a run for his money with the leg back?!"

Adam Roynon* "Ofcourse we love it..no other reason to be doing this madness! At Mildenhall, missed the new airfence too! Haha. FML! Rest up marra!"

Nicolai Klindt* "just been at the bank to get some very usefull informations. fx it will only be a 5% deposit for me when i want to buy a house #learning"

Nicolai Klindt*
"might sound daft bout i found out where i jinxed it on saturday. put everything on left leg first when i changed and not like normal #bummer"

Chris Neath*
"not daft mate, I have to put everything on the left first! Funny how little things like that make you feel good! Superstitious"

Nicolai Klindt*
"and just thought at another meeting i only put my boot on the left first and had a shit one aswell #alwaysdoitthesameway"

Chris Neath*
"it makes all the difference! In our heads anyway! #Neath2theleftKlindt2theright"

Greg Hancock* "u know how the Ol handshake agreements work in some situations! A handshake has not the same respect there as with us!"

David Watt* "Always got something to do ! #missmybed"

Paul Burbidge* "Hans Andersen admits some property investments which went wrong have hurt his speedway scores for the past 2 years"

Fredrik Lindgren* "Cleaned up a little outside yesterday have cleaned up inside today. Is it boring or what? But it's got to be done #lifeislife"

David Howe* "Good day in workshop, was nice seeing someone else wash two long track bikes. Carbs took me nearly all day ;)"

Fredrik Lindgren* "When I was 14 I won the Swedish Youth Championship"

Sam Masters* "My last night in UK tonight and flying to the sunshine tomorrow will miss everyone here especially my English family!!"

Dakota North* "hungry subway"

Sam Masters* "#aussiesubway :(jelous as"

18th October

Nicki Glanz* "Is soaking wet, would be good if I was a woman"

Shane Parker "The reason for choosing Ipswich as my first club was the chance to ride for John Louis with his experience as an ex-rider, and one of my main aims has always been to entertain the fans."

Greg Hancock* "Some Chris Baldwin has sent out email to my sponsors & speedway community asking for money to publish a book involving me! I AM NOT INVOLVED"

Jonathan Barber* "........he is a con man mate....gave track shop bouncy bouncy cheque once.......last time we dealt with him funnily enough"

Greg Hancock* "This alleged book by Chris Baldwin is called Speedway, The Art of Sliding! I have nothing to do with & not cool what he did!! #moneygrabber"

Chris Holder* "Woke up this morning with the post man delievering a parcel from mum #toogoodtobetrue"

David Watt* "Achieving alot today already ! That's what happens when you get woken up at 6:30 #imissmybed"

Fredrik Lindgren* "Tonight I'm aiming for my fifth Olympique title! With a starting handicap system overtaking is a must! Tapes up 19:30 Wolverhampton"

Rory Schlein* "CVS said he would give me a call about riding in it still waiting ha ha ha good luck Fred see ya Friday"

David Howe* "its scunny awards night and don't wanna get messed up if I'm riding #dontdohangovers"

Chris Neath* "way to old for hangovers and speedway nowadays!!"

Thomasz Gaszynski "Tomasz [Gollob] will be staying [at Gorzow] and it's unfortunate for some of the riders who have to leave because of the rules, but such is life."

Josh Auty "I'm not unhappy at Sheffield, but I think it'd be good for me to learn on a smaller track for a year. I wouldn't rule out coming back, but I do think I need a change."

David Watt* "I knew something was wrong ! Bloody collarbones !!"

Scott Nicholls* "What they gonna do about it wavey?"

David Watt* "gotta go for a scan as they think I have done something in the shoulder too !!"

Scott Nicholls* "nice! So is the end broken or has it separated? Not good either way. Good luck with it"

David Watt* "it's in 3 pieces but I have a problem on the inside of the AC joint too. I think that's right anyway ! gotta wait and see"

Mark Lemon* "yep, gotta love the ol collar bone fella! no envy"

Jonathan Barber "I did see something I'd never seen before at a speedway meeting – Adam Roynon fell off twice and didn't go to hospital"

Nigel Pearson* "Had enough of speedway but my boy loves it so a quick visit to Wolves speedway for the Olympique is in order tonight"

Mads Korneliussen* "Have hat a good day in London, with louise. So must to see, and our feet hurts. Get fit hat my pic. Taken in front of Big Ben"

Sam Masters* "The start of a long trip home on way to heathrow now not looking forward for this flight #toofar"

David Watt* "don't start. Lucky bastard !!"

Kevin Long* "starting work on Shane Parker's rhyme for Thursday - any requests for specific inclusions?"

Chris Neath* "Just had a 3 hour wait to get some crutches cos I'm sick of hopping"

Gary Havelock* [on facebook campaign to get him on I'm a Celebrity 2011] "Check this out. Unreal"

Nigel Pearson* "Big meeting of speedway bosses today, waiting for more info on how it went ahead of AGM. Can't afford another shambles of a winter"

Gary Patchett* "Shouldn't have bothered today. Lawns needed cutting and a better use of my time #wasteoftimeachievednothing"

Jan Staechmann* "Gary you appear surprised for some reason??"

Shawn Moran* "WOW, way 2 go Freddie. 4 n a row with 5 out of 6. Think the track likes u. Thats a good record bub. Got nice season ender"

Chris Neath* "Some t#@t at the pub reckons speedways easy. Guess he's another 'if I rode as much as u, I'd be world champ' #hearditallbefore"

Fredrik Lindgren* "Nice to get that fifth Olympique title tonight! Celebrated with Indian food now off to Stansted!"

Chris Neath* "awesome dude. For someone who don't like Monmore you got that place dialled. Well done mate #WolvesLegend"

Scott Nicholls* "Well that's me done 4 2011.not the best of seasons but I couldn't have done it without my tremendous sponsors,so a massive thank u to them & To my family,friends,mechanics & supporters.When u have a rough season,it's all these people that help get me through. Very grateful,thank u"

Fredrik Lindgren* "'Fast Freddie' is a name that aren't always flattering on your performance. #justsaying"

Bob Tasker* "Lindgren lads like their handicap events! #countto5andchasethemdown"

19th October

Greg Hancock* "Just emailed all my sponsors to let them know about the Chris Baldwin book! Not Happy! Thanks to all of you, I now remember who he is!"

Dakota North* "Back out the quarry today! Busy you could say!"

Jonathan Barber "Nick [Barber] started our end of [Belle Vue] season in August so it's been the longest end of season sale ever"

Fredrik Lindgren* "Landed at Skavsta Airport and started getting hiccups, only thought I got that while drinking gin, weird"

David Watt "I rode in both legs of the Elite League Play-off final with the injury, so this makes no difference. I've told the management I'll be at Belle Vue and raring to go. I'm not surprised that these further tests has shown this. From the first moment I crashed I thought I had broken a bone in my shoulder, but have tried to recover even though they said there were no breaks."

Jan Staechmann* "News from Sweden filtering through this morning that a wage cap is being proposed for 2012"

Gary Patchett* "I understand it's already agreed. Contracts have to be lodged with SVEMO and subject to audit. Ceiling can be broken but penalty is a similar sum which will go to fund development of junior speedway. That's what I heard!"

Jan Staechmann* "news out today says it will be up for vote in November at AGM. proposed penalty is an admirable cause. Very good."

Paul Burbidge* "Wage caps in speedway will never work. Riders could just get the difference from 'sponsors'. Hard to enforce."

Jan Staechmann* "we know that Paul. Just spreading the news"

Paul Burbidge* "Sure, we've all been around speedway long enough to know when there's a will, there's a loophole"

Chris Holder* "How come everywhere else in englnad can't be as cool as Poole"

Gary Patchett* "you should try Birmingham mate. It's bloody freezing ;-)"

Nigel Pearson* "In orange shop - farewell Blackberry, hello iphone. Very nervous. #oldtimer"

Jan Staechmann* "be strong Scoop! May the force be with you, LOL"

Nigel Pearson* "The bloke is explaining about apple registration, email setup and this and that. HELP. scared"

Bob Tasker* "good God man, don't listen to the shop techie bloke - MAN UP, or the next thing will be reading the manual :-P"

Gary Havelock* "I phone is idiot proof #greatestdeviceevermade"

Adam Roynon* "Hyperbaric time! ..to try get fixed up for the weekend!!"

Paul Burbidge* "Harris refuses to commit future to Belle Vue beyond the end of 2011. On a 7.97 ave, can't see Coventry letting him go"

Ian Adam* "Another week another *Speedway Star* cover"

Nicki Pedersen* [1st ever tweet] "i promised i would do a tweet when i got 2000 Followers ;o) lets see when the next comes out ;o)"

Chris Holder* "On way to belle vue"

Rory Schlein* "2 maxs this year not bad for some one who hates the place"

David Gordon "It's the first time I've heard of ticket touts operating at a speedway match"

Rory Schlein* "Stuck on the M6 massive traffic jam"

David Watt* "Well this traffic on M6 can suck a fat one !!!"

Cornishfisherman "Jaybea of Enjay Designs was injured in a car accident on the way to the Belle Vue/Poole KO Cup final today. He sustained a broken hand but is in good spirits. Photographer Phil Hilton was also in the van at the time but fortunately sustained only minor injuries"

Mads Korneliussen* "Got to stansted, not likeing the 7-30 flight tomorrow, but atleast it's the last one this year"

Dakota North* "I'm waiting for so much stuff in the mail I've forgotten what in waiting on"

Linus Sundstrom* "Time for some sleep after a long day, worked overtime today! Not much going on with speedway atm, hope i got all my clubs sorted soon #2012"

Scott Nicholls* "Nice to see people wanting me to race for their club next season. I do not have a clue where I will be,but will tweet when I do. Thanks"

Rory Schlein* "Paid 13 and won by 2 track was ok ish ha ha but we will give it our best 2moro love Darcy Ward dive bomb in heat 13"

David Watt* "I've said it before and I'll say it again, the M6 can suck a fat one !!"

Chris Holder* "how many fukn diversions!!"

Darcy Ward* "tell me a about trying it In and too many corners"

Chris Holder* "save it for the motorways bro"

Mike Bennett* "heading home after a week visiting my money that I left here last year! :-)"

20th October

Nicolai Klindt* "i cant breath #blockednose cold winter"

Dakota North* "when was it ever summer?"

Nicolai Klindt* "three years ago i recon"

Scott Nicholls* "Wow! My worst season for about 12 years & I'm in more demand than ever! How bizarre. Feels nice though ;-)"

Bob Dugard "A lot of people haven't got Sky Sports and can't watch the Grands Prix at home"

Nigel Pearson "It wasn't nice for the unfortunate ones, but how nice was it to see a capacity crowd and folk being turned away at Poole in the Elite League Final? The UK has taken a battering from riders and fans alike as a 'second rate' Speedway nation behind Poland and Sweden, but the capacity crowd last Monday coupled with another massive turnout at Cardiff in the summer for the British GP shows we are still a country which enjoys our speedway.....But the biggest success for me has been the Elite League itself. By accident, the league became 10 after the prolonged dispute between two clubs and the BSPA was resolved, although the wounds are struggling to heal. And my one wish for this winter is that the sport has a more peaceful and straightforward time of it. What happened last winter was completely unacceptable and, whilst listening to both sides of the story, the wider public really don't care who was at fault and who fell out with who. That needs to be remembered because the sport as a whole is bigger than any club or individual ego.....As for the Premier League, congratulations to Glasgow for their wonderful success - but the league has missed a trick. Of the three leagues in British racing the Premier is the only one which doesn't follow the play-off system because it's not fair on the team that finishes top of the league. Time to change that view. I refer once again to the thousands of fans who packed into Poole to see them lift the title as opposed to the numerous meaningless PL meetings for a large part of the season because the title has been in the bag for some time. And I'm told the crowd at Ashfield was pretty poor to see them win the title. Time to look at the bigger picture, PL bosses."

Jan Staechmann* "good write up Scoop. #talkingsense"

Sam Masters* "Aussie is good 28 degrees not a cloud in the sky"

Chris Holder* "Ahh way Better at belle vue last night odegrees and a lovely track"

Scott Nicholls* "Omg!Feelin the love,thanks.If only u lot were promoters! I could coin it in,Haha. Will go wherever I think will be best for"me"not just money"

Olly Allen* "mildenhall it is then! ;)"

Thomas H Jonasson "I explained to Matt Ford at the start of the week that I have not been well. I am due to race in America at the weekend, but my schedule was to ride for Poole before flying out. I am not due to ride in the States until Saturday, so I decided I would use the purchased ticket for Wednesday rather than buy another one. Right now, I am in no state to ride speedway. Travelling is one thing, but racing is a completely different story. I have no strength. I have enjoyed my time in England with Poole and the last thing I want to do is let down the public. I feel disappointed that rumours are circulating that I am okay and off on holiday."

Matt Ford "Thomas and I have had several conversations on the phone and he's not well. He wouldn't let the team down. End of story. I see no reason why he shouldn't travel to America. There's a world of difference being able to sleep on a plane to try and recover or try and race at the highest level in sport. He's unwell and he is unable to race at the present time. If he had told me he wasn't riding and was withholding services, we would still have still operated rider replacement for him, so it makes not a jot of difference to our current dilemma. It's frustrating for us because we have been severely weakened by his absence. I wish him a speedy recovery but as a management we have to focus on a potential team of heroes in blue and white."

Paul Burbidge* "Perfect venue for next SGP round out of Europe. Come on Mr Bellamy -FIM Las Vegas SGP has a good ring to it!"

Adam Roynon* "Last night was a case off #loosingiphoneleadstodepression My life was put on hold until I got it back! How sad"

Chris Neath* "I swear Charlie knows more people in Worcester than me!!!"

Alun John Rossiter* "My house full of Aussies and Danes can't move #justsayin And eating me out of house and home"

Bob Dugard "We've done okay financially and possibly even made a small profit. That is a massive turn around which is largely due to race night and sticking more consistently to Saturdays as well as the team's success. Of course team success is a major, major factor."

Nicolai Klindt* "going jovial later for a "fans night". have a swindon robins race-shirt with me aswell for highest offer!"

Niall Strudwick* "slightly bummed not riding twice this weekend, but riding once is better than missing ANOTHER week of racing"

Rory Schlein* "My high light from tonight was chasing Chris & Darcy's back wheels couldn't guess what line to take"

Adam Roynon* "A bobby on the beat queuing at the bar for a bevy! ..only happens in Barrow! #whatashithole"

Ricky Ashworth "It's been a financial disaster for me this year; I'm having massive gaps between racing and just not getting the meetings in. If you are riding regularly you get in the zone and the points flow, but if not it makes everything harder."

Dennis Andersson "Hasse [Holmqvist] lives in Avesta where I live and when I started racing 500cc I didn't really have the equipment. I asked him if he wanted to do my first tuned engine and that was the start of my team. Now he does all my engines. I have 11 engines at his place for use in Sweden and England."

Elvin King "Second place is there for the taking if they [Ipswich] want it badly enough"

21st October

Avtar Sandhu "Even though I won't be involved in the team in any capacity after this season, the club is certainly not closing down and we have one or two potential buyers, but as yet no takers. We are still pressing on and putting an exciting team together for 2012 no matter what happens in the next few weeks and I will insist that both Colin [Pratt] and Rosco [Alun John Rossiter] are part of any club sale, as that will give continuity and a lot of reassurance to the fans. I need to make sure the club is protected and can keep progressing in the decisions I take next but I am a Bees fan first and owner second. The club is in a strong shape."

Rob Godfrey "We've been in the Conference League for seven years now and we feel we're coming to the end of the road with finding new talent and riders moving on. It's a drain financially and on resources as well. Next year we want to concentrate our resources on winning the Premier League. It's very, very likely that we're going to take a year out. It could be the last year for a long while we see National League racing at Scunthorpe or Sheffield. It's getting increasingly easier to find riders from abroad that are at a higher level. Certainly we need to be ahead of the game if we want to win the Premier League."

Chris Holder "It's one of the worst rules in British speedway. They want to have good riders here, but if you have an eight-point average, you run the risk of not getting a team place. If you had an eight-point average four or five years ago, you weren't even a heat leader. How can you only have one guy with an eight-point average? It's all going to be to spite Poole and break us up. There's no other reason than that they don't want us to have me and him [Ward]. You can't put it into words. It's all a huge fight right now. Hopefully they put their heads together and come up with a solution."

Darcy Ward "The decision is on the BSPA as to whether they want me to ride in Britain or not, but Matt Ford is there and he'll sort something. Clubs should build a team underneath the limit, not by this one-rider-over-eight rubbish. They only made that rule for the two teams that came into the league and that was fair enough, but let's just go back to the normal rules. If I am not at Poole, I am nowhere."

Speedway Star The Heathens chairman, who refuses to hold a promoter's licence in order to avoid a conflict of interests with his broadcasting duties

John Campbell "The scuffle was created by Glasgow's track staff and why they believe they have got to fight, I don't know. It could easily have been sorted out with a discussion between James [Grieves] and Kevin [Wolbert]."

Alan Dick "There was a bit of pushing and shoving but no-one got hurt and everyone seemed to shake hands at the end of it so that is the end of it."

Nigel Pearson "Whilst I believe that the infrastructure of the [Dudley] club is all in place to ride at a full-time level, we must remember that Wolverhampton are the primary tenants at Monmore Green....If we were to be successful in our pursuit of some land for a track of our own, then I feel we would have to move into the Premier League at least, maybe even the Elite, but that's where my involvement would end. On a personal level I couldn't give the time to a full-time professional club, it takes up enough of my spare time now. Chris, Gary, Will Pottinger and myself are doing this in our spare time, it is very much a passion for us all."

Ulrich Ostergaard* "Almost 200 followers maybe i should tweet a bit more"

Fredrik Lindgren* "On my way to Skavsta Airport, final push in this years speedway season. The Midlands Bowl Vs Bees! Coventry tonight & Monday Wolverhampton"

Nicki Glanz* "Cruising flat out with abit of Elvis"

David Howe* "Last few meetings of the season starts today! Plymouth tonight, off to Newport sat then Rye House on sunday, I'm sorry that I had to stop being on standby for rye but berwick gave me a definite booking and this time of year have to take them"

Lewis Rose* "Made the switch to speedway signing contract later today for kings lynn young stars pumped"

Nicki Glanz* "Started smoking again....stress Jason Lyons"

Bev Barber "Jaybea is being released from Leighton Hospital in Crewe this morning. Nick has gone to get him. Had surgery yesterday afternoon and all went well, hand has been wired and pinned. We spoke to him last night and he was very high on drugs!!! He categorically denies speaking to any of us last night lol and has been told that he has been chatting up the nurses constantly!! That sounds like my brother!!"

Claudia Staechmann* "going to the Swindon dinner and dance tonight to drink champagne with my Danish Prince. Happy days!"

Nicolai Klindt* "oh well, more traffic....."

Chris Holder* "Not alot goin down today!"

Gary Havelock* "how's the i phone scoop has it blown your mind"
Nigel Pearson* "must be honest mate I am converted. It's unbelievable and easy to use!!"

Adam Roynon* "Getting some last minute treatment ready for tomorrow!"

Taylor Poole* "Bike washed... Ready for workington tomorrow! #mustwin #losingisnotanoption"

22nd October

Nicolai Klindt* "thanks to all the robins supporters whos been backing us all year - the team did their best and ended up first from the bottom. #notthatbad"

Darcy Ward "If I'm not at Poole, I don't think I'd ride in Britain."

David Watt "There isn't a huge abundance of money to go around and clubs can't afford to have everyone they want. We have to remember there are only a certain amount of speedway clubs, not a huge amount, and they're only trying to be fair and have teams that are equal and can race against each other. These rules are put in place for that – to try and save money and keep clubs on level playing fields. Unfortunately, that means the pawns in this game are moved around and not always put in the right place in the eyes of some people."

Nicolai Klindt* "decent meeting at coventry tonight. can really feel its late season, but thats how it is. better luck on monday!"

Hans Andersen "No disrespect to some of the riders, but people are paying Elite League prices to get in, but it's not Elite League riders on display."

Paul Burbidge* "In the least surprising transfer deal of the winter, Chris Harris returns to Coventry for 2012"

Chris Harris "Coventry want me back, and the deal was quite quick and easy. They were always going to be my first choice, with living down the road. I know the people well and it was an easy decision. It's been a tough time at Belle Vue but I enjoyed it up there, I learnt a lot and it was good for me. It's probably done me good to have a year away, and I'm looking forward to coming back."

Josh Auty   "It is a good club [Coventry] but there has been some turmoil there this season."

Trevor Swales   "Our owners have put a tremendous amount of time and money into the club and we need to repay them by delivering success on the track."

Jon Cook   "It's been a very confused season in terms of never quite reaching the goals we set ourselves, but we haven't fallen as far short as some people believed we would."

Terry Russell   "In reality I've deliberately had little say in the team line-up for the past two seasons, but as co-owner since 2003 I now totally realise that this club and its fans want a successful team."

Scott Nicholls   "There are only a couple of tracks I'd rule out but that has more to do with logistics and travel. Swindon is a track that has never been kind to me in a way, but I don't regret going there and I don't rule out returning if they want me and we agree a deal."

Daniel Nermark   "If I had a choice of clubs in the UK then I have to say Birmingham would be my choice. The supporters are brilliant, the track has been good and the management have always been very fair with me."

Trevor Swales   "We are obviously hearing all the rumours about one rider over eight points rule possibly changing and have drawn up a Plan A, Plan B and Plan C."

Alan Dick   "In the past we tended to go for the cheap option"

Stewart Dickson   "I didn't buy into the Ipswich thing, I saw Kevin Doolan as their one heat leader. I didn't get the hype, I don't know where it was coming from."

Alan Dick   "There was no key person, absolutely not. Josh [Grajczonek] was hoping to be our No.1 and he had a magnificent season up until his leg break at Plymouth on Friday, June 3. It was an horrendous crash and to hear that boy on the track squealing with agony was terrible. It was very bad, the bone fractured in three places, it was a terrible accident."

Stewart Dickson   "The old track became a bit of a gater's paradise, it was very difficult to pass. I remember last year a rider, it might have been a reserve, popping out and leading Joe Screen. Joe chased him for four laps and was quicker but he couldn't get past and if Joe Screen can't pass on it, then we have got trouble."

Alan Dick   "We budgeted for round about £7-8,000 in track maintenance and expenses but it ran to almost three times that, just to reshape it. It ran to almost £23-24,000."

  Rory Schlein*   "Watching a Bruce Lee movie at the mo feel like fighting"
  Nicolai Klindt*   "you can't kill a spider"
  Rory Schlein*   "you seen me rolling around on the grass at Swindon"

Nicolai Klindt*   "tired after a good 2nd half of the d&d! a shame Scott Nicholls, Claudia & Jan Staechmann and Sophie Blake went to bed early, boring"

Nicolai Klindt*   "i was on it on the way down with my coke-zero tho"

Rory Schlein*   "Just sat watching the Wolves swansea hoping to see goals please as there is f@£k els on telly"

  Taylor Poole*   "In traffic on the M6 #fml #couldbelate"
  Jan Staechmann*   "M6 north blocked from 10a to 14 #avoidlikeplague"

Lewis Kerr*   "Reserve for worky tomorrow at Leicester.. Just hope I get a ride yeeeewww"

Mads Korneliussen*   "No looking forward to claening this shit"

  Niels Kristian Iversen*   "Had another round of golf today. Off the pace again again again. Think i need a trainer. Struggle"

  Nicolai Klindt*   "your just crap"

  Niels Kristian Iversen*   "This guy with a battery trolley, He forgot to turn it off while putting, and it went strait into the lake.. He got so angry he slammed his Cap into the ground. Guess he didnt think it was as funny as the people around him #funnyshit hahah golf"

John Campbell "I think it took him [Kalle Katajisto] half the season to work out that he wasn't here on holiday and when he got down to concentrating on his racing, he found it more difficult than he expected."

Nick Mallett "Not sure if there is another sport in which you can get started for £35, but you can in speedway, so nobody should complain about lack of opportunities."

Tim Allen "Meanwhile, improvements at [Smallbrook] stadium are currently underway. The toilet block behind the pits has been finished and the telephone booth for the clerk of the course has been revamped."

Fredrik Lindgren* "Beware of the wolves! Fast Freddie & Co out in Wolverhampton tonight"

Nigel Pearson* "Might be on here a while. No interest in Saturday night TV, utter garbage. Can't believe a nation gets excited by it"

David Watt* "That's what Sky + is for !!"

Nigel Pearson* "I'd rather be in Luton Airport passport control. That's how strongly I feel about the rubbish!!"

Nicolai Klindt* "looking forward to start my diet on the 1st of #novemberoctoberalwaysmessmeup"

Scott Nicholls* "My Twitter's not working,pants! :-("

Rene Bach "Gotta love a Night out with the boys!! #justsaying #funnyshit"

Olly Allen* "Fun night racing at Eastbourne, nice to get one over Cameron Woodward aka bubba in heat #15crashorwin"

Cameron Woodward* "First or floor. You rode wicked mate. I had no answer"

Olly Allen* "love your style man...win it or bin it!! was good to see you cam, have a good winter downunder! i hope its really cold!!"

Casper Wortmann* "15 girls and 5 guys. Lovely paty. Love it flatout party"

Hans Andersen* "hvor er min invitation ?????"

Casper Wortmann* "man skal gøre sig fortjent til damer ! De blir ved med Og komme. Vi i undertal !"

23rd October

Malcolm Vasey "It's been a great season up until the last three or four weeks when we have since fallen away through a mixture of injuries and engine problems. No-one can take away from us that we have finished top of the National League table, and although we have been beaten in the play offs and the cup we have not disgraced ourselves this season."

Kevin Long* "league table shows that Ipswich speedway finished 3rd, on race points difference. Dont think it matters tbh,no one ever remembers 2nd/3rd etc"

Paul Burbidge* "Off to Leicester today for my last meeting of 2011. The next speedway I see will be in North Brisbane on January 7 #cantwait"

Shane Parker* "Well here we go my final meeting today! Mixed emotions with what's happened to Simoncelli. But I'm going to enjoy today. Braaap"

Michael Lee "I have been talking to people who have been watching speedway for 50 years and they haven't seen something like this. I've seen a bit and I was shaking."

Greg Hancock "I've been getting Twitter messages and there are a lot of people talking about this whole thing with Zielona Gora. People are sending me messages saying, 'you're not going to be in the team, but you're welcome back here anytime.' That's news to me. I have a contract until the end of November with Falubaz. Technically, you're not allowed to make any agreements with anybody or talk to anybody until then. My club is saying they might change the rule again. But how long are we supposed to wait? It's dog-eat-dog when it comes down to it because everyone wants to ride in Poland. I want to be in the top league; I don't want to be in a lower league. You need to be where the best guys are. But some guys, and it could even be me, are going to end up in the First Division just because there are no places in the Ekstraliga."

Paul Burbidge*   "In an almost laughable turn of events, Greg Hancock could be left without Polish Ekstraliga club for 2012"

Taylor Poole*   "And the fours is on today. Just in Leicester reading speedway star"

Mark Lemon*   "I love motorsport but I also hate it at times! Marco [Simoncelli], you were a breath of fresh air to MotoGP. Condolences to all Marco's team & family"

Lewis Kerr*   "On way to Leicester with the boys..#letsdothis comets"

Jon Cook   "I really believe that Peter [Ljung] could be a very top rider and that it's not too late for him to achieve that goal. I also believe riding in the UK and mastering tracks like ours can help him to achieve that aim."

Stuart Douglas   "It's not my team, and it's not my business, but I strongly feel that if this rule is maintained with the sole, mean spirited purpose of separating the fantastic pairing of Holder and Ward at Poole – and trust me, there are those very capable of behaving in such a manner - then that would be a disgrace. Those two riders are marquee names when they ride together, and that is very good for speedway in general in this country. Whilst I firmly believe in building to an even strength, it should be Poole's choice whether to run a top heavy team or not. I guess we will have to wait and see."

Jon Cook   "[Kauko Nieminen] will have to think long and hard about a return to lower level racing in 2012 as his overseas commitments are plentiful but as ever he was an absolute gentleman to deal with."

Jon Cook   "We wasted no time at all in signing [Kim Nilsson] on a full HAMMERS contract at a fee of £12,000 and we feel that will prove to be excellent value in the seasons to come. His last meeting of the year at Belle Vue was a sign of what we have to look forward too and he is one of the reasons why next season can't come quick enough. No prizes for guessing the other reason, one Mr Robert de Mearo. Words can fail to outline achievements of this young man justice, but let's try. A season out of the sport, the season before ended early by injury, holding down a full time job and taking trade exams as well.. Result? An ever present, an average nearing 5 and some performances both home and away that had us all jumping for joy. Robert is a role model for what any aspiring young British rider should do; be confident and go for a career in the Elite, don't hang around the PL too long; seize your moment. As a result of his endeavours, Rob has established himself in great company and perhaps as soon as next season he may have to put his full time job on hold to chance Continental opportunities. One thing that will not happen is his availability to double up next season, that would be huge step back."

Jon Cook   "Our average crowd increased very slightly and we had some true highlights, including a crowd of 2700 against Eastbourne on Good Friday and then another 2000 plus figure against Coventry. Poorest crowds were the Sky match v Wolves with only 625 and the KO Cup match v Birmingham, when on a wet night just short of 800 of you visited. All in all our crowds figures now make us one of the four best supported teams, week in week out, in the Elite League and our season ticket holders, who showed extraordinary faith to back us during the winter of uncertainty, are the second highest total of any club in the country."

Jon Cook   "We probably lost something in the region of £7,500 on the [NL Hackney] matches run [at Lakeside] in total and that certainly would have had a detrimental effect on the main team, had it not been for Linda and George [Barclay] and also the excellent Russell Paine "Ride and Slide" days"

Chris Harris   "It's a new start next year and I've built a new team that wants to improve and progress. The team was stale and nothing was moving forward. You've got to have the right people who want to move forward with you and I feel I am getting that now. We've put a lot of hard work into this year and it has been a lot of stress to get where we are now, but it's working. I'm going to train hard and we're going to do a lot of testing this year. We didn't do any last year. But the new team is keen to have a good push for the World Championship. They want to go out testing and work on the bikes, which we are going to do. We'll have a good go at it again."

Jon Cook "Our Asset list increased by one rider this year with the addition of Robert and Kim at a joint cost of £22,000 and the sale of Joonas Kylmakorpi for an undisclosed fee. In full, our retained list reads:

Henning Bager
Daniel Davidsson
Jonas Davidsson
Jerran Hart
Shane Hazelden
Paul Hurry
Peter Ljung
Robert Mear
Andreas Messing
Kauko Nieminen
Kim Nilsson
Marc Owen
Lee Richardson
Stuart Robson
Adam Shields
Piotr Swist
Lubos Tomicek

Jon Cook "In time, we hope our near neighbours Ipswich return and perhaps one more team will make the move up, to give us a strong 12 team [Elite] league. To show our support for Birmingham and Kings Lynn we have decided not to push for a specific points limit, but instead to give our vote on that matter to those clubs, we hope our Elite league colleagues will do the same. Our other wish is that the "one over 8 point" rule is rewritten to allow teams to keep more than one rider over eight from the previous season if both are assets of that club and have been for 12 months. We feel strongly that there is no point whatsoever in signing and developing riders and then having to release them because they go over a certain figure. The points limit after all creates movement."

Nicki Glanz* "OMG my farts stink!! #justsayin #brutal #rotten"

Paul Burbidge* "Leicester's Magnus Karlsson is on the motorway and racing to Beaumont Park for the PL Fours. 5 mins until tapes up"

Paul Burbidge* "Magnus Karlsson has arrived at Beaumont Park. We've got the huge queue of fans in, so time to race"

Derek Barclay "In truth I'm usually among the more bullish in saying that there should be hope in our hearts about getting something out of the larger Olympics Park/Eton Manor grounds site but yes, you're right, brave hopes won't win anything there needs to be action...A leading local promoter has said he'll sit down and chat with me about thoughts on the (London speedway) subject once the season's over, so let's see what transpires... At the end of the day though, we'd need people with financial commitment asnd I'm afraid I certainly ain't in a position (next year THREE kids at university!!) to provide any of that...! Went visiting Central Park in Sittingbourne yesterday and what an ideal venue for Speedway that is, and there's PP - so though not London clearly, there IS real hope for a new and top class venue at that here in the south-east... Simple train journey from the capital too"

Paul Burbidge* "New rules for the PL Fours. Each team has 4 tactical rides if they're 8 or more behind leaders. We just had 3 riders on tacticals in 1 race"

Chris Holder* "Me and Darcy did a lawn mower insurance race today! So fun! Endurance race! Not insurance race!!"

Lewis Kerr* "Tough night! Only got one ride! Crashed! Everyone was crashing patchy"

Scott Nicholls* "Sorry if I'm not replying,my Twitter's playing up still!"

Stuart Parnaby "On one hand it was a disaster and on the other hand absolutely fantastic. Mildenhall came here believing they were dead and buried before they started but they've pulled it superbly. They've whitewashed us really and it was only the last few races where we started to compete"

Alison Chalmers "So, the curtain comes down on a special season. 5 trophies for my beloved Tigers - League, Pairs, Scottish Cup, Spring Trophy and Super Cup. I still find it a little difficult to believe we actually did it. To be honest, it was not quite as exciting as in 93 but that was the first ever after a 47 year wait."

Shane Parker* "Well its all over the last two meetings have been wet and awful. But I have enjoyed every minute of it! Finished of with a win!"

Magnus Karlsson "My flight from Stockholm was delayed by four hours due to a technical fault, so it was a stressful day."

Lasse Bjerre "I have been to Leicester three times now and I like the track. It has tight corners and it is nice."

24th October

Niall Strudwick* "what a match last night. Unlucky not to be NL champs but still KOC champs with Mildenhall"

Rob Godfrey "To say that after thirty heats you win by one point - it's mind-blowing what happened"

Ian Maclean "Shane [Parke] rode what he said is his last race in heat 13 yesterday. It had rained between 3 and 4pm and the [Glasgow] track was difficult at first with slower times. The track held up very well and no one fell. Shane had three seconds but we all knew he wanted to win heat 13 and he did it in style with the fastest time by far all afternoon – what a talent. I went to the pits to see him before the match to say how much I appreciated and enjoyed his time with us. He was mobbed by young fans wanting autographs and photographs. He is as you know very good with fans especially children. After the match he put on a great show of wheelies, doughnuts and the firecracker thing much to the delight of the crowd. Anji and the children were on the centregreen and it was a very happy occasion. Again it is what is special about speedway."

David Gordon "[Chris Harris] was never part of our 2012 plans. He didn't deliver what Belle Vue expected and required. It was clearly a tough season all round."

Backless "On the other side of the [Newcastle] pits, "Plymouth" turn up with R/R for Kyle Hughes (which, to be fair, proved to be a match winning selection for Somerset earlier in the season at Sheffield) and two guests replacing a combined average of over 11 points.... with 2 NL guests who quite frankly never looked like scoring a point between them other than off each other until Mark Jones evidently tired in his 6th ride of the night, with the match all but mathematically tied up. Not for the first time, there was no managerial or promotional representation at a northern fixture. Surely SOMEONE at Plymouth has a sat nav? This total disregard for the Premier League should be tolerated no longer. The PL part of the BSPA are apparently going to admit that they got it wrong with the 2nd Phase (really? who'd have thought) & should be man enough - and protective of their own businesses - to admit an error inadmitting this shambolic promotion into the league. Mildenhall were originally refused admission into the NL & came back with an acceptable alternative. The same should be applied to this lot. Crowds at Plymouth may well be above average for the PL (perhaps attracted by the always likely added attractions provided by the Brian Rix impersonator & his "oops, there go my trousers" antics, but repeatedly sending out substandard collections of miscellaneous riders, seemingly, irrespective of their ability does nothing but damage the financial stability of those forced to host their shambolic circus. Hell, if the mechanics races had been held as a curtain raiser, Scott Robson wouldn't have been the only one being tapped up as a late replacement! Plymouth: by all means book NL guests. Book a team of them (oh, you did - apart from Ricky Wells & Ben Barker!). That's what the National League is there for, awaiting your return."

Roger Martin "Is it the man behind the running of the Plymouth team you have something against, or is it him and the Plymouth supporters you have something against, because i don't know what the crowds at Plymouth have anything to do with the running of the team, if your saying that Mike Bowden is a disgrace to the PL then i agree like all the Plymouth supporters do, but keep it to him, don't bring supporters or riders into it, because like you we love speedway, there is only one culprit in all this, and thats a man who hasn't a clue how to run a speedway team, and is only interested in home meetings, because he can make money from us mugs that are called supporters, because money is the only drive he has, speedway riders and supporters don't come into it, he proved that on friday when Ben Barker went into the fence on bend one, and was only interested in how much damage was done to the fence when Ben was down still on the track, then when the supporters let Mike Bowden know there feeling he put one finger up to them, thats what he thinks of riders and supporters, a complete disgrace, i think the only way ahead for Plymouth speedway is for his licence to be taken away, and for someone else to take over, if that takes a year or two to get the right man, then so be it, because he is making a mockery of a great league."

Backless "Nothing against the good people of Plymouth & surrounding areas - why would I? Their mention has been justified in your summary of the clown "in charge" - they turn up in numbers, line his pockets & are (presumably) well entertained by a string of well organised PL teams each Friday. Nothing against the riders who turn out for Plymouth - why would I? That includes the NL riders last night - they're not going to turn down a booking that'll presumably provide them with more cash - even as a small guarantee - than an average NL meeting. Good luck to them for getting it. But, if I wanted to watch National League, I'd go to a National League fixture. The "Premier League" fixture last night was a NL Select (Starke, Taylor, Cockle & Franchetti - who isn't anything other than a journeyman NL rider with the wrong passport), R/R & a couple of "star guests" in Barker & Wells. Didn't Ricky Wells "guest" along with Ryan Fisher in a team made up of American second halfers & holiday makers recently? THAT wasn't a PL fixture either. Harsh on those supporters of Plymouth to remove his licence but it's equally harsh on those fans of the other teams to inflict Plymouth matches on them. The difference being of course the other fans have the choice of a week off, & therefore it's a financial penalty inflicted on those very promotions who provide quality teams who turn up at Plymouth each week."

Niall Strudwick* "planning for 2012, lets see what happens for next year :)"

Troy Batchelor* "Heading for the Egyptian sun"

Charlie Webster "I've always used sport as my release, my outlet. When I was younger I had about as much self-esteem as I could fit in my little finger, and I have small fingers, but I was overwhelmed with pent up frustrations and emotions that sometimes felt like they were drowning me. I discovered sport or sport discovered me, either way it guided me through a tough upbringing and made me who I am now. It continues to do so."

Rory Schlein* "News... Signed for Hammarby in Sweden very happy to be bak in 2012"

Nicolai Klindt* "signed for hammarby? ur sure that they didnt mis-spelled ur name and thought u wad bomber harris?"

David Howe* "Both bikes done ready for last speedway of the season at Berwick Friday"

Nicolai Klindt* "last meeting of the year. good finish to the season with paid 8 from 4. pk gave me a free parking ticket in bend 3/4 thank you"

Alun John Rossiter* "u could of had more know what I am saying"

Nicolai Klindt* "i know boss i know.... gotta work on it!"

Taylor Poole* "3 sleeps left with my hair :P #maybeinteresting #dreddingthis"

25th October

Gary Spiller "I have got a lot of ideas for next year. It's a case of looking at things after the season has ended and working on it. I have talked to several riders, including some of the guests and there are discussions going on, but they are at a very early stage – almost embryonic."

Taylor Poole* "How I MISS Umina Beach #wontbelong"

Nicki Glanz* "Kevlars, covers and gaurds ordered #NeverBeenThisOrganisedBefor"

Chris Neath* "Decorating the new house today. Painting is definitely not my strong point!!"

Nigel Pearson* "do what I do son - pay someone to do it"

Chris Neath* "len doesn't pay me enough for that scoop!"

Nigel Pearson* "paperwork, paperwork, paperwork, blah, blah, blah #gottabedone"

Rory Schlein* "Season ova what a great year loads of ppl to thank my family and friends all my sponsors and to the fans speedway would be nothing without u"

Darcy Ward "It has become a bit of a protest. There are a lot of people who want to keep us at Poole. But there are a lot of idiots who want to change it. I'm not saying it's the BSPA; it's just other promoters who are against Matt. It's not about me and Chris. It's just speedway. If they can get some advantage, they'll do it."

Mick Horton "I know there are a few people interested and I am certainly one of them. I've had a few years out of the sport and really want to get back in. Coventry have a great history and a great crowd base. It is a very professionally run club and a place where riders want to ride."

Ludvig Lindgren* "what is this that i hear about diets and winter training? every1 knows that the October month for a speedway riders is Beer diet and dancing"

Nicolai Klindt* "sorted out most stuff and bikes ready to go. maybe go and meet up with ludde, fredster and mr nermark later...#hellowintergoodbye season"

Linus Sundstrom* "On the way to ikea with Johanna, buying kitchen today! #spendingallmymoney"

Ludvig Lindgren* "i feel for ya bro!!"

Adam Roynon* "Looking forward to steak night at Weatherspoons later on YUM"

Mads Korneliussen* "Nothing like a Late night in the workshop, love being in the workshop when it's dark outside #IAmNotNormal"

Ulrich Ostergaard* "your just A's normal as All other #speedwayriders:-)"

David Watt* "Been a busy day. So much going on right now. Can't wait for Aussie !!"

Rebekah Walpole* "saw Mads Korneliussen in tesco car park earlier my son was very chuffed!"

Rye House fans* "Chris Neath raced in his 350th meeting as a Rocket on Sunday, now third in the Rockets appearance list, behind Garrad & Mullarkey"

Gary Havelock* "curry night tonight"

Olly Allen* "legend [Shane Parker]...will be missed in the uk"

Derek Barclay "As chance would have it I was stranded in Sittingbourne for some hours on Saturday (clutch burnt out on my car on the M2!!) and so I went down to Central Park to see what's going on. Luckily too they were doing maintenance to the dog track: involved a tractor going round and round (no, it WASN'T driven by Mr. Arnold!) - so was able to sneak in and have a look-see.... they have 'pegged-out' the dimensions of a circuit on the centre green - and this is more than directly inside the dog track so a liitle smaller than it could be. This is a good idea imo as it will contribute cost and building-wise to make it easier to lay..I have to say that this venue is absolutely fantastic...! And location-wise (deep, deep into a vast industrial estate - one notices the distances more when on shanks' pony!!) it beggars belief that anyone was able to bring up issues about noise... But equally explains why the Planning Cttee effectively dismissed those complaints - albeit also responding to Roger Cearns' belt and braces approach of sound barrier and early curfew..The facilities are first-class; the stadium (built mid-90s and well maintained since) clearly amongst the best in the UK. This venue would instantly upon opening be in the top five tracks in the country in terms of facilities from a stadium point of view. AND remember there IS planning consent... I am so excited about the prospect of Speedway happening at Central Park and we should all be... Let's just pray there are no more unexpected glitches or hiccups and the dream can become a reality...: for next year.."

Linus Sundstrom* "Byebye £3,5k , hellohello a new ikea kitchen!"

Lee Richardson* "that's cheap mate!! Started doing my kitchen 2 weeks ago and already upto £14,000 and not even finished!! #crying"

Linus Sundstrom* "your one is not from ikea though! I can only afford ikea #needtoscoremorepoints"

Adam Roynon* "hey lækker! Are the bikes cleaned yet!? ..or ready for P+P next year? :-)"

Ulrich Ostergaard* "nah mate still dirty:-)wanna do a hole season dirty:-)jokeing all clean and ready for next year.du sej adam #funnyshit :-)"

26th October

Ludvig Lindgren* [at 04.15] "live ur life 2 the fullest!!! u only got one!"

Rory Schlein* "Getting some jobs done today so we can head up to Manchester early 2moro. shopping,relax,and then get on it like a car Bonnet at D&D"

Mike Bennett* "and the award for most pedantic slow and rude security staff goes to. . . .Norwich International Airport !! Thats 3 years in a row!"

Jeff Scott* "do they recognise kindred spirits?"

Mike Bennett* "oh do keep your tweets coming Jeff- each one adds to the case that our lawyer is working on against you as we speak!"

Jeff Scott* "?"

David Howe* "Another day in workshop, cleaning all junk out ready to build new bikes 2012 speedway"

Claudia Staechmann* "5 years today I married my danish prince"

Shane Parker "I've been collecting custom-made chopper bikes for a while. I've bought equipment back home and I've got some stuff here, so I want to get into it when I get home. It's something I'd really like to do long-term, whether it gets off the ground as a business I don't know but I'm going to give it a shot. After speedway I don't want to get home and do a job that I don't enjoy. I need to find something I enjoy doing. I watch all the chopper programmes on telly and it fascinates me."

Paul Burbidge* "Nicki Pedersen is ready to race in the Polish First Division if he can't reach a deal in the Ekstraliga"

Jitendra Duffill* "some muppet at cineworld gave Mudga and me 3D glassses with lenses the wrong way round, not cool wearing spex upside down in public #eyedeal"

Ludvig Lindgren* [at 13.00] "lets get this party started!"

Jonathan Barber* "boredddddddddddddddddddddddddddddddddddddddddddd"

Paul Hunsdon "Shame [Nigel Wagstaff] didn't manage to pay Greg Hancock or Chris Mills (plus others as well I'm sure) out of the proceeds of that 2000+ crowd! Reading had 3000+ for Legg and Holloway's last meeting - does that make them credible as well?"

Chris Neath* "Been flat out workin on the house again today. Man speedway seems easy after all this!!"

Rory Schlein* "I said I had some big news well it's not far away ppl"

Taylor Poole* "Tomorrow when I shave my head its all for this. My Nan is a survivor and I love her. I hope we raise"

27th October

Mick Bratley "I have enjoyed my time immensely with the Brummies, winning the Premier League Fours in 2010 was a special occasion for all associated at the club and making a success of running in the Elite League in 2011 was an even bigger achievement in my opinion. I obviously wish the new owners good fortune and success and would particularly like to thank the staff, sponsors and supporters for two very special seasons, that I will always remember with fondness."

Neil Machin "We knew nothing about Josh's decision to look for another deal until it appeared in the press and that shows an alarming lack of courtesy for people who have paid his wages for the last three years. It's probably typical of young riders these days, but it shows bad manners and is unprofessional. One person he should apologise to is Eric Boocock, who has nurtured his career since it started. I expect a written apology if these broken fences are to be mended."

Taylor Poole* "Last sleep with my hair :'(at least I had a good dream rip"

Jerran Hart* "cany get a tank or nothing so no point taking part bro x"

Mark Lemon* "Extra tank,fitted. Carbohydrates,loaded. Energy levels,up. Fitness,?? Van packed. Am ready,yes! 16lapper Ipswich speedway lets rip up"

Gary Havelock* "rather you than me bro!!!!"

Mark Lemon* "you love it still haha, well maybe not Ipswich or 16laps..."

Gary Havelock* "don't mind Ipswich it's just the 16 laps part #toooldforallthat"

Lee Richardson* "My middle son Jake has just smashed the screen on my 50 inch plasma tv!!! We got no kitchen and at the moment and now tv is f***ed #nothappy"

Linus Sundstrom* "oops, did he play wii?"

Lee Richardson* "no he threw and domino! He's in his bedroom now !!"

Chris Holder* "Jus dropped all my bikes back to Mr Hagon! It's nearly home time"

Chris Neath* "Me against the world #loveinit"

David Watt* "Feeling angry and frustrated. I need to get some sunshine !! #nothappy"

Mike Bennett* "very busy Eastern airways flight back to Naaaarich tonight? Must have missed the sign that said "free soup this way!" :-)"

Chris Holder* "Looking forward to the weekend! Last one in Uk for 2011... guna be big I rekn"

Lee Richardson* "Signed a new contract to stay in Vargarna (norkoping) for next 2 years. nice"

Linus Sundstrom* "Just been NEB Engineering to visit Nigel and Craig to pick up my new clutches for 2012"

Chris Holder* "welcome to the swedish pirates fella !"

Rory Schlein* "wow dackarna gonna be pissed"

Chris Holder* "yeh well can't please everybody"

Linus Sundstrom* "thanks man!"

Emelie Hedburg* "Dackarna got Darcy Ward, Jonas Davidsson and keeping Fredrik Lindgren instead"

Gary Havelock* "The captain, team manager and 2 chief mechanics just won the quiz. Get in there!!!!"

Chris Holder* "Celebrity juice jus kickin off yeeeh"

Bob Tasker* "cracking tribute to Maurice Gordon, top gentleman. RIP Maurice"

Bob Tasker* "your books may only be liked by some (!) but where else would the likes of Maurice be recorded? For that you should be praised"

Roman Chyla "Polish speedway website www.sportowefakty. pl reports revolutionary changes that are about to happen in the way the BSI are running SGP. Here is translated text."... After another refusal to accept GP wild card the organizers , BSI, will probably be forced to introduce a solution that so far has been unprecedented. Riders officially are reporting that they are not interested in accepting a permanent SGP Wild Card. The first one who did it officially was Matej Zagar, whose name was considered in the event that BSI's proposal will not be accepted by Darcy Ward. The Australian, in the same way as Krzysztof Kasprzak and Martin Vaculik (successive riders from the Grand Prix Challenge after Piotr Protasiewicz) are also not interested in the Wild Card. Piotr Protasiewicz announced yesterday at the press conference that he has chosen Polish Ekstraliga over the SGP. The controversial ruling of the Polish Ekstraliga limiting the number of GP's riders in one Ekstraliga team means that riders do not want to take permanent Wild Card, which block their way to take up a place in the best and best-paid speedway league in the world! This means that BSI are thinking on introduction of a revolutionary solution. We are informed by people associated with the Grand Prix organizers, that it is quite possible that in the next season a greater number of a single wild card will be given. Until now, each of the individual organizers had an option to put forward one candidate for the wild card in his tournament. It is quite possible that from next season, the number of single wild card will be increased up to 5! There is also probability that the top eight riders from the last season will have permanent places in the GP series and the other eight will be selected for each individual tournament.'

28th October

Dakota North* "Last night was too big to have work the next day"

David Watt* "Want to go to sleep for a few weeks You know you're up too early [07.20] when you can watch the sun come up ! I'm supposed to be on holiday !"

Greg Hancock* "That's kids for ya man! It won't be like that forever though. Not that bad in Sweden though. Sun up about 7:30 now"

Steve Mallett "I am asking every fan who has ever watched this club over the years to come and support us in our final meeting of the season against Edinburgh. This is very much a 'Save the Wasps' plea from us all here at Newport and unless we have a good turnout, then what else are we to deduce from it? We won the Knockout Cup and have a chance to finish fourth in the Premier League and at the risk of repeating myself, speedway in this city is the only winning sport with all the rugby and football clubs struggling."

David Howe* "Will I need to pack my shorts for Berwick tonight?"

Adam Roynon* "Ouch..£100 just gone in the tank to go to Plymouth today! Looking forward to riding there again though..not rode it since '07!!"

Lewis Kerr* "On the forklift"

Nicolai Klindt* "Just been NEB Engineering to visit Nigel and Craig to pick up my new clutches for 2012 makethemstarts"

Linus Sundstrom* "21st birthday today, time goes so quick!"

Mark Lemon* "Last bike wash for the season. Guess its going to have to be a proper job! #thenthebarisopen"

Amanda Saunders "Work will start on the [Reading] site in the next three years but there is no date set for it to begin."

Chris Holder* "Gotta go get pimped out for this end of season party... The only time u see me in a suit other then speedway suit"

Rory Schlein* "so ya off to get a suit our D&D is tonight I'm all pinned striped up bro"

Mads Korneliussen* "On our way to Harwich ferry"

Gary Havelock* "Just seen the feral youth's doing Britain proud in tesco"

Lewis Kerr* "Stuffed... Feel pregnant..winter Training starts Monday.. 6:00 am run"

Gary Havelock* "Radio one. Banging tunes"

Rory Schlein* "Rory Schlein rides for the aces in 2012 and will become a full time ace"

Madgalena Zimny-Louis "I absolutely do not see any chance of speedway revival in Great Britain or Scandinavia. The question is whether speedway as a sport will survive by thriving only in Poland? The organizers of the Speedway Grand Prix failed - as it was planned - to make speedway popular worldwide. They were defeated in new areas, not because they were doing it wrong. It has been now several years since the first memorable Grand Prix in Wroclaw, where I had the pleasure of interpreting at the news conference. We were all bewitched, we wanted to believe that it would begin a new, truly global era of speedway on TV, in the media, in finances, at the Olympics. Those who were talking about those visions, did not lie, they believed in it. The reality of the 2012 speedway season is that - it will consist of two elements: One is the Grand Prix, the second is the Polish Extraliga. Other leagues, other speedway events will not arouse much emotions, because we all know in advance that Poland, as a team. Will again be World Champion team in 2012"

Magdalena Zimny-Louis "Today's Elite League is getting weaker due to lack of funds available to clubs, but this does not mean that there is no emotion and entertainment value. The British are running speedway the way they can afford it. The promoters are risking their own, private money and do not like to lose them. In Poland, huge sums are pumped into speedway, sometimes, like in my home town of Rzeszow, to no avail."

Magdalena Zimny-Louis "British speedway had its time. There was no breakthrough that suppose to happened with the sponsorship and live coverage on the Sky Sports television. The clubs, yes, they got some money from the Sky, but in reality they were money to cover losses resulting from the fact that speedway was on television. At a time when I ran the Witches, it was about 40-60 thousand pounds a year for the club. In Poland now it would not be enough to keep a junior. It is true that SKY shows live speedway, doing it in an extremely professional and attractive way, but this does not translate into obtaining sponsors in such a scale as it was promised. Even before the crisis they failed to bring in serious companies with serious money, now is even worse. Riders also did not feel that being on TV translates into tangible money. Let's add to that decaying stadiums, the large number of matches that were off-putting to some riders, increasing ticket prices and eventually competitions, namely football, the queen of sport in Britain. The average fan cannot afford two tickets a week for a sporting event, no matter how much they love the sport. In Poland there is no competition, football is pathetic, and I know because sometimes I watch it."

Trevor Gordon "I read with interest where the BSI is thinking of making the top 8 go through to next years GP with up to 5 or 6 wildcards for each round. What happens at the end of each year as the top 8 who have gone through will compete in every event and I assume that the wild cards will not so surely the top 8 would have the advantage of staying in each and every year. Seems it's getting harder to get out of the GP than it is to get into it."

Philip Rising "BSI/IMG pay a considerable sum of money to the FIM (putting money back into the sport) that they wouldn't otherwise have, SVEMO use their income from GPs to benefit youth speedway, likewise the DMU. We live in a commercial world. Do FIFA not make money out of the World Cup? Your argument should be about what happens to the money the FIM receive. We do have a proper World Championship but you just can't see it."

Chris Brown Not like you to appear on a thread supporting the wonderful job BSI/IMG do for the sport Philip. Perish the thought people do not share your view. I am entitled to my view as you are without it being rubbished. No I am no GP fan, never have been and never will. The fact that its in such a mess now says it all for me, they seem to be struggling to persuade riders to take up a freebie gift to ride in it. I totally accept others views that the GP is wonderful, just wondering who its wonderful for. I do find it amazing how quick you are to defend the GP series on just about every thread that starts. As for the comparison of FIFA taking money out of the World Cup, yes of course they do, but BSI are not the governing body, they are a commercial organisation who take money out of the sport and in my opinion couldn't give a t*ss about the sport or the fans, my opinion that's all. IMO the FIM should be the ones making the money not some external organisation. Can you imagine FIFA allowing someone else to run the World Cup and keep a large slice of the proceeds. That is a far better comparison than the one you make"

Philip Rising "*Speedway Star's* post-GP sales don't vary at all and as we add 16 pages to every edition the week after a GP (at a cost of around £1,600) it has no financial benefit.
I am a fan of the GP because I think through originally John Postlethwaite and now IMG the level of professionalism and presentation puts speedway's premier event on a par with any other sporting occasion. It is impossible to equate some of the benefits of the SGP series right down to your local track but it is up to the BSPA and its members to do that. SVEMO use revenue gleaned from the SGP to filter down to invest at lower levels rather than reducing the cost of entry or the price of a programme which is what you appear to want. There is no doubt that many young riders are attracted to speedway because of the SGP, they aspire to race on big occasions in big stadiums and on television around the world. It is these riders who eventually put bums on seats and help provide the revenue at tracks everywhere. Sadly that may not be as true in Britain as it is in many other countries but you cannot blame the SGP for that. Of course IMG are in it to make money but they make huge investments in the SGP infrastructure and take a long term view which is something that was lacking in the past. I make no apology about canvassing for the SGP because I see it as something speedway can be proud of rather than embarrassed about."

Philip Rising "YOU cannot judge rider income generated through the SGP by prize money alone"

Rob Peasley "Surely if the Grand Prix riders received thier fair share of the cake, then there would be no problems. The GP riders are massively underpaid - the prize money is a joke. That's why riders are putting Poland first. Even British Speedway pays better than the GPs."

Philip Rising "Racing in the SGP isn't all about the money. Crump is one of many who believes that their careers have been considerably enhanced and enriched by racing at stadiums like the

Millennium in Cardiff and competing in such a series and that memories will be worth much in later years.... There are lots of examples of other sports where contestants place winning before financial gain. It's called something like ambition. The world will be a poorer place without it."

Philip Rising "I saw many World Finals when the title was all but won before the last race, quite often they ended in an anti-climax. And these days, like it or not, TV is the major consideration. They way everything to go to the wire whether it be GP speedway or one-day cricket. Speedway on TV has to try and appeal to non-afficiendos as well as the diehard fans. When I wrote daily newspaper stories for the Express a million years ago I was constantly told by the Sports Editor that they weren't simply going in fort the benefit of speedway fans. That's why household names mean everything and why, at present, speedway in the UK is ignored while in Poland it (Gollob) is headline news."

Derek Barclay "Sorry Phil but this could not be further from the truth.. Each GP may well indeed end up with a grand final but many times (especially under the current format..)the actual significance of who wins it in the context of the ultimate champion is totally marginal.. I've said it before and I'll say it again but I've been to many very important events over a range of sports but NONE even come close to comparing to the sheer breathtaking excitement of the old World Speedway Final. I can't in truth believe that you, Phil, with soooo much more expereience of those than I have can't agree..: which, as others have suggested, does make me now wonder why you say otherwise."

Philip Rising "PLENTY of World Finals left me stone cold ... 1974 was a typical example. Michanek made five starts and that was that. But that doesn't make me right and you wrong or the other way round. It's all in the eyes of the beholder."

Philip Rising "Have you spoken to Ward? Probably not. He is a young man, actually quite sensible beneath his Aussie Jack the Lad veneer. Of course he is tempted by an offer from Torun worth a lot of money. But there is more to it than that. Riding in the SGP demands a lot of organisation, extra responsibilities for mechanics, more bikes, etc, etc. He believes that at present he may not be quite ready for that side of the GP and that he needs more sponsorship too. He knows he is good enough on the track. It is possible, though less likely, that he would have declined an invitation for 2012 even if he had also been able to accept a contract from Torun. He has time on his side. He witnessed what happened to Woffinden. He will get his chance again and deservedly so. Far great judges that I could ever aspire to be, including ex and current top, top riders, believe him to be an exceptional talent. We should be grateful that he has emerged and that isn't wholly down to Britain. He spent days and days riding round the Torun track improving his technique. It will be a great shame if he doesn't compete in the SGP next year but it will only heighten the anticipation of when he does. Before long hopefully he will be joined by riders like the Pawlicki brothers, Janowski, Sundstrom, young Danes and (fingers crossed) a rejuvenated and reformed Woffinden who has it within his grasp to become a World class rider."

Graham Hambly "Persistent rain during the week had found its way into the [Plymouth] electrical system and a power failure plunged the track into semi darkness as referee Stuart Wilson released the tapes for the first race. The red stop lights were not working and some of the riders completed the four laps before realising the race had been stopped. Racing resumed after a 20-minute delay but the lights went out again befor Heat 2 took place."

Philip Rising "If there were millions and millions to be made out of speedway no doubt the FIM would plunder a bigger share of the spoils. But, as said here before, my understanding is that speedway is the second biggest contributor to the FIM coffers"

29th October

Rory Schlein* "Just getting in from a night on the town in manchester great night hope all aces fans are happy with the news. And a big thanks to the fans from Coventry and mr. Sandho and Collin Pratt I won't forget my time at cov 05/06/07 great seasons. But must look a head and times look good for the aces and look forward to being apart of it"

Neil Machin "It's no secret that the NL has to change. We never wanted it to become a retirement home for older riders – and we've all been guilty of going down that road – because it should be a development stage for progressive youngsters. It is not a third professional league or a watered down Premier League, it has to be about bringing through the next generation of youngsters"

Jan Staechmann "I think that we all know the riders who compete in the SGP do so because of personal ambitions to become World Champion. When I had a go in the inaugural GP series in 1995, the winner was paid $10.000, plus we got our hotel room for two nights. No. 18 received 1.500. In 2011 the winner of a GP received $11.000... (no added extras). No. 18 received $2.100. That's an increase of $1.000 to the winner in 16 years?! I wonder where that lies in terms of rate of inflation... I know the riders have tried for years to get their prize money changed to € instead of USD, but to no avail. BSI is not to blame for this because it is the FIM who pay the prize money. The FIM is a wealthy organisation, so I am sure there is a plausible explanation to all of these questions, or maybe not. The carrot for a rider in the GP series, if you will, is a combination of things, but it is mainly the exposure that being in the SGP series brings. This in turn the riders can "sell" to sponsors, and that will increase their value. Club wise yes, Poland is at the top of the tree, and pay the most in terms of sign-ons and points money. I read that the restriction of one GP rider per team was a cost cutting excercise, and yes of course it is. Not all 10 Ekstra League clubs have council aided budgets akin to that of Gorzow, Torun or Zielona Gora, and not all teams have a sponsor like Azloty in Tarnow, or Unibax of Torun? (Apologies in advance if I've left any obvious details out, or have inaccurate facts) So they (PZM) are doing the right thing, in my opinion. If restricting the teams to 1 SGP rider means stability to the League, and the survival of some of the teams that are less fortunate in terms of funding, then surely that is the way forward? I also think whoever mentioned the order of leagues in terms of earning potential was spot on, in that it is Poland, Sweden, England, and then Denmark. I am not sure where the Czech Republik, Germany, and Italy figure currently in that list, but I would hazard a guess at the end of it. I think Dave Howard is right on the money as well when he hints that the riders mentioned, Jason and Nicki et al, are getting paid deservedly well for what they do, because they are x times World Champion. I will add to that, that they also get paid for what they bring to the club. The promotors know who will put it all on the line in every race the rider goes in, they know who is a great motivator and help for younger riders, who is good PR for a clubs sponsors, etc. etc. Modern era speedway has become big business, for the top riders 2-3 full time employed mechanics, dozens of bikes, a couple of vans and workshop facilites etc. etc. is the norm. League speedway are the cogs that make this whole machine go around, pays the wages, the investments into R&D, and generally trying to go faster to compete in the SGP Series, to chase that elusive World Championship."

Speedway Star "It would also mark the end of his youth as Ward would need to give maximum focus to his SGP bid, instead of enjoying life in the same way as most people of his age do."

Scotsman "A SERIES of electrical failures and a huge crowd waiting to get in caused a big delay to last night's Premier League speedway clash between Plymouth Devils and Edinburgh Monarchs. And when power was eventually restored to the St Boniface Arena, sadly it was Monarchs who remained switched off."

Steve Mallett "The National League has been a disaster this year. The team hasn't ridden well and the people have faded away. I didn't come into this to do National League. Don't get me wrong. Given that Nick came through as a junior, we wanted to do something to help the kids. But we want to be with the big boys. That's the whole idea of it. If we're running, we're only doing Premier."

Casper Wortmann* "Morning..... Its #racingtime yewwww #cantwait"

Chris Harris "If I'm given a good surface to perform on, I can perform."

Chris Holder "It's an inferior product. They want to keep costs down but are watering down the product. If they want to make the Elite League in England 'the Elite League', they should bring all the top riders over."

Linus Sundstrom* "Going for some sponsor meeting today, hopefully it comes out with good news :) #planningfor2012"

Steve Mallett "We've lost an absolute fortune without a shadow of a doubt. The crowds haven't been good enough at all. I get told off for being negative, but I'd get told off if I shut the stadium on a whim. So what should I do?"

Kevin Doolan "Funnily enough, none of our averages are very high because we've had such inconsistent seasons. We probably won't be able to track the same [Ipswich] team next year, but it won't be too far off."

David Watt* "Might have had enough of this now !"

Gary Havelock* "and you call us whinging poms. Jeez you can moan bro"

David Watt* "Been here too bloody long !!"

Gary Havelock* "it's not even cold yet. You wanna try being up here in Boro in January"

David Watt* "Nah ! I just tough it out in Australia. Thanks for the thought though. I'll think of ya when I'm there"

Gary Havelock* "who needs bondi beach when you got Redcar beach!!!!"

Paul Burbidge* "Bloke tried to get me into his car near Arc de Triomphe by offering me modelling work. Come up with a plausible way to kidnap me numbskull"

Nicolai Klindt* "thanks to everyone for a good dinner and dance with wolverhampton wolves. now heading back home to prepare for next year!"

Ian Maclean "Shane is someone I have admired for a long time and I'm glad he got out without anything happening to him in his final year. We are going to the Tigers dinner this evening - who will be rider of the year. For once we have a choice, it ought to be Screen who hasn't had a last place at home all season but what about young Morris and Grieves has had a very good season?"

Keith Denham "The way the league has been done this year, with the second phase fixtures, has put everyone in trouble as they have been racing in worthless matches…. You need to keep people interested. The system this year has been ridiculous and people cannot afford to come and watch worthless fixtures."

Adam Roynon* "Just crossed the Severn-bridge and the weathers just gone shite! 'Rain rain go away' and all that!!!"

Chris Holder* "Who's goin big tonight then….?"

Casper Wortmann* "So good to be back on a bike … Wish it could be more than just a couple of times every year #missitbigtime #winnthelottery #iwillbeback"

Adam Roynon* "speedway is crazy, I've just guested twice for the monarchs yestday and tday and then tomoz I'm against them guesting for Workington!"

Nigel Pearson* "think of the dosh. See you Friday kid"

Nigel Pearson* "Meanwhile in speedway I've talked to promoters who want to scrap the one rider over 8-pt rule in the last 24-hrs. Interesting!!"

Alun John Rossiter* "self interest o well let's get on with it"

Nigel Pearson* "speedway rule of one rider over 8 was with new clubs in mind so everyone got a no.1. Prediction: EL Pts Limit 41, 8+ rule scrapped"

Alun John Rossiter* "fantastic mate I am boing boing boing all over the place mick Horton confirmed don't judge a book by it's cover #justsayin"

Nigel Pearson* "I was on here in the week urging folk to give Mick a chance. Needs to rid himself of a family reputation that's all. #cleanbreak"

Jan Staechmann* "Interesting news coming through that Mick Horton is the new owner of Coventry"

Alun John Rossiter* "fact mate"

David Tattum "I thought we did the [KO Cup Final] occasion justice with our presentation"

Philip Rising "SADLY it is the case that some riders at a particular club this year hadn't been paid for sometime. Don't ride? Look what happened to Hans Andersen a couple of years back when he rebelled against not being paid"

Chris Van Straaten "One rule I think needs looking at is the replacement facility for riders who are missing for reasons other than crashing in a speedway race, which it seems is a growing syndrome…right now, all a rider has to do is moan that he has got a cold or doesn't fancy flying over and it's fine… the 'withholding services' phrase is something which was used rarely 10 years ago but it's something which is becoming more and more common, and something needs to be done about it."

Bob Dugard "Trevor and Mike are very keen on it [Speedway Champions League], as are the BSPA. But I follow Polish and Swedish speedway all the time via satellite TV and I've got to say I don't think it is worth it. They are so strong in their home countries that we would get absolutely blitzed."

Philip Rising "THE Mayor of Bydgoszcz was voted out of office largely, we are told, because the city lost its GP status. The new mayor of Daugavpils is desperate to get the GP back. The mayors of Torun and Gorzow are heavily involved. I think you misunderstand the prestige enjoyed by these Polish cities being associated with the GPs. There is massive political capital to be gained. The city of Gothenburg is now actively involved, anxious not to lose the GP like other sporting events in Sweden to Stockholm... YOU simply cannot compare speedway's status in the UK to that in Poland. Places like Leszno, Torun, Gorzow, Bydgoszcz and Zielona Gora are fanatical speedway cities. Their speedway clubs are much more akin to soccer clubs in places like Manchester, Birmingham and Liverpool. Mayors in Poland know the political capital to be gained by supporting speedway, whether it be with the construction of new stadiums or hosting a SGP round."

Jason Doyle "The first six weeks is pretty much do or die. If I don't look after myself and keep the sling on, then I'll pretty much need another operation because the four anchors inserted in my bone will come out."

Graham Drury "It is a measure of what an attractive sport we still have when, despite difficult economic times, three different parties have shown an interest in becoming the new owners of Birmingham Speedway."

Mads Korneliussen "I remember when I first came over [Neil Street] taught me so much. I laughed with Neil so many times when I was there with him. He taught me a lot when I was at Newport, and back when I left I thought: 'oh, that's Neil Street, I'll never see him again'. But then, now and again, he would show up at Swindon in the pits. He would give me a hug and give me advice, and say things like: 'You've been on the gas; I have seen your lap times in the *Speedway Star*'. He was one of a kind. One of the things with Neil – if he really liked you, he would follow you to the bitter end. He would always look after you. I don't like getting close to people, but he was one of the only few men who hugged me in the whole world. That was Neil."

Chris Neath "Len [Silver] knows how loyal I am to the club and I know how loyal he's been to me."

Philip Rising "IF memory serves me correct Meridian Lifts were the sponsors of the rain-affected meeting in Gothenburg and obviously, judging by Andy's comments, he wasn't satisfied but I doubt whether he can speak for all the other sponsors throughout the year. I do know companies like Nice and Doodson were very pleased with their involvement and in these tough economic times I would image BSI/IMG were satisfied overall."

Jordan Frampton "day meetings, you are really on a hiding to nothing because when the sun comes out and the track dries, it becomes very slick very quickly."

Michael Palm Toft "When I first came over, I had quite a lot of confidence and I enjoyed my first three meetings when my Dad was here with me, but then he took off and I went down a hole. My mechanic helped me at that time and he said to me, 'you have to start enjoying your time over here', so I tried to change a bit of my personality and that really helped me. Every time I go out now, I am going out to have fun and enjoy it."

Peter Oakes "Meetings at West Row had often been tedious affairs – punctuated by mix-ups between the promotion and medical staff over start-times. Clouds of dust rising high above the track high into the sky were a sure indication that it was race-day and generally meetings were run in an off-hand, uncoordinated manner."

Karl Mason [25] "I've had a great 18 years in speedway, but I feel it's time to move on, and this has been a brilliant year to end with."

Philip Rising "WILD cards are chosen after discussions between representatives of BSI and the FIM, including Tony Olsson, Ole Olsen and Roy Otto, Director of the CCP. I agree that at this particular moment it is a tough decision, not because they are spoilt for choice but exactly the opposite. Darcy Ward was the obvious candidate outside of those who competed this year but he was practically alone. Hopefully within the near future the number of suitable riders will increase as some young Poles, Danes, Swedes and, indeed, Aussies further their careers and, as stated earlier, perhaps Tai Woffinden will grow into the role. In the not too distant future we are likely to see Tomasz Gollob and Greg Hancock retire from the SGP scene and speedway as a whole and the SGP in particular desperately needs some of the young talent to step up to the plates we enter a new era."

Arnie Gibbons "A slightly Ango-centric view. Polish and Swedish form would put Grigori Laguta up there with Ward, but his absence from the World Cup must count against him (with some justification I think). I guess this is going to come down to politics, with BSI and the FIM sitting down together to try and work out how to compel the riders they want to compete in the GP"

Steve Williams "Not many people know, but [Karl Mason's] van engine blew up right at the start of the season, and he's done the whole year having to use hire vans at his own expense. Despite that, he's never let us down and he's been an ever-present for the team."

Rob Godfrey "I think it's universally accepted that play-offs will return to the Premier League next year. If I was a betting man, I'd bet my house on them coming back."

30th October

Rory Schlein* "Rum and coke while intaking it it's brill but today not so good 2 nights 2 D&D 1 specials show I'm all party out"

David Watt* "Must have bumped my head last night because I've got a headache now ! That's the only logical reason right ?"

Stein Waalen "It seems like the Speedway Grand Prix Highlights DVD sets are only available in GBR. Like Dale I can`t find them anywhere else than on Amazon.co.uk and the only shipping available is to GBR. That is just plain stupid....... .anyone knows why?"

Chris Neath* "Big day today. Might not be to important to some but i wanna try and get my name on the trophy #AceOfHerts"

Paul Burbidge* "Congrats Chris Holder & Darcy Ward on sharing Pirates' Rider of the Year. Polled same no. of votes!"

Nicolai Klindt* "now is it time to go home to the main land denmark.... van packed, bags are packed and i'm ready! on the 18hr ferry later"

Lee Richardson* "Midday drink....why not....better get in training for next week!!"

Philip Rising "CANNOT be 100 per cent sure but I think [Alf Weedon] has celebrated his 90th birthday"

Lewis Kerr* "On way home from Norwich from veterans speedway lunch.. Good day out. Met some cool legends"

Chris Holder* "Anyone work for DHL or fed ex in the Uk..? Need to send Some bikes back to Aussie"

Roman Chyla "As previously reported Darcy Ward has signed 3 year contract with Tourn. Rumor has it that if he actually gives up the call up by the BSI then, his Australian Federation will ban him for 3 years (up to 2014). That means he won't be able to even take part in the eliminary rounds of the SGP. The news was apparently broke to him by the BSI. So the young Australian has now a choice. The money or the glory"

Colin Barber "If that is the case it is an utter disgrace, after all he did not actually qualify in the preliminary rounds and the bosses at the Aus.Fed should have their backsides kicked. Too many GP rounds and as has been said on here many times that the SGP will do no good to domestic speedway, the very spawning grounds for the GPs."

Robin Goodall "If there was a competition for the most tedious speedway meeting ever, then this one [Heathersfield Helmet] would be up there as a strong contender."

Chris Neath* "Gutted I had to pull out tonight, wanted it so bad, probably to bad but we all love winning ay"

Olly Allen* "mate the form you've been on at rye this year I don't think it's a shame at all that I didn't race you!"

Chris Neath* "Been a gd season though and stoked to win a couple of awards for the year #LoveRyeHouse"

Lewis Bridger* "Thanks to Dave Mason for the lend of a motor due to all equipment being prepared for 2012 season"

Kevin Doolan "It's just a shame that the season is finishing now. I've had a bit of a dip in my form this year, and I wasn't really happy mid-way through the season. Fortunately, everyone at Ipswich rallied around me and really got me going again, and I've put in some great meetings in the last month. This is just the icing on the cake."

Ray Blackwell "Deepest sympathy to all at Coventry"

31st October

Alun John Rossiter* "Think I over cooked it on the dancing this weekend struggling #hangover"

Lewis Bridger* "2011 season officially to a end.. Raced the Ace of hearts last night on a national league motor borrowed from Mr Mason :-) #nospeed But Mr Mason was never going to lend me his best National League motor was he :-) ? Haha but at least I didn't let Len Silver down #topbloke"

Jonathan Barber* "bored"

Nicki Glanz* "You know you been staying at the same hotel for Ages when they go "welcome back Nicki" when u walk in"

Nicolai Klindt* "good to be back home now! but busy again tomorrow where the work starts for next year"

Lewis Kerr* "Been bike pimping All night in the cave.. 2012 bikes gonna look Sick!"

Chris Holder* "even after all these yrs Neathy you still an excitement machine :-P"

Chris Neath* "still life in the old dogg yet bro!!"

Acknowledgements

In addition to the record of note that is the *Speedway Star*, (obviously) club websites have all the latest information. In addition lots of other print & media media outlets cover speedway. Those read and/or visited – with gratitude and thanks - in the course of compiling this book on the 2011 season include:

Birmingham Mail, *Bournemouth Echo*, *Bridgewater Mercury*, *Brighton Argus*, British Speedway Forum, BSPA, *Courier Mail*, Coventry Speedway Chat, *Coventry Telegraph*, *Daily Mail*, *Daily Mirror*, *Dorset Echo*, *Eastbourne Herald*, *Edinburgh Evening News*, *Express & Star*, *Evening Gazette*, FIM Live, *The Glaswegian*, *The Herald*, LoveSpeedway 24, *Lynn News*, *Manchester News*, *Mid Sussex Express*, *News of the World*, *Peterborough Evening Telegraph*, *Scotsman*, *Sheffield Star*, Sky Sports, *South Wales Argus*, Speedway GB, Speedway GP, Speedway Plus, Speedway Updates, Speedway Yahoo Forum, Speedway 365, *Sunday Mercury*, *Swindon Advertiser*, *Sydney Daily Telegraph*, This is Staffordshire, *Times & Star*, Twitter, World Speedway.

For more information on the Speedway Riders Benevolent Fund, future events or to make a donation – please visit

http://www.srbf.co.uk/

SPEEDWAY RIDERS BENEVOLENT FUND